# BARGAINING WITH THE STATE

# BARGAINING WITH THE STATE

*Richard A. Epstein*

PRINCETON UNIVERSITY PRESS PRINCETON, NEW JERSEY

Published by Princeton University Press, 41 William Street,
Princeton, New Jersey 08540
In the United Kingdom: Princeton University Press,
Chichester, West Sussex


***Library of Congress Cataloging-in-Publication Data***

Epstein, Richard Allen, 1943–
Bargaining with the State / Richard A. Epstein.
p. cm.
Includes bibliographical references and index.
ISBN 0-691-04273-X
1. Police power—United States. 2. Taxing power—United States.
3. Eminent domain—United States. 4. United States—
Appropriations and expenditures. 5. Compensation
(Law)—United States. I. Title.
KF4695.E67 1993
320.973—dc20 92-46793 CIP

This book has been composed in Trump

Princeton University Press books are printed
on acid-free paper and meet the guidelines
for permanence and durability of the Committee
on Production Guidelines for Book Longevity
of the Council on Library Resources

3 5 7 9 10 8 6 4

TO

**Eileen, Melissa, Benjamin, Elliot**

FOUR PEOPLE, MY FAMILY

## Contents

# Preface

In *Bargaining with the State*, I have continued a project that, in spite of the best intentions of its author, has been in the making now for twenty years. The limited nature of my original goal was to work out a set of comprehensive rules that could answer (at least to my satisfaction) one of the outstanding problems of the tort law—to figure out which harms suffered by one person could be attributable to the actions of another. In order to get a handle on that question, however, it quickly became necessary to work out a theory, not only of causation, but also of property rights, for unless it could be established what one owned, it could not be explained why that person could recover for that loss. But the question of ownership does not lend itself to easy answers, either for person or property, and the upshot was an effort to develop a theory of individual autonomy, and a persuasive justification for the acquisition of property, both topics discussed at length in this book.

Any theory of autonomy and property carries with it both great promise and substantial limitations. On the promise side, the theory is better able than any of its rivals to explain vast chunks of the legal terrain, not only in the common law systems, but also in the civil systems based on the Roman law. The inviolate nature of the person is a strong peg on which to hang the law that protects all persons against murder, rape, and theft. It establishes the set of initial entitlements that makes coherent exchanges of both labor and property, and thus accounts for many of the ingredients of a well-functioning market system. It is no wonder that the natural law theories have always gravitated to autonomy based rules, because they do far better than any rival in explaining the rules of conduct that govern our daily interactions.

But this autonomy theory has its dark side as well, and without modification, it often leads to results that have long been rejected in practice by all legal systems, and which are to most persons morally repugnant, or practically unworkable. Thus a theory of autonomy not only says that persons are under no duty to rescue a stranger in dire need (a result that most people find uneasy, but when pressed correct), but also that the owner of property could actively prevent a stranger from coming onto his land to rescue a third person who was lying there in desperate need of assistance. And it allows the owner of property to refuse the right of entry to persons in imminent peril of life and limb, even if they are ready and willing to pay for any damage that they might cause. On the public law side of the equation, an autonomy based theory is sufficient to explain why government should protect liberty and property from the invasion of others. Yet, by the same token, it cannot account for how it is that any state could be called into being, or how it could finance its operations even within this limited sphere. The institution of taxation (regressive, flat, or progressive) presupposes a coercive transfer by the state, which is imposed on persons who have committed no wrongs against their neighbors, and who have made no promises, express or implied, to assist them. A theory which specifies a role for government is thus unable to account for funding the government that marks the end of Hobbesian anarchy and the onset of civilized life.

It seems clear, then, that some principle is necessary to account for the defects of an autonomy based theory if that theory is to retain any credibility for the good work that it can accomplish over large portions of human activities. While many modern thinkers are quite happy to abandon any reliance on this theory, my approach is to cast about for a second principle that preserves the basic theory where it works well, while allowing for exceptions when and where needed. It is important that the exceptions be limited in number (one is ideal) in order to avoid a long list of epicycles that call any theory into question. Here again the common law, and its intuitive approach, supplied the key principle: forced exchanges with just compensation under conditions of necessity. This one rule seems to answer the major objections to the autonomy based theory with which I began, while preserving its use in the areas where the autonomy principle seems the strongest.

Basically put, the theory of necessity is critical at two junctures of the inquiry where the autonomy theory is weakest: first, to explain the origins of autonomy and property, and then to explain the origins of the state. In between, the autonomy based theory works quite well to explain the rules for the protection of person and property against aggression (the tort problems that were the focus of my original academic interest), and the rules of voluntary transfer of labor and property that form the core of the law of contract. But before any person can sell labor or property, these must be owned, and, as developed in chapter 3, theories of necessity explain better than any rival why each person owns his or her own body, and the external things that are reduced to possession—here to the exclusion of the rest of the world. But at the back end, a theory of necessity explains why property may be taken from all persons in the form of taxes, which can then be used to pay for the police and court systems that protect individual freedom, private property, and the social order. In both cases the necessity in question refers to the large transaction costs barriers (not present in the ordinary contract for sale or employment) which make it quite impossible for all persons to agree (not tacitly, impliedly, or fictively, but by ordinary contracts) on the allocation of rights in the initial position or in the distribution of the tax burden necessary to maintain any system of private rights so established.

The next stage in my generation-long project was therefore to develop a body of rules that deal with the taking of property and just compensation, the subject of my 1985 book *Takings: Private Property and the Power of Eminent Domain.* Throughout that book I took a view of private property which derives not from the customary public law view of the subject, but rather from my own work as a common lawyer concerned with the articulation and limitations of the rules of property, contract, and tort. In dealing with that issue, I argued that a taking of private property could not be understood simply as the forcible dispossession of a person from land or chattels that had been acquired under the first possession rule, or acquired by voluntary transaction (sale, gift, will, mortgage) from someone who had previously obtained valid title. Instead, the idea of taking necessarily embraced all forms of government activity—regulation, be it of the power to use or dispose of property; taxes of all kinds and descriptions; and the modification of the liability rules, whether of trespass or nuisance, that are used to protect property.

In adopting that position, I claimed in effect that any form of standard legislation or adjudication that altered the common law framework was a taking. The state then had to show that the taking was justified in one of two ways: either to prevent wrongful conduct by private individuals, or, where it did not, to provide compensation. Here the link to the common law theories of tort must be explicit, for once that link is abandoned, then there is no separate conception of private wrong that limits the scope of state activities, and we reach the dangerous position that we are at today where virtually all government restrictions on use or disposition of property meet what low constitutional standards remain.

Alternatively, where no private wrong was committed, necessity might justify the taking *with* just compensation. The point of this compensation requirement was to insure that no single individual bore the costs of government projects that were said to be for the common good. More than considerations of intuitive fairness justify this just compensation requirement, which also has a clear economic function: to keep the government from undertaking foolish projects (i.e., those that cause more harm than they do good). It does this by the simple constitutional expedient of making the government show that there are no individual losers. In some cases that showing can be made by identifying the in-kind benefits (e.g., protection supplied by taxation, or reciprocal restrictions on land use that inure to the benefit of neighboring landowners) that the government activities generate, and in other cases by making cash payments to persons who would otherwise be the losers from government intervention. The purpose is to insure that only projects with a positive expected value are undertaken by the state.

The question then arises as to how the gains of useful government action should be divided. In *Takings*, I spent very little time dealing with that question, or at least dealing with it in a satisfactory fashion. In *Bargaining with the State*, I return to that question in far greater detail, for the key question that unifies the many disparate themes in this book is this: where the government does undertake projects that promise some positive gain, how can the size of that gain be maximized, and what implications does the task of maximization have for the division of the gain across citizens? This topic does not have quite the dramatic sweep of a takings analysis because its intention is to see that useful projects go forward in a sensible fashion, not to strike down unwise projects that should not go forward at all. Stated otherwise, once the New Deal has been declared unconstitutional (as only an academic can do), it is hard to do it a second time. In order to deal with the division of gains from useful projects, however, it is necessary to canvass a wide variety of subjects of private and public law, and to show in particular why and how the ordinary accounts of "coercion" cannot be limited to the threats and use of force as that is understood in a purely autonomy based system. Instead the idea of coercion has to be brought to bear in connection with a wide variety of bargaining transactions that take place under conditions of necessity, where the state exercises its monopoly power alone or in conjunction with its power to tax and spend. The purpose of this book is to give systematic answers to this set of inquiries.

My answer to this set of problems has developed in two stages. Initially in the spring of 1988 I was asked by the editors of the *Harvard Law Review* to write the foreword for their Supreme Court issue for the 1987 term. I accepted their gracious offer, and a long article, "Foreword: Unconstitutional Conditions, State Power and the Limits of Consent" (102 *Harv. L. Rev.* 4 (1988)), was the result. When the dust settled on that project, I had the uneasy sense that far more work had to be done on the question, which was really one of book length proportions. I hesitated about whether to undertake that project until I was approached by Jack Repcheck, then the economics editor of Princeton University Press, who encouraged me with the promise of publication to undertake the longer study, which, while it has preserved much of the original material, has easily grown to more than twice its former length. In particular I have added at the beginning of the book a far longer theoretical explanation of coercion and the legal paradox of unconstitutional conditions. I also have added discussions of many topics not considered in the earlier book (including many forms of taxation and licensing), and updated and revised the discussion to take into account the materials, both academic and judicial, that have appeared on the subject in the four years since I completed work on the "Foreword." Philosophical writers on the subject of identity may debate whether the book is a continuation of the older "Foreword" or a brand new work, or, as seems to be the truth, a composite of the two. Nonetheless I hope that the ideas that it contains will interest people both in and out of the law concerned with the fundamental matters of political and constitutional obligation, whether or not they have read the original "Foreword."

In dealing with a work of this sort, I am of course in debt to many people. In particular, I presented various portions of this book at the Constitutional Law Panel on Unconstitutional Conditions held at the Annual Meeting of the American Association of Law Schools in 1989 (which resulted in the publication of an excellent volume, *Unconstitutional Conditions Symposium* (26 *San Diego Law Review*, in which my contribution was "Unconstitutional Conditions and Bargaining Breakdown," 26 *San Diego L. Rev. 189* (1989)). In addition, I presented parts of this paper at workshops or lectures, at Boalt Hall, the law school of The University of California at Berkeley, the University of Kansas Law School, Chicago-Kent Law School, Harvard Law School, and the University of Chicago Law School.

I have benefited from the assistance of many people in the preparation of this manuscript. The editors of the Harvard Law Review, especially its President Dan Kahan and its executive editor Gregory Katsas, did yeoman work in rounding the "Foreword" into shape within such a short time span. They constantly supplied me with cases and materials to take into account, and they edited the original manuscript with sympathy and appreciation for its overall conception, and with a careful and attentive eye to detail. In addition, there are many people who have read parts of this manuscript in the various stages of its production: Larry Alexander, Albert Alschuler, Douglas G. Baird, Gerhard Casper, David P. Currie, Frank H. Easterbrook, Larry Kramer, Jonathan Macey, Michael W. McConnell, Frank I. Michelman, Randal C. Picker, Charles Smith, David A. Strauss, and Cass R. Sunstein. Richard A. Posner found time in his overcrowded schedule to read and supply detailed and insightful comments on the completed version of the manuscript. In addition, I am grateful for the excellent help of Daniel Klerman, Annalisa Pizzarello, and Jay Wright, my three research assistants who over the past two years went over more times than I care to recall the entire manuscript. I also wish to thank Charles Dibble for his excellent and meticulous copyediting of the original manuscript, and Peter Dougherty for his energetic assistance in turning a submitted manuscript into a completed book. My secretary Kathryn Kepchar helped in the preparation of this manuscript, and my family, to whom this book is dedicated, once again endured the distractions of a husband and father who perhaps too often took his work to the dinner table.

*Chicago, Illinois*
*September 21, 1992*

# Part One

## THEORETICAL FOUNDATIONS: THE PROBLEM OF COERCION

CHAPTER 1

# Givings and Takings

## TAKINGS AND BARGAINING RISKS: HEREIN OF THE PARADOX OF UNCONSTITUTIONAL CONDITIONS

In this book I shall explore the extent to which, as a matter of political and constitutional theory, it is proper to impose limits on the power of the state to bargain with its citizens. The inquiry in question is in large part a continuation of some of the themes that I had previously developed in my book *Takings*.[1] As with that earlier book the inquiry is conducted at two levels. The first level is abstract, and seeks to determine the answer to this question within the framework of an ideal constitution. The second level, in contrast, is intensely practical, and seeks to address the limitations on the state's power to bargain within the context of a wide range of government programs and initiatives, many of which are the creature of the modern welfare state, but some of which predate it by hundreds of years.

At bottom, a belief in constitutional government entails an acceptance of some limitations on government power. One of the most obvious of these is directed at the power of the government to take property (here broadly defined) from some individuals in order to give it to others: confiscation, seizure, destruction, and regulation of private property must be subject to some external limitations if constitutional government is to survive political faction and intrigue. Even though there are vast differences of opinion as to what these limits might be, there are strong, widespread intuitions that untrammeled government power to coerce its citizens is a fatal mistake of constitutional dimensions. The entire logic of the takings clause, and many of the other specific constitutional guarantees in our constitution (protection of contracts, the free exercise of religion, the guarantees of due process) are efforts to delineate the appropriate limits of that most fundamental, most necessary, and most dangerous of government powers: the power to take.

That analysis is enormously complicated because the government itself is not some disembodied entity. Just as corporations are elabo-

[1] Richard A. Epstein, *Takings: Private Property and the Power of Eminent Domain* (1985) [hereinafter *Takings*].

rate networks of shareholders, so too states are elaborate networks of citizens endowed with rights and burdened with obligations of bewildering complexity, criss-crossing in every direction. Whenever property (however defined) is taken from some person, in the same breadth, or by the same act, property is given to some other people as well. Property is taken from some, not so that they will lose, but so that others, who control the political process, will win. A complete analysis of the takings question requires a full consideration of what happens to persons who do *not* bear the direct brunt of government action, as well as to those who do.

The same set of problems arises with respect to the other side of the transaction—where government *gives* things to certain individuals. At root, these ostensible gifts are gifts of property that has been taken from other persons, so these transfers necessarily implicate important questions of takings theory and practice. Normally someone is not allowed to give or sell what he does not own: *Nemo dat quod non habet* is the original Roman law maxim, which has been faithfully carried over into the common law.[2] The full rigor of this maxim applied to the state means the government must establish the legitimacy of its taking in order to legitimate its subsequent transfers of the property so taken. Otherwise it is little better than the thief who attempts to convey good title to a third person, especially to a purchaser in bad faith, that is, one who knows or who has reason to know the defect in the state's title. The concern with the legal title to government property is surely the proper subject of a treatise that deals with the constitutional limitations on the power to tax, although these are slender or nonexistent today.[3] But questions about the legitimacy of taxation may be raised in more than one context, and it often turns out that where taxpayers themselves are unable to mount a direct challenge upon government activities, program recipients, either actual or potential, should be allowed to do so.[4] One of the constant risks to which I shall refer to in analyzing bargaining with the government may be termed the *takings* risk.

[2] See, e.g., Campbell Printing Press v. Walker, 22 Fla. 412, 418, 1 So. 59, 62 (1886). The doctrine was of great importance in the early law in part because of the limited exceptions to it. Thus in commercial law one perennial conflict is whether a person in possession of a chattel can convey good title to a good faith purchaser, even if he is not the owner. See, for the early history of the doctrine, Saul Levmore, "Variety and Uniformity in the Treatment of the Good Faith Purchaser," 16 *J. Legal Stud.* 43 (1987). In the ordinary case, however, the buyer cannot acquire a title any better than that of the seller; if the rule were otherwise, then a subsequent sale would serve to insulate a prior theft.

[3] See infra chap. 9.

[4] See infra chap. 14.

Yet the difficulty with government givings is not confined to origins of the state's title to the property that is given. In addition, there has been extensive and widespread concern with the form that the gift (or grant, contract, or benefit program) assumes when viewed from the position of its *recipient*, who may be asked to take the gift subject to conditions or restrictions imposed by the state. The second side of the problem therefore might be termed the *bargaining* risks that are associated with government behavior: what kinds of conditions may the state impose on citizens in the course of their mutual dealings? In many circles this recipient concern is often set out as a kind of a paradox, which in legal circles travels under the name of the "paradox of unconstitutional conditions": the government (sometimes conceived as an individual, sometimes not) may be able to withhold certain benefits absolutely from a person, or it may be able to confer those benefits to a person unconditionally. Although it is possible for the government to adopt either of these two extreme positions, the doctrine of unconstitutional conditions nonetheless insists that the state is *not* entitled to take certain intermediate positions, whereby it conditions the transfer it makes upon the individual waiver of constitutional rights.

Stated in its canonical form, this doctrine holds that even if a state has absolute discretion to grant or deny any individual a privilege or benefit, it cannot grant the privilege subject to conditions that improperly "coerce," "pressure," or "induce" the waiver of that person's constitutional rights. Thus, in the context of individual rights, the doctrine provides that, on at least some occasions, receipt of a benefit to which someone has no constitutional entitlement does not justify making that person abandon some right guaranteed under the Constitution.[5] In other instances, the doctrine prevents the government from asking the individual to surrender by agreement those rights that the government could not take by direct action. For example, although a state may absolutely forbid foreign corporations from doing business within its borders, it cannot allow them to do so on condition that they waive their right to federal diversity jurisdiction, any more than it could divest them of this right by statute.[6] In

[5] See generally William W. Van Alstyne, "The Demise of the Right-Privilege Distinction in Constitutional Law," 81 *Harv. L. Rev.* 1439, 1445–49 (1968).

[6] Diversity jurisdiction, of course, refers to suits between citizens of different states. The initial Supreme Court decision, Doyle v. Continental Insurance Co., 94 U.S. 535 (1876), upheld the power to divest the federal courts of their diversity jurisdiction over the dissent of Justice Bradley who made early use of the phrase "unconstitutional conditions." "Though a State may have the power, if it sees fit, to subject its citizens to the inconvenience, of prohibiting all foreign corporations from transacting business within its jurisdiction, it has no power to impose unconstitutional conditions upon

still other instances the doctrine closely resembles an equal protection norm, barring the state from making certain privileges available to individuals only if they consent to terms more onerous than those demanded when the same privileges are made available to others. Again, the state may prevent foreign corporations from doing business in the state altogether, but it may not allow them to do business in the state only on condition that they pay higher taxes than their local competitors.

The problem of unconstitutional conditions arises whenever a government seeks to achieve its desired result by obtaining bargained-for consent of the party whose conduct is to be restricted. There is, for example, only an ordinary First Amendment issue involving the use of government power when the government seeks to impose prior restraints on publication or broadcast of news stories. That question is transformed into an unconstitutional conditions issue when some government benefit is conditioned upon acceptance of some prior restraint on publication or broadcast. Similarly, there is a traditional equal protection claim when the government imposes heavier criminal penalties on blacks than it does on whites, or vice versa. The unconstitutional conditions overlay is relevant only when the government sells goods or services to blacks on more onerous contract terms and conditions than those it offers to whites. But even so the potential scope of the doctrine is enormous. Thus it is possible for the contract conditions, if left unchallenged, to single out a select class of individuals for more onerous treatment than others. There is nothing that requires all persons to have an equal chance to comply with the conditions in question, although many of the conditions examined in this book are of this second (and generally less insidious) type.

There is a special conceptual problem with the doctrine of unconstitutional conditions that does not arise in connection with ordi-

---

their doing so." Id. at 543. An earlier hint of the doctrine is found in Lafayette Ins. Co. v. French, 59 U.S. (18 How.) 404, 407 (1856): "This consent [to do business as a foreign corporation] may be accompanied by such conditions as Ohio may think fit to impose; . . . provided they are not repugnant to the Constitution or laws of the United States." The condition sustained in *French* required the corporation to accept service of process as a condition for doing business in the state.

At the time of *Doyle*, states were allowed to impose such conditions. *Doyle* was significantly restricted, however, by Barron v. Burnside, 121 U.S. 186 (1887), which returned to the earlier position of Home Ins. Co. v. Morse, 87 U.S. (20 Wall.) 445 (1874), by striking down a similar condition. *Doyle* was definitively overruled, and the position of *Morse* and *Barron* reaffirmed, in Terral v. Burke Constr. Co., 257 U.S. 529, 533 (1922). See infra at chap. 8.

nary constitutional limits imposed on the exercise of government powers. Why does the doctrine exist at all? Why should there be any limitation on a system of government power that rests on the actual consent of the individuals whose rights are thereby abridged? To be sure, even a robust system of free markets contains some limitations upon the principle of consent in ordinary contracts between private individuals. Duress, force, misrepresentation, undue influence, and incompetence may be used to set aside contracts that otherwise meet the normal requirements of offer, acceptance, consideration, and consent. But none of these conventional grounds accounts for the doctrine of unconstitutional conditions, which comes into play only after all these conventional hurdles to contract formation and validity have been overcome.

The analogies to ordinary contract law thus give rise to a persistent puzzle that can be formulated in both conceptual and practical terms. To revert to the foreign corporation cases, if a state can exclude a foreign corporation, why can it not admit the corporation subject to whatever conditions it wishes to impose? Justice Holmes dismissed the entire doctrine of unconstitutional conditions as a logical and conceptual error: "Even in the law the whole generally includes its parts. If the State may prohibit, it may prohibit with the privilege of avoiding the prohibition in a certain way."[7] Sometimes the puzzle is stated in terms of a greater and a lesser power. The greater power to exclude might be said to include the lesser power to admit on condition.[8]

The objection to the doctrine of unconstitutional conditions can also be stated in functional terms. Under present law, unionized workers have the right to strike for economic reasons. The state may, if it chooses, give welfare to its unemployed citizens. It now

[7] Western Union Tel. Co. v. Kansas, 216 U.S. 1, 53 (1910) (Holmes, J., dissenting). There is an obvious tension between Holmes the jurist and Holmes the scholar. Holmes the scholar embodied the entire legal realist movement in a single sentence: "The life of the law has not been logic: it has been experience." Oliver Wendell Holmes, Jr., *The Common Law* 1 (1881).

[8] Cf. Posadas de Puerto Rico Assocs. v. Tourism Co., 478 U.S. 328, 345–47 (1986) (holding that "greater" power to ban gambling includes "lesser" power to ban advertising promoting gambling). The formulation is somewhat misleading, however, because greater/lesser problems can arise even when the issue of consent or the form of a conditional grant is far removed from a case. For example, any case of selective enforcement of criminal or civil sanctions might be said to give rise to a greater/lesser problem: if the state has the greater power to punish both blacks and whites, then it has the lesser power to punish only blacks or only whites. Although such cases do not give rise to an unconstitutional conditions problem as that term is used here, the greater/lesser language is still applicable.

chooses to withhold those benefits from workers who are out on strike.[9] How can striking workers complain that they have not received benefits to which they have no absolute entitlement? The state has made an offer—abandon the strike to receive the welfare benefits—that any worker may choose to accept or reject. There has been no use or threat of force. As long as individuals know what is best for themselves, they can enter into only those bargains that leave them better off than they were before. Some workers have taken the bargain and others have cast it aside. All workers are free to make whatever decisions they choose, but must live with the consequences of their decisions once made.[10] The same point could be made about bargains made with members of distinct racial groups. Under this view, for example, blacks cannot complain because they are better off with the bargains they made than they were before the state contracted with either blacks or whites.

These examples are intended to show that the Pareto principle for measuring social welfare makes it unnecessary to adopt any doctrine of unconstitutional conditions. As originally developed, the Pareto criterion attempted to make social judgments about alternative states of the world without resorting to problematic interpersonal comparisons of utility. It avoided the necessity and awkwardness of such comparisons by prescribing a test that allowed each person to compare his own private welfare before and after the legal change. Thus if no person in state A is worse off than he was in state B, and at least one person is better off in state A than he was in state B, then state A must be judged as superior to state B. The criterion of judgment is social in the sense that the welfare of every individual is taken into account; yet the stringent condition that no person be worse off in state A than in state B obviates the need for any comparison of welfare across separate persons.

The Pareto formula has often been attacked for being too restrictive on government, for it appears to invalidate any social program that provides enormous benefits so long as one person is left worse off.[11] Nonetheless, where the relevant universe involves only two self-interested parties, any voluntary agreement or grant satisfies the test, for the agreement is formed only if it makes both sides better off

[9] Lyng v. International Union, UAW, 485 U.S. 360 (1988).

[10] For a celebration of this bargain theory, see Maurice H. Merrill, "Unconstitutional Conditions," 77 *U. Pa. L. Rev.* 879 (1929). There are shades of the same position in the dissenting opinion of Justice Rehnquist in First National Bank of Boston v. Bellotti, 435 U.S. 765, 823–27 (1978) (Rehnquist, J., dissenting).

[11] See, e.g., Jules L. Coleman, "Efficiency, Utility, and Wealth Maximization," 8 *Hofstra L. Rev.* 509 (1980).

than before, given that each is the best judge of his own welfare. The use of this Pareto formula presupposes that the status quo ante is the baseline against which shifts in individual welfare are measured. Thus when people reject a bargain or grant offered by the state, they are no worse off than they were before. When they accept the bargain or grant subject to the condition, they are better off. Either way, they are not in a position to complain. The state for its part is treated (and this assumption will become controversial) as though it were a single person that knows "its" own preferences when measured against the same baseline of the status quo ante. If its bargain or grant is rejected, then it will be no worse off than before; if that grant or condition is accepted, then it will be better off. In both cases the stringent Pareto conditions are satisfied so that there is no reason to worry about the terms and conditions that the government attaches to its bargain or grant. No matter what its outcome, the proposed transaction appears unassailable.

At first blush, then, a categorical rejection of the doctrine of unconstitutional conditions seems to square with both traditional conceptions of sovereign power and modern tests of social welfare. A position with so strong an apparent pedigree should be hard to dislodge on any ground. Yet the doctrine of unconstitutional conditions tenaciously endures, notwithstanding charges by figures no less distinguished than Justice Holmes that it is both logically incoherent and corrosive of sovereign power.[12] Originating during the nineteenth century, the doctrine of unconstitutional conditions is no novel judicial concoction of the post–New Deal welfare state. Nor is the doctrine anchored to any single clause of the Constitution. Like the police power, it is a creature of judicial implication. It roams about constitutional law like Banquo's ghost, invoked in some cases, but not in others. It has been used as an aid in construing the scope

[12] Holmes's most famous statement of his position is found in McAuliffe v. Mayor of New Bedford, 155 Mass. 216, 29 N.E. 517 (1892): "The petitioner may have a constitutional right to talk politics, but he has no constitutional right to be a policeman. There are few employments for hire in which the servant does not agree to suspend his constitutional right of free speech, as well as of idleness, by the implied terms of his contract. The servant cannot complain, as he takes the employment on the terms which are offered him." id. 155 Mass. at 220, 29 N.E. at 517–18.

A similar freedom-of-contract rationale is found in some of Holmes's tort opinions. See, e.g., Lamson v. American Axe & Tool Co., 177 Mass. 144, 145, 58 N.E. 585, 585–86 (1900): "[The workman] complained, and was notified that he could go if he would not face the chance. He stayed, and took the risk. He did so none the less that the fear of losing his place was one of his motives" (citations omitted). Justice Holmes reiterated these principles in the context of unconstitutional conditions in *Western Union Telephone.* See supra note 7.

of Congress's spending power[13] and of the states' police power.[14] It has been engrafted onto substantive protections afforded to speech,[15] religion,[16] and property.[17] It also has found expression in decisions under the equal protection[18] and due process[19] clauses.

The ubiquitous presence of the unconstitutional conditions doctrine thus provides powerful reason to subject it to close scrutiny. Nonetheless, it is a mistake to believe that the doctrine can be fully understood in conceptual isolation from the takings risks that are also present whenever the government bargains with its citizens. A full account of the place of the limitations on the power of the government to bargain requires both risks to be taken into account simultaneously. In principle, therefore, there are four cells to be filled, and it becomes important to see which cases fall into which cells. The first cell contains transactions that involve takings risks, but no bargaining risks. The second is the converse situation, in which the transaction involves a bargaining risk but not a takings risk. The third situation involves *both* a takings risk and a bargaining risk, where the two risks may point in opposite directions, and apparently require different outcomes. The dual constraints imposed upon the system mean that certain types of government programs—the denial of unemployment benefits to religious observers, the provision of health care and counseling to pregnant women, the funding of the arts[20]—place the law in an impossible position no matter how skillfully they are designed. The fourth category is in a sense the easiest, for it involves government transactions in which neither of the two risks are present, so that government choice is wholly insulated from private attack. In setting out the problem in this fashion, it should be clear that any complete analysis depends on the *overall* social situation.

[13] See Child Labor Tax Case, 259 U.S. 20 (1922); South Dakota v. Dole, 483 U.S. 203 (1987); infra chap. 10.

[14] See Nollan v. California Coastal Comm'n, 483 U.S. 825 (1987); Posadas de Puerto Rico Assocs. v. Tourism Co., 478 U.S. 328 (1986); infra chaps. 12, 13.

[15] See, e.g., City of Lakewood v. Plain Dealer Publishing Co., 486 U.S. 750 (1988); Arkansas Writers' Project, Inc. v. Ragland, 481 U.S. 221 (1987). For discussions of these cases, see infra chaps. 11, 15.

[16] See, e.g., Hobbie v. Unemployment Appeals Comm'n, 480 U.S. 136 (1987); Thomas v. Review Bd. of the Ind. Employment Sec. Div., 450 U.S. 707 (1981); Sherbert v. Verner, 374 U.S. 398 (1963); see discussion infra chap. 16.

[17] See, e.g., *Nollan*, 483 U.S. 825; see discussion infra chap. 12 .

[18] See, e.g., Southern Ry. v. Greene, 216 U.S. 400 (1910); see also discussion infra chap. 8.

[19] See Frost & Frost Trucking Co. v. California R.R. Railroad Comm'n, 271 U.S. 583 (1926); Western Union Tel. Co. v. Kansas, 216 U.S. 1 (1910); infra chap. 11.

[20] See infra chap. 18.

The scope of this inquiry, it must be stressed, is enormous. Indeed, with only a little exaggeration, it may be said that cases in which citizens bargain with the state are far more numerous and important than those cases in which the government simply takes property for public use. The systems of taxation and regulation, which have been traditionally analyzed under takings doctrines, often involve implicit bargains between the government and the citizen. The only form of tax, for example, which looks like an unambiguous taking, is a poll or a head tax, which imposes an obligation on the citizen to pay some fixed amount to the government regardless of what course of conduct the citizen adopts. The typical poll tax says that each person, regardless of income, owes $10,000 per annum for the upkeep of the state. Few, if any taxes take this form, and even here a bargaining problem arises if the citizen does not have the $10,000 for the government to take. Most taxes are conditional in the sense that they take a fraction of the income that the citizen earns, or impose a tax conditional on the size of the transaction. In essence the government says that *if* you choose to earn or to sell, then we will take so much from you, where the citizen has the option to reduce the amount of the activity in order to mitigate the tax. Similarly, minimum wage laws do not command private citizens to hire workers at given wages. Instead they only impose the conditional command which says, if you wish to hire certain workers, then you must pay them certain wages. These various government initiatives can therefore be understood as take-it-or-leave-it offers that are extended by the government to all individuals.

In other contexts, the bargaining component of interaction between citizen and state is more explicit. A developer applies to the local government for a construction permit, and is told that it will be granted only if certain conditions are complied with.[21] The power to refuse the permit sets the stage for extended and protracted negotiations between the two sides, where the fundamental legal question remains as before: are there any limitations on the terms and conditions that the state can impose on the project in question? In dealing with this inquiry, there is a certain irony and an evident reversal of roles and forensic positions. Devotees of freedom of contract in the private sphere (I count myself as one) are enormously suspicious of the exercise of government power through contract and grant. Yet persons who are suspicious of freedom of contract for private parties often gravitate to the view that the government has vast (if not total) discretion on the terms and conditions that can be imposed on private parties. The irony is, I think, clearly resolved by noting that the

[21] See infra chap. 12 .

ultimate question in these cases is not, do we believe in freedom of contract, but rather, do we believe in limited government and in what sphere? Where the belief in limited government holds, the pattern of response is to limit *both* the power of the government to regulate and to contract. Where the belief in limited government ebbs, then the power to regulate and the power to contract are both regarded as legitimate means for expanding government power.

It is this theme that allows for the unification of both givings and takings. In dealing with takings, my view is that the government should use force where bargaining and holdout problems prevent the reaching of a competitive solution. By the same token, government power to condition contracts or grants is limited to exactly the same end. The question in all cases, therefore, is whether the actions of the government tend to drive us closer to the desired end, or whether they tend to lead us further astray. For those who see only social peril and danger in competitive markets, the presumption is reversed. If direct regulation is allowable to control the excesses of the market, then the same must be said of government granting and contracting behavior.

## A CRITIQUE OF PAST SCHOLARSHIP

The argument thus far has shown that the problem of bargaining with the state is of sufficient complexity to require a comprehensive approach to the subject. Indeed I believe that many of the failures in dealing with this subject rest upon the implicit effort to consider one corner of the problem without attending to the overall situation. The weaknesses of this approach are I think evident in many of the numerous important and comprehensive articles that have dealt with its justification and scope.[22] The received writing usually focuses on the bargaining risks associated with the unconstitutional conditions problem, but then does not integrate that analysis with a concern for the parallel takings risk that is always present with gov-

[22] See, e.g., Vicki Been, "'Exit' as a Constraint on Land Use Exactions: Rethinking the Unconstitutional Conditions Doctrine," 91 *Colum. L. Rev.* 473 (1991); Seth F. Kreimer, "Allocational Sanctions: The Problem of Negative Rights in a Positive State," 132 *U. Pa. L. Rev.* 1293 (1984); Albert J. Rosenthal, "Conditional Federal Spending and the Constitution," 39 *Stan. L. Rev.* 1103 (1987); Kathleen M. Sullivan, "Unconstitutional Conditions," 102 *Harv. L. Rev.* 1413 (1989); Cass R. Sunstein, "Why the Unconstitutional Conditions Doctrine is an Anachronism (With Particular Reference to Religion, Speech, and Abortion)," 70 *B.U. L. Rev.* 593 (1990); William W. Van Alstyne, "The Demise of the Right-Privilege Distinction in Constitutional Law," 81 *Harv. L. Rev.* 1439 (1968).

ernment action.[23] Then, when dealing with the unconstitutional conditions portion of the problem, it seeks, by an elaborate explication of the idea of "coercion" to make unconstitutional conditions cases resemble garden-variety duress or coercion cases,[24] as is made evident by the constant discussion of differences between "penalties" or "fines" on the one hand, and "subsidies" or "benefits" on the other.[25] Yet if common law duress were present in these cases, the recipient of the grant would be able to attack the offending condition without resorting to any special doctrine of unconstitutional conditions. As long as the condition is obtained by coercion or duress, it can be set aside as a matter of right, regardless of its content. In contrast, the doctrine of unconstitutional conditions, much like the doctrine of substantive unconscionability in modern consumer law,[26] is directed towards the substance of various conditions, regardless of the course of negotiations between the individual recipient and the state. As with the private law doctrine of unconscionability, the area is one filled with pitfalls, for it is usually necessary, both in the public and private contexts, to have a precise understanding of the disputed terms or conditions in order to decide whether it should survive judicial scrutiny.[27]

The balancing tests commonly suggested by commentators to explain the doctrine show that it cannot be explained by analogy to common-law coercion.[28] The proposed balancing does not ask courts to weigh different sorts of evidence that might support or undercut

[23] A charge to which I have to plead guilty, at least in part. My Harvard "Foreword" did not articulate the interactive effects of these two risks in its theoretical section, but only stumbled on the importance of the problem in dealing with the abortion funding cases. Richard A. Epstein, "Foreword: Unconstitutional Conditions, State Power, and the Limits of Consent," 102 *Harv. L. Rev.* 4 (1988).

[24] See, e.g., Kreimer, supra note 22, at 1293; Steven Shiffrin, "Government Speech," 27 *UCLA L. Rev.* 565 (1980); William W. Van Alstyne, "Cracks in 'The New Property': Adjudicative Due Process in the Administrative State," 62 *Cornell L. Rev.* 445 (1977); Van Alstyne, supra note 5, at 1445–49.

[25] Stressed in *Sullivan*, supra note 22, at 1420, 1428. See infra chap. 10 (discussing the *Child Labor Tax Case*); infra chap. 16 (discussing Sherbert v. Verner, 374 U.S. 398 (1963)); infra chap. 15 (discussing Bob Jones Univ. v. United States, 461 U.S. 574 (1983)); infra chap. 16 (discussing Lyng v. International Union, UAW, 488 U.S. 360 (1988)).

[26] For an exhaustive account of the relevant literature, see E. Allan Farnsworth, *Contracts*, 319–43 (2d ed. 1990).

[27] For my defense of specific contract terms struck down on grounds of unconscionability, see Richard A. Epstein, "Unconscionability: A Critical Reappraisal," 18 *J.L. & Econ.* 293 (1975).

[28] See Kreimer, supra note 22, at 1349–51 (criticizing attempts by Van Alstyne and others to defend this balancing approach).

the claim that a certain gesture is an implied threat of the use of force.[29] Rather, its close involvement with the substantive terms and conditions of the statute—for example, whether the use of state highways is conditioned upon agreeing to service of process in all cases, or only on those arising out of highway use—distances us from the process-oriented issues that dominate ordinary duress cases. But without a strong substantive theory that explains both the use and the limits of individual consent in its larger social setting, the use of balancing tests in this context leaves far too much room for the legal imagination. Balancing must be in the service of a general theory. It cannot be a substitute for one.

Efforts to explain the doctrine on the basis of "dignitary" interests are equally unsatisfactory.[30] These dignitary theories rest on the belief that it offends the dignity of all persons who are asked to make certain choices, to sacrifice some interests for the benefit of others. The theory has had its greatest appeal in connection with welfare rights, where the contention is that it is improper for the state to condition the receipt of welfare benefits upon a waiver of right to a hearing before termination.[31] Yet this theory runs into the same difficulties in this context that it does in all others.

First, it is unclear how individual dignity is advanced when restrictions are placed upon the individual right to contract, or even receive welfare payments. Can one respect the dignity of the individual, and at the same time hold that a person, although of full age and competence, cannot make the decisions of greatest importance to his or her life prospects? How does one enhance dignity by restricting choice? Theories of dignity are often used to support notions of individual autonomy, yet here they are invoked to limit the ability of the individual to enter into desired agreements with the state.

Second, the dignitary theories are undermined by their exclusive focus on the individual upon whom the condition is imposed. As far back as Hohfeld, if not before, it has been understood that the crea-

[29] For a common law illustration of the difficulties, see Courvoisier v. Raymond, 23 Colo. 113, 47 P. 284 (1896).

[30] See, e.g., Jerry L. Mashaw, "Administrative Due Process: The Quest for a Dignitary Theory," 61 *B.U. L. Rev.* 885 (1981).

[31] See, e.g., Goldberg v. Kelly, 397 U.S. 254 (1970). Justice Brennan, the author of the opinion, defended its result in William J. Brennan Jr., "Reason, Passion, and 'The Progress of the Law,' The Forty-Second Annual Benjamin Cardozo Lecture," 42 *The Record of the Association of the Bar of the City of New York* 948 (1987). See infra chap. 17.

tion and recognition of a right or privilege in one person will impose correlative obligations on others.[32] The art (or science) of government is to apply some social criterion, such as the Pareto test, that helps decide which interests, including dignitary interests, should be protected, and which not. In this inquiry, of course, it is useful from the individual's perspective to identify the benefits of having certain conditions removed from state bargains or grants. But again the analysis is incomplete unless the correlative costs of their removal to other persons are taken into account as well. So long as resources are scarce, individual rights, even constitutional rights, must have some correlative duties. Thus, any complete analysis must take both sides of the same problem into account, but dignitary theories generally fail to do so.

One of the most ambitious effort to organize the unruly law of unconstitutional conditions is that of Professor Kreimer, who recognizes that standard notions of coercion are unable to account for the doctrine.[33] In Professor Kreimer's view, the greatest difficulty with the coercion question is identifying the appropriate baseline against which the possibly coercive effects of government action may be evaluated. When the baseline gives a right to the government, government may condition the benefits that it imposes. When it gives the right to the individual, then the government's extraction of a concession amounts to impermissible coercion.[34] Kreimer proposes

[32] See Wesley N. Hohfeld, "Some Fundamental Legal Conceptions as Applied in Judicial Reasoning," 23 *Yale L.J.* 16 (1913).

[33] Kreimer has also pointed out the limitations of simple contract models that focus exclusively on force and fraud. See Kreimer, supra note 22, at 1318: "While there is a contemporary philosophical school that attaches unique status to rights of bodily integrity and freedom from physical force, it is hard to imagine any modern constitutional theorist taking the position that only a direct threat of violence would violate constitutional rights." He attributes this model to Robert Nozick, Charles Fried, and me. See id. at 1318 n.77. In part, this book seeks to go beyond that simple libertarian model in the context of state grants and bargains. For my own concerns with the libertarian model, published after Kreimer's observation, see *Takings*, 334–38, and Richard A. Epstein, "The Classical Legal Tradition," 73 *Cornell L. Rev.* 292, 298–99 (1988).

[34] See Kreimer, supra note 22, at 1352: "My conclusion is that the distinction between liberty-expanding offers and liberty-reducing threats turns on the establishment of an acceptable baseline against which to measure a person's position after the imposition of an allocation." The use of baseline analysis is extensive in the treatments of coercion in both the philosophical literature and the common law. The most exhaustive treatment is the excellent study by Alan Wertheimer, *Coercion* (1987), which treats coercion as a function of the interaction between the two parties to a transaction, and not in light of its systemic social effects.

three baselines against which the constitutionality of any government bargain can be measured: history, equality, and prediction.[35]

Although an account of baselines is essential to any general analysis of unconstitutional conditions, Kreimer's inability to offer a single baseline for assessing conditional government benefits renders his account problematic. For example, the historical baseline may allow the states selectively to grant access to the public highways in a way that the equality norm prohibits. Consistent and determinate baselines can be generated only with aid of a theory that links the substantive guarantees provided under the Constitution to the set of government practices and processes that can undermine them. The desired theory, moreover, has to be functional, not intuitive: it must explain how some social improvement is obtained by striking down the condition in question. So much at least is demanded by any theory that treats the substance of bargains, not the process of their formation, as its subject matter. What is needed is a more systematic examination of the overall consequences of certain bargaining strategies undertaken by government. It is just that theory that this book seeks to supply.

[35] See Kreimer, supra note 22, at 1359–74. History refers to the use of tradition and the status quo ante as a baseline, so that coercion occurs when a previously enjoyed benefit is lost. See id. at 1359–63. Equality refers to equal treatment under the law, and invokes equal protection ideals generally. See id. at 1363–71. Prediction is the hardest baseline of all to grasp because it requires a counterfactual judgment of what a government would have done had it been asked to adopt a policy without reference to the constitutional rights that it is asking the individual citizen to waive. See id. at 1371–74.

## CHAPTER 2

# The Plan of Action

IN THIS BOOK I hope to start anew to develop a comprehensive approach to the problem of bargaining with the state, integrating the discussion of unconstitutional conditions with a discussion of the takings risk. That inquiry is itself an exceedingly complicated one. The canonical statement of the unconstitutional conditions inquiry, for example, leads one into a discussion of baselines and coercion, and rests upon the widespread agreement that a discussion of the latter depends upon the proper identification of the former.[1] Efforts to expose the greater/lesser fallacy therefore take extensive detours into the private law analogies that serve as the best testing ground for these constitutional theories. No adequate inquiry into the problem of bargaining with government can proceed in ignorance of the proper rules that govern bargains between private parties. Accordingly this book shall begin with an extensive inquiry into the fundamental building blocks that show the uses and limits of baselines, coercion, and bargaining within ordinary private transactions. The inquiry has to begin cautiously at its foundations, and proceed by increment and indirection to its final analysis of the unconstitutional conditions problem.

The first half of this book develops the conceptual framework. Its inquiry is overtly functional and utilitarian. Bargains are interactions thought to advance some overall measure of social welfare. They are not regarded as absolutes in themselves. Essentially, we want to enforce bargains when and only when they satisfy two criteria. First, does the bargain create joint gains for the contracting parties? Second, does the bargain respect the interests of third persons who are not parties to the bargain? Within a libertarian framework, the first criterion is satisfied by refusing to enforce bargains induced by force and fraud. Similarly, the second criterion is met by refusing to enforce bargains that contemplate the use or threat of force or fraud against third parties. As stated, these criteria account for many of the necessary limitations on the common law regime of contractual freedom. Although this model addresses some of the possible

[1] See, e.g., Alan Wertheimer, *Coercion* 202–21 (1987).

externalities that are created by contractual agreements, it ignores monopoly and collective action problems, even though these may induce individuals to take actions that benefit their private but not the social interest. Each of these phenomena offers compelling reasons why certain private bargains are not enforced. The problems each poses arise with equal or greater intensity in the context of state bargains. The reasons that lead us not to enforce some private bargains can thus explain why certain bargains between the government and the individual are not enforced. Once those reasons are explicated, we can provide a more systematic consequentialist argument for why the doctrine of unconstitutional conditions limits the ability of individuals to consent to the surrender of constitutional rights.

Bargaining does not take place in a vacuum. The literature on unconstitutional conditions makes constant reference to choosing the baseline, that is, the system of property rights against which government grants, benefits, and contracts are to be assessed. It is therefore necessary to understand something about how these baselines are established, both as a matter of general political theory and ordinary legal practice, before turning to how they are interpreted at various stages in our constitutional history. This inquiry is the main task of chapter 3, which seeks to explain in principle how considerations of transaction costs drive us to the conventional baselines in person and property (both public and private property) that have been accepted in the common law.

Chapters 4 and 5 then show how the theoretical problems identified in the third chapter should be attacked from the point of view of bargaining theory generally. In these chapters, I argue that the linkage between "coercion" and the protection of its victims should be understood only as a powerful but imperfect proxy for making judgments about the overall social distribution of goods and services. The chapter first considers the relatively uncontroversial applications of coercion which involve the threat of force or fraud. It then moves beyond these obvious cases to a broader class of "coercive offers" that do not involve the use or threat of force: monopoly, prisoner's dilemma games, necessity, blackmail, and tender offers. Thereafter it examines how the takings risk manifests itself whenever government makes decisions on the use or allocation of "its" property.

The discussions of the difficult issues in chapter 4 and 5 should, I hope, be of interest in their own right. They also set the stage for the transition from private to public law, a task which is accomplished in the next two chapters. In some contexts at least, the bargaining problems identified in chapters 4 and 5 should be overcome by government coercion in order to create a viable and ongoing state, capable of enforcing the legal norms developed in private law. A full account of the legal order must do more than articulate the rules of acquisition, the rules of protection, and the rules of exchange. A system of limited government is for good reason *not* a robust libertarian system in which initial individual liberties and property rights can be removed only with the consent of the holder of the right or to provide rectification to the victims of those wrongs. In addition, the state may institute a wide range of forced exchanges, where these exchanges produce an overall level of social improvement that is not obtainable by voluntary exchanges of preexisting property rights.

Chapter 6 examines that network of forced exchanges with special attention to the traditional just compensation requirement in takings law. The chapter seeks to show why a sensible constitutional order requires both a comprehensive account of what constitutes a taking, and a strict just compensation requirement. The decision to make each person whole after a given exchange is commonly defended as a requirement of fairness in the individual case. Yet it is better understood, I believe, as an effort to discipline the acquisitive behavior that lies behind so much legislative action. Indeed the chapter shows that the entire problem of just compensation is rendered moot in any (utopian) system where legislatures have public-seeking motivations and reliable information about the consequences of their action. It also offers some explanation as to why the risk of judicial abuse is an acceptable price to pay to control the legislative abuses that all too often do occur.

Chapter 7 then extends the analysis to its second stage once the objective of just compensation is achieved. At this juncture two related inquiries arise. First, what techniques help insure *the maximization of the social surplus* from forced exchanges initiated by government? Second, what rules determine each person's share of that surplus? By answering these questions it will be possible to lay bare the inadequacies of the greater/lesser power argument. The baseline against which bargains with the state should be judged therefore is subtly transformed. No longer is it sufficient to show that some government action leaves everyone better off than they would have been if there had been no exchange at all. Instead it becomes critical to show that none are left worse off than they would have been if the *optimal set* of social exchanges had been imposed by the state. The doctrine of unconstitutional conditions is thus directed toward the preservation of the total surplus of government action, and concerned with its proper distribution among various actors.

The remainder of the book is concerned less with general theory and more with practical doctrine. Before addressing the material in each chapter, several additional layers of complication first have to be taken into account. Ours was not a perfect constitution at the time of its formation, and its basic structure has been heavily battered by over two centuries of interpretation. The approach taken toward the question of unconstitutional conditions will therefore mirror the shifts in judicial attitudes to the exercise of all government powers. To what extent is government activity viewed under a presumption of distrust? The usual private law approach to this question is that individuals generally act out of their own self-interest, and seek to maximize their own private returns, subject to the legal constraints under which they labor. The regulations against theft, monopoly, and breach of contract are set, however imperfectly, to minimize the likelihood that they will be able to achieve some private gain at some net social cost. To be sure, this presumption of distrust is somewhat overdrawn. There are many individuals who will come to the aid of those who are in trouble, without so much as the thought of payment to themselves. Many people would never think of abusing their partnership control to cheat their partners. These cases are important for any overall assessment of human nature, but they are not the cases against which the legal rules are directed. Honest and honorable people will behave well regardless of the legal framework in which they act. The law must be directed against that fraction of the total population for whom self-interest is the sole beacon of conduct—Holmes's famous "bad man" who wants to know the law only to skirt its commands.[2] For such people, the assumptions of the law fit all too well with the behavior that the law seeks to control.

The question—what are the mainsprings of human nature?—carries over to the constitutional context with equal significance. If it is assumed that government officials and the private parties who influence them are prone to the corrosive influence of self-interest, then the legal rules should strictly scrutinize whatever behavior they undertake. If the direct use of government coercion is subject to serious constitutional scrutiny, then government bargains should be subject to a similar level of scrutiny. The doctrine of unconstitutional conditions thus becomes an inseparable part of constitutional law, atten-

[2] Oliver Wendell Holmes, Jr., "The Path of the Law," 10 *Harv. L. Rev.* 457 (1897). Needless to say, the law addresses other constituencies, including citizens who wish to comply with it and judges and administrators who apply it. But the acid test of a clear law is whether its commands are accepted by those who would love to violate it.

dant to any and all exercises of government power. Alternatively, if government officials are assumed to act with benevolent motives when they regulate, then they should be assumed to act with similar motives when they contract. The low level of scrutiny found under modern, rational-basis review would carry over from regulation to bargains, and the doctrine of unconstitutional conditions would play only a marginal role in our legal firmament.

There are today many competing general constitutional visions, which bear on the question of how courts should regard government figures. Some theories stress the virtues of republican self-government;[3] others the satisfaction of "dignitary" interests;[4] still others the protection of economic liberty or the niceties of utilitarian calculation. Other constitutional theories rest upon the sanctity of private property and the fear of the democratic excesses of the populist masses.[5] For present purposes, the correctness of these basic orientations is not the critical point. The various theories only direct attention to those areas in which the political process is viewed with distrust. It is precisely in those areas that the doctrine of unconstitutional conditions will take root and flourish. It is therefore necessary to trace the ebb and flow of the unconstitutional conditions doctrine through changing attitudes of constitutional law. More concretely, there are in general two basic stages of that historical evolution that bear separate comment.

First, it is necessary to examine the doctrine of unconstitutional conditions as it worked in the pre-1937, pre–New Deal, constitutional world, which at the risk of some oversimplification, stressed two fundamental values: the protection of private property against government regulation, and the insistence upon a strong system of federalism in which the federal government could legislate only in certain enumerated and restricted domains and, correlatively, in which states had powers that they could exercise independent of federal control. It was a world in which many individual property rights were beyond the direct power of regulation of the government at all levels, and in which, when regulation was permitted, the states could act without taking their lead from the federal government. The presumption of distrust of government officials was thus re-

[3] See, e.g., Frank I. Michelman, "The Supreme Court, 1985 Term—Foreword: Traces of Self-Government," 100 *Harv. L. Rev.* 4 (1986). For a more recent discussion, see Symposium, "The Republican Civic Tradition," 97 *Yale L.J.* 1493 (1988).

[4] See supra at 14–15.

[5] The framers' concerns in this regard are set out in Michael W. McConnell, "Contract Rights and Property Rights: A Case Study in the Relationship Between Individual Liberties and Constitutional Structure," 76 *Calif. L. Rev.* 267, 270–71 (1988).

flected both in the analysis of government powers and in the protection of individual rights.

Second, there is the post–1937 world where the landscape has been sharply altered. Now the protection of property rights has been sharply reduced, although not fully eliminated. A parallel development, however, marks the rise of other individual rights associated, for example, with speech, religion, and reproductive freedom. This new hierarchy of legal rights increases the scope of permissible taxation and regulation, and thus the scope of the takings risk. Simultaneously, it makes the doctrine of unconstitutional conditions especially difficult to apply to complex modern statutory schemes that implement explicit or implicit transfers of wealth for purposes now regarded as unquestionably legitimate—for example, to regulate land use, or to help the needy or unemployed. Many programs have both effects in varying degrees, and often work their transfers along forbidden lines, such as political or religious affiliation. Frequently, the question arises how to disentangle the multiple strands of a single statutory scheme, subjecting each to its appropriate level of review—minimal scrutiny for ordinary rights, strict scrutiny for fundamental rights and suspect classifications. The coerced transfer of property from A to B may be allowed today in general economic areas, but it will not be tolerated along (say) religious or political lines. Where the state seeks those forbidden objectives through contracting, its actions will be met with the same hostility as when it proceeds through direct regulation or taxation. In such contexts, we find the continued, indeed expanded, vitality of the doctrine of unconstitutional conditions in modern times.

To make matters still more difficult, the older order of federalism has been transformed so that the federal power is no longer constrained within narrow enumerated heads. Today the states have to struggle to maintain their own powers free of federal influence when Congress chooses to act. But while there is virtually unlimited federal power, much law has been made about the tensions and rivalries between states in those areas where the Congress has not acted, especially with respect to state taxes and regulations that may burden interstate commerce. There is now in place an active and extensive body of Supreme Court jurisprudence covering the kind of actions that individual states may take to burden and obstruct interstate commerce. To that extent, at least, the earlier concern with the maintenance of the competitive order still remains an important feature of the modern constitutional system.

The doctrine of unconstitutional conditions, then, has survived in these two very different constitutional environments, and any adequate theory of the subject cannot be moored exclusively to either underlying vision of the constitutional order. The point must be stressed time and again because, even though I am a devout and unrepentant supporter of the earlier vision of constitutional order,[6] many of the arguments advanced in this book survive even if I am wrong in my stubborn allegiance to discarded doctrine. The concern with unconstitutional conditions, resting as it does on a general view of bargaining theory, can apply with equal vigor in both settings. The same applies to the comprehensive takings risk, given the expanded powers of taxation and regulation commonly afforded the state.

There is a second strand of the doctrine of unconstitutional conditions that also merits mention at the outset. The doctrine of unconstitutional conditions is beset with the serious problem of being a "second-best" approach to controlling government discretion. In many cases, the Supreme Court has held that Congress or the states have absolute discretion with regard to matters such as allowing foreign corporations to do business within the state or allowing commercial vehicles to use public highways. This discretion increases the risks of government misbehavior. In some cases, the doctrine of unconstitutional conditions is used to "take back" some of the power which had been conferred upon government officials in the first instance. In principle, the doctrine's application would be unnecessary if the Court had restricted the scope of the government power in the first place.

Often the unsatisfactory nature of the doctrine of unconstitutional conditions arises from its status as a mop-up doctrine when other forms of constitutional restraint have been abandoned. Within these contexts, it is often very difficult to decide whether the doctrine does more harm than good. When the government is told that it cannot bargain with individuals, the empirical question arises whether government will deny them a useful benefit altogether or grant them the benefit without the obnoxious condition.

Using this framework, the second half of the book shows how the doctrine of unconstitutional conditions does, and should, function in a variety of contexts as a check against the political perils of bargaining and takings risks. In principle there are two ways to organize the discussion. The first is to examine how the doctrine works with respect to its distinct limitations upon the "prices" people have to

[6] I am one of the few explicit supporters of the pre-1937 understandings on both counts. See, Richard A. Epstein, "The Mistakes of 1937," 11 *George Mason L. Rev.* 5 (1988); Richard A. Epstein, "The Proper Scope of the Commerce Power," 73 *Va. L. Rev. 1387* (1987).

pay in order to obtain benefits from the government. Thus, there could be a discussion of the First Amendment protections of speech and religion, the takings clause, the due process clause, and the like. I have chosen not to follow that course, at least not fully. Instead, I have adopted an approach that first identifies the different heads of government power (the power to extend privileges of incorporation, to grant access to highways, to tax) and then shows how the doctrine of unconstitutional conditions plays itself out with respect to their exercise. By beginning with the powers and not the limitations, it is easier, I think, to follow both the doctrine's historical development and its institutional framework.

The examination of doctrine is divided into two parts. Part Two, which includes chapters 8 to 14, deals with a wide range of economic issues that have been, and often continue to be, litigated before the Court. Chapters 8 through 10 deal with a cross between issues of federalism and economic issues. Chapter 8 addresses the limitations on the state power of incorporation. Chapter 9 then turns to the question of discriminatory taxation. Finally, chapter 10 deals with the tensions between the United States and the individual states. Matters of federalism are of less importance in the next three chapters which again deal primarily with economic and property issues. Chapter 11 addresses the issue of state control over public roads. Chapter 12 then extends the inquiry to state regulation of land use under the police power. Chapter 13 carries the police power theme forward to cover the general licensing of business and professions. Chapter 14 then deals with the same issues in connection with contracts of employment.

Part Four then carries the analysis forward to the welfare state. Chapter 15, a transitional chapter, addresses the general problem of tax exemptions in cases of religion and speech. Chapter 16 turns to unemployment benefits, and chapter 17 to welfare benefits. Finally, chapter 18 covers the contemporary problem of conditional grants for educational, religious, and artistic purposes. The hope is to present a comprehensive view of a subject which pervades all corners of general legal theory and constitutional law, both historical and modern.

CHAPTER 3

# Baselines

## AWAY FROM THE CORNER

The material contained in the first chapter left an overarching project that requires us to identify the baselines against which claims of coercion can be measured. Baselines offer the initial positions against which the propriety of subsequent individual or government action can be judged. The selection of these baselines is the first part of any inquiry into bargaining with the state, and it forms the subject matter of this chapter. The difficulties of the inquiry are always compounded because it is unclear whether these initial baselines should point toward collective or individual entitlements. The choice is not one of mere words, but, owing to the frictions that prevent optimal readjustments against initial mistakes, will influence the ultimate system for controlling resources as well. Where the entitlements are individual, there is a movement to markets, and where they are collective, there is a movement to government ownership and control.

The subject obtains its difficulty and importance because there is little sentiment in favor of adopting initial baselines that exclusively lead to either extreme position, that is, to a corner solution where all property is either public or private.[1] Intuitively, we all believe that some mix between private and public (or at least common) property will yield more desirable outcomes than a solution that embraces one system of control to the exclusion of the other. A system that uses only collective means to determine all questions of allocation and distribution runs into the insuperable problems of centralized planning. The information necessary to make intelligent decisions and the incentive structures to see that the decisions, once made, are properly executed, cannot be obtained by any system of command and control. The failures of the socialized economies of Eastern Eu-

[1] A corner solution arises when an all-or-nothing trade-off is optimal between two goods. If the choice is between the production of guns and butter, a corner solution is preferable when the total value of the output is greatest with the production of either guns or butter, but not both. See generally David D. Friedman, *Price Theory: An Intermediate Text* 10–11 (2d ed. 1990).

rope and the Third World offer graphic evidence of the widespread dislocations and suffering that are brought about when economic decisions blend into political ones, and when both are concentrated exclusively in the hands of a powerful bureau or agency. Most everywhere the sentiment is in favor of moving toward market institutions as a way to liberate the forces of production from the heavy hand of the state.

By the same token, however, there is sharp resistance to the other extreme, that of political anarchy, in which the uncoordinated decisions of separate actors come together to form a cohesive and attractive whole. It is very difficult to regard as ideal a world without any resources owned and controlled by the government. Competitive markets have enormous resilience, but they cannot sustain themselves against all forms of external shock. Within the framework of a secure state, many individual markets may develop customary norms and informal enforcement mechanisms within any given industry.[2] Still, it is far cry to assume that the same process of voluntary coordination would take place with equal precision without the background institutions of state enforcement that allow these industry practices to mature and flourish. A pure system of private ordering cannot protect a system of voluntary, competitive, or even functioning markets. The anarchist vision that social control can come out of unanimous voluntary consent has never been tried, or if it has been tried, it has never succeeded. Economic markets, then, need political markets to support and sustain them. Politics will not succeed without markets, and markets will not function without politics.

Indeed, it is difficult to accept a somewhat weaker thesis, namely that the only proper function for publicly owned resources is to enforce a system of private rights. A well-functioning state may well have some resources that by law are not reducible to private ownership and may be shared by others: waterways are the stock example of resources held in common in the original position; public highways, open to all, are in many contexts superior to private toll roads. Some forms of property are better held in common than privately. So long as that proposition is true, then it will not be possible to move to a world with all private and no public, or common, property. The hard question is to find out what form of "mixed" economy will work the best for the social system at large. The most a priori arguments can do is to eliminate either extreme while leaving

[2] See Lisa Bernstein, "Opting Out of the Legal System: Extralegal Contractual Relations in the Diamond Industry," 21 *J. Legal Stud.* 115 (1992).

open an enormous range of options for the relative proportions of state and private control of both resources and decisions.

In order to answer that particular question, both as a general matter and for particular cases, it is not sufficient to rely upon simple maxims or presumptions whose literary appeal outweighs their analytical power. Thus it has been said by Thomas Jefferson that "those who govern best, govern least," or by Ronald Reagan, that "government is not part of the solution, but part of the problem." As statements of political sentiment I heartily agree with both, at least if their sole import is to suggest that smaller government, fewer administrative regulations, and lower taxation would lead to an overall improvement in social welfare. But read literally, these statements do more than suggest a rough presumption for abandoning the existing status quo in favor of a system with less central control. They logically imply that there should be no government at all and, less clearly perhaps, no public or common property. Thus, if to govern best is to govern least, then the optimal size of government is zero because, so long as the government has any positive size, then its domain could still be shrunk. Similarly, if government is the source of the problem and not the solution, then the total elimination of government is the necessary solution to the problem. Let casual maxims control and there is no stable stopping point short of the corner solution, which is one of two solutions that can be ruled out of bounds on a priori grounds.

## BACK TO THE CORNER

The construction of a viable intermediate position, then, has to be the outgrowth of some theory that does not rely solely on the use of some conclusive presumption for or against government power or public ownership. That presumption must be moored to a distinctive substantive outlook or approach. Yet to find that theory from first principles alone is very hard, unless the inquiry can be broken down into smaller components, themselves amenable to analysis. In this context the language of presumptions plays, after all, an indispensable part in reaching by increments some optimal social solution. Suitably bounded, the legal idea of presumption is a precise parallel to the mathematical technique of solving difficult problems by a sequence of successive approximations, a technique which works best when direct analytical methods do not yield well-defined general solutions. It is that method that I propose to follow here, first as a matter for general social theory, and then as a matter of constitutional law and theory in deciding how individuals bargain with the state over its full range of activities.

The first question in this inquiry therefore takes the following form: What should be the initial baseline from which we make deviations under this analytical regime of successive approximations? One obvious answer is to start at the "midpoint" between the two ends on the ground that this point is closest to the ideal solution. But the middle is not a unique point even if we continue to use the metaphor of continuous, well-ordered points within the closed interval. It is very difficult to develop any theoretical measure of what counts as the middle position, for there are any number of distinct ways that various activities could be assigned to government or to the private sector, or to common or private ownership, and these are, or at least appear, to be consistent with this middle point. So the strategy of reaching the ideal point by repeatedly subdividing the total array of possibilities into ever smaller units will not work. And the measurement and uniqueness problems that are inherent in choosing *any other* interior baseline as the initial presumption remain, no matter what interior solution is chosen. The irony in a sense is complete. The only feasible starting points for the analysis are our two end points, all and none. These two are the very same, indeed the only two points that we can rule out in advance as representing the correct ultimate solution.

## WHICH CORNER?

Thus chastened, we now have to look closer at our two end points in order to assess the magnitude of the difficulties that beset each of them. With all resources owned in common and directed by central government planning, nothing intelligent can get done. Where government regulation works at all (as in the procurement of military personnel and equipment), it is often rendered feasible by a set of prices generated within a market, prices that convey some information about the opportunity cost of using certain resources in a particular fashion. The Hayekian theories of "spontaneous order" stumble when they move from particular industries and trading communities to general societies, that is, when they move from local to general equilibrium models.[3] So too any model of government behavior

[3] Richard A. Epstein, "*International News Service v. Associated Press*: Custom and Law as Sources of Property Rights in News," 78 *Va. L. Rev.* 85, 126–30 (1992), arguing that a stable system of property rights in news depends on a stable system of property rights generally.

suffers from a fatal intellectual flaw if it assumes that if some government regulation works well in a mixed system, then total government regulation necessarily works better. Quite the opposite; private benchmarks often supply the information necessary for government decisions on allocating goods and services. As a starting point for analysis, the all-government, all-political markets end of the spectrum seems to be highly unattractive. The number and difficulty of the corrections necessary to bring us back to some sensible social position seem vast indeed, which is why the restoration of even modest elements of a market system seem to be pose such radical problems for Eastern European and Third World nations.[4]

The same objection cannot be lodged (at least with equal force) against a baseline that begins with the world of no government ownership. Thus if we start with a decentralized, or Lockean, assumption that each person owns his or her own labor, it is easy to envision how a productive society and a competitive market in labor might emerge from this setting. Start with the simple case of persons who engage in any actions that satisfy their desires. The presumption in favor of liberty of action rests on this simple observation: we know that at least one person is better off from the action that is undertaken, and as yet we have no information that any other person is left worse-off in consequence of that action. Setting the presumption in favor of individual liberty thus looks to advance general welfare, subjectively defined, and it is up to others who wish to resist that action to indicate why that presumption should be overridden.

That burden is not insuperable for A's act to kill or maim B, an act that imposes external losses on B that look to any untutored eye to dwarf A's gains. That proposition can be tested by asking people whether they would prefer a world in which (a) they could neither kill nor be killed, *or* (b) kill or be killed for any reason at all. Even if one's odds of surviving and killing in situation (b) were well over 50 percent, I suspect that there would be few, if any, takers for that solution, which is why the purchase of social order at the expense of absolute individual liberty has in general been sought for so long from so many quarters, most notably by writers such as Hobbes and Locke who founded the modern social contract tradition.

That same model that supports an initial presumption in favor of individual liberty supports the parallel presumption in favor of freedom of contract for the exchange of labor, which is one of the elements so critical to forming a competitive market. The exchanges

[4] For one set of essays that addresses this problem, see Symposium, "Approaching Democracy: A New Legal Order for Eastern Europe," 58 *U. Chi. L. Rev.* 439 (1991).

between immediate trading partners will, given the ordinary descriptive norm of individual self-interest, generate mutual gains for both parties. Each side will normally undertake actions that work to its exclusive benefit so that the agreement of both bodes well for their combined future fortunes. The endowments that are acquired in one set of transactions can then be repackaged and resold in a second set of transactions, allowing the complex patterns of human interaction to develop through voluntary coordination—again, if market structures can be sustained against external attack. It is one of the major strengths of Robert Nozick's historical theory of entitlements that it stresses the repeated prospects for exchange from any preexisting baseline.[5]

This line of argumentation rests upon the implicit assumption that all persons (of full age and competence) own their own labor and are allowed to dispose of it as they will. That assumption is defended in many quarters as the necessary consequence of a commitment to individual autonomy and political freedom. Its denial is tantamount at some level to a system of slavery. But the situation clearly requires more attention than this simple antislavery defense of autonomy would suggest. A system of slavery allows some persons to stand in a position of ownership with respect to others, whose preferences they can disregard save to the extent they harm themselves thereby. (Everyone can pray, let the dominant party be me, but under this game all can never succeed, for someone must be dominated.) It is quite easy to reject any norm of domination as an offense to equality of position among equal individuals in some initial position. The equality constraint in and of itself, however, does not lead to the legal norm of individual autonomy. Although the equality norm is consistent with the autonomy norm, it is also consistent with a Rawlsian system of common ownership of individual talents, whereby each person has identical fractional interests in the talents and output of other all persons within the group, or indeed the world.

The hard question is whether, and if so to what extent, any system of common ownership is superior to one of individual self-ownership. That inquiry cannot, I believe, be answered on a priori grounds, but requires at the very least some empirical appreciation of the strengths and weaknesses of human behavior under these alternative institutional arrangements. In line with the pathbreaking work of Ronald Coase,[6] I believe that the choice of institutional arrangements depends heavily upon the transaction costs generated by

[5] See Robert Nozick, *Anarchy, State, and Utopia,* chap. 7 (1974)

[6] See Ronald Coase, "The Problem of Social Cost," 3 *J. L. & Econ.* 1 (1960).

each. Again, to move swiftly to the limit, assume at the outset that we had a zero transaction cost world, so that each person could effortlessly monitor the actions of all other individuals. At this point there would be no strong objection to a universe in which each person owned a tiny fraction of the labor and output of every other person on the face of the earth, a fraction equal to the minimal fraction owned in his own labor and output. Since both inputs and outputs are costless to monitor, the level of production should be left undiminished even if the stick and not the carrot were the only way to police behavior. The widespread patterns of individual cross-ownership would not only be perfectly consonant with claims for equal dignity and equal rights in the original position, but it would also have the additional advantage of allowing all risk averse individuals to perfectly diversify their risks of good fortune and bad, without (since monitoring is perfect in a zero transaction cost world) having to make any sacrifice in overall levels of output. In a zero transaction cost world, the familiar maxim—to each according to his need, and from each according to his ability—would no longer be the sign of a dogmatic Marxist; it would be a perfectly rational plan for making out a just social order, that is, one that maximized ex ante utility across the board. The questions of distribution of gain and creation of gain can be kept separate in this zero transaction cost world, so why resist the impulse to have the best of both worlds simultaneously?

This model, however, is far from robust. Quite the contrary, it is exceedingly sensitive to the slightest deviation from the zero transaction cost assumption. Let there be 1 billion persons on the face of the earth, and then perfect diversification requires around $5 \times 10^{17}$ separate contractual ties under a single master agreement.[7] Within a zero transaction cost world, the total enforcement costs of these connections remain at zero. However, once contracting has the slightest positive costs, the cost side of the model explodes: it becomes clear that perfect diversification comes at administrative and allocative costs that would surely exceed the total level of resources produced. By the logic developed above, it is far better to start from the other side of the line, that is, with a presumption of total individual self-ownership of labor and talents, which can then be disposed of through voluntary transaction in some organized labor market.

[7] The applicable formula is $n(n - 1)/2$, where $n = 10^9$, or $5 \times (10^{17} - 10^8)$, approximately $5 \times 10^{17}$. For a discussion of these span-of-control problems, how they drive organizations to the usual hierarchical structures, see Robert Clark, *Corporate Law*, Appendix A, 801–15 (1986).

Now there are only the costs of self-governance and restraint in the original position, since the number of contracts needed to move labor from one position to another is relatively small. As before, the inflexible assumption of absolute individual rights, forfeited only by misconduct or consent, becomes untenable as a final solution because it supposes a zero level of taxation and hence no political institutions at all. The case of common ownership of labor is only a subset of the basic presumption of government ownership of all resources, which should be rejected as the initial point of departure for the reasons set out above. Analytically, absolute individual self-ownership is the proper point of departure. The hard-line libertarian, who shuns all forced exchanges, thus captures a good portion of political wisdom, but unfortunately ends the analysis where most of us would begin it. But notwithstanding his adamant stance, I think that we can be confident at the outset that the place where the analysis begins is not the position where it ends.

## THE INITIAL POSITIONS IN EXTERNAL THINGS

The analysis of the ownership of material things is parallel to that of the ownership of labor. As before the polar positions are two: at the one pole, it is possible to assume that all things are owned by all persons in common in the initial position, so that no one can acquire individual rights to anything save through the consent of all. At the second pole, assume that no things are owned by any one in the initial position, and that all are acquired, typically by a rule that assigns ownership of things to those persons who unilaterally take first possession of external things, be it by the seizure of chattels or the occupation of land. In deciding which rule is appropriate it is again instructive to begin with the zero transaction costs assumption. With that assumption it is certain that all holdout and bargaining problems among individual persons can be resolved in zero time. No matter what the ideal allocation, each individual thing gets assigned to the right owner, such that any distributional problems are resolved by costless side payments between individuals. As with the ownership of human capital, it is possible to have the perfect marriage between distribution and allocation by the infinite and costless set of voluntary moves that drives assets to their ideal position while ensuring that all persons share in the overall distribution of the gain.

Yet, as was the case with personal labor, the desirability of this initial position instantly collapses with the slightest deviation from the zero transaction costs assumption. Once that assumption is abandoned, the question becomes, what is the best way to assign initial property rights in order to minimize the total cost of two inversely related transactional difficulties in the original position? The first of these problems is the *holdout* problem alluded to above. If there are large numbers of individuals with fractional interests, or veto positions, over certain material things, their inability to coordinate their behavior could lead to a ruinous stalemate: no one gets anything. Stated most graphically, if the unanimous consent of all individuals were required before any single person were entitled to put any resource to productive use, then we would all starve first.[8] One thousand, let alone one billion, people cannot agree on lunch or on anything else. The transaction costs questions here are no longer a matter of abstract economics. They have become a matter of life and death.

Yet there is a second side to the problem as well. When any person claims ownership of a given thing by excluding others, his action imposes a *negative externality* on those who in conditions of scarcity are denied the use of the resource.[9] The usual conclusion then follows: there will be too much reduction of land and goods to private possession too soon, as individual parties do not have to bear the full costs of their decisions for early privatization. But the existence of this imperfection is not decisive against this rule, for it has two offsetting advantages that cannot be ignored. The first possession rule allows for the decentralized acquisition of individual things that works notwithstanding the obstacles of space, time, and culture. It sets up a situation in which original possessors can trade the resources so acquired with each other for mutual advantage. The legal system thus can start with three sorts of common law rules: acquisition, protection (against theft and destruction), and exchange, which roughly correspond to the common law areas of property,

[8] A point well understood by John Locke. See his *Second Treatise of Government* §28 (1690): "And will anyone say he had no right to those Acorns or Apples he thus appropriated because he had not the consent of all Mankind to make them his? Was it a Robbery thus to assume to himself what belonged to all in Common? If such consent as that was necessary, Man had starved, notwithstanding the Plenty God had given him."

[9] Here the externality is often described by economists as pecuniary and not technological. See Richard A. Posner, *Economic Analysis of Law* 7 (4th ed. 1992). But the term "pecuniary" conceals a lot of difficulty because it assumes that the distribution of gains and losses is unimportant, which in practice it is not, and that they are in any event of the same magnitude, which may be false as well. For a discussion of the relationship between holdouts and externalities, see Richard A. Epstein, "Holdouts, Externalities, and the Single Owner: One More Salute to Ronald Coase," 35 *J.L. & Econ.* (1993) (forthcoming).

tort, and contract, and which are echoed in the theories of "historical justice" that were developed on abstract philosophical grounds by Robert Nozick in *Anarchy, State, and Utopia.* The imperfections with respect to this system will become apparent over time, but for these initial purposes the right question to ask is not, "Are there shortcomings of the rule in question?" to which the answer is always "yes." Rather the question is, "As between our two initial baselines of common ownership, or no ownership, which causes the greater dislocation?" And the answer to that second question is easy: a bit of premature acquisition of valuable resources brought on by the first possession rule is far preferable to mass starvation.

It should not be thought, however, that the arguments just made always point us in the direction of private property/initial acquisition rules for the initial baseline. The more complete answer to this question is in fact heavily dependent on the nature of the resource over which the private or communal rights structures will be imposed. In this regard, it is instructive to draw a comparison between the common law approaches to property rights in land and property rights in water, for while the individualistic first-possession rule outlined above dominates for land (and chattels), it has never achieved any headway as an initial system of allocation for water rights. Quite the opposite; the language of absolute rights has always been muted. Instead one is told that flowing rivers are in some sense a common property which could not be partitioned or alienated by those individuals who had partial, or usufructuary (literally, the use and the fruits) interest in the water. The exact systems of demarcation of rights in flowing water differ from place to place and from time to time, and are heavily dependent upon the type of water flow on the one hand, and the achievable set of beneficial uses for that water on the other.[10] The natural flow system of England, with limited rights to remove water for riparian uses, gained a foothold in the American Northeast, where it was in time supplanted by the reasonable use theories, to allow for the development of mill power.[11] Yet these theories did not gain much headway in the American West, where prior appropriation theories were adopted to maximize consumptive uses at the expense of low-value instream uses. Finally, in Hawaii customary property rights under local water law differed

[10] I discuss these alternative systems in Richard A. Epstein, "Why Restrain Alienation?" 85 *Colum. L. Rev.* 970, 979–82 (1985).

[11] For elaboration, see Carol M. Rose, "Energy and Efficiency in the Realignment of Common-Law Water Rights," 19 *J. Legal Stud.* 261 (1990), tracing the shift away from the English system of natural flow in New York during the nineteenth century.

from all the American schemes to take into account the runoffs from the high mountain.[12] The set of property rights in water for any given river or stream does not necessarily remain constant over time, but often varies notwithstanding the very high transitional costs of moving from one legal regime to another.

Yet beneath all this substantial diversity, the same problem of social utilization remains in a world of positive, indeed prohibitive, transaction costs. The risks of externalities and holdouts are far greater than those which normally apply with respect to land, and more complex rights structures are needed to cope with the problems. If riparians and others could remove water from a river at will, their uncoordinated actions could destroy its "going concern" value for other riparians and for other users of the river. Assigning exclusive rights of passage over discrete portions of navigable rivers to the riparians on either side destroys the value of the river as a highway, for it places an endless row of toll stations along its banks. The alternative set of rules that allows free and open navigation to all, subject to customary rules of the road, does a far better job of capturing the navigation use than any rule of private ownership. The implicit limitations, caught by the usufruct rules, permit a mix of consumptive and instream uses that, by the crude proxies that are available, maximizes the value of the river or stream as a whole. The optimal mix of competing uses depends in some sense on their relative values, for as mills become workable, it is probably sensible to allow some deterioration in the use of a river for navigation, although it is difficult in the abstract to say how much.[13]

The precise answers to these questions are outside the scope of the study, which is concerned with the setting of initial baselines from which the further moves within the game can be played. Still, some general observations should be offered. If the goal is to minimize the transaction costs that have to be incurred in order to place physical resources to their best social use, then there can be no universal presumption that all resources should be owned privately, and the common law (without any formal appreciation of the role of transaction costs) did a good job in choosing specific initial allocations for the various resources. With land, the corrections should be made from a baseline of individual private ownership. With water (at least where transportation is in issue), they should be made from a baseline of universal access subject to the customary rules of the road. The same basic concern with minimizing transaction costs is

[12] See Robinson v. Ariyoshi, 753 F.2d 1468 (9th Cir. 1985).

[13] Rose, supra note 11, at 273–74.

capable of generating both private and public baselines in various forms of property.

To draw an analogy, consider the way in which several different components can be assembled into a complete electrical circuit. Normally there are two choices: connection in series and connection in parallel. Where elements are in series, each one proceeds or follows the other, so that all elements of the system have to work in order for the system to work. For a system that works in parallel, one element of the system can be a substitute for another, so that the system can operate even if some of its components are inoperative. Where the elements are arranged in series, each element within the system has to operate if the whole system is to work at all. If all elements of a system had perfect reliability, then redundancy would impose a cost without offsetting benefits. But given that elements fail, redundancy has powerful advantages.[14] Where there are competitive markets, the individual units operate in parallel, so the greater their individual autonomy, the more effective the operation of the system. But with certain forms of property rights, such as those with water and highways, the units operate in series, so that all elements must be brought into harness in order for the system to operate at all. Within this context, individual autonomy necessarily leads to a frustration of the overall success of the system, since the breakage, or holdout, at any one component immobilizes the entire operation.

The way in which the various components can be assembled into complex wholes thus plays a large part in determining the definition of the proper original position. Here again the key element to note is that the costs of externalities and holdouts, both relative to each other and in absolute terms, may vary systematically depending upon the appropriate set of end uses. An increase in the number of rights holders in an initial position has an ambiguous effect upon the bargaining difficulties that will emerge once the initial position has been correctly defined. Thus, in some circumstances it is possible to conceive of recombinations of initial endowments that require the consent of two (or very few) initial rights holders: it is as though the initial units operate in parallel in the sense that some portion of the system remains fully operative even if other parts are not. Under those circumstances there will normally be a reasonably thick market, so that any given person will be able to seek out the best offer

[14] The point is not only true with mechanical systems, but also with biological systems, where redundancy of some organs (lungs, kidneys, etc.,) is a dominant feature. For a discussion of this point in insects, see George Oster & Edward Wilson, *Caste and Ecology in Social Insects*, chap. 1 (1978).

from a large number of competing offers that the market can generate. In this situation of contracts between two (or very few) parties, the thicker the market and the greater the number of its participants, the more efficient the operation of that market will be and the weaker the case for any form of coercive state intervention.

In some cases, however, an increase in the number of relevant rights holders vastly complicates the bargaining games that must be played in order for the initial rights to be redeployed in some Pareto superior fashion: it is as though the units have to be assembled in series. Thus if each river had only one or two adjacent landowners, it might be possible to overcome their joint coordination problem by voluntary agreement (even if the two riparians had some locational monopoly rents that they could extract from the hapless public). But the longer the river and the more numerous the riparians, the more critical it is that the initial rights structure include open access for navigation, for the possibilities of correction by voluntary renegotiation are just not available. It is just not plausible to believe that all the holders of land that borders the Hudson River could agree on a division of tolls. Keeping the river open for navigation in the initial position is critical to its successful use.

There are some cases where the coordination problem shifts rapidly from one extreme to another. Thus the division of land into relatively small building parcels may facilitate a competitive real estate market. But if many plots have to be assembled into a single unit to develop a large-scale plant, then the holdout problems that ensue turn the initial allocation of the land into a liability,[15] and one has to seriously think of eminent domain, forced takings solutions as a way to overcome the difficulties that will ensue. A fortiori, if a long highway has to be built, the diffuse ownership structure makes it impossible to overcome these difficulties in advance, so some system of central coordination of land acquisition has to be entertained. There is no unique and ideal initial position that facilitates a smooth course to the ideal end use in the full array of social scenarios. The initial baselines that are set up are presumptive, and the presumptions can be overridden when changes in external circumstances change the relative value of different uses for some particular resource. There are, then, bargaining difficulties that are associated with markets, and bargaining difficulties that are associated with politics. The major task is to develop a set of rules that minimize the sum of the bargaining failures that arise in both domains. Damage

[15] See, for a general discussion of these problems, Lloyd Cohen, "Holdouts and Freeriders," 20 *J. Legal Stud.* 351 (1991).

control is the raison d'être for the formulation of sound legal institutions and arrangements. And the issues that are salient for transactions between individuals are salient as well for transactions between individuals and the state.

The absence of a clean solution means that a sound social order always lies astride politics and the market. It depends on taxes for its revenues, and exerts coercive power over subjects that violate its laws, so that its use of these powers raises the questions of takings. The state also enters the marketplace to purchase many of the goods and services that it needs for its operations, which raises the problem of unconstitutional conditions. In order to decide when the state should coerce and when the state should purchase, it is necessary to explore first the relationship between political control and economic markets, and thereafter the boundaries that separate them from each other.

CHAPTER 4

# Coercion, Force, and Consent

ESTABLISHING property baselines in the original position was achieved through a strategy of reverse engineering. The desired outcome is to use resources where they generate the greatest social benefit. The strategy is to make that initial assignment of rights that is most likely to achieve this end. The difficulty is that no individual or group has the knowledge to make those assignments perfectly. The best that can be done, therefore, is to make that initial assignment of rights which allows subsequent adjustments to be made with the lowest level of friction and drag. The assignment of rights in persons and things developed in the previous chapter worked for that goal in two separate ways. Where effective utilization of resources could be achieved by contracts between two (or very few) persons, then individual assignments of rights are preferred—assignments that may then be altered by voluntary exchange. But where the unanimous cooperation of many persons is required to achieve a favorable outcome, then some form of common property may be preferred. In each instance, however, the creation of rights, individual or common, is not looked upon as an end in itself, but as a means to facilitate the redeployment of resources, both of labor and of property, at the lowest possible cost. The strategy for achieving overall social welfare is to minimize the transaction costs along the way. Distributional issues have nothing to do with this inquiry.

The creation of the initial baselines, therefore, is only one step in the overall project. The next question that arises is the subject of this chapter: what sort of moves may be made once the initial baselines have been established, and what subsequent moves are out of bounds? Since the basic strategy was to choose baselines that admit of easy correction, it follows that there must be some proper moves, e.g., voluntary exchanges, that are allowed from the original demarcation of property rights. Yet, by the same token, there cannot be a system of "anything goes" after the original baselines have been determined with such care. There must be some moves that are regarded as off-limits within the game as it is played. The effort to work out the line between these two classes of moves is intimately tied to the distinction between coercion and consent. But, although the distinction has great relevance, it does not have conclusive validity. There are some cases in which coercion should be permitted, and some cases in which voluntary exchanges should be regarded as invalid, even though consent was obtained. But the scope of the exceptions can only be understood after the logic behind the initial presumption in favor of consensual exchange is well articulated. As before, I shall put the question of enforcement of individual rights off until chapter 6, and ask only what moves should be allowed when a well-functioning state is in existence.

In developing this analysis of coercion it is useful to begin with the distinction between coercion and the use of force. It is well illustrated by a comparison between two cases.[1] In the first, X goes and beats up Y for the sheer pleasure of the occasion. X has no ulterior motive for the beating. No matter what Y was willing to do for X to forestall the beating, X only wanted to beat up Y. This is a clear case of coercion in a loose sense, but in a more precise sense it only involves the use of force. The point behind the distinction is this: force alone is involved whenever something is done for its own sake, not as an initial step in a subsequent bargaining relationship. Coercion for its part may in the end involve the use of force, but initially it involves the *threat* of force which the party who engages in coercion makes in order to achieve some collateral end.

If a robber R says to the victim V, "your money or your life," the threat to use force supplies the element of coercion. R is in a position to inflict force, but at some cost and risk to himself. The deal that is offered is one that says to V, if V abandons her right to resist the use of force and hands over her money, then R will not inflict any harm upon her. R is better off because he has no particular interest in (that is, gain from) the death of V. His object is to obtain the money, and her surrender of it reduces the risks to him attendant in using force, including the possible harms that determined resistance by V could inflict. Indeed, killing V to gain her money may leave him worse off than if she handed it over voluntarily if it increases the likelihood of police investigation and criminal liability. V for her part is better off as well. Although she values both her money and her life, she values the former far less than the latter, and if put to the choice will gladly sacrifice the one in order to preserve the latter. V will, for example, cheerfully pay a higher price in order to purchase a better car. She

[1] For these and other examples, see Robert Nozick, "Coercion," in *Philosophy, Science and Method: Essays in Honor of Ernest Nagel* 444 (S. Morgenbesser, P. Suppes, & M. White, eds. (1969)), stressing that a threat of force (or other wrongful act) is distinguishable from a warning or prediction of some adverse natural event.

also believes that the surrender of the money will help get her preferred state of affairs, because she rightly understands that R has no intrinsic interest in killing or hurting her. Although R has the power to impose his will by force, he will not use it. Instead he will make a threat (usually credible) to use the force, and that threat will constitute coercion, properly conceived. Viewed in this particular way, coercion (but not force) is the first step in a bargaining game. In order to decide that coercion is, or is not, properly invoked, it is necessary to get a sense of the outcome of the game as it is played.

Stating that coercion sets the stage for a bargaining game raises this puzzle. Most contracts are mutually beneficial to the parties, and the agreement between R and V is no exception to the rule. Both are better off if the threat is not carried out and the money is handed over voluntarily. Nonetheless, this bargaining game should not be tolerated where the threat involves the use of force against the person or property of another individual, even though the victim is "free" to reject the threat and to face the use of force. One feature of this threat/with/offer condemns it socially. Before the transaction took place, V had the right to both her money *and* her life. The first was hers under the autonomy assumption that every person owns her own body. The second was hers because she acquired it by the use of her labor, or by the sale of property acquired through lawful means, and so on.[2] As both of these initial entitlements were justified by the arguments made in the previous chapter, the question of coercion is explicitly linked to a general analysis of social welfare. Thus the money transferred in the particular case does not, presumptively, have greater value to R than it does to V. At best, the transfer is a wash, for the only way that R could restore V to her prior position is to retransfer all the money that had been taken. Nonetheless, the forced exchange itself consumes resources of both the at-

[2] There are cases where the money that R seeks to take from V is money that V has taken from X, which therefore V does not lawfully hold. There is a long, sound legal tradition which says that, in these settings, R is *not* allowed to raise the defense of ius tertii, the right of a third person (X) to the property, as a defense to his own actions with respect to it. The theory is that X is able to maintain any action against V to recover his property. V for her part is owner against the rest of the world, for under any other assumption, once property ceases to be in the possession of its lawful owner, then it forever becomes fair game for all and may never be reduced to a form of protected ownership. Thus if R can take the property from V, then surely another robber S could take the property from R, and so on, destroying all stability in ownership. It is therefore permissible to treat all cases as though V were the true owner, noting that where the assumption does not hold, some individual has the right of suit needed to rectify some previous wrong. See, e.g., Ray A. Brown, *The Law of Personal Property* §§3.1–3.5, 4.1–4.3 (Walter B. Rauschenbush, ed., 3d ed., 1975).

tacker and the victim, whether the threat of force is successfully executed or not. These deadweight losses benefit neither side. Stated otherwise, the standard case of coercion represents a bargaining game marked by high bargaining costs and no social gain, even on the favorable assumption that what is taken, e.g., money, is as valuable to the robber as it is to the victim. Once that last assumption is relaxed so that other forms of property may be surrendered to coercion, the social losses are more pronounced. People who fence stolen goods typically receive ten or twenty cents on the dollar for the goods that they have taken, and it is doubtful in the extreme that the valuation attached by either the thief or the subsequent purchaser is anything close to its value in the hands of the original owner, and in the unlikely event that it were, a voluntary exchange could easily have been arranged.

There is, of course, the further caveat that differences in wealth levels might be sufficiently large to change the relative utility calculations. But even if that were the case (which it will not be when poor people are the victims of local criminals), a system of redistribution through taxation surely dominates any self-help mechanism that could be devised. The arguments of differential utility have for this reason never been advanced as a legal justification for criminal behavior, even though they have been used to rationalize why people might resort to it. The prohibition against private theft makes sense even if a society is committed to the social redistribution of resources.

It is proper, then, to conclude that the outright case of theft always generates social losses. When force becomes coercion those losses are only increased, not decreased, by the interposition of a bargaining game which can yield catastrophic results if the threats do not achieve their stated end. When one says that the threat of force is coercive, the conventional focus is on the relationship between the victim and the initiator of the threat. In his detailed study of coercion, for example, Alan Wertheimer,[3] following the general legal view on the subject,[4] breaks the coercive transaction into two components: the *choice* prong, which addresses the position of the victim, and the *proposal* prong, which addresses the position of the party who makes the threat. The position of the victim is clear, for by virtue of having to respond to the offer she is rendered worse off than she would have been if no offer had been made. Yet, by the same token, the party who makes the threat is left better off as well. If the

[3] *Coercion*, 31–46 (1987).

[4] See *Restatement (Second) of Contracts* §492 (1981).

issue were only about the relative position of the two parties, then why should the position of the victim be preferred, given the correlative restrictions imposed on the party making the threat?

The key point here is that judgment of these transactions is not merely about the individual rights of the victim. Since the arguments about the social losses that flow from the threat of force are universal, we can also say that the victim's loss is a *perfect proxy* for the social loss. Because we know the structure of the bargaining game, there is a one-to-one correspondence between offers of this sort and net social losses. Where the offer is of the form, "your money or your life," it should be regarded as an illegal *threat* because of the net social losses that invariably accompany it. The bargain was only about *which* forced surrender of initial rights should be undertaken, not whether there should be any surrender at all. The context that surrounded the voluntary exchange is what renders it fatally defective. Our moral intuitions are happily the strongest where the social losses are the greatest.

The above example of a coercive threat occurred in a context in which the victim was asked to choose between an entitlement to personal autonomy and an entitlement to personal property. That same kind of illicit choice can arise where some property has been exchanged for the right to a future performance under contract. The problem, captured at common law under the instructive name of "duress of goods," arises in the following simple situation. A man brings his shirt into the cleaners, and the cleaner promises to clean it for $10. Once the shirt is cleaned, the cleaner insists that the man pay $15 in order to secure its return. In essence, he has been left with a choice between his shirt and $15, and, if forced to pick between them, he will gladly part with the $15 in order to recover possession of a shirt that is worth perhaps ten times as much. Nonetheless, even though this subsequent renegotiation of the original contract works to the mutual benefit of the two sides—the customer prefers immediate possession of his shirt to the extra $5, and the cleaner is willing to part with possession for the extra $5—the offer is rightly regarded as coercive because of the way in which it destabilizes the preexisting exchange relationship between the parties. If the cleaner is entitled to unilaterally revise the terms of the deal after she receives possession of the goods (indeed after she makes a binding contract), then the security of exchange is effectively destroyed. The price calculations that individual traders have to make will be compromised because they can always be undone, and the inability to trust others with your own work leads to a reduction in the division of labor and the concomitant gains from trade. The bargaining games that ensue will, like the bargaining games with the robber, consume resources without directing those resources to higher-value uses, as the sole effect of this renegotiation is to reduce the anticipated wealth of the customer and increase that of the cleaner. It is a game whose redistributive consequences, lead to negative overall outcomes. There is therefore a good reason to call these exchanges out of bounds, as the phrase "duress of goods" itself suggests.

The situation is, however, more complicated than the previous case because with exchange relationships it is often possible to think of "good reasons" why the price readjustment may be appropriate. There are cases in which the original contractor will not be able to complete the work at the original price because a sharp run-up in costs is sufficient to threaten bankruptcy, which would leave the original trading partner high and dry.[5] That trading partner may prefer to pay an increased cost to get the work done, especially if the transaction overall is viewed as a net gain. The legal literature has spent an enormous amount of time and effort to determine when these justifications are of sufficient strength so that the original promisee is bound even though he has waived the benefit of the first bargain in order to induce the intended performance, albeit at a somewhat higher price. But lest these cases complicate the analysis unduly, it should be recalled that duress of goods cases are easy to make out where cost conditions are constant, the work has already been done, and the provider of services insists upon a price increase solely to exploit a holdout position. It becomes critical to allow the original party both to pay the excess in order to gain immediate possession of the goods, and then to sue for a restoration of the overpayment (with penalty and costs) in order to preserve the integrity of the exchange relationship.

The arguments about social losses from coercion can be extended to other cases. Take a situation where the robber steals from the victim a watch that has a market value of $100 and a sentimental value to its owner of $150. There is no coercion involved because the victim was not asked to hand over her watch, which was stolen from her desk while she was out of the office. Now suppose that subsequent to the original theft, the thief offers to exchange the watch for $125. Taken in isolation, that second exchange meets the usual test of mutual gain from trade: the thief prefers the $125 to the watch, and the victim prefers the watch to the money. Nonetheless there is

[5] See, e.g., Goebel v. Linn, 47 Mich. 489, 11 N.W. 284 (1882).

a strong sense that this offer, although not backed by the use of force, should be regarded as illegitimate notwithstanding the joint benefit it promises.

The explanation is not, I believe, hard to find once we take into account not only the gains from a subsequent voluntary exchange but also the losses from the original theft. Thus suppose that when the robber stole the watch there was no money in the victim's desk. If the robber knew that he could only keep the watch or sell it in the open market, then the maximum value of the theft would be $100, and its likely value would be far less, say $20, owing to the usual discount in fencing transactions. Allowing the subsequent transaction has two consequences, one to permit the victim to increase her welfare from $125 (the cash paid over) to $150 (the watch's subjective value), which should be welcome, assuming that the initial theft could not be reversed or prevented. But at the same time it also allows the thief to increase his welfare from $20 (his sale price to a fence) to $125 (the cash paid over). In and of itself, that increment of private welfare should be regarded as positive on the social calculus, but that happy conclusion is quickly tempered when we recognize that the subsequent exchange also allows the robber to increase the gains from the initial theft, which in turn increases the probability that he will undertake it. We therefore are reluctant to tolerate the "ransom" because of the perverse incentives it creates to engage in kidnapping in the first instance. And the social response is strong; in cases of kidnapping, for example, the state may properly freeze the assets of the parents and may often make it impossible to ransom back the child, solely to discourage any future escapades of this sort. The individual victim is made, as it were, hostage to the class of potential victims because one beneficial exchange is prohibited in order that other destructive transactions may not take place. The social consequences of the second transaction cannot be viewed in isolation, but must be nested in their larger context.[6]

The same scenario has its analogue in the public sphere, which moves us closer to problems of bargaining with the state. The original taking could be by way of taxation, and the proceeds of the tax are then returned to the individual as part of a deal which requires him to surrender some independent right, which the government might not be able to acquire directly, say, because of some juris-

[6] For an articulation of this point in the context of secured transactions, see Randal Picker, "Security Interests, Misbehavior, and Common Pools," 59 *U. Chi. L. Rev.* 645 (1992).

dictional limitation. Attacking the subsequent contract may look odd because it meets the mutual gain provision. But again we have a mutually beneficial "offer" which becomes coercive when it is placed in its larger transactional context. As before, this offer should be condemned as coercive because of its negative social consequences, even though it is subsequent to the initial use of force.

Finally, it should be evident that there are certain cases in which the threats of force are fully *justified*. The most obvious case is one where a threat of force is made in self-defense where the victim seeks to preserve her autonomy by threatening to harm the assailant. The use of force in this case is designed to preserve, not undermine, the original baselines between strangers. To be sure, in some cases the force is excessive for its stated end of repelling aggression, as is the case when a powerful athlete kills a puny attacker whom he could brush aside with the back of his hand. In still other cases the force could be disproportionate, even if strictly necessary: if removing someone's hands from your shoulders, for example, requires the use of deadly force. For these purposes, we do not have to inquire further into the limitations of self-defense, which are reasonably well set out at common law.[7] Rather, it is quite enough to note that coercion as the threat of force (or breach of contract) should be regarded as wrongful, even when it leads to an agreement between the parties because of the tight correspondence between the victim's losses and the overall social losses of aggressive practices.

As a matter of principle these cases are relevant to the constitutional issues later on because they indicate that coercion cannot be understood as a unidimensional concept. In our zeal to limit the power of the state to commit bargaining transgressions, it is critical to remember that the legal rules have a dual role to play: not only must they constrain the state, but they must also restrict the abuse of the individuals with whom the state does business. Oftentimes, it is not clear who is the aggressor and who is the victim when there is a potential for abuse on both sides. These two concerns of social control move us in opposite directions. Rules that place ideal limitations on state power may pave the way for private abuse, just as rules that place ideal limitations on private power may usher in massive

[7] For a convenient summary see Fowler Harper, Fleming James, and Oscar Gray, 1 *The Law of Torts* §3.11 (1986). One difficult case is that where persons occupy property but do not threaten physical damage. To ask them to leave will be futile, but to use force to eject them is likely to be necessary but disproportionate, so that the best course of action is often to wait them out. The sit-in strikes of the labor movement in the 1930s and of the civil rights movement in the 1960s both had this character.

forms of public abuse. Minimizing the sum of the two forms of error is the order of the day, and it is unlikely that any corner solution will achieve that result. Indeed, a priori, it is doubtful that dominant attention should be given to either form of misbehavior relative to the other. Any party that is left unregulated is apt to engage in selfish conduct. The rates of substitution are not uniform, for the strenuous effort to remove the last bit of abuse from one side is likely to be very costly and invite far more abuse from the other.

The above discussion indicates some of the cases on the boundary between coercion and consent. Nonetheless, there are many instances in which consent represents, not a yielding to improper threats, but the acceptance of beneficial offers.[8] In line with the previous discussion, the distinction between illicit threats and legitimate offers (or more briefly, threats and offers) cannot be located in the mutually beneficial nature of the immediate exchange, for that is a feature common to all the threat situations that were outlined above. Instead, the distinction must rest in the way in which this immediate transaction nests into the overall social outcomes of the result in question. In order to see the point, it is instructive to begin with a case where the offeree is subjected to a hard choice not dissimilar, from her point of view, to those considered in the previous section. Thus suppose that an employee has been working on a contract at will for her employer at a salary of $1000 per month. Quite out of the blue, the employer announces that the employee will be faced with this hard choice: accept a reduction in wages to $800 or be faced with termination. On any view this offer comes as bad news, and perhaps as a deep disappointment. But unless one wants to label all offers as coercive (in which case the term loses its sting),[9] this employment case has to be distinguished from a coercive one by looking at its larger setting.

The offer involved does not involve the threat or use of force; nor is it one that asks the employee to sacrifice any of her initial entitlements or any derivative entitlement protected by contract. At this point, there is every reason to believe that the nature of the shift in the offer is perfectly consistent with the smooth operation of a competitive market, so that to deny the employer the wage relief is necessarily to insist that he keep high-cost labor when his rival is able to procure low-cost labor for similar work. The process of tough offer

[8] See Wertheimer, supra note 3, at 202–41.

[9] See Robert L. Hale, "Unconstitutional Conditions and Constitutional Rights," 35 *Colum. L. Rev.* 321 (1935) taking this unfortunate position. See also the criticisms of Robert Nozick, "Coercion," supra note 1, where the point is far better understood.

and acceptance therefore represents an effort not to achieve an exchange that always reduces social worth, but to preserve a competitive equilibrium in which all labor receives its market value. If the employer has guessed wrong about the operation of the market, the employee can sell her labor elsewhere. The situation therefore is one in which hard bargaining and hard choices produce overall social gains. At this point, therefore, any effort to treat the unfortunate plight of the employee as though it were a reliable proxy for social loss is misguided notwithstanding the psychological pressures under which she labors.

It is worth noting today that these at-will contracts, and the concomitant wage renegotiations, are under attack in the courts in part on the ground that "inequality of bargaining power" renders these renegotiations suspect. Here it is the profound uneasiness with competitive markets (and the failure to understand their socially desirable features) that drives critics of the at-will contract to call these offers coercive and hence illegal. And the point is well taken. It is only if one can develop an account of why markets work well that it is possible to justify the initial baselines of the last chapter—that the employer owns his capital and the employee her labor—and conclude that this wage renegotiation is efficient. I believe that this conclusion can be made out precisely because business incentives make it highly unlikely that employers will "just" choose to demand wage reductions when no shifts in external market conditions justify that position: if the worker leaves, then the employer is faced with the heavy costs of finding and training a suitable replacement, and the reputational losses will increase the cost of maintaining good relations with other workers. The use of at-will contracts, and the threats of renegotiation that they allow, have social results that are radically different from those involving threats to use force, or even threats to exploit the advantage of some monopoly position.

The basic outcome may be complicated when there are other impediments to market mobility—labor unions, minimum wages, and the like—and where those institutions do gain sway, then the definition of coercion will in practice be altered to take into account the shift in the relevant social baselines. In a regulated economy, it will be regarded as a coercive offer for an employer to insist that a worker take below a minimum wage, or that a worker abandon her union in order to keep her job.[10] The new set of entitlements works into the old theory of duress: the worker is still given a choice between A and B, both of which are protected legal rights when (by assumption) she

[10] See National Labor Relations Act §8(a)(3).

is entitled to have both. The attack on the finding of coercion in this setting requires that one undermine the implicit baseline established by the legislative or judicial foray into the labor market. That inquiry, in turn, demands a demonstration of the superiority of competitive markets over all possible alternatives, an inquiry that carries over to the next chapter.

## CHAPTER 5

# Competition, Monopoly, and Necessity

THE ARGUMENT in the previous chapter has been designed to erect a libertarian fault line that allows us to distinguish between coercive threats and ordinary market offers. Illegitimate coercion arises where a threat of force is used to acquire an entitlement, or where some prior use of force allowed a person to obtain the resource that is then offered for resale to its original owner. I think that there is little reason to believe that any modification should be made on this side of the divide. Apart from the case of self-defense and similar issues,[1] there is very little sentiment anywhere for treating offers backed by the threat of force as anything other than coercive. The more controversial side of the analysis covers those offers which are not backed by force but which should be regarded as coercive, such that the consent, although procured, can be ignored by the party that gave it. I have already given reasons why in general hard bargaining in competitive markets should not fall into this class. But it is now useful to set out the formal conditions under which certain offers are regarded as coercive even though they do not involve the threat of force or of breach of contract.

### BARGAINING STRUCTURES

#### *Perfect Competition*

The initial point of demarcation requires us to return first to the world of perfect competition. We begin with an idealized spot market that contains many buyers and many sellers. Fraud and duress are made illegal, as is the power of either sellers or buyers to contract among themselves over output or price. In this type of market an optimal social equilibrium emerges in the sense that all the possible

[1] One such issue is the recapture of chattels that have been taken by force from the owner. The question then arises, "what force if any may be used to take back the chattel from the thief?" on which, see, e.g., Kirby v. Foster, 17 R.I. 437, 22 A. 1111 (1891). Fowler Harper, Fleming James, & Oscar Gray, 1 *The Law of Torts* §3.16 (1986).

gains from trade are exhausted by voluntary exchanges. Within the ideal competitive equilibrium, there will be a unique price at which all goods of uniform quality will be traded, and that price will be set equal to the marginal cost of the marginal producer.[2] Accordingly, no seller and no buyer has any discretion over price. The seller who tries to raise his price above the market will find no takers. The seller who tries to lower his price below the market will find that he cannot make a profit on the sales that are concluded. A system of perfect economic freedom yields a set of rules in which no player finds it to his advantage to engage in any bargaining tactics at all. The ideal competitive market yields an ideal social situation in which all the gains from bargains are captured at zero bargaining costs.

The outcomes of a competitive market, it must be cautioned, are not so benevolent when looked at from the viewpoint of disappointed competitors: individuals who are not hired for coveted jobs, or firms that have lost lucrative contracts or have been plunged into bankruptcy. These so-called pecuniary externalities are generally ignored by economists in their overall calculations of social welfare.[3] The explanation is that the losses which are sustained by any individual actor in any given transaction are more than offset by the gains to other individuals in virtue of the movement in price and quantity of the various goods and services supplied. While the operation of markets appears from an ex post perspective to have severe distributional consequences, from the ex ante perspective the opposite is true. The expected prospects of any person, systemwide, are far greater if individual failures are allowed to take place than they are if entry into markets is allowed, say, only after established firms are bought out by their new competitors.[4] This alternative protective regime induces a round of costly renegotiation to achieve a set of desirable outcomes better achieved in a regime of free entry on either side of the market.

This point may be restated by pointing out that pecuniary externalities created in competitive markets are not all negative. Many

[2] In real markets, nonprice terms introduce additional complexity that must be taken into account. These terms—such as warranties and delivery provisions—usually lead to adjustments in the price term. Also, in practice, firms seek supracompetitive returns by finding new "niches" for their products to obtain, in the short run at least, some discretion over prices. The resulting monopoly gains are typically subject to erosion in the long run by new entry, a phenomenon generally inapplicable to political markets.

[3] David D. Friedman, *Price Theory* 463 (2d ed. 1990).

[4] See Harold Demsetz, "Some Aspects of Property Rights," 9 *J.L. & Econ.* 61 (1966).

externalities are positive as well. For every disappointed competitor, there are satisfied consumers. So long as the overall size of the social pie is enhanced, everyone shares the benefit of having greater opportunities to buy and sell goods in the marketplace. The pecuniary externalities with negative signs are ignored because they are systematically offset by positive externalities of larger amounts. What looks to be a capricious redistribution from the vantage point of an isolated transaction, is far closer to a general improvement when looked at from behind the veil of ignorance. If all parties were forced to choose between a regime that (a) allowed free entry in all competitive markets, and (b) required a buyout of established firms before entry were possible, the first scheme would dominate the second. It is for this reason that the competitive outcome is the one we should seek to achieve in setting the baselines (now called property rights) for subsequent exchange transactions.

## *Monopoly*

The polar opposite to perfect competition is monopoly.[5] Here the market is controlled by a single seller who can set terms for sale that maximize his own profits. In general, the monopolist will seek to maximize his own profits by selling a smaller quantity of goods at a higher price than is found in the competitive market. This private strategy yields lower total social output than is achievable under pure competition. The social losses in question arise from three distinct sources. First, when the monopolist raises his price, he prevents some mutually beneficial exchanges. Thus, if the competitive price of a good is eight and the monopoly price is ten, any consumer who values that good at more than eight units but less than ten will no longer purchase it. The benefits of that foregone exchange are thus one form of loss created by monopoly.

A second source of social loss is also critical. With respect to transactions that do occur, the price increase from eight to ten units seems to result in a pure transfer of wealth from consumers to producers without any attendant social loss. Nonetheless this transfer itself is not costless to achieve. Monopolies do not come down from heaven, but are acquired by purposive and costly human action. The prospect of obtaining increased prices is a private gain for which any prospective monopolist will pay. The costs of acquiring a monopoly,

[5] For an excellent general discussion of the differences between competitive and noncompetitive markets, see Friedman, supra note 3, at 247–84.

whether by buying out a competitor or obtaining government protection from competition, are real costs incurred to obtain simple wealth transfers. The result is that some fraction, and perhaps all, of the potential social gain from the transaction is wiped out, thereby creating a second form of loss.[6]

Finally, monopolies generate a third form of social loss. Outside a regime of pure competition, there is no unique price at which goods can be bought and sold. The advent of a bargaining range—a series of prices at which both buyer and seller are willing to transact—gives rise to a problem of "strategic bargaining," or more generally, "strategic behavior." Parties now have a tendency to "act strategically," to conceal preferences, to lie, to haggle, to hold out, to dicker, to build coalitions, and to price discriminate, all of which cost money but none of which produces real gain.

The losses that arise from strategic behavior can perhaps best be seen if we take an extreme situation, the bilateral monopoly, in which there is a single buyer and single seller. The buyer might be willing to pay 200 units to purchase, and the seller to accept 100 units to sell. The opportunity for a mutually beneficial exchange is present. A costless bargain at any price in the interval generates 100 units of total gain and leaves both sides better off. If the price is 150, each side obtains 50 units of that gain. But 150 does not offer a stable resting point. The seller, for example, may be too tempted to spend, for example, 10 units in time and effort in the hopes of being able to raise the sale price to 170, while the buyer may be tempted to spend 10 to reduce the purchase price to 130. Both strategies cannot be simultaneously successful. If each side's efforts cancel each other out, then the sale is still at 150, but bargaining behavior reduces the total gain by 20 units, or 10 per person. Nor is the overall result changed by any shift in the contract price from the midpoint price of 150. The total gain is still reduced by the level of bargaining costs, which could exhaust much of the total 100 units of potential gain. Therefore, any set of institutions that could reduce the bargaining costs without preventing the consummation of the bargain would generate important social benefits that could be shared by both parties to the transaction.

The dangers of monopoly have led to powerful legal restraints against freedom of contract for private parties under both the Sherman and Clayton Acts. Thus, an aggrieved consumer may bring a private antitrust monopoly action against a monopolist from whom

[6] See generally the essays in *Toward a Rent Seeking Society* (J. Buchanan & G. Tullock, eds. 1980).

he has made a direct purchase.[7] That consumer is better off having made a purchase from a monopolist than he would have been if he had done without the good. The exchange is still Pareto efficient. In the example above, he might have valued at 11 units a good for which the monopolist charged 10, but for which the competitive price was 8. Nonetheless the antitrust damage action for two units (ignoring trebling of damages) is permitted, notwithstanding the consumer's consent to pay ten. The baseline norm is not the state of affairs before any contract, but the achievable state of affairs under the competitive equilibrium that is the social optimum. In effect, the plaintiff is regarded as a suitable private attorney general and can sue, even though he was a willing party to the contract. Yet, by the same token, the consent given is not wholly inoperative: the purchaser is not free of all obligations under the contract. He must, for example, properly maintain the goods in order to bring successfully an action for breach of express warranty, just as he would if he had purchased at a competitive price.

### *Necessity and Bilateral Monopoly*

Similar limitations on consent are often found in cases of bilateral monopoly where only a single buyer and single seller are in the market for a particular good. This situation is rarely encountered in dealing with markets for ordinary goods and services, but it has great theoretical importance in understanding bargaining with the state, given the monopoly power that government has over the use of force. There are, moreover, private law examples of how these markets operate. A good illustration of the process is the common law response to private necessity as it relates to the law of both tort and contract. For example, when a ship is caught in a storm and the crew can save itself only by docking at a single dock, there is a powerful bilateral monopoly problem that invites the use of strategic bargaining. The dockowner may be able to make a gain if he allows the use

[7] In most cases the purchases are not made directly, but through intermediates. To simplify the process of private enforcement, the law today authorizes the direct purchaser to recover the monopoly profits from the seller, even if that purchaser has passed on all or part of the cost to its buyer further down the chain. See Illinois Brick v. Illinois, 431 U.S. 720 (1977), discussed in William M. Landes & Richard A. Posner, "Should Indirect Purchasers Have Standing to Sue Under the Antitrust Laws?: An Economic Analysis of the Rule of *Illinois Brick*," 46 *U. Chi. L. Rev.* 602 (1979). The basic analysis of the role of consent remains the same regardless of these enforcement complications.

of his dock for any sum greater than 10 units, while the ship's crew may be willing and able to pay 1000 just for the temporary use of the dock. If the matter were resolved by a voluntary bargain, the price settled upon might be anywhere within the total range of 10 to 1000, leaving both sides better off. Worse still, there might be no bargain at all, if the dockowner, who has so little to lose by holding out for a high price, refuses to accept a more reasonable offer.

The doctrine of "conditional (or incomplete) privilege," developed at common law, offers an effective counter to bargaining problems created by the necessity situation.[8] In essence the privilege allows the shipowner to use the dock upon payment of compensation equal to the rental value of the dock, plus damages for any loss inflicted during the storm. The right to exclude, a normal incident of property, is suspended under conditions of necessity.

Modifications of the law of contract parallel those in the law of property. For example, it has long been the law in admiralty that a salvor is not allowed to take advantage of the position of a ship in distress at sea by driving a hard bargain. Even if such a bargain has already been concluded, it will not be enforced, and compensation will be set in accordance with a formula that takes into account both the risk to the salvor and the gain to the rescued ship[9]—a principle easily extended to contracts made in the dock case. What goes for price terms applies equally to conditions that might otherwise be set. Thus a contract that said, "I will rescue you only if you agree not to enter into competition with me in the real estate market and to vote Republican," would not be enforced either.

[8] See Ploof v. Putnam, 81 Vt. 471, 71 A. 188 (1908) (recognizing a privilege to enter the land of another when acting under private necessity); Vincent v. Lake Erie Transp. Co., 109 Minn. 456, 124 N.W. 221 (1910) (requiring compensation to be paid for damage caused when using another's property under conditions of necessity). See generally Francis H. Bohlen, "Incomplete Privilege to Inflict Intentional Invasions of Interests of Property and Personality," 39 *Harv. L. Rev.* 307 (1926).

[9] The Supreme Court has stated the rule as follows: "Courts of admiralty will enforce contracts made for salvage service and salvage compensation, where the salvor has not taken advantage of his power to make an unreasonable bargain; but they will not tolerate the doctrine that a salvor can take the advantage of his situation, and avail himself of the calamities of others to drive a bargain; nor will they permit the performance of a public duty to be turned into a traffic of profit. The general interests of commerce will be much better promoted by requiring the salvor to trust for compensation to the liberal recompense usually awarded by courts for such services." Post v. Jones, 60 U.S. (19 How.) 150, 160 (1856) (citations omitted). For the determinants of salvage price, see William M. Landes & Richard A. Posner, "Salvors, Finders, Good Samaritans, and Other Rescuers: An Economic Study of Law and Altruism," 7 *J. Legal Stud.* 83, 100–06 (1978).

These limitations on contractual freedom could not be justified if the only reason to invalidate contracts were to counteract force and fraud, both of which are absent in the situations just described. Rather, the rules are a judicial effort to maximize the overall value of the use of the dock in the one case, or of salvage activities in the other, by preventing the gameplaying that parties might otherwise engage in, given the large bargaining range. The rules impose a single price at which the dock must be rented, or ships salvaged, which is set roughly to allow the rescuer a competitive return on his costs while preserving the remainder of the cooperative surplus for the party subject to the external necessity.[10] The legal rules are set in a way that, subject to the usual imperfections of measurement, imitates the outcome that a competitive market would generate. The moment the crisis is over, the ordinary rules of property and contract are restored. The dock can be used by the shipowner only with the owner's consent; the salvage crew keeps full control over its equipment. Calm seas and safe journeys bring with them a return to the ordinary property rights regime.[11]

Thus far our evaluation of the necessity case assumed that it is possible for the state to override the ordinary rights of property owners to exclude others from their land. In so doing it dramatically contracts the scope of the bargaining range, which originally ran from the rental value of the property at the low end to the survival value of the plaintiff (or the full subjective value of his property) at the high one. The substitution of a single point of exchange for the entire bargaining range means that no bargaining at all is allowed between the parties. The landowner must stand aside to allow the stranger to use his property. The sole negotiation after the fact is over rental value or the extent of property damages, if any.

It was of course possible to choose another unique outcome that falls outside the bargaining range. Confident in the social judgment that the dock is worth more to the shipowner stranded at sea than it is to the landowner, the law could allow the dock to be used without

[10] There is, to be sure, an important difference between the salvor situation and the casual dockowner. The former has to make heavy investments in specific capital which can only be recovered from salvage operations, and the rate of compensation has to take these costs into account, as is done under the standard formulas. See generally Wayne T. Brough, "Liability Salvage—By Private Ordering," 19 *J. Legal Stud.* 95 (1990).

[11] In Calabresi's terms, the necessity situation reduces the dockowner's protection to that afforded by "liability rules"—a damage action against loss. "Property protection" means that control over the asset can only be lost by consent, the normal situation. *See* Guido Calabresi & A. Douglas Melamed, "Property Rules, Liability Rules and Inalienability: One View of the Cathedral," 85 *Harv. L. Rev.* 1089, 1105–6 (1972).

any payment of compensation either for rental value or property damage. This allocation is superior to a rule that allows the dockowner to exclude the shipowner, for it is better that people be rescued than docks be undamaged. The rule of absolute privilege is preferable to the common law rule of absolute exclusion, even though it trades in a large holdout problem for a small externality problem. Nonetheless in all likelihood this allocation is inferior to the rule of conditional privilege, because it places the shipowner in a position where he controls the use of someone else's resource but is not accountable for the damage that ensues. But the just compensation rule combats both problems simultaneously: the dangers that the party in peril will ignore the welfare of the dockowner is counteracted at the (acceptable) price of some increase in the administrative costs of the system.

But let us suppose that someone who was opposed to the abrogation of the exclusive rights of property for the dockowner nonetheless sought to constrain the bargaining problems endemic to the common law regime. In order to do so, he could propose the follow ingenious stratagem that brings us closer to the puzzle of unconstitutional conditions: the dockowner will be left the absolute right to exclude, but if he chooses to admit, then it can only be on condition that he accept a compensation package limited to the rental value of the dock, plus the property damages caused by the owner—that is, the same bundle of benefits that is now provided under the conditional privilege rule at common law. The use of this two-point distribution in effect rules out all intermediate solutions and thus makes it impossible to haggle over the price within some large range. In particular, the dockowner cannot insist on capturing the net worth of the shipowner, so that the bargaining problem is therefore effectively obviated.

What will the result of this constrained bargaining game look like? Unlike the traditional common law rules, there is some uncertainty as to which pole the dockowner would migrate. Although we cannot speak of certainties, we can still speak of probabilities. Suppose we therefore examine the returns that are available to the dockowner under the two alternative scenarios. If he exercises the option to exclude, his return is zero, and ship is destroyed or the shipowner drowns. But if he allows the shipowner to use the dock, then he gets the competitive rate of return on an otherwise idle asset, plus full protection against property damages. As an initial guess, it looks as though the dockowner will choose this second alternative, for it gives him an income stream unobtainable under his other choice. But some dockowners may chafe under the restriction of having to allow entry, and would therefore choose not to be bothered with enormous losses on the other side. Yet a simple expedient can reduce that probability without going back to the common law conditional privilege or the open bargaining game: provide the dockowner with a multiple of rental value (say threefold) which will induce him to allow the use of the dock by making the exclusion alternative more costly than it was before. In essence it is possible to sweeten the pot so that it is in the interest of the dockowner to allow entry under an all-or-nothing choice even though he has the absolute right to exclude.

The use of the all-or-nothing choice operates as a second best alternative that could, and should, be adopted if the first best alternative—the straight conditional privilege—were beyond the power of the state to impose. Yet it seems clear that this option is not the best way to avoid the problem of coercive bargaining precisely because we know which horn of the dilemma we wish to embrace. It seems preferable to allow the shipowner to force the entry as of right; if there is a concern that rental value plus damages understates the appropriate level of compensation, then the multiple of rental value and/or damage can be built into the just-compensation formula just as it was done with the bipolar choice model that respects the absolute right to exclude. But be this as it may, it should now be clear why the language of coercion applies to threats to exclude in these necessity situations. The constraints against force and fraud are insufficient to define the set of illicit transactions. Although coercion starts off as being tied to threats of force and misrepresentation, by degrees the term *coercive offer* expands to cover any bargaining tactics that leads to suboptimal social results. And the tactic that is most central to the inquiry is the extraction of a price (far) above the opportunity cost of the resources when these are sold or exchanged in a monopoly situation, one governed by firm property rights but freed of all complications of force or fraud.

## *Blackmail*

The discussion of coercion and necessity also has important implications for the law of blackmail. Under the criminal law, blackmail involves any transaction in which the person who possesses unfavorable information about another person agrees to keep it silent in exchange for a monetary payment or other transfer of property or favor: the exact nature of the consideration furnished by the blackmailer is of secondary importance here. The information may have to do with past criminal conduct of the target, in which case it could be argued that blackmail serves the useful social function of supplementing the criminal law system.[12] Yet blackmail is not limited only to those cases, but also covers the suppression of any information about the target, e.g., family background or military service, which the target has chosen not to reveal or indeed actively to conceal.

The paradox of blackmail is this: it is lawful to keep the information quiet: if A knows that B's wife, C, is a reformed prostitute, he is not obliged to inform B of that fact. Yet it is also lawful to disclose that information to B. Especially in light of recent case developments, C has no legal recourse should A broadcast true knowledge of C's activities to B or indeed to the entire world. Since the right of action is denied, the proof of extensive personal anguish, and loss of friends and associates counts for naught. The statement is true, and it was not obtained in breach of any confidential relationship. There is therefore no defamation and no breach of contract, and hence no liability.[13] As a matter of private law, the individual who possesses true, damaging information about another person is left with a complete choice of whether to disclose or to conceal.

How then should this choice be exercised? Even before the question of blackmail is raised, the question of whether disclosure is proper conduct is surely vexing.[14] There are many people who regard it as a solemn duty to allow the past to be buried even if they should inadvertently stumble upon true and incriminating information about a friend or a business associate. What possible good is there in inflicting gratuitous harm on people who have struggled to put their

[12] See, e.g., Richard A. Posner, *Economic Analysis of Law* 600–602 (4th ed. 1992), which tries to link blackmail to the optimal enforcement of the criminal law. The line, which is carried over from his second edition is criticized in Richard A. Epstein, "Blackmail, Inc.," 50 *U. Chi. L. Rev.* 553, 561–62 n.15 (1983), and in Walter Block, "Blackmail, Extortion and Free Speech: A Reply to Posner, Epstein, Nozick and Lindgren," 19 *Loy. of L.A. L. Rev.* 37, 39–40 (1985).

[13] See Melvin v. Read, 112 Cal. App. 285, 297 P. 91 (1931), where the revelation of plaintiff's previous history as a prostitute and murder defendant was held actionable in a case generally not followed today. Sipple v. Chronicle Publishing Co., 154 Cal. App. 3d 1040, 201 Cal. Rptr. 665 (1984) (revelations of secret homosexual relationship in newspaper column, action denied). See generally Cox Broadcasting Corp. v. Cohn, 420 U.S. 469 (1975) (publication of the name of a rape victim constitutionally protected).

[14] For a thoughtful discussion of this question, see the judgment of Scrutton, L.J., in Watt v. Longsdon, [1930] K.B. 130 (Eng.), where the question arose in the context of determining privilege for honest mistakes in a defamation suit brought by one private party against another. One case put by Lord Justice Scrutton was whether an obstetrician who in attending the wife of his friend should disclose a marital infidelity that he has discovered during his medical work.

lives back in order? The artifices are not frauds, but benevolent white lies, of the kind that all of us practice in order to smooth out the daily frustrations of everyday living.

Yet other people (I suspect a minority) take exactly the opposite and more judgmental point of view. They could view the silence of the person about his past as a continuing fraud, or at least an active concealment, against a spouse or a business associate; they could see it as an effort to continue close personal relations on false pretenses. Once the truth is disclosed, the victim of the disclosure suffers his just deserts.

In still other cases the motives for disclosure are much more complex. Take the practice of "outing," whereby gay groups reveal the sexual preferences of concealed gay men. Those who practice outing may well believe in the presumptive privacy of certain information that others find distasteful, but they think outing is justified in order to advance a general social cause with which the victim of the disclosure might (or perhaps should) identify himself: greater protection for gay men. In their view, it is hypocritical to gain the advantage of legislative and political struggles without taking part in bringing about the desired social or legal changes. In essence, the argument for outing is that closeted gays are free riders on a larger cause. So long as the revelations are true, it is quite clear today that outing is not actionable as either a tort or a crime, but is a protected form of free speech,[15] solely because the speech is true and not because it is wise.

With all these complications, the basic question remains: should one then conceal or disclose? I confess that I have nurtured both sentiments from time to time, but that in practice over the years I have kept quiet unless something of immediate consequence turned on the disclosure, and then only in cases where I thought I had standing to intervene. Yet I could not delineate an easily applicable working set of principles of when I would want to disclose damaging information about someone whom I knew. Still less can I articulate a set of principles that would tell me when the law should either compel or forbid the disclosure. I do not think that I am alone. The absence of any legal prohibition in this area is a direct consequence of the inability to structure any authoritative norms. We cannot state with any conviction which of the two end points—disclosure or concealment—is superior to the other.

This social uncertainty, I believe, helps provide some explanation as to why blackmail is generally regarded as illegal. In effect the law

[15] See *Sipple*, 154 Cal. App. 3d at 1045, 201 Cal. Rptr. at 667.

of blackmail says that the possessor of harmful information may (like the owner of the dock in my earlier example) choose either of the two end points with perfect liberty. But he is unable to choose the middle position by selling to the victim his right to speak. The paradox arises because the immediate transaction *is* for the mutual gain of both sides. As Walter Block, the most articulate defender of the legality of blackmail, writes: "It is easy to see how the blackmailer gains from trade. He is paid merely for holding his tongue. But the 'victim' also gains. Both parties gain from a voluntary trade, and this is as true of the exchange of money for silence as it is for any other case."[16]

It is not possible to deny the truth of this point. But, by the same token, it is critical to set the immediate bargain into its proper social context. When that is done, the case looks very close to the private necessity situation and the bargaining complications that it generates. James Lindgren, who has trenchantly criticized all previous explanations (my own included) as to why blackmail should be made criminal, alludes to this point when he observes: "The blackmailer is negotiating for his own gain with someone else's leverage or bargaining chips."[17] Lindgren has clearly grasped the germ of an idea, but I think he misfires when he treats the information about the past as though it were the "property" of either the victim or third party to whom it might be revealed. If that information belonged to the victim, then there would be a duty to remain silent, which there is not; and if it belonged to that third party, then there is a duty, as it were, to return the property to its owner, that is, of mandatory disclosure. The property rights analysis thus requires that either the victim or the third party be the owner, but not both. But either position is inconsistent with the admitted choice that the party who possesses the information has to disclose or remain silent.

Rather than stress the property portion of his analysis, Lindgren's reference to "bargaining chips" shows that the root of the difficulty with blackmail lies in the destructive bargaining games that it generates.[18] Like the necessity cases, blackmail does not arise in competi-

[16] Block, supra note 12, at 39.

[17] James Lindgren, "Unraveling the Paradox of Blackmail," 84 *Colum. L. Rev.* 670, 702–3 (1984).

[18] Blackmail also generates some mischievous externalities because it encourages fraud against the third parties whom the target of blackmail wishes to deceive—a point I emphasized in "Blackmail, Inc.," supra note 12. But I have come to think that the bargaining difficulties lie closer to the heart of the problem, which is consistent with the dominant intuition that the target of a blackmail is a victim because of the impossible choices to which he or she is put.

tive markets. Quite the opposite, it always arises in a bilateral monopoly situation, typically with a single blackmailer. Given the aura of secrecy that surrounds blackmail, this bilateral monopoly situation engenders difficult and perilous bargaining problems for both sides. For starters, the victim of blackmail knows that she cannot pay her entire money up front to the blackmailer. Once the blackmailer has the money, there is little to prevent him from leaking that information to some third party. The blackmailer has obtained all that he can get, why not release the information? If the victim knows that the information will be subsequently released, then why pay the huge exaction?

Nor is it easy to see how contractual protections can stop the problem. If there were a contract that required the blackmailer to pay liquidated damages to his victim in the event of the release of information, suing on such an agreement would be nightmarish given the difficulties of proving the breach, locating a fund, finding the blackmailer, and republishing the harmful information. Legal or not, blackmail by nature is a venture that requires continuous payments of small amounts of consideration: large enough to keep the blackmailer happy, but small enough to keep the victim alive for another round. In a sense the game is as difficult for the blackmailer as his victim, but with this one critical difference: the blackmailer can always choose to exit unilaterally, while the victim cannot. Indeed, the complications are so acute that it is doubtful that *two* independent blackmailers could ever succeed over a prolonged period of time, given the likelihood that their combined demands would prove excessive.

The prohibition against blackmail therefore has as one of its objects to knock out all the destructive bargaining games that could exist were the institution legalized. Even though blackmail will take place because its victims are reluctant to come forward, the law has at least this collateral benefit: it forestalls the formation of Blackmail, Inc., the firm that would arise if blackmailing were just another legal contracting activity. Therefore the paradox of blackmail is very close to the paradox of unconstitutional conditions, with which it is often discussed.[19] There are the mutual gains from trade, yet they are no longer evidence of a preferred social outcome, given the setting in which the bargain takes place. The greater power to

[19] See, e.g., Howard Abrams, "Economic Analysis and Unconstitutional Conditions: A Reply to Professor Epstein," 27 *San Diego L. Rev.* 109 (1990); Kathleen Sullivan, "Unconstitutional Conditions," 102 *Harv. L. Rev.* 1413 (1989).

disclose does not justify the lesser power to threaten to disclose.[20] There are no bargaining games between blackmailer and blackmail victim once disclosure has taken place.

Once the bargaining problems are taken into account, there is strong justification for the all-or-nothing rule on disclosure that characterizes the blackmail situation. With the necessity case there seemed little reason to give the owner of the dock the choice to exclude or to admit for a fixed compensation. We know which choice in the all-or-nothing distribution dominates: access to the dock. But with blackmail, all we know is how difficult it is to choose between the two extremes, so that neither can be excluded with any confidence.[21] But we also know that the intermediate solutions that allow silence to be bought and sold consume resources without advancing us to a higher social state. Ex ante there is powerful reason to think that just about everyone is better off with the prohibition against excluding people in times of necessity. The same is not quite true with blackmail: while we cannot choose which outcome is preferable, we can conclude that the bargaining turmoil that blackmail induces is a social cost which generates no comparable social gain: still the nondisclosure it produces is not necessarily a good. Set in its larger context, the threat to expose is socially destructive, even if the disclosure by some lights is not. Once we recognize why this offer reduces overall social welfare, then we can conclude that this practice too is illegitimate and coercive, even though it does not involve the use of force or fraud.

## PRISONER'S DILEMMA GAMES

The problem of coercive offers also arises in connection with prisoner's dilemma games. Their basic structure is well known and will be set out only briefly here. Suppose each of two prisoners acting alone finds himself driven to confess, even though both prisoners would be better off if they could coordinate their efforts and remain

[20] As Holmes noted, without quite understanding why, "[w]hen it comes to the collateral questioning of obtaining a contract by threats, it does not follow that, because you cannot be made to answer for the act, you may use the threat." Silsbee v. Webber, 171 Mass. 378, 381, 50 N.E. 555, 556 (1898). Ironically, Holmes was one of the staunchest opponents of the unconstitutional conditions doctrine.

[21] For those who are curious, my views here differ from those in "*Blackmail, Inc.,*" supra note 12, because I am less certain that the fraud or concealment practiced is one that the law should suppress. But I still think that Blackmail, Inc. is a firm that should be allowed to collect no revenues.

silent. To see how this situation might arise, assume the following sentences await each prisoner: if both confess, each gets a five-year sentence; if prisoner A confesses but prisoner B does not, A gets a one-year sentence and B gets a ten-year sentence; if B confesses but A does not, B gets the one-year sentence and A gets the ten-year sentence; if neither prisoner confesses, each gets a two-year sentence.[22] If A and B could coordinate their behavior, both would remain silent, and each would escape with a light two-year sentence. Acting separately, however, each will confess and therefore receive a five-year sentence. Consider A's situation. If B confesses, A should confess in order to receive a five-year sentence instead of a ten-year sentence. If B remains silent, A should confess in order to receive a one-year sentence instead of a two-year sentence. No matter what B does, there is a dominant strategy for A: A is always better off confessing. Parallel arguments apply to B, so both A and B confess. Their uncoordinated activities lead to their mutual destruction.

The moral of the story is clear. If the two prisoners could engage in cooperative action, then both could keep silent and beat back the harsher sentences that they would otherwise receive. But since they cannot remain silent, each of them enters into the fatal deal with the police. It seems clear that the prisoner's dilemma generates enormous losses to the parties who are forced to play that game. But in assessing the social desirability of these prisoners' dilemma games, it is important to recognize that their occurrence may be a problem that society should try to avoid, or in the alternative should be a dilemma that it either tolerates or actively fosters. The prisoner's dilemma leads to the social good if the confessions secure the maximum punishment of criminals. Whether the offer is regarded as "coercive" or not is almost beside the point. If it is coercion, then the coercion is surely justified by the end it obtains.

[22] A chart of the payoffs looks as follows, where the first entry in each box is A's expected sentence, and the second entry is B's:

| | | B: confess | B: keep silent |
|---|---|---|---|
| A | confess | 5,5 | 1,10 |
| A | keep silent | 10,1 | 2,2 |

The prisoner's dilemma set out here is one that seems socially beneficial because it tends to forestall crime. But sometimes, as in the bankruptcy case, each creditor finds himself in a prisoner's dilemma game with his co-creditors that leads to a negative social outcome, namely the destruction of the going-concern value of the business. For various articles discussing the prisoner's dilemma, see *Rational Choice* 34–107 (J. Elster, ed. 1986).

Similarly, ordinary competitive markets give rise to prisoner's dilemma games for the sellers of goods or the providers of labor. If all of them were able to coordinate their activities, then they could maintain a system of monopoly prices, and divide the gains among themselves. The business cartel and the labor union are thus rational responses to the prisoner's dilemma game. As before, it is critical to distinguish between the private and the social justification. Overcoming the prisoner's dilemma game is an advantage to the sellers of goods or the providers of labor, but it is not an advantage to the society at large. By coordinating their behavior they are able to reduce output and to raise prices (or wages) like the classical monopolist. Their behavior therefore generates the kinds of social losses characteristic of monopoly activity. It may well be that the state will find it too costly to enforce an antitrust law against these practices, but it surely can refuse to enforce agreements in restraint of trade, and it most definitely need not prop up the monopoly by giving legal restraints against entry (as with the raisin cartel)[23] or with mandatory collective bargaining provisions under the National Labor Relations Act. Here the external losses that are inflicted on others exceed the gains to the parties by overcoming their prisoner's dilemma.

In other contexts, however, the want of coordination exemplified by the prisoner's dilemma produces not only losses from the parties but for society at large. Thus in the ordinary case of the fishery, or of the oil and gas field over many separate plots of land, the individual strategies of capture undertaken by each potential claimant of fish or oil and gas lead to a premature destruction of the common pool. A system of regulation that coordinates their behavior—restriction on the catch limit, or oil well spacing regulations—produces gains for the private parties that justify the administrative costs in question. But unlike the competitive situation, these private gains are not tied to external costs of greater magnitude. The increase of supplies at a lower price works to increase social welfare, so long as the coordinated activity that captures the natural resource does not lead to the formation of a cartel that restricts, after resources have been privatized, its sale in the open market. Stopping prisoner's dilemma games with these natural resources can be a social good if done at reasonable cost.

Prisoner's dilemma games can have destructive social consequences in other collective action settings. Suppose in bankruptcy that there is a single common debtor with a large number of indepen-

[23] See Parker v. Brown, 317 U.S. 341 (1943).

dent general creditors.[24] Assume further that the debtor's business has a positive "going concern" value that could not be captured if its assets were sold off piecemeal in order to satisfy creditors' claims. If the business should become insolvent, the way to maximize the total return to the creditors would be to keep the business intact and to provide each creditor with a portion of the earnings it generates, prorated to his share of the debt. Nonetheless, any debtor has powerful incentives to take individual action to defeat this ideal collective solution. Thus, one creditor may prod the debtor for full payment of his obligation by threatening suit. To stave off disaster, the debtor may agree to make this payment, even at the cost of the piecemeal sale of assets. Once any given creditor takes this course of action, other creditors will also hasten to protect their positions. Each creditor will therefore race for early payment and seek a "preference" from the debtor. The debtor, who might survive if the creditors stay their hands, can be brought down by the onslaught. Acting individually, the creditors will manage to destroy the going concern value of the business, probably ensuring that many creditors will receive only partial payment, and some none at all. Moreover, all of the jockeying consumes enormous resources which could have been saved if the creditors had acted as a unified group from the outset.

The problem of coordination has also arisen in the modern corporate tender arrangement. To see the problem in its stripped-down form,[25] suppose the bidder corporation seeks to acquire the shares of a target corporation from its individual shareholders. In essence the bidder adopts a two-part strategy. It first offers a substantial front-end premium to shareholders who are willing to tender in the voluntary market.[26] Thereafter it exercises its condemnation powers to buy out (without their consent) the remaining shareholders who did not tender at a price equal to or above the pre-tender offer market price. In essence the shareholders of the target corporation are faced with a prisoner's dilemma situation.

[24] See, e.g., Douglas G. Baird & Thomas H. Jackson, *Cases, Problems and Materials on Bankruptcy* 31–35 (1985); Thomas H. Jackson, *The Logic and Limits of Bankruptcy Law* 10–13 (1986).

[25] Many modern tender offers do not assume this form, as there are state regulations that restrict the use of front-end loaded tender offers, and there is some uncertainty as to whether they expose the offeror to suit from disappointed shareholders. But it is the theory, not the current practice, that is of interest here.

[26] On the need for the initial premium, see Lloyd R. Cohen, "Why Tender Offers?: The Efficient Market Hypothesis, the Supply of Stock, and Signaling," 19 *J. Legal Stud.* 113 (1990).

Assume that the market price for each of 100 shares is $50 per share. Assume that none of the shareholders wants to sell at any price below $70 per share, but will sell at above that price. An offer to purchase 60 per cent of the shares comes in at $75, where the remaining 40 percent of the shares will be purchased at $55 per share, above the prebid price. Here the shareholders as a group agree that the value of the firm to them equals $7,000 (the $70 × 100 shares). The total value of the two-part offer ($75 × 60) + ($55 × 40) = $6,700, which is $300 less than the shareholders acting together would accept. Yet in an uncoordinated fashion, the shareholders feel compelled to accept the offer. Thus suppose that 40 percent of the shareholders refuse to tender: now their decision allows the remaining shareholders to tender at $75, or $5 more than their reservation price. But that maneuver forces the nontendering shareholders to surrender their shares at $55 per share, which is lower than the front end of the bid. Anticipating the second stage of the game, they will also tender at the initial stage. In the end the average share goes for the blended price of $67 per share (usually prorated across shareholders), which is less than the $70 per share that all the shareholders desired.

Now the question is whether this offer should be regarded as coercive, as has often been portrayed in the literature. There is surely an element of coercion involved in the game, for the back-end transaction requires an involuntary purchase which, if not traceable to some prior consent to that maneuver in the original corporate charter, represents a use of government power that is inconsistent with strict libertarian principles. In this sense the state supported takeover is surely coercive. But the word *coercion* also implies the unjustified threat of force, and it is on this point that positions can differ, depending on the baseline chosen for analysis. One first has to decide that takeovers are desirable because they displace the flabby incumbent management, and are thus not harmful simply because they hurt suppliers, creditors, and workers of the firm.[27] More critical to this discussion, even if the tender offer is thought to be a good thing, there can be extensive arguments about the baseline against which the just price is measured. If the baseline is the prior state of affairs, then the coercive tender offer is fully justified for two reasons. First every person (including the back-end shareholders) is left better off

[27] See the Pennsylvania statute that allows corporate officers to take this interest in account to defeat the tender offer. Law of 1990, Dec. 19, Pub. L. 834, No. 198, §102 (codified at 15 Pa. Cons. Stat. Ann. 515(a) (1992)).

than before the tender offer was made so that the new position is strictly Pareto superior to the old one. Second, the frequency of tender offers will increase because the bidder will be able to preserve a larger portion of the total gain. Nonetheless the tender offer will be viewed differently if the baseline is the amount that the shareholders could have obtained if they had been able to negotiate as a single owner, here the $70 per share. In that case it can be said that the strategy of divide and conquer has left them as a group poorer by $3 per share.

The choice between these two views does not depend upon the mechanics of the prisoner's dilemma game. It depends rather upon the prior judgment that asks whether these tender offers are substantively desirable. Where the judgment is that tender offers are good (because they displace incompetent management), then the offers are not regarded as coercive. The nontendering shareholders are said to be protected against exploitation by the rule that allows their forced surrender of shares to proceed, but only at a figure greater than the premarket price. Where there is a sense that the transaction may reduce the social value (the bidder values the shares at only $68, enough to win the offer, but not enough to match the private value of the existing shareholders) the offer is described as coercive. The actual judgments are invariably clouded because there are important empirical judgments about the existence or size of any premium that existing shareholders attach to their shares, and the costs of running tender offers and resistance to them. But for these limited purposes, the basic point is clear: when the prisoner's dilemma game is judged to lead to social misallocation, the baseline chosen is the reservation price each person holds for the firm's share; accordingly the transaction is deemed coercive. When the transaction is judged socially beneficial, then the baseline chosen is the prebid price of the shares, and the offer is regarded as noncoercive.[28] The judgments about coercion depend upon the choice of baselines, a point that is well enough understood. What is less well understood is that the choice of baseline depends upon the perception of the overall social welfare of the transaction in question. Coercion is parasitic on baselines. And the choice of baselines is parasitic on conceptions of social welfare.

[28] See, e.g., Daniel R. Fischel, "From *MITE* to *CTS*: State Anti-Takeover Statutes, the Williams Act, the Commerce Clause and Insider Trading," 1987 *Sup. Ct. Rev.* 47, 59–63; Lucian A. Bebchuk, "Toward Undistorted Choice and Equal Treatment in Corporate Takeovers," 98 *Harv. L. Rev.* 1693 (1985).

## EXTERNALITIES

The last of the social problems that lead to limitations on freedom of contract is the need to protect strangers to the agreement.[29] It is here that the libertarian prohibition against the use of force shows its greatest strength. Assume that A is not entitled to take the property of B without B's consent. Any contract between A and C that allowed or required A to take B's property would not be enforced. It is obvious of course that B could not be made to hand the property over. In addition, however, C should have no remedy against A in damages if the property is not taken, for to give the remedy is to encourage by indirection the illegal taking. At the very least therefore, the A/C contract is not enforceable. Indeed, in most jurisdictions a contract to take property from a stranger itself forms the basis of a conspiracy offense, punishable even if the theft does not take place.[30] This network of prohibitions is necessary in order to forestall destructive behavior that would otherwise undermine any stable system of social organization. If A and C could bargain away the rights of B, why would B and D not bargain away the rights of A? And so on, ad infinitum. An unending series of costly bargains could be used to secure the transfer of wealth, but little would be done to secure the creation of wealth in the first instance. The general legal rule allowing persons to exchange only those resources that they own creates powerful incentives for the creation of wealth, and with it the satisfaction of human desires.[31] The rule that allows them to buy, sell, or consume resources owned by others only leads to the dissipation of wealth. Private law must therefore protect all individ-

[29] The seminal discussion of this issue is found in Ronald H. Coase, "The Problem of Social Cost," 3 *J.L. & Econ.* 1 (1960). I have stated my own views more fully in Richard A. Epstein, "Causation—In Context: An Afterword," 63 *Chi.-Kent L. Rev.* 653, 653–57 (1987).

[30] See, for a representative view, *Model Penal Code* §5.03 (1962). See generally George Fletcher, *Rethinking Criminal Law* §3.6 (1978).

[31] There are exceptions to the rule, for example, for persons who purchase property in good faith from a person not entitled to convey it. But all of these exceptions are hedged in with limitations that prevent major abuses and generally facilitate rather than retard commerce and exchange, given that the original owner is usually in a better position than the ultimate purchaser to protect against the risks in question. See generally Saul Levmore, "Variety and Uniformity in the Treatment of the Good-Faith Purchaser," 16 *J. Legal Stud.* 43 (1987). Where the risks of error are too great, systems of recordation, such as those for land and motor vehicles, provide effective institutional ways to remove that risk at relatively low administrative cost.

uals against the contractual machinations of strangers. The rights that A and C each have against B cannot be enlarged by an agreement between A and C alone. The temptations for strategic contracting would be too great.

The problem of externalities can also arise in the public sphere in any situation in which unanimous consent is not obtained. Within any government system, taxes are imposed by majority will. The revenues so obtained could then be used to purchase property, which could then be conveyed to some preferred groups via "bargain sales," at a fraction of its true value. There would be no exploitation of the happy buyer, but there would be a risk that the state as trustee would have abused its power in relation to the other citizens it represents, all of whom received less than fair value in exchange for the property transferred. This pattern of abuse would result not only in a systematic deprivation of the interests of some citizens but also in an overall efficiency loss, as the controlling group will not only expend resources to obtain the transfer, but will be willing to acquire the property even when it values it less than the state did.[32]

To take a simple case, assume that there are five persons in the society at large, and that a majority faction of three arranges to buy a public asset worth \$500 for \$300. In a static analysis, the wealth of each of the two minority shareholders decreases by \$40 (one-fifth of the state's \$200 loss in the transaction), assuming that the asset has equal value for all concerned. The wealth of each of the three dominant shareholders, ignoring assets not involved in the transaction, increases from \$200 before the transaction (\$100 in cash, plus \$100 for his interest in the public asset) to \$227 after the transaction (\$60, or one-fifth of the publicly held cash, plus \$167, or one-third of the \$500 asset). As a first approximation, there is only a redistribution not substantially different from that of an ordinary takings case. In dynamic terms, however, there will be not only a simple shift of wealth, but a total reduction as well. Not only are transaction costs incurred in making the shift, but the winning coalition may be able to profit from the public sale if they value the asset at more than \$300, even if they value it at less than \$500. Hence there is a systematic divergence between private and social costs, analogous to the one found in the monopoly case. The winning coalition forces the transaction even when the property is worth *less* in private hands than it was in public hands. The insistence that full value be paid for any transfer of property from the state is necessary to stop this problem.

[32] See Richard A. Epstein, "The Public Trust Doctrine," 7 *Cato J.* 411 (1987).

The problem here is not one of bargaining breakdown, so the doctrine of unconstitutional conditions is inapplicable. It is the takings risk that is most salient in this context, although the two issues are often confused. The most available weapon to combat this abuse on a general is the public trust doctrine. But the doctrine in many cases lacks a firm constitutional basis,[33] and in any event its development is decisively hampered by undue willingness of courts to treat the government just as if it were a private owner of property, capable of dealing with "its" property just as it sees fit. The model does not work well because the model of absolute rights on which it depends permits government action of all kinds and descriptions to work redistributions of wealth among private citizens by a wide range of strategies. The failure to take into account the losses that may be imposed by the majority has resulted in serious constitutional dislocations, both in the area of property rights generally, and with specific guarantees of individual rights.

*Hunter v. City of Pittsburgh*[34] shows the dangers that arise when the state is given untrammeled power to reorganize its political subdivisions. A Pennsylvania statute allowed any city council to initiate a referendum in which both its citizens and those of a contiguous city could participate; if a simple majority vote of the two cities combined had approved the union, then the larger city could implement that union by "annexing and consolidating" the smaller. In *Hunter*, Pittsburgh initiated a statutory referendum covering itself and the contiguous city of Allegheny. Allegheny had already financed its needed general improvements. Pittsburgh, for its part, needed to levy extensive taxes in order to service the debt on prior municipal improvements (parks, water, boulevards), and also planned expensive additional improvements in the near future. The annexation threw the burden of the Pittsburgh improvements on the taxpayers of Allegheny whose political remedy was wholly inadequate under the voting procedures established under the statute. The case thus involved an externalization of costs through the political process.

The constitutional challenge that followed rested on the proposition that the skewed distribution of taxation and improvements

[33] See Illinois Cent. Ry. v. Illinois, 146 U.S. 387 (1892). *Illinois Central* does not locate the public trust doctrine in any particular clause of the Constitution. On the public trust generally, see Carol M. Rose, "The Comedy of the Commons: Custom, Commerce, and Inherently Public Property," 53 *U. Chi. L. Rev.* 711 (1986), and Joseph Sax, "The Public Trust Doctrine in Natural Resource Law: Effective Judicial Intervention," 68 *Mich. L. Rev.* 471 (1970).

[34] 207 U.S. 161 (1907).

wrought by the annexation were a taking without compensation, prohibited by the due process clause of the Fourteenth Amendment. The only cases that might have supported that contention were prior decisions under the contract clause which held that third-party creditors of local governments could not be deprived of their claims by having the state first liquidate and then reincorporate its municipal debtors under a different name or charter.[35] Those cases, however, did not extend to situations, such as that in *Hunter*, where the redistribution of benefits and burdens was solely internal to the citizens of the two cities. The due process challenges raised against these decisions received the back-of-the-hand treatment by the Court, which celebrated the extensive power of the state to make and remake municipal government and other subdivisions as it sees fit.[36] The absolute power of state government as regards "its" internal affairs was thus celebrated in print two years after *Lochner v. New York*,[37] showing once again how perilous it is to allow individual cases to define constitutional eras. The elaborate nineteenth-century power that limited the incidence of special assessments under the due process clause[38] was not carried over to structural changes in government that worked a substantial redistribution of wealth, perhaps because of the difficulty of fashioning some remedy either to block the acquisition (without the consent of the majority of the citizens of the city taken over) or to limit the taxing power of the acquiring town after annexation.

Over time there has been some erosion of unfettered power attributable to state governments. *Gomillion v. Lightfoot*[39] took great pains to distinguish away *Hunter* when it struck down as a violation of the Fifteenth Amendment protections of voting an Alabama statute which converted the town of Tuskegee from a square into a grotesque 28-sided object, when all the voters excluded by the new boundaries were black. For these purposes, what is striking about *Gomillion* is that it solemnly invokes the unconstitutional condi-

[35] See, e.g., Shapleigh v. San Angelo, 167 U.S. 646 (1897); Mobile v. Watson, 116 U.S. 289 (1886).

[36] "The State, therefore, at its pleasure may modify or withdraw all such [local government] powers, may take without compensation such property, hold it itself, or vest it in other agencies, expand or contract the territorial area, unite the whole or a part of it, with another municipality, repeal the charter and destroy the corporation." *Hunter*, 207 U.S. at 178–79.

[37] 198 U.S. US (1905). Elsewhere, as well; see discussion of Atkin v. Kansas, infra chap. 14.

[38] See Stephen Diamond, "The Death and Transfiguration of Benefit Taxation: Special Assessments in Nineteenth-Century America," 12 *J. Legal Stud.* 201 (1983).

[39] 364 U.S. 339 (1960).

tions doctrine to deal with a case that involves only a takings, but not a bargaining risk: at no point did any of the black citizens of Tuskegee have any choice as to whether to take or reject some burden as the price for receiving some benefit. So closely did Justice Frankfurter conceive the relationship between the two risks that he did not see fit to distinguish between them. Both were treated together because they represent serious difficulties of the political process. The only difference between *Hunter* and *Gomillion*, was that the former involved only economic issues, while the latter involved economic manipulations that crossed racial lines.

The key gap in these cases is the weakness of our current constitutional structures to place effective constraints on the ability of government to deal with property to which it has legal title. Thus the same risk of redistribution through regulation of government lands can arise today under any of the specified guarantees of individual rights under the Constitution. Perhaps the most poignant illustration of this process is Lyng v. Northwest Indian Cemetery Protective Ass'n.[40] There the Forest Service (long the nation's most inveterate roadbuilder) decided to build a road which seriously disrupted the burial grounds and other sacred sites of three Indian tribes (the Yurok, Karok and Tolowa Indians). The question was whether the decision to build this road was an infringement of their First Amendment guarantee of freedom of religion, to which Justice O'Connor's short answer, in a 5 to 3 decision, was no: "Whatever rights the Indians may have to the use of the area, however, those rights do not divest the Government of its right to use what is, after all, *its* land."[41] In essence government is treated as though it were the absolute owner of the property in question, endowed with the strong right to exclude.

The case takes on a very different appearance, however, when the impact of the decision on various groups within society is assessed. Any decision by the Forest Service to build a road to collect logs is implicitly suspect. Even if there is no suitable alternative road site to a given tract of land, it is hard to establish why any particular government lands have to be harvested at all, especially when cheap private alternatives are available. Yet for their part the Indians come out huge losers in the case, because it is doubtful that any system of cash transfers would make them indifferent to the loss of their sacred religious sites. The weakness of modern public trust and takings law precludes any direct property rights attack on the Forest

[40] 485 U.S. 439 (1988).

[41] Id. at 453 (italics in original).

Service's decision to build the road, and induced the Indians to mount a free exercise claim instead. That case too rests implicitly on the idea that government property interests are never absolute, but are subject to easements and other prescriptive rights obtained by the Indian tribes under, of course, the standard rules of property as developed at common law.[42]

Now the broader message should be clear: the belief in limited government leads to a strong system of private-property rights and freedom of contract for private parties. Yet that same concern with government power leads to exactly the opposite conclusions for property that is held in public hands. Public property may often be impressed with some sort of public trust that limits the power of the government to dispose or use it in certain fashions. And government freedom of contract is now subject to restrictions, given the risks of extraction attributable to its evident monopoly power. *Northwest Indian Cemetery*, like *Hunter* before it, is simply illustrative of a case where the takings risk is manifest when the bargaining risk is nonexistent, and is thus lumped with the unconstitutional conditions doctrine because of the nagging suspicion that questionable government behavior received an uncritical pass in the Supreme Court.[43]

The arguments thus far have developed these conceptions largely in connection with private transactions. The set of issues that have been raised here—the definition of baselines, the problems of necessity, and monopoly—have their precise parallels in the domain of public and constitutional law. In the next two chapters, I leave the private law analysis of coercion and move to the ways in which these arguments have their analogues in the public area, where they give some clues on limitations about bargaining, both at the formation of the state, and during the course of its operation.

[42] See Ira C. Lupu, "Where Rights Begin: The Problem of Burdens on the Free Exercise of Religion," 102 *Harv. L. Rev.* 933 (1989).

[43] See, e.g., Sullivan, "Unconstitutional Conditions," supra note 19, at 1455–56, which recognizes that the case is "not an unconstitutional conditions case," but discusses it for the light it sheds on the coercion question.

## CHAPTER 6

# Forced Exchanges and Just Compensation

### FROM THE DEFINITION TO THE ENFORCEMENT OF PROPERTY RIGHTS

The previous discussion of baselines sets the stage for the analysis of coercion. Broadly speaking, coercion is the adoption of some bargaining strategy that leads to an unacceptable deviation from the original set of entitlements. These cases fall into two classes. The first, and obvious, cases involve the threat of force or fraud. The less obvious cases are those which arise from taking certain bargaining strategies in monopoly, necessity, or prisoner's dilemma situations. These are not coercive in the first sense because force and fraud have been ruled out as bargaining strategies. Nonetheless, in both cases the bargaining strategies adopted by one party can lead to a deviation from the optimal social outcome. A strong libertarian framework takes the first class of cases into account, but ignores the second. The ambiguity arises because in some contexts coercion is thought to involve the use of force, and in others coercion is thought to involve an illegitimate bargaining move. There is an overlap between the two sets, as there is a strong presumption that force and fraud are illegitimate, while other moves (i.e., offers of contract) are not. Matters become more complicated by a second ambiguity. Some forms of coercion are regarded as legitimate, but others are not. Stated otherwise, the presumption against coercion (in either form) is not absolute. The threat (like the use) of force can be regarded as legitimate under some circumstances, while other types of threat may be considered illegitimate, depending on social context. No wonder the term "coercion" is so elusive in its descriptive and normative import.

Thus far the inquiry has posited that there is a well-functioning state that can enforce its various prohibitions in a cheap, honest, and reliable fashion. Yet there is always some question as to how that state system of enforcement arises. Unanimous consent is not obtainable for state enforcement of individual rights, given the well-known coordination and holdout problems that block that obvious approach. The next stage of the inquiry therefore follows quickly on the heels of the previous chapters. If a system of well-defined property rights is (or is even close to) Pareto superior to a system in which no one may acquire any rights in anything, how are these rights to be enforced? This question in turn requires us to revisit the issues of coercion and coordination which were so closely linked in the original inquiry to the structure of property rights. The private use of coercion, that is, both the use and especially the *threat* of force, represents the major source of destabilization of any system of property rights. An insistence upon individual self-ownership of labor counts for naught if some individuals are allowed through force to reduce other individuals to chattel slavery, or even to prevent them from moving freely about or from entering into social or trading relationships with other persons. The exclusive ownership of land and chattels will come for naught if those who sow are barred from reaping: who will plant if others can freely harvest? Similarly, systems of common ownership, such as those involved with navigable waterways, will turn out to be unstable if any single individual is allowed to blockade the river against use by the public-at-large.

These obvious forms of coercion represent efforts to obtain the unilateral and egoistic redefinition of property rights brought about by some solely for their private advantage.[1] If the social calculus has set the baselines for labor and external resources correctly, then these private moves represent a backward slide that takes place only because they provide substantial gains for the users of force, but gains that are dwarfed by the losses imposed on others who must pay the price. The move from the state of nature to a well-run society requires not only the proper *definition* of initial property rights (justified in the end by transaction cost considerations) but also their successful *enforcement and protection.*

## THE TRANSACTIONAL BARRIERS

There is, however, no effective system of voluntary transactions that allows a coordinated social response to the use of force. To be sure, some persons can form various voluntary self-protective organizations that will lend some measure of security to their memberships.[2] But if these organizations are based only on voluntary membership and not on exclusive control within well-defined territories, then several associations will operate in the same place at the same time.

[1] See Guido Calabresi & A. Douglas Melamed, "Property Rules, Liability Rules and Inalienability: One View of the Cathedral," 85 *Harv. L. Rev.* 1089 (1972).

[2] See Robert Nozick, *Anarchy, State, and Utopia*, ch. 2 (1974).

Where there are various offenses committed against the legal order, it may not be clear who has done them, but there may be no ability for multiple separate organizations—it is difficult to say how many would exist in equilibrium—to coordinate their efforts to track down and punish the rights violator within the system. If one organization refuses to respect the just claims (or even claims perceived as just) of a rival organization against one of its own members, then conflict between protective associations could shatter any uneasy peace that exists among them. It is largely for that reason that our constitution contains a full faith and credit clause, which mandates some level of comity and cooperation among the states.[3] Competition in enforcement does not yield uniformity in results and may well magnify private quarrels into major social disruptions. Unless some forced exchanges are allowed as a matter of first principle, those associations offer the only prospects for social order.

It is clear why this outcome is inefficient. To return to the metaphor of the last chapter, the elements of the legal system operate in series, and not in parallel: partial concurrence is insufficient, everyone must be bound by the common set of rules, for so long as the use of force is left unchecked, each person has to fear the actions of his worst enemies. Private protection depends on multiple pairwise agreements and is highly unstable for that reason. If there are 1000 persons who might try to kill me, what prospects are there of making agreements with all of them that secure my bodily integrity? The failure of any one connection could result in death unless by other agreements I am able to secure the protection of others to enforce the agreements that I have made with some enemies and to protect me against other enemies who have refused to deal. The transactional network here is likely to collapse of its own weight. The situation, moreover, is a far cry from those cases where agreements work well, namely, in seeking out trading partners in a world in which the collective use of force has ruled out private aggression. In those circumstances, I need only search for the trading partners who offer me the best deals, and once these are concluded I need not worry about doing business with persons who are indifferent or hostile to me.[4] Collective force therefore works best to achieve a simple standard-

[3] Full Faith and Credit shall be given in each State to the Public Acts, Records, and Judicial Proceedings of every other State." Art. IV, §1. For a discussion of the complexities that this simple provision generates, see Roger C. Cramton, David P. Currie & Herma Hill Kay, *Conflicts of Law Cases—Comments—Questions* (4th ed. 1987).

[4] On the difference between the use of force and the refusal to deal, see Richard A. Epstein, *Forbidden Grounds: The Case Against Employment Discrimination Laws*, chap. 2 (1992).

ized form of social arrangement: everyone keeps off. It is quite hopeless to articulate the detailed relationships of exchange that characterize market interactions.

The coordination problem, then, blocks the easy consensual answer to the coercion problem in the realm of rights enforcement just as it did in the realm of rights definition. The major question of social theory, with strong echoes in constitutional law, is how to develop the needed institutions for the enforcement of property rights, however defined. While in the original position it is in the interest of everyone to have a system of centralized enforcement, it is not in the interest of all to join in so long as others are able to free ride while staying outside the group, claiming the benefits of peace that it promises without being forced to contribute to its perpetuation. In this context, the players in the prisoner's dilemma game are all members of society, so there are no other individuals outside the group who receive positive externalities to offset the losses to the players. This prisoner's dilemma game is therefore corrosive. The only way it can be overcome is through the use of collective coercion which, when used to prevent private coercion, takes on a legitimate coloration.

Yet there must also be limits to the use of state coercion, for the dangers of excessive force and improper bargaining practices carry over from the private to the political arena. The traditional Hobbesian insistence that the state must exercise a monopoly of force within its jurisdiction in order to prevent the war of all against all recognizes only the need to restrain private violence by central coercion. But it does not recognize that the creation of that monopoly power in the hands of a few public officials itself poses a great danger of abuse. In some markets the government has a high degree of monopoly power. It may be the only party that can operate the public roads, issue building permits, or allow firms to do business in corporate form. Unlike the private monopolist, its power cannot be eroded by the entry of new firms, but is perpetuated by a legal prohibition against entry by new rivals. The major task of constitutionalism, therefore, has been to forge a system in which these government excesses are curtailed while leaving the state sufficient power to discharge the necessary tasks of governance. A system of unrestrained political power does a poor job in setting the right balance.

The risks of resource misallocation identified in private bargaining transactions carry over into the political arena as well. There is an obvious need for limitations on the direct use of coercion. By the same token, if the monopoly and necessity cases are any guide, there are obvious reasons to limit the capacity of the government to bargain with its individual citizens. Just as the dockowner in the private necessity case is limited to a fixed rate of return when the dock is used by others and forbidden from imposing collateral or unrelated conditions on that use, so too the state, when it provides resources of which it is the sole supplier, should be limited both in the concessions that it may exact from private owners and in the conditions it may impose on them. Similarly, government action often creates the risk of collective action problems. As a single unified entity, the state may be able to make offers to widely dispersed individuals who find themselves faced with a prisoner's dilemma game. Each person acting alone may think it in his interest to waive some constitutional right, even though a group, if it could act collectively, would reach the opposite conclusion. By barring some waivers of constitutional rights, the doctrine of unconstitutional conditions allows disorganized citizens to escape from what would otherwise be a socially destructive prisoner's dilemma game.

Finally, the problem of externalities, as it arises from majority rule, must be taken into account. The state is an association of a large number of individuals with diverse interests and inconsistent desires. Yet it must make decisions that bind them all. In principle it would be ideal if all collective decisions could be made by unanimous consent, which would forestall the problem of the majority exploiting the minority. But any unanimous consent requirement would lead to government paralysis because any single individual would be in a position to bargain strategically by holding out for a lion's share of the gain from social action. For better or for worse, some system of majority rule is a necessary evil, and one that forces us to confront explicitly the expropriation problem in the political context.

A sound constitutional order must address all these problems. The theory of limited government that restricts the government's use of force also should restrict the government's ability to get its way by contract, and it is no wonder that from Holmes to the present, the strong detractors of the unconstitutional conditions doctrine are those who desire, or at least accept, the large government structures of the welfare state.

## TWO PIES AGAIN

The best way, I believe, to examine the expropriation question is to return to the diagram of the two pies with which I began my earlier book on *Takings* (see diagram). The logic of the system is as follows. The initial endowments in the original position represents the world of well-defined property rights without a system of collective en-

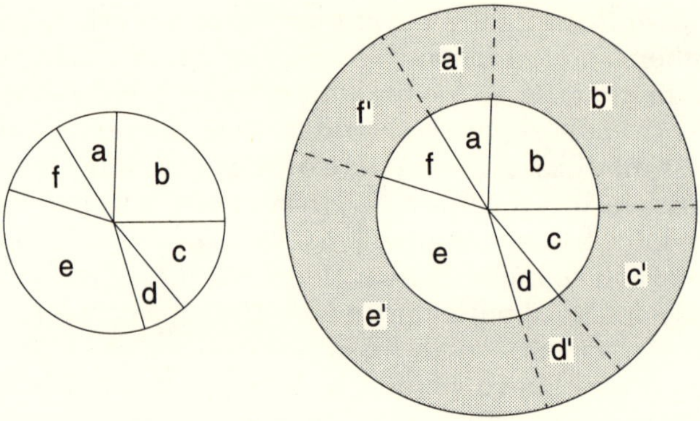


forcement. The boundaries that separate the various slices are the boundaries that must be respected if the private use of force is to be controlled. These should be defined in the ways indicated in the discussion of baselines, for the transactional reasons set out in chapter 2. The outer pie represents the social gains that can be obtained if there is some collective solution of social order to which all contribute and from which all derive benefit.

As diagramed, it looks as though these benefits are equally distributed in accordance with private holdings before state enforcement took hold, but that assumption needs far more elaboration, postponed until the next chapter. At present, it is sufficient to note that the use of social coercion could promise that there is an outer ring, representing the social gains that are derivable from a system of taxation (itself a coercive exaction not sanctioned by individual consent) whose proceeds are used to fund the enforcement machinery of the state. Once state coercion is instituted, two further inquiries are appropriate. The first concerns the guarantee that no person is left worse off after the collective action takes place. The second, which is central to this book, concerns the maximization of the outer ring, that is, the collective social surplus generated by the proper use of coercive arrangements.

## JUST COMPENSATION AND THE COORDINATION QUESTION

Start with some forced redeployment of individual rights, be it taxation to secure individual liberty and property, or the taking of land for a public highway. Should the individual losers from the state action be entitled to receive just compensation for their losses from the state?

At the highest level of analysis, the answer itself is far from clear. The standard social welfare literature describes two alternative definitions of efficiency, one of which embodies a compensation requirement (Pareto) and the other which does not (Kaldor-Hicks).[5] A social change is desirable under the Pareto test only if it makes at least one person better off and leaves no one worse off. That test has nothing to say about the distribution of the surplus from collective action, but it requires only that after the fact each person be left at least indifferent between the present and previous state of affairs. This test has a precise analogue under the just compensation requirement that is imposed for government takings. Where the taking is found, it will be allowed to go forward only if it produces no losers. The division of the surplus is not specified by a demand for just compensation, which is again consistent with the Pareto test as well.

The Pareto test of just compensation frequently has been criticized on the ground that it leaves no play in the joints: so long as one person is left worse off by the particular change, then it is blocked no matter how great the gains that are obtained by other individuals. The emergence of the Kaldor-Hicks standard of social welfare is an effort to overcome this stringent obstacle without foresaking one of the main strengths of the Pareto system—its willingness to take all individuals and their preferences just as they are without treating some as "illegitimate" and not worthy of consideration in setting the social calculus. Thus according to Kaldor-Hicks, so long as the winners could in principle compensate the losers and still remain better off by their own lights, then the change could be regarded as a desirable one, even if the compensation required has not been paid. If this test is correct, then the just compensation requirement no longer need be satisfied in either of the two contexts in which it is frequently invoked: the initial delineation of property rights, or their enforcement by the state sovereign, and their redeployment by state action. The logic of the Kaldor-Hicks system is to produce positive sum games without the transaction costs drag associated with satisfying the compensation requirement.

The best, and perhaps even the only, way to decide which of these two tests is more desirable is to invoke the familiar inquiry behind the veil of ignorance: if any person knew something about the gen-

[5] See, e.g., Jules L. Coleman, "Efficiency, Utility, and Wealth Maximization," 8 *Hofstra L. Rev.* 509 (1980), for discussion. For a discussion of variations on the theme, see David D. Friedman, "Does Altruism Produce Efficient Outcomes? Marshall versus Kaldor," 17 *J. Legal Stud.* 1 (1988).

eral behavior of individuals, but lacked specific knowledge as to his role in the overall setting, which rule of governance would be chosen? The logic of this decision procedure is structural. Where persons cannot identify the role that they will possess once a general rule is put into effect, they will have a strong incentive to choose that rule which maximizes the value of the whole, for only then will they have some assurance that they will maximize their own individual prospects once their places within the system are subsequently revealed.[6] The question that has to be addressed, therefore, concerns the relative efficiency of a system that seeks in some way to respect a compensation requirement as against one that does not. Will the amount of surplus that is created be greater or lesser if a just compensation requirement for all persons is incorporated into the system?

One way in which to assay this choice is to make assumptions about the way in which state officials will exercise their powers in regimes in which just compensation is and is not required. In making this argument is it useful to take into account the usual vices that undermine the correctness of human action, or at least human action in which some persons, here the state officials, are required to act in a fiduciary capacity for other persons, here the citizens of the state. These are, simply stated, the use of power when faced with individual self-interest and imperfect knowledge. The case for or against a *just compensation* requirement for government takings depends on how these two issues are confronted.

## POWER, KNOWLEDGE, AND SELF-INTEREST

Begin with some strong assumptions. If state officials knew for certain that particular redeployments of resources worked a positive redistribution of wealth, and if these officials always operated without faction or favoritism so that the evaluations they made were never clouded by partisan political pressures, then there would be no reason at all for the ideal constitution to contain any explicit just compensation requirement for the takings (including regulation and

[6] See *Takings*, chap. 14. One very difficult question is whether the system of legal rules needed to satisfy that question would leave any play for compulsory redistribution of wealth. I have argued that the enormous political risks and administrative costs of that venture preclude all forms of compulsory redistribution. See Richard A. Epstein, "Luck," 6 *Soc. Phil. & Pol.* 17 (1988). But the general consensus is surely otherwise.

taxation) of private property. So long as all problems of knowledge and self-interest, by assumption, are wholly neutralized, then the only forced changes in property rights that would take place within the legal system are those that move existing resources from lower- to higher-valued uses. That any given person may be subject to losses in one instance would be of little consequence. Individual persons could diversify their holdings, with mutual funds for example, and they could use insurance to protect their special investments in particular pieces of property where necessary.

If one only looked at a single transaction, there would be conspicuous winners and conspicuous losers, but with no social significance. Because state officials act with long-term public welfare in mind, we do know that each and every one of these transactions will satisfy the Kaldor-Hicks standard of welfare: the gains on net are greater than the losses, as measured by the hypothetical compensation criterion which the knowledgeable state faithfully and accurately applies. The state, of course, engages in literally thousands of transactions which trench on the private property rights of ordinary citizens, so that the social calculation of relative advantage must be made on a cumulative basis, netting out the gains and losses on the full set of transactions. Individual losses sustained in the one setting would be offset by the gains that were generated when this flawless government machine took property from other persons in the same or unrelated transactions. Over the long haul, the massive number of takings, regulations, and taxes would each generate not only social gains, but also net gains for each individual citizen, through the benevolent operation of the law of large numbers. Behind a veil of ignorance, it would be difficult to find any person uncertain of his role who would prefer to be left in the status quo ante, given the virtually certain likelihood that his own private position would be improved. Stated otherwise, although each transaction is governed by some Kaldor-Hicks test, in the end it would (asymptotically) satisfy the Pareto test as well.[7] As the number of transactions increases, the probability of finding even a single net loser in the long run moves ever closer to zero. Within this benevolent system, there is no occasion for bearing the heavy costs of operating the just compensation requirement—of valuing the assets to be taken through litigation and appraisals. Everyone would be better off if spared the direct and indirect administrative burdens that must be borne individually and

[7] I develop this point further in Richard A. Epstein, "The Utilitarian Foundations of Natural Law," 12 *Harv. J.L. & Pub. Pol'y* 713 (1989).

through taxation.[8] The concern with just compensation would be satisfied without explicit calculation, first by the inexorable rise in wealth, and then through the rise in the subjective utilities of all concerned.

This is not our world. In traditional constitutional thought, the Republican concern with "corruption" and the Madisonian concern with "faction" both point to the same set of difficulties. In politics there are gaps not only with information but also with power. No system of representative government will work to ensure that all persons are as well protected as if they retained the exclusive right to deal with their own property. The problems of power and self-interest, which the prior analysis assumed away, now come back to haunt the system. A determined majority, or even a concentrated minority, can work to make collective decisions that benefit only private ends, that is, take actions where the Kaldor-Hicks requirement is not satisfied. The ordinary private person, even in government, is tempted to measure the private benefit from government action against its private costs. The private benefits obtained by others, and the private costs borne by others are excluded from the calculations if those persons are not part of any winning political coalition. Thus if the private gains to the winners are 100, and their private costs are 50, they will adopt the measure even if the benefits to others are 5 and their costs are 100. On the winners' private calculation, 100 is greater than 50; yet on the social side, 105 (the sum of all private benefits) is less than 150 (the sum of all private costs) so that the project should not go forward.

There is no reason to assume that all decisions made by an unconstrained legislature will have this unfortunate tendency. Yet constitutional protection is needed even when the legislature or other public officials misbehave only part of the time. The only question worth asking is whether the protection against misbehavior through the full range of government activities—taking, taxation, regulation, changes in liability rules[9]—is sufficiently great to justify the exten-

[8] Parallel arguments can be made, for example, with the issuance of secured debt. In a world without misbehavior (whether of creditor or debtor), the capital value of the firm is independent of the way in which the claims against it are arrayed. See Randal Picker, "Security Interests, Misbehavior, and Common Pools," 59 *U. Chi. L. Rev.* 645 (1992); George G. Triantis, "Secured Debt Under Conditions of Imperfect Information," 21 *J. Legal Stud.* 225 (1992); Franco Modgiliani & Merton H. Miller, "The Cost of Capital, Corporation Finance, and the Theory of Finance," 48 *Am. Econ. Rev.* 261 (1958). The use of secured credit is only relevant as a way to combat the various imperfections that exist given the risk of debtor and creditor misbehavior.

[9] As argued for in *Takings*, chap. 8.

sive administrative costs needed to combat it. But given the temptations that are available when all external constraints on legislative behaviors are lifted, these outcomes will occur with sufficient regularity that it becomes important to try to find a way to distinguish between legislation that advances the common good, by any of these standard tests, from that which advances only a factional interest.

The just compensation requirement responds to that challenge. By forcing the winners to fully compensate the losers for the deprivation of their rights, the losses that the winning coalition could otherwise externalize on losers are brought back to bear on them. In the above example, the outsiders must receive from the insiders 95 units in compensation in order for political exploitation to be avoided. But once the winning coalition has to face those costs, then it will change its decision on whether to proceed: if it garners only 50 units of gain from the transaction, it cannot be better off if it has to pay 95 units out to the outsiders. The compensation requirement preserves a sense of fairness across parties that is captured in the Paretian formula. It also changes the mix of legislative schemes that are generated by altering the incentives to all the players within the system and hence the selection of projects that go forward and those which do not. While the just compensation rule is stated in distributional form, and is motivated largely by distributional concerns of fairness, its allocative consequences cannot be neglected either and, rightly understood, wholly dominate the distributional concerns. By weeding out poor legislative schemes, these allocative consequences are always positive and, in most instances (if historical experience is a loose guide), seem to justify the substantial administrative burdens that they impose.

The just compensation requirement also responds to the problem of knowledge. To see why, assume that there was a self-interested majority within the legislature, while the court had the capacity to tell perfectly which schemes promised net social benefits and which did not. In contrast to the perfect world that was outlined above, this system requires judicial review to function well, for otherwise all self-interested legislation would become law, as in the example above. But judicial review under this system would not have to depend upon any requirement of just compensation. Since the courts could accurately monitor the most complex legislation without effort, they would simply approve those statutes which on balance promised net benefits and invalidate those which did not, and make the cut between them with a zero error rate. Compensation could be required if there were some desire to even up the individual accounts for each particular transaction, but, so long as only benevolent social legislation passed judicial muster, any short-term inequities would be washed out in the long run, just as if the legislature had passed only benevolent legislation in the first place. So the issue of compensation becomes a minor detail, with no obvious allocative or distributional consequences.

Indeed it is possible to go one step further. On the assumptions just made, the problem of compensation would, strictly speaking, never arise. Since the judicial monitoring is, by assumption, perfect, no legislation would ever have to be struck down, save in the rare cases where the winning faction inadvertently miscalculated costs and benefits. No faction would ever seek to pass a statute that promised private gain and social loss because it would know that the statute could not survive judicial scrutiny. Why then incur the administrative costs of a struggle that promises no gain? The power of courts to strike down unwise legislation would render any just compensation requirement redundant.

Yet the assumption that courts can monitor legislation flawlessly is no better than the assumption that legislatures always act benevolently. Social legislation is ordinarily exceedingly complicated, especially when its indirect effects have to be taken into account, and the ability to marshall either theoretical or empirical evidence of the overall desirability of a social scheme is usually well beyond the competence of any court. Some judges and commentators have regarded these difficulties as a reason to abandon judicial review of economic and (much) social legislation altogether, but that conclusion exposes us to the greater peril of self-interested regulation which would (as it has) flourished without any judicial check.[10] Given the information problems that beset the judicial role, the use of a just compensation requirement here, as in the private necessity cases, has a very salutary effect. While it is not a perfect constraint (as shall become evident) against legislative abuse, it is an effective constraint against some forms of abuse.

Take the simplest model where the law only addresses the question of whether the individual target of some government taking (e.g., land for a military base) has been hurt by the legislation. If a court insists that this person be fully compensated for the property that is lost, then there is some increased reason to be confident that the net social gains exceed the costs that are imposed upon that person. To be sure, if the system of taxation used to collect the funds is

[10] This position has become most closely associated with Justice Scalia. See his dissent in American Trucking Assn's v. Scheiner, 483 U.S. 266, 303 (1987). *Scheiner* is discussed infra chap. 9.

left outside the scope of judicial review (itself a mistake),[11] then there can be no confidence that the legislation is desirable just because the parties who propose it have been able to buy off the property owners whose property has been taken. It could well be that some political coalition has been able to deflect the taxes raised to finance the taking onto some groups within the society who do not benefit proportionately from it.

In a world rife with imperfections, however, it is a serious mistake to treat the best as the enemy of the good. A single constraint on government action reduces the opportunity for political manipulation, and, by forcing the funding question back into the political realm, it becomes more costly for the dominant coalition to force the losses onto other citizens who may be able to organize to resist the tax. The right question to ask is whether the constraints that a just compensation requirement imposes on the legislature are sufficiently valuable to justify the costs of running that requirement. Given the strength of the combined problems of faction and knowledge, the answer has to be yes.

## VALUATION

In order to make this system work, however, it is necessary to respond to the problem of valuation within the judicial setting. Where there is a single individual, or small number of individuals who are isolated for separate treatment, it is often possible to do the calculations the long and hard way: (1) determine the value of the affected property before the restriction is imposed; (2) determine its value to the owner afterwards (zero in the case of total takings, and positive in all other regulatory cases); and (3) award compensation *in cash* for the difference, all the while taking into account any benefit that the property owner received under the legislation in question. But for many schemes of comprehensive legislation, such as wage and price controls, direct accounting, done person to person, is too costly to operate, so that the system has to find some indirect proxy by which to measure its effect.

Here it is necessary to return once again to the veil-of-ignorance methodology that underlies this whole discussion. The disproportionate impact test (with a suitable stress upon all three words) is one effort to use indirect means to determine whether the targets of legislation have been compensated by the state.[12] Where all persons

[11] See *Takings*, chap. 18.

[12] For more extensive discussion, see *Takings*, chap. 14.

are in the same rough position ex ante, and all persons are left in the same relative position ex post, there is good reason to think that the statute does not work a taking without providing compensation to those who did not support it. The winners here have themselves suffered the same burdens and received the same benefits from the statute. In order for them to gain, they have to pass measures that allow others to gain, and by roughly equal extent. The theory here is that there is in fact actual in-kind compensation of the sort required under the Pareto test, but without the direct payments that would be necessary by using cash compensation to balance the account. Instead the instinct is simple: as all persons are made to march lockstep, it is acceptable to allow any single person to make the move if it leaves him better off. Since the choices are all or nothing, in the sense that a person provides the same deal (positive and negative) to everyone else, they are left better off as well, in (which becomes critical in the next chapter) the same proportions.

The measure is, of course, not perfect because its effectiveness depends on the ability to ensure that there is both an identity of initial conditions and, perhaps more importantly, an identity of subjective valuations for all persons involved in the forced exchange. In some cases small but critical differences in initial positions, or in subjective valuations of different persons, could create complications that the test could not reach in practice. A single example shows the problem with respect to a statute to run a railroad line through a small bucolic town.

Suppose that there are 200 landowners in the community, who fall into two groups, and that all individuals in each group have identical plots, each with a market value of $100. The subjective value associated with the plots are, however, widely different. The 80 members of Group A, a political minority, all wish to preserve the bucolic nature of the current setting, and would not sell at the market price of $100 because they value the land at $175, which would be their reservation price. The 120 members of Group B value their property at $100 and are indifferent between retention and sale, for they attach no special weight to the bucolic setting.

Since Group B constitutes 60 percent of the whole, it is able to provide for a highway to run through town by legislative means. The highway will raise the market value of all plots (net of the allocated costs of construction) to $125. Under the disproportionate impact test, it looks as though this scheme should be allowed because gains and losses, measured in market terms, are equal for both the inside and the outside group. That is surely the result under the present law which attaches total dominance to market values and tends to ignore subjective ones. Nor should one say that the current legal constraints are wholly idle, for they do impose certain important limitations in some contexts. Surely this situation is better than one where the road increases the market value of Group B plots to $125 while reducing the market value of the Group A plots to $50, a shift that would be caught by the disproportionate impact test. But even though the disproportionate impact test is satisfied, the proposed change need not amount to a social improvement after the position of Group A is taken into account. For while the market price of their lots is raised to $125, the subjective value of those plots may well be lowered from $175 to $135. Their total losses now equal $3,200 (or 80 persons at $40 per head), while the total gains to to the members of Group B are equal to only $3,000 (120 persons at $25 per head). When keyed to a standard of market value, the disproportionate impact test allows the state to impose a transaction that generates a net loss, here of $200, whose effect is heavily skewed, so that there are some clear winners and some clear losers. Nonetheless, on the assumptions given, there will be no market sale of plots by the losing group because the sole consequence of the government action is the reduction of their owner's surplus of $65 (from $75 to $10), brought on by the decrease in the total net valuation by $40. Yet as all (or in practice, some) of them remain inframarginal, none will reach either the market, or be protected by the law.

It follows from this example that a disproportionate impact test is in an important sense seriously underinclusive because it will not catch unwise social schemes whose sole consequence is to reduce the surplus of property owners disadvantaged by the regulation, so long as they retain any surplus at all. The consequences of course are predictable. Private owners value subjective value surplus as much as they do market value, so that we can expect the members of Group A to oppose fiercely the legislation in part because they know that they will not receive any compensation from the system at large. The inability to measure the size of the changes in surplus of all participants directly is an important structural weakness of the disproportionate impact test. The question is, how can one go further? In order to answer that question, it is necessary now to divert our attention from the just compensation requirement, which protects the original level of entitlements before government action, to the outer ring, and to ask what (if anything) should be done to maximize its size? That is the subject of the next chapter, and answering that question allows for the clean theoretical resolution of the paradox of unconstitutional conditions raised in the opening chapter.

## CHAPTER 7

# Maximizing Social Surplus

### A CLOSER LOOK AT THE OUTER RING

In the previous chapter, I offered an explanation as to why a just compensation requirement offered an effective, if imperfect, limitation against government excesses. The analysis in that chapter did not, however, exhaust the subject because it did not address the division of any surplus created by government action. That surplus, of course, has first to be found, for if none is created, then the just compensation requirement cannot be satisfied for all persons simultaneously, save in the improbable case where a statute (which costs money to enact) leaves everyone in exactly the same position as before. Accordingly, any scheme that generates any net losses should fail on constitutional grounds, for someone must have emerged a net loser to account for the shrinkage in the overall size of the pie.

Where, however, there are gains from legislation, the just compensation requirement should insure that no person will be left a loser. Nonetheless, the inquiry is not at an end, for there is still the question of how these gains should be allocated. In ordinary private markets that are not characterized by strong bilateral monopoly patterns, the proper approach, generally followed in the case law, is to let the surplus lie where it falls. In competitive markets the problem will not arise given the unique price for both buyer and seller. But in the myriad of transactions between buyer and seller with some play in the joints, we can be confident that the parties will structure their obligations to maximize their joint gain. In virtually all cases, both sides will enjoy some fraction of the surplus, for otherwise the deal would not go forward.

Indeed there is some reason to believe that, for purely egoistic reasons, each side wants the other side to receive some portion of the transactional surplus in order to obtain insurance against future nonperformance, and to encourage the formation of a long-term relationship that makes future deals possible. If in steady state, A has one unit of surplus and B has 100, B must fear that any exogenous shock that reduces A's return by 2 units could precipitate his defection from the agreement, jeopardizing all or some B's 100 units of gain. Thus if there is a 10 percent chance that A will defect, and if that occurs B's surplus will be reduced from 100 to 20 units, then B, if risk neutral, should expect ex ante a gain of 92 units (reflecting the 8 units of probable loss). To obviate that risk, B is better off by giving A at least 8 additional units of surplus at outset if that adjustment reduces the risk of defection to zero. Given the uncertainty, the larger surplus for A (not too large, of course) is also in the interest of B. A is likely to have similar motivation not to press to the limit, so there should be some tendency for parties to bargain for some acceptable division of surplus. Greedy people (those who seek to extract all the surplus) do not prosper in business over the long haul.

Given these tendencies of private agreements to stabilize, any public intervention to reallocate surplus among participants is likely to prove counterproductive. The administrative costs are likely to be high, and even the most careful examination of each transaction is likely to generate substantial error because the level of surplus obtained by each is not directly observable by outside parties. The evidence from consent only shows that a party is better off with the deal than without it. It does not give any clue as to how much better, much less any clue as to relative size of the gains to the two parties, assuming that these can be measured in some common unit, such as dollars.

In a sense, the problem cuts deeper, for more is at stake than the limitations of external measurement and observation. Even the parties to the transaction will often be unaware of the precise extent of their own surplus from the transactions that they have made. People usually make precise calculations of gain and loss only when they are at or near the margin, that is, in situations where these calculations are apt to influence their future decisions. Where individuals anticipate an extensive surplus from a given transaction, they will ordinarily enter into it without calculating how much. It is only when there are relatively sharp increases in relative prices that anyone has to decide whether to eliminate or reduce transactions of a certain sort. To seek to isolate and measure transactional surplus in any private transaction therefore is to ask for information that in many cases the parties themselves could not report on truthfully, even if asked to do so. Crude approximations have to be used and at great cost. These expensive procedures must be funded either by exactions from the parties themselves or from general tax revenues; either way the effort to "fairly" allocate the surplus will lead to its systematic destruction.

The soundness of this position is well recognized, if only by common practice, in dealing with key elements of income taxation. In principle the correct definition of income is one that speaks of increments to net worth plus consumption during a particular period.[1] In most cases the individuals who gain from consumption will receive a greater subjective benefit than the cost of their consumer goods. The purchase of a five-dollar ticket to the movies will normally generate some consumer surplus to the buyer. Yet the standard accounting principles never seek to measure the surplus associated with those ordinary consumption behaviors. Instead the subjective value of the consumption expenditure is invariably (and falsely) posited to be exactly equal to its cost, so that the taxpayer is simply denied a deduction for the expenditure that is made. There is no taxable income for the surplus that the transaction predictably generates.[2] In some sense this measure results in a systematic shrinkage of the tax base, and it creates some efficiency loss since individual taxpayers are induced to give excessive weight to this form of nontaxable income, relative to its taxable substitutes. But abandoning the hope of perfection is the source of wisdom. The exclusion of surplus as a matter of course creates no discernible built-in bias between persons, for in the millions of consumption transactions virtually everyone has some consumer surplus whose amounts are difficult to correlate with income, type of expenditure, or anything else. The administrative simplification from ignoring surplus is enormous; so too are the benefits from restraining the use of political discretion that might lead to selective enforcement of the tax laws. In the end, the best political strategy in this case is a categorical refusal to take into account the subjective gains obtained by *anyone* under the tax system, *ever.* The admitted allocative distortion is less dangerous than the administrative peril that replaces it.

The results in the tax area are today a matter of sheer administrative necessity, not of high constitutional principle. But the basic approach to the problem of the tax base has strong constitutional implications. It would surely be intolerable to have any policy that allowed government efforts to exploit the size of the consumer sur-

[1] See Henry Simons, *Personal Income Taxation* 50 (1938): "Personal income may be defined as the algebraic sum of (1) the market value of rights exercised in consumption, and (2) the change in the value of the store of property rights between the beginning and the end of the period in question." Note that Simons refers to the market value of consumption items. He does not touch the subjective value question.

[2] See generally Alvin C. Warren, "Fairness and a Consumption-Type or Cash Flow Personal Income Tax," 88 *Harv. L. Rev.* 931 (1975); William D. Andrews, "Fairness and the Choice Between a Consumption-Type and an Accretion-Type Personal Income Tax: A Reply to Professor Warren," 88 *Harv. L. Rev.* 947 (1975); Richard A. Epstein, "Taxation in a Lockean World," 4 *Social Phil. & Pol.* 49 (1986).

plus as an object of taxation, even if the policy were announced as some general social rule. Behind this uniform policy lies the judgment that political actors will often take steps that will destroy the collective surplus from government action by trying to reallocate it. A judicial rule that prevented the partisan efforts to capture surplus would have substantial social merit if it could be framed and implemented in an intelligent fashion.

How then should the surplus be maximized? In principle the arguments with respect to cooperative surplus are identical to those involved with the inner circle in the two pies diagram. To develop a rule that allows the transaction to go forward so long as no one is left worse off and someone is made better off will satisfy all the concerns of the just compensation requirement and the strict rules of Pareto optimality on which it rests. A rule requiring just compensation whenever there is a deviation from the original baseline can be justified from behind the veil of ignorance as a way to prevent the dissipation of social wealth. Nonetheless, the just compensation requirement, standing alone, is *underinclusive* because it leads to the conclusion that the surplus generated—the size of the outer ring—may be allocated through political action in any way whatsoever. Where those gains are large, interested groups will strive to obtain the largest share of the surplus for themselves. These efforts cost time, money, and resources to mount. None of these efforts to reallocate the gain will increase social wealth; they will only decrease its overall size. At the limit it is possible that the full amount of the surplus could be dissipated by the efforts to direct it to one group or another, although in many cases the level of dissipation may be less, especially if a dominant faction is able to control political outcomes at low cost.[3]

The next two stages of the argument follow from the analysis of the just compensation requirement. If legislatures were all-knowing and all-benevolent, then these concerns with factional losses of surplus would disappear. It would be no more necessary to impose legal constraints on the allocation of surplus than it would be to impose a just compensation requirement that protected initial entitlements. Similarly, if courts were flawless evaluators of legislative proposals, a system of judicial review that simply said "yea or nay" would be sufficient as well. Inferior schemes would always be defeated because they failed to maximize the cooperative gain, so that self-interested legislators would be induced to maximize the value of

[3] See, e.g., Marilyn R. Flowers, "Rent Seeking and Rent Dissipation: A Critical View," 7 *Cato J.* 431 (1987).

the whole in order to satisfy the partisan interests of any constituents. But as this assumption is highly unrealistic, some substantive constitutional constraint on the process also seems to be appropriate. Only here it is wholly insufficient to insist on a just compensation rule, for its capacity has been exhausted by ensuring that no individual is left worse off than he or she would have been prior to the legislation.

The question then arises: how should the surplus be allocated? As before, it is useful to go behind a veil of ignorance to ask what division of surplus people would prefer before they knew their particular social roles. In this case, two possible approaches come to mind. The first seeks to identify those solutions that help to advance competitive situations in their own right. The second approach speaks about the pro rata division of the gain from collective action which, as in the case of income taxation, becomes critical where competitive solutions are not possible but constraints on government behavior are nonetheless imperative.

The argument about competition takes the following form. In the earlier discussion, I noted that any switch in a legal regime that moves us from a monopoly to a competitive position should be welcomed as a matter of principle, given the increase in total output that it achieves. Since the gains themselves are dispersed throughout the larger society by the operation of market forces, there is no need (or ability) to apportion these gains under the legislative plan. The transformation of market form is a pretty solid guarantee that everyone will be able to garner some fraction of the benefits simply by participating in the market. Any inquiry to "even out" the gain, or to direct some of it to favored parties, is both costly and mischievous and as a general rule should not be undertaken. In this case the same general arguments that explain why just compensation is provided implicitly and in kind also explain why the adoption of a particular legislative scheme secures the protection of cooperative surplus as well.

There are, of course, many contexts in which noncompetitive means may be resorted to in order to increase the total output of the system. The imposition of well-defined property rights over a common pool situation, such as a fishery or an oil and gas field, cannot arise from a simple government decree that secures open access to all comers within a competitive market. Instead there has to be a conscious effort to undo the existing set of rights and to substitute another in its place. In the absence of any clean market solution, two variables have to be taken into account simultaneously. First, choose that allocation of the surplus that maximizes the likelihood that the beneficial social change will be brought about by the legislature in the first place. Second, minimize the administrative costs associated with the operation of the system. These two elements are often in tension with one another, for the ideal incentive structure may be obtainable only with costly administrative rules. It is, therefore, necessary to look at the two elements separately.

Starting with the incentive point, there are grounds for adopting a rule that additional gains should be supplied to those particular parties that have initiated the gains, for by so doing it would increase the likelihood of their occurrence. The precise analogy here is to a "going private" transaction in corporate law, whereby the insiders in a public corporation wish to take the entire business private by buying out the passive shareholders.[4] In this setting, the moving parties are more likely to go forward with a transaction if they can capture a disproportionate share of the surplus that is generated by the deal. The analogy also applies to the standard hostile takeover bid, when the surplus is divided between the hostile raider and the shareholders of the target corporation who are willing to sign on to the initial tender offer. In both cases involuntary participants are protected by a rule that provides them with just compensation, that is, the prebid market value of their shares. These examples suggest that an effort to skew the gains toward the side that proposes the innovation makes sense, so long as the other parties are not required to suffer any diminution in overall utility once the changes are put into place. In order to encourage the transaction in the first instance, it looks as though an effort to skew the gains from the transaction will maximize the overall wealth.

The argument, however, is tricky in a number of respects. First, within its own terms, it is a mistake to assume that the likelihood of a successful transaction increases uniformly with the gains awarded to the party that initiates it. The likelihood of success depends upon a delicate interplay between the willingness to initiate on one side and the willingness to resist on the other. To the extent that success depends upon the behavior of persons outside the initiating group, a rule that allocates all the surplus to the initiators may well doom the project by inducing stronger resistance from those who garner no part of the surplus. The situation is not dissimilar from the ordinary private transaction in which excessive demands can lead to unstable outcomes. In addition, if the outsiders perceive that they will (by

[4] See, e.g., Frank H. Easterbrook & Daniel R. Fischel, *The Economic Structure of Corporate Law* 134–39 (1991); Victor Brudney & Marvin A. Chirelstein, "A Restatement of Corporate Freezeouts," 87 *Yale L.J.* 1354 (1978).

errors in valuation, for example) be left worse off by the change in legal order than before, then the likelihood of a struggle increases. One reason therefore to gravitate toward the other position—a pro rata division of the gains—is that it minimizes the likelihood that the coerced transaction will flunk the just compensation test.

The optimal division of the total gain in these semi-private corporate transactions is thus unclear, given the concern with both initiation and resistance. The difficult question for these purposes is how these private analogies to the division of surplus carry over to the political setting. At this point, there are a number of important differences that should be noted, of which perhaps the most critical is the absence of any clear market price benchmark against which the overall fairness of the public transaction can be adjusted. If the question is whether foreign corporations should be admitted to doing business within a given state only if they surrender their right to sue in federal court, then no set of market prices indicates the value of their holdings before and after the condition is imposed.

In addition, the object of the legal system is not merely to make sure that people are not hurt by the proposal, relative to the baseline of their prior entitlements. It is also an effort to maximize the total gain in question. Therefore, if there is some reason to believe that these social gains can be achieved by adopting some alternative rule—here (say) one that calls for the pro rata allocation of the gains, across all participants—then so much the better. A legislative proposal on the incorporation of businesses and the construction of (some) public highways promises enormous social gains, so it is very unlikely that the interest groups that support these changes have to capture all the surplus in order to press for the passage of the legislation. Thus if it costs $100,000 to initiate a proposal that promises literally millions of dollars in social benefits, the firms that capture only 50 percent of the benefits are likely to make the proposal even if other people take a large fraction of the gain. There is room for some useful social free riding.

The conclusion involves a certain irony because it suggests that the pro rata rule, despite the limitations that were discussed in the previous chapter, has a set of often unappreciated virtues in handling the proper allocation of social surplus in cases when competitive solutions are not easily obtainable. Recall that the basic weakness of the disproportionate impact test is tied to its exclusive reliance on market values as the measure of individual welfare in alternative social states. It is just that gap between market and subjective values that explained why environmentalists could in principle oppose improvements that increased the market value of their holdings.[5] It was possible to envision situations that featured both an increase in someone's market value and a reduction in subjective value in response to some critical social change. The pro rata test would therefore allow the change to pass muster even though it led to transactions that are inefficient even under the most generous of all the social welfare criteria—the Kaldor-Hicks formulation.

With the types of unconstitutional conditions cases that are covered in the second half of the book, there are relatively few instances in which the initial position of the various actors differs because of their different subjective values. There are, however, numerous cases where persons who look to have the same initial position are subject to explicit discriminatory treatment in consequence of the application of the rule. The pro rata test, which attacks these forms of discrimination, therefore has one virtue: it leads to the *automatic* proration of the surplus across all contenders. In so doing it does little to diminish the efforts to adopt the preferred set of legal rules. Indeed as all members of the relevant group are similarly situated, there will be no opposition to the proposed reform once it is in fact proposed. Faced with an all-or-nothing choice, all participants will prefer to adopt the desirable outcome because they know that there is no solution available to them which allows them to garner the benefits of the legal change while simultaneously denying it to their adversaries. Since there is no way to obtain private gain by defecting from the social solution, there will be widespread support of the measure. In addition, there will be no factional efforts to impose conditions whose effect is to reallocate (and thereby diminish) the surplus created by legislation.

In many instances, it is likely that uniform rules on parties similarly situated will generate uniform gains across the board, so that the pro rata constraint is satisfied. But for these purposes, it is quite immaterial if it turns out in fact that some person or group enjoys a larger share of the gains from some other group. So long as there is rough parity in initial expectations, the law has done its job. Calling the division of surplus *pro rata*, therefore, is a bit optimistic, for it is unlikely that this condition will be precisely satisfied, given a wide variety of natural differences between persons. But treating the gains *as though* they were perfectly pro rata makes sense because it ensures that they will not be dissipated by pointless factional strife. The disproportionate impact test, measured by a formal criterion,

[5] See supra chap. 6.

therefore, leads to the same place as it does in connection with just compensation rules when direct measurement of gains and losses is neither feasible nor desirable: because it covers both assignment of original endowments and the gains from subsequent collective action, it powerfully protects the social surplus generated through government action.

## SOLVING THE UNCONSTITUTIONAL CONDITIONS PARADOX

We have now undertaken sufficient preliminaries to allow for a definitive solution to the paradox of unconstitutional conditions. In essence the puzzle arises because the position of the individual party is judged against the position that was enjoyed before the collective action took place. Thus it seeks to identify the social optimum with the satisfaction of the just compensation criterion, and completely ignores the issues concerning the proper division of the cooperative surplus. Once that surplus is taken into account, it is clear that collective solutions that advance competitive behavior, or which promise pro rata gains to the various participants, should be preferred because they promise the greatest likelihood of yielding the social optimum. It follows therefore that rules that satisfy the just compensation test may be inferior to alternative rules that can be proposed and adopted. The parties will accept them if put to the all-or-nothing choice, for they compare what is offered with what they have. But the social system should not respect that choice because it leads to a deviation from the preferred social outcome. The relevant information can be gathered together by considering six different scenarios, which for the sake of simplicity involve two groups, A and B, of equal size, both of which possess initial endowments equal to 100. The six scenarios are given on the facing page.

These tables lay out the different problems that have been canvassed in the last two chapters. Under the first scenario there is no problem by any of the relevant tests. The regulation is appropriate because it advances the welfare of the members of both groups, and it does so in equal proportions that speak of formal equality and equality of impact. It is hard to oppose that change, as far as it goes. The question is whether one can do better or worse when the basic regulation is overlaid with certain conditions.

Scenario 2 indicates the class of conditions that are good because they improve the situation from either the prior state of affairs, *or* from the regulatory intervention without the attached condition. Again there is a formal equality and a parity of outcome, so that this

*Scenario 1: No Conditions*

| | Group A | Group B |
|---|---|---|
| (a) Before regulation | 100 | 100 |
| (b) After regulation | 150 | 150 |

*Scenario 2: Virtuous Conditions*

| | Group A | Group B |
|---|---|---|
| (a) Before regulation | 100 | 100 |
| (b) After regulation | 150 | 150 |
| (c) With regulation and good condition | 160 | 160 |

*Scenario 3: Oppressive Conditions*

| | Group A | Group B |
|---|---|---|
| (a) Before regulation | 100 | 100 |
| (b) After regulation | 150 | 150 |
| (c) With bad condition that flunks Pareto test (or) | 170 | 90 |
| (d) With bad condition and costly but just compensation | 155 | 100 |

*Scenario 4: Unconstitutional Conditions*

| | Group A | Group B |
|---|---|---|
| (a) Before regulation | 100 | 100 |
| (b) With regulation | 150 | 150 |
| (c) With regulation and unconstitutional condition | 160 | 130 |

*Scenario 5: Problematic Conditions*

| | Group A | Group B |
|---|---|---|
| (a) Before regulation | 100 | 100 |
| (b) With regulation | 150 | 150 |
| (c) With regulation and efficient condition | 160 | 170 |

*Scenario 6: Perverse Conditions*

| | Group A | Group B |
|---|---|---|
| (a) Before regulation | 100 | 100 |
| (b) With regulation | 150 | 150 |
| (c) With regulation and perverse condition | 130 | 130 |

case is no more problematic than the one before. Indeed it looks less so, since the size of the overall gain is increased. We should expect its adoption, for in any head-to-head comparison between Scenario 1 and Scenario 2, Scenario 2 strictly dominates Scenario 1.

Scenario 3 shows evident signs of pathology. The condition imposed reduces the overall level of wealth below that which it reached when the regulation was adopted without the condition, as in (b). Nonetheless the problem here is caught by the ordinary just compensation test because Group B can complain about the outcome and block it, given that their holdings have been reduced to 90 from the prior state of 100. The just compensation test thus works to guarantee the preservation of the surplus by forcing the transaction back to level (b) where each group has 150.

Still the just compensation test is not ideal, as is indicated at step (d). If Group A could develop a tax system that transferred 10 units of wealth to members of Group B at a cost of 5 units of wealth, then Group B could not be in a position to protest if the just compensation rule alone were in effect. The 10 units of compensation work to raise Group B to their preregulation endowments of 100, but the 15 units of loss suffered by members of Group A still leave them 5 units ahead of the position that they would have occupied by returning to (b). Nonetheless this new distribution at (d) (155, 100) generates only 55 units of surplus while stabilization at (b) (150, 150) generates 100 units of surplus, a clearly superior outcome. Only those who think that on average 5 units to the members of Group A are worth 50 to Group B would prefer (d) to (b) in Scenario 3.

Scenario 4, the unconstitutional conditions scenario, is designed to prevent the unfortunate move from (b) to (d) of Scenario 3. In essence the doctrine treats the *outcome in (b)* as the appropriate baseline against which the success or failure of the subsequent condition is measured. It is as though the process took place in two stages. First the basic regulation was imposed, and only thereafter was the condition in (c) attached. If the condition flunks the Pareto test relative to the baseline in (b), then the condition is struck down, even if the members of Group B are better off in state (c) (130 to 100) than they were in state (a). Without the doctrine of unconstitutional conditions all persons faced with an all-or-nothing choice will choose (c) over (a) because access to (b) is blocked. By adopting the unconstitutional conditions doctrine, (c) is blocked, so that all persons have to choose between (a) and (b), in which case they will choose (b) unanimously.

This case is one where mutual gains from a prior historical baseline do not establish the social optimum, and therefore should not be respected. It thus becomes clear why the greater/lesser argument is improper. It presupposes that the relevant comparison in Scenario 4 is between (a) and (c) when in fact the right comparison is between (b) and (c). The question is whether the condition advances overall social welfare, and there is no guarantee that this will happen just because it is consented to by the individual actor. As the earlier discussion of coercion indicates, the risk of an inappropriate outcome is not controlled by stopping the use of force, or even by requiring just compensation. It has to do with the social outcomes that are generated when individuals play certain bargaining games. By blocking certain bargains between the individual and the state, it becomes possible to improve overall social welfare.

Scenario 5 adds one measure of complication to the overall picture because it sets out a situation in which the condition produces gains that are not pro rata on the one hand, but which maximize the overall size of the pie on the other. Therefore it is a close question whether one wants to equalize the gains or tolerate the imbalance. If only a random set of cases fell into Scenario 5, then there would be little reason to alter its distribution, which is as likely ex ante to work out in favor of the members of Group A as it is the members of Group B. There would be attendant administrative costs that produced no allocative gain. But if one thinks (as I do) that most conditions with unequal gains will *not* generate the benevolent outcomes in this scenario, then candidates for Scenario 5 should be treated as falling within either Scenario 3 or 4 where the conditions are invalidated. Perhaps the presumption that Scenario 5 is an empty set should not be made absolute, but it surely should be overridden only with very powerful evidence under some test of compelling state interest.

Scenario 6 completes the possibilities by setting out a case of perverse condition—one which satisfies the pro rata test, but which leaves everyone equally worse off. Formally, it is impossible to distinguish between Scenario 2 and Scenario 6 because in both cases there is formal equality and equal impact. Nonetheless, theoretically we should expect Scenario 6 never to occur because it presupposes that interest group politics will generate a set of outcomes from which no one benefits. The disproportionate impact test therefore goes a long way to rule out unfortunate cases and to simplify the general inquiry.

At this point it becomes clear why the doctrine of unconstitutional conditions is in its theoretical aspect so difficult to resolve. First, it is impossible to decide the question of whether a condition is inappropriate solely by looking at its effect upon the ostensible victim of the wrong. That party is left better off than before, and prudently has consented to the change of affairs. The term *coerced* to describe his personal state seems on balance to be singularly inappropriate for the situation at hand, given his private improvement over the prior state of affairs. But the doctrine of unconstitutional conditions offers a way to pierce the consent by using as its baseline, not the status quo ante, but a *best achievable* state of affairs in which the program is put forward without the conditions attached. Here the person who takes subject to a condition is aggrieved relative to the world as it might have been. He is also in the best position to challenge the new legislation with the condition, since he is prejudiced by it. Extending the term *coercion* to cover this case thus links it back to the less problematic cases where individuals are made worse off by threats relative to the previous state of affairs. Coercion is thus an effective label (but not an accurate description) to allow certain persons to initiate actions that will improve not only their own private position but also the overall state of affairs.

Now the object of the inquiry is to maximize the total cooperative surplus from the government action. Given this complex inquiry, the trick is to fashion a test that can distinguish good conditions from bad ones. The first point is typically to establish some use of monopoly power by the state, as with its control of access to public highways. Then it is necessary to examine the conditions that individuals must accept in order to gain access to public roads. A rule that all persons on the highway must agree to answer for their torts seems to be the benevolent kind of condition.[6] In imposing it the state acts as a mutual agent of all citizens in a way that advances their ex ante welfare by increasing the protection all individuals have against accidents. Alternatively, a toll that is twice for people whose last names begin with A through L, relative to those whose names begin with M through Z, looks like a perverse condition with no allocative gains. Similarly, a condition stipulating that all commercial haulers who use the highway must agree to accept the regulations imposed on common carriers looks like the type of condition that reduces the total size of the social surplus by allowing it to be redistributed through factional intrigue.[7] A strong unconstitutional conditions doctrine is one effective way to control this public abuse and to ensure full preservation of the social surplus created from the use of highways.

[6] See infra at chap. 11.

[7] See infra chap. 11, discussing Frost & Frost Trucking Co. v. California R.R. Comm'n, 271 U.S. 583 (1926).

In dealing with unconstitutional conditions, the stakes are not limited only to dollars and cents, or even to property and economic liberties; conditions might impinge upon individuals' political and religious liberties as well. Thus it would be wholly improper to condition use of the public highways on the willingness to participate in religious services, or to renounce religious affiliations. Here too, the factional gains dominate and the condition should be struck down, even if the individual values the access to the roads more than he or she dislikes the condition.

# Part Two

## GOVERNMENT RELATIONS WITHIN A FEDERAL SYSTEM

CHAPTER 8

# State Incorporation Powers

## THE DISTINCTIVE STATUS OF LIMITED LIABILITY

The doctrine of unconstitutional conditions cuts across areas of substantive law because the question that it addresses—the relationship between coercion and consent—is an ubiquitous one for the law. Historically, however, the cases which gave birth to the doctrine tended to gravitate to those areas of the greatest political and legal concerns of their own times. It is not surprising therefore that the origins of the doctrine of unconstitutional conditions were intimately tied to state powers of incorporation, a source of bitter nineteenth-century dispute. When the issue of corporate status first came to the Supreme Court, the precarious juridical status of the corporation was captured in Chief Justice Marshall's observation in *Trustees of Dartmouth College v. Woodward,*[1] that the corporation is only an "artificial being" that owes its existence to the state. Perhaps the strongest reason for this view is that the dominant consequence of incorporation (as opposed to a mere partnership or joint association) is that of limited liability—a rule that limits the liability of contributors to a corporation to the amount that they have contributed to the corporation for the purchase of their shares.

This rule is commonplace everywhere today and thus has not (at least until recently)[2] been the subject of any special attention or debate. Nonetheless, as a theoretical matter, the rule is of great moment because it confers upon corporations and their shareholders a privilege against the rest of the world that they could not obtain under the usual rules of property, contract, and tort. Thus if a group of individuals sought to form any kind of joint venture, they would be entitled to allocate the rights and responsibilities, and the gains and losses of that venture *among themselves* in whatever matter they saw fit. But any effort to limit liability *to strangers* by contract

[1] 17 U.S. (4 Wheat.) 518, 636 (1819): "A corporation is an artificial being, invisible, intangible, and existing only in contemplation of law. Being the mere creature of law, it possesses only those properties which the charter of its creation confers upon it, either expressly, or as incidental to its very existence."

[2] See, e.g., Frank H. Easterbrook & Daniel R. Fischel, *Economic Structure of Corporate Law*, chap. 2; Henry Hansmann & Reinier Kraakman, "Toward Unlimited Shareholder Liability for Corporate Torts," 100 *Yale L.J.* 1879 (1991).

would fail under the ordinary common law rule that a contract only binds the parties to it. (To hold otherwise as a general rule allows contracts to authorize endless theft.) Since the officers and directors of the corporation are all agents of the shareholders, the usual rule of vicarious liability (the same rule that binds the assets of the corporation to the wrongs of its employees) would allow strangers to initiate suit against any shareholder of their choosing and to collect tort judgments from the personal assets of any or all individual shareholders. The disincentive to invest in the corporate form under such a rule is manifest. In an effort to facilitate the large amalgamations of capital needed for major industrial ventures, the law has conferred limited liability on corporate shareholders, usually equal to the amount of their invested capital.[3]

The rule in general is a wise one and paradoxically advances the position of third parties to the joint venture. The larger aggregation of capital will supply third-party victims with a fund of wealth greater than that possessed by ordinary individuals, especially those who are insolvent, or who might have otherwise conducted their own dangerous activities as sole proprietors or small general partnerships.[4] The key to understanding limited liability is to recognize the externalization of harm it *prevents* as well as that which it causes. In addition, there are some intermediate solutions that can control some of the externality problems that remain. Explicit insurance requirements can control some abuses, and others can be counteracted by policies that allow the piercing of the corporate veil for thinly capitalized firms, especially business subsidiaries of larger corporations.[5] These intermediate responses accept the principle of limited liability while seeking to curb its excesses.

[3] In many banking contexts, there was during much of the nineteenth and early twentieth centuries a rule called "double liability" of banking corporations. Under these rules the shareholders (or their assignees in good faith) were liable, first for their invested capital, and then for their private funds in an amount equal to that invested capital. For an exhaustive analysis, see Jonathan R. Macey & Geoffrey P. Miller, "Double Liability of Bank Shareholders: History and Implications," 27 Wake Forest L. Rev. 31 (1992). The double-liability option offers an effective means to expand the scope of creditor protection without going to the extreme of unlimited liability. Miller and Macey show that it is likely that this system is superior protection for depositors without the enormous moral hazard problems associated with government guarantees of deposits.

[4] See Stephen Wiggins & Al H. Ringleb, "Adverse Selection and Long-Term Hazard: The Choice Between Contract and Mandatory Liability Rules," 21 *J. Legal Stud.* 189 (1992).

[5] See Robert Clark, *Corporate Law* §2.4, at 71–81 (1986). For free-standing firms, allowing thin capitalization has, of course, benefits as well as costs. It encourages new entry and stimulates competition. The tort risk must be kept in perspective.

The problem of incorporation is examined here, however, not for its intrinsic merits, but for its intimate connection to the law of unconstitutional conditions. There is in general no obligation for the state to supply a system of limited liability for individuals who wish to undertake joint ventures. The question then arises whether the state can condition the privilege of incorporation upon the waiver of constitutional rights that the ordinary individual might possess. Is it permissible for the state to insist that corporations must waive their right to due process of law in criminal proceedings, or in the more modern context, their right to sponsor political advertisements, make campaign contributions, or lobby legislators in the same manner as ordinary citizens? The question is an old one, and I start with some nineteenth-century cases before turning briefly to some more modern applications.

## NINETEENTH-CENTURY SPECIAL CHARTERS

During the nineteenth century, the corporate form was both novel and controversial. Corporations were not the general vehicle for conducting business, and resort to the corporate form did not emerge full-blown at a single point in time. There were serious questions of where corporations, being creatures of the law, were situated; how they could sue or be sued; whether they could undertake business ventures outside the frame of reference of their corporate charter; who could assume the role of shareholders; and how corporations were to be regulated and taxed. In consequence, the issuance of corporate charters was not regarded as a routine ministerial act, but one of high political import for which special justification and cause had to be shown. Corporate charters were valuable forms of property, issued by the state legislature on a selective basis. Which individuals should, or will, receive certificates of incorporation, and on what terms, can raise all the potential for abuse associated with government discretion.

Consider what happens in a regime in which the state has complete discretion in awarding charters. First, state legislators will be able to extract enormous payments (including bribes) from the private parties who wish to obtain the benefits of incorporation. Second, granting a certificate of incorporation to one firm while denying one to its competitors creates enormous externalities. The public at large is denied the benefits of competitive product markets, while the rival firms are relegated to doing business in the inferior partnership form, with unlimited liability for their members.

These two concerns are not simply hypothetical. One of the major issues of political reform in the nineteenth century revolved around the once common practice of issuing individual, special charters of incorporation, the abuses of which have been well documented.[6] The situation was corrected largely through competition between states in the chartering market, rather than through application of any constitutional principle. Over time, the result was a regime of general incorporation that essentially allows any group of individuals the benefit of the corporate form as long as they can meet certain minimum requirements designed to protect the public at large from abuse: minimum assets or insurance to protect tort creditors, and a willingness to accept service of process in the corporate name.

Although not prompted by application of the doctrine of unconstitutional conditions, the shift in the method of chartering corporations shows the social utility of limiting the state's discretion. It makes excellent sense to say that the state may choose not to grant any individuals a charter of incorporation, or may choose to grant it to all comers on equal terms, but cannot use the ostensibly lesser power of picking and choosing among applicants. To see the point, consider a very simple and stylized example. Assume two firms—firm A and firm B—desire corporate charters. If neither firm A nor firm B gets a charter, then each will have a value of $100. If firm A gets a charter and firm B does not, then A will have a value of $120 and B a value of $90. If firm B gets a charter and firm A does not, then B will have the value of $120 and A the value of $90. If both firms get the charter, then each will have a value of $115. These values do not reflect the costs of getting a charter. The payoffs of the various alternatives are put in tabular form in the notes.[7]

[6] For a judicial account, see Louis K. Liggett Co. v. Lee, 288 U.S. 517, 557–64 (1933) (Brandeis, J., dissenting). For an explicit public-choice analysis of the abuses under the special charter system, see Henry N. Butler, "Nineteenth-Century Jurisdictional Competition in the Granting of Corporate Privileges," 14 *J. Legal Stud.* 129, 138–52 (1985). See also John W. Cadman, Jr., *The Corporation in New Jersey* 61–72 (1949), which reports that in the early part of the century (between 1804 and 1824), the state legislature reserved the right of the legislature to purchase bank stock at a favorable price if it so chose. See also Vicki Been, "'Exit' as a Constraint on Land Use Exactions: Rethinking the Unconstitutional Conditions Doctrine," 91 *Colum. L. Rev.* 473 (1991) (arguing that exit rights constrained the state's power to misbehave). For criticism, see infra at chap. 12.

[7]

| | | Value | | |
|---|---|---|---|---|
| | | A | B | total |
| Structure | 1. No incorporation | $100 | $100 | $200 |
| | 2. A only | $120 | $90 | $210 |
| | 3. B only | $90 | $120 | $210 |
| | 4. Both A and B | $115 | $115 | $230 |

In a regime of selective incorporation, firm A and firm B will both bid for a charter, and each would be prepared to pay up to $20 to the legislators to obtain an exclusive charter. If either party starts down this road then the other will have to respond, because one rival's incorporation reduces its competitor's net worth from $100 to $90. There will be a complex political struggle whose outcome is quite unclear. What is clear is that these bargaining costs reduce the total gains from incorporation, both for the firms and the society at large, even if the fourth, and preferred, outcome is achieved. In an extreme case, dual incorporation with bargaining costs taken into account could leave both firms with a value of only $100. Political intrigue can wipe out the efficiency gains of incorporation for firm members, suppliers, and customers.

We can now see the value of a rule rejecting the argument that the greater power (to keep all firms from incorporating) includes the lesser power (to keep some firms from incorporating). If the state is forced to grant charters of incorporation to every firm if it grants a charter to any, then the second and third possibilities are eliminated. The state is forced to choose between Alternatives 1 and 4. The two firms will no longer be in a position to compete with each other for charters, so the level of intrigue will be diminished. In addition, political dynamics will tend to force the outcome to Alternative 4, as the legislators will be very hard-pressed to resist an outcome that benefits both firms and the public at large. The upshot is that the power of *selective* incorporation is the greater power while the all-or-nothing choice is the lesser power.[8] Whatever the formal appearances, selective incorporation gives political actors a greater opportunity to extract economic rents. [9] The rule forcing the state to incorporate all firms or none is, as a first approximation, a better protection against individual and public abuse. The parallels to the arguments regarding blackmail and necessity appear to be complete.[10]

---

This chart underestimates the value of Alternative 4 because it does not include the gains that the public achieves from general incorporation, including greater technical innovation and more competition in product markets. This point does not affect the analysis; if anything, these gains tend to show the greater social preference for Alternative 4.

[8] Kreimer makes this point explicitly: "Often it is only by ripping a problem from its historical context that selective denial can be viewed as a lesser power. In reality, selective deprivation may be the less controlled and hence the more dangerous power." Seth F. Kreimer, Allocative Sanctions: The Problem of Negative Rights in a Positive State, 132 *U. Pa. L. Rev.* 1293, 1313 (1984) (footnote omitted).

[9] See Fred S. McChesney, "Rent Extraction and Rent Creation in the Economic Theory of Regulation," 16 *J. Legal Stud.* 101 (1987).

[10] See supra chap. 5.

One piece to the puzzle is still missing, for not all conditions are harmful. Some conditions can and should be uniformly imposed upon all firms seeking incorporation; for example, requiring insurance or minimum capitalization to protect tort creditors, and requiring firms to accept service of process. These requirements can be stated in a general form, however, so that public protection is possible without conferring enormous discretion upon state authorities In addition there are strong practical reasons why this restriction should be imposed on corporations. Thus far the analysis has addressed the question of what legal rules should be adopted in order to prevent government abuse in situations that promise overall net gain. The problem of abuse, however, should be understood as being *bilateral*, just as it is in the private sphere. With insurer and insured, with buyer and seller, with tortfeasor and tort victim, the question is *never* how to design a contract scheme that will minimize the abuse of buyers, insurers, and tortfeasors. Instead, it is how to minimize the abuses that both parties to the relationship will practice. A rule that drives abuses on one side of the relationship to zero often will allow greater abuses to flourish on the other side of the relationship, to the overall detriment of the system at large. Strict rules on sellers could lead to abuses by buyers, and so on. The incorporation problem is no exception to this general rule. Some state-imposed conditions therefore are not exploitive, but preventive, and included on that list are those directed to insurance, capitalization, and service of process. It is clear therefore that there are powerful reasons for rejecting the greater/lesser dogma in order to prevent political abuse and to advance the overall competitive situation. But the fear of unconstitutional conditions cannot be translated into a working rule that treats all conditions attached to incorporation as unconstitutional. Some empirical estimations are inescapable adjuncts to an overall solution to the problem.

## TWENTIETH-CENTURY APPLICATIONS

### *Within the State*

The question of incorporation has generally subsided in the twentieth century, but in recent years it has resurfaced in a number of important cases that deal with the regulation of speech in the corporate form. In *First National Bank of Boston v. Bellotti,*[11] the Supreme Court struck down a statute that made it a criminal offense for cor-

[11] 435 U.S. 765 (1978). Mass. Gen. Laws Ann. ch. 55, §8 (West Supp. 1977).

porations to make contributions or expenditures "for the purpose of . . . influencing or affecting the vote on any question submitted to the voters, other than one materially affecting any of the property, business or assets of the corporation."[12] The statute also provided that matters concerning the general taxation of income or property shall be "deemed" not to affect the corporation. The Court struck down these restrictions as violative of the First Amendment without addressing the unconstitutional conditions issue head-on.

That question, however, was squarely raised in Justice Rehnquist's dissent, which relies on *Dartmouth College* to claim that because the corporation is a creation of state law, the state can legitimately withhold from the corporation those liberties not "incidental" to the corporation's state-defined purpose.[13] At one level, even Rehnquist accepts the unconstitutional conditions doctrine, for he would not allow the state to prevent the corporation from speaking out on issues of direct, and not merely incidental, concern to its shareholders. But he offers no explanation as to why the practical difference should make any theoretical difference, given that the content of a contract is, under the bargain theory he adopts, utterly irrelevant to the validity of the bargain so made.

The weakness of Rehnquist's argument is of major consequence, for *Bellotti* illustrates the very risks that the doctrine of unconstitutional conditions should combat. The analysis is best conducted in two stages. The first question is whether there are gains or losses achievable from general incorporation. So long as the arguments about limited liability are sound, there is surely a gain to be preserved by allowing incorporation across the board. The world of incorporated businesses becomes the best achievable outcome against

---

In a sense this restriction applies evenhandedly to all corporations. But it is selective among business entities as a larger class, exacting an implicit tax on speech by corporations that reduces the gains from incorporation for private parties. The statute is not designed to prevent any abuse of the corporate form. In my view it could be struck down not only on First Amendment grounds, but also as a differential tax that violates the takings clause. The argument here follows familiar lines. The restriction on speech operates as a limit on the purposes to which corporate assets may be turned, and thus as a partial taking of corporate property. There is no justification for this taking under the police power, given that the regulated speech is neither deceptive on the one hand nor a threat to use force on the other. Since the regulated corporations suffer a singular disadvantage, it follows that they are not compensated for the taking to which their holdings were subject. See *Takings*, 283–305. The First Amendment analysis in *Bellotti* is similar to that applicable in the highway cases, discussed infra at chap. 11.

[12] Mass. Gen. Laws Ann. ch. 55, §8 (West Supp. 1977).

[13] See 435 U.S. at 822–28 (Rehnquist, J., dissenting).

which any further regulation is evaluated. In this situation, the further restriction is directed to corporate political speech. It seems clear that if forced to choose between political speech and the privileges of incorporation, the firm will sacrifice the former to save the latter. But the doctrine of unconstitutional conditions spares it that choice because a world with both incorporation and limitations on speech is worse than the world with incorporation but without those speech limitations.

The reasons go to the heart of First Amendment discourse. The limitations in this case related to participation in political discourse. It was limited by both content and persons. Thus it represents the class of selective limitations that, when applied to ordinary individuals, constitutes the greatest threat to freedom of speech.[14] The restriction should be struck down notwithstanding the seductive appeal of the greater/lesser logic.[15] To be sure, this conclusion depends on delicate empirical judgments that are hard for judges to make, but no more so than in any other First Amendment area where selective restrictions by person or content are imposed. Similarly, the state is most unlikely to eliminate the right of incorporation altogether, for the price that other individuals and firms (not to mention the state coffers) would have to pay is just too high. Even though the state is not under a duty to provide for incorporation, it will not exercise its greater power even if it is deprived of the option to exercise its lesser power.[16]

[14] For an exhaustive analysis, see Geoffrey R. Stone, "Content Regulation and the First Amendment," 25 *Wm. & Mary L. Rev.* 189 (1983).

[15] The argument in favor of the restriction is one that says that persons of power and influence should not be allowed to participate in public debate, which cuts against the libertarian grain of the First Amendment and applies both to individual and corporate speech. See Owen M. Fiss, "Free Speech and Social Structure," 71 *Iowa L. Rev.* 1405 (1986).

[16] Cases subsequent to *Belotti* in general have made only passing reference to and placed weak reliance on the point that the state has special powers to regulate the corporation, given its control over corporate charters. See, e.g., Austin v. Michigan Chamber of Commerce, 494 U.S. 652, 658–66 (1990), which upheld a prohibition against the use of independent corporate funds (i.e., those not raised as political contributions and placed in segregated accounts) to support candidates for state elective office. The drift in these cases is to dilute the compelling state-interest test so that state regulation is justified to prevent the "corruption" of the political process by corporate funds. The opinion does not take into account the diversity of views that corporations may have on important political issues, nor recognize that businesses with out-of-state shareholders may have greater need for participation by voice since they do not have the vote. For a trenchant criticism of *Austin*, see Jill Fisch, "Frankenstein's Monster Hits the Campaign Trail: An Approach to Regulation of Corporate Political Expenditures," 32 *Wm. & Mary L. Rev.* 587 (1991).

### *Foreign Incorporation*

Although the battle over general incorporation laws during the middle of the nineteenth century showed the dangers of government discretion, it was not cast as a debate over the doctrine of unconstitutional conditions. Rather, the doctrine arose from the conflict over whether a foreign corporation had a right to do business in a state under the same terms and conditions as a domestic corporation. A state's power to exclude foreign corporations creates a monopoly situation, for no matter where a firm is incorporated, each state has the sole right to decide whether a corporation from another state can do business within its territory. While in many contexts federalism provides a set of competitive governments which private entrepreneurs can play off against each other, that is not true in this case, where governments operate in series and not in parallel.[17] The firms that want to do business on a national basis have no choice but to obtain the consent of *every* state in order to do business. They are not in a position to play one state off against the other, as would be the case where a manufacturing firm has to choose to locate between, say, Pennsylvania and New Jersey.[18]

Professor Vicki Been in her exhaustive study of zoning and other land use restrictions claims that the exit right—the right to go elsewhere if demands on the political system are not met—exerts sufficient control over state and local governments that there is little if any need to superimpose the doctrine of unconstitutional conditions on the exit right.[19] No one should ever dispute the importance of exit rights for keeping the political system in order, but there is a vast difference between a desirable condition that helps promote social optimality and a sufficient condition for social optimality. In particular Been fails to distinguish between the parallel and series situations noted above. The exit right may work to constrain state abuse where states are in competition with each other for business, but it will not work in the case where each state has a holdout position

[17] See supra chap. 2 .

[18] Just that competition is noted in Been, supra note 6, at 536 and n.300. For criticism, see Stewart E. Sterk, "Competition Among Municipalities as a Constraint on Land Use Exactions," 45 *Vand. L. Rev.* 831 (1992).

[19] Her conclusion is overstated in yet a more mundane respect. She records countless instances where corporations were able to get their special charters with some jockeying for position and some delay. These are costs, which while not overwhelming, are positive, and are eliminated by a regime of general incorporation statutes. Stated otherwise, an exit right may be more important in some contexts than a general incorporation statute, but the two in tandem do better than the exit right alone.

against a firm that wishes to do business on a national scale. The opportunities for political maneuvering should be especially evident in this second context, even if they are relatively absent from the first. Firms will compete to gain entrance for themselves and to exclude rivals, just as they did when special charters for incorporation within the home state were the general rule.

The legion of nineteenth- and early twentieth-century cases on discriminatory taxation and regulation are evidence of the magnitude of the problem that remained even with the passing of the era of special incorporation.[20] Allowing the foreign firm into the state makes that firm better off than it was before, but, unless the unconstitutional conditions doctrine applies, the home state may extract surplus. The usual negative consequences follow: the bargaining games between the foreign corporation and the home state consumes valuable resources, and the uneven terms on which foreign and local corporations do business in the home state distorts the competitive balance in product and labor markets. The best way to combat the problem of discrimination is by a strong, categorical rule granting foreign corporations the same right to do business in the home state *on the same terms and conditions* available to its local corporations. In effect, the desired equilibrium could be established between domestic and foreign corporations by eliminating the power of selection—as long as no state would be prepared to disenfranchise its local firms in order to keep out foreign rivals. By forcing states to select between the first and fourth alternatives noted in footnote 7, the doctrine of unconstitutional conditions, as applied to this interstate context, again would result in the state choosing the fourth alternative.

The obvious—and correct—constitutional vehicle for reaching this position is the privileges and immunities clause, which provides that "The Citizens of each State shall be entitled to all Privileges and Immunities of Citizens in the several States."[21] That line of attack, however, was decisively foreclosed in *Paul v. Virginia*,[22] which held that corporations were not "citizens" within the meaning of that clause. The position so adopted necessarily conferred a broad range of discretion upon the state, which *Paul* sets out with extraordinary clarity:

> Now a grant of corporate existence is a grant of special privileges to the corporators, enabling them to act for certain designated purposes as a single individual, and exempting them (unless otherwise specially

[20] See, e.g., Welton v. Missouri, 91 U.S. (10 Otto) 275 (1876).
[21] U.S. Const. art. IV, §2.
[22] 75 U.S. (8 Wall.) 168 (1869).

> provided) from individual liability. The corporation being the mere creation of local law, can have no legal existence beyond the limits of the sovereignty where created. As said by this court in *Bank of Augusta v. Earle*, "It must dwell in the place of its creation, and cannot migrate to another sovereignty." The recognition of its existence even by other States, and the enforcement of its contracts made therein, depend purely upon the comity of those States—a comity which is never extended where the existence of the corporation or the exercise of its powers are prejudicial to their interests or repugnant to their policy. Having no absolute right of recognition in other States, but depending for such recognition and the enforcement of its contracts upon their assent, it follows, as a matter of course, that such assent may be granted upon such terms and conditions as those States may think proper to impose. They may exclude the foreign corporation entirely; they may restrict its business to particular localities, or, they may exact such security for the performance of its contracts with their citizens as in their judgment will best promote the public interest. The whole matter rests in their discretion.[23]

The Court thus took a very relaxed attitude toward the question of governmental abuse. The implicit repudiation of any form of judicial scrutiny in *Paul* carried forward the original argument in *Dartmouth College* that corporate privileges are the subject of legislative grace, and exposed the Achilles' heel of that earlier decision which, in protecting existing charters, expanded the power of the state to regulate business affairs of new corporations.[24]

*Dartmouth College* necessarily rejected the theory that the welfare of a corporation is simply the welfare of its individual shareholders, all of whom are collectively prejudiced by the inability to do business in other states.[25] The sharp disjunction between the right of individual traders to enter foreign states on equal terms with local

[23] Id. at 181.

[24] The effects still linger. See CTS Corp. v. Dynamics Corp. of Am., 481 U.S. 69, 88–91 (1987) (upholding state anti-takeover regulation in part on the ground that corporations are creatures of state government). For a brief discussion of the point, see Comment, "The Personification of the Business Corporation in American Law," 54 *U. Chi. L. Rev.* 1441, 1442 n.3 (1988). It is worth noting that one of the most horrible of the Supreme Court decisions on race relations, Berea College v. Kentucky, 211 U.S. 45 (1908), which allowed states to prohibit any incorporated educational institution from teaching white and black students together, rested in large measure on the proposition that states retain extensive powers to regulate the corporations that they had created.

[25] The implication of *Dartmouth College* was made explicit in Bank of Augusta v. Earle, 38 U.S. (13 Pet.) 519 (1839), which held that the power of a corporation to act, within or beyond its home state, is limited by the provisions of its charter.

citizens and the inability of foreign corporations to do the same constitutes a fundamental weakness in *Paul* that was not lost on the leading commentators of the time, all of whom reverted to aggregate theories of the corporation to conclude, in the words of Victor Morawetz:

> [T]he rights and duties of an incorporated association are in reality the rights and duties of the persons who compose it, and not of an imaginary being. . . .
>
> [T]here is no reason of immediate justice to others, why a number of individuals should not be permitted to form a corporation of their own free will, and without first obtaining permission from the legislature, just as they may form a partnership or enter into ordinary contracts with each other.[26]

Even if a corporation is not a "citizen," its shareholders surely are, and it is they who are denied legal protection against selective exclusion.

Although *Paul* prevented the privileges and immunities clause from ensuring nondiscrimination, other constitutional avenues that could have constrained the level of state discretion conferred by *Paul* soon opened up.[27] Most notably, the term "person" as used in the due process clause had been construed to cover the same corporations deemed not to be "citizens" under the privileges and immunities clause.[28] By the 1890s it had been held that the words "without due process of law" were to be construed, at least in some contexts, to mean "without just compensation,"[29] so that takings jurispru-

[26] Victor Morawetz, *A Treatise on the Law of Private Corporations Other Than Charitable* §1, at 2 (1882); id. §29, at 24. The development is outlined in Comment, supra note 24, at 1457–58. Note the use of natural-right rhetoric to support market structures that can be justified on consequentialist grounds.

[27] The contract clause line of argument had already been foreclosed, with Chief Justice Marshall and Justice Story dissenting, by the earlier decision in Ogden v. Saunders, 25 U.S. (12 Wheat.) 213 (1827), which denied the clause any effect with respect to future contracts. I have defended the prospective view of the contract clause in Richard A. Epstein, "Toward a Revitalization of the Contract Clause," 51 *U. Chi. L. Rev.* 703 (1984).

[28] See Santa Clara County v. Southern Pac. R.R., 118 U.S. 394, 396 (1886). Note that Congress could not have limited state discretion during this period, because *Paul* had also held that local insurance contracts were matters of local commerce (or more decisively, that they were not commercial transactions at all) and thus beyond the reach of the commerce clause. See *Paul*, 75 U.S. (8 Wall.) 168, 182–85 (1869).

[29] See Chicago, Burlington, & Quincy R.R. v. Chicago, 166 U.S. 226, 235–41 (1897). That textual ploy is doubtful, but not necessarily wrong. The connection between substantive and procedural due process is most apparent in cases of judicial bias, where the unfair treatment increases the likelihood that property will be taken incorrectly. See generally Richard A. Epstein, "Takings: Of Maginot Lines and Constitu-

dence, which often uses a disproportionate impact test to determine whether just compensation has been provided,[30] now applied to the states. The disproportionate impact of a discriminatory tax seems clear enough. If the tax is a taking, then its discriminatory impact is clear evidence that the party so taxed has not received just compensation for the moneys paid to the state. The same kind of argument could be made in principle under the equal protection clause. If foreign shareholders are entitled to the same rights as domestic ones, then any discrimination between them must be justified by the extra costs that foreign corporations impose on local governments, of which there seem to be none. Any sensible use of either due process or equal protection doctrine would have resulted in an end run around *Paul,* without recourse to the doctrine of unconstitutional conditions. Under this "strong rights" thesis, the state would *not* have the power *either* to exclude foreign corporations from doing business within its borders *or,* to tax foreign corporations differently from local firms. The outsider comes in on equal terms, and nothing more need be said.

Because this position did not take hold in the late nineteenth or early twentieth century, however, the stage was set for the Court's use of the doctrine of unconstitutional conditions, under both the due process[31] and equal protection[32] clauses of the Fourteenth Amendment[33] as the "second-best" means of controlling government discretion.

---

tional Compromises," in *Liberty, Property and the Future of Constitutional Development* 173, 177–79 (E. Paul, and H. Dickman, eds. 1990).

[30] See *Takings,* 204–9.

[31] See Pullman Co. v. Kansas, 216 U.S. 56 (1910); Western Union Tel. Co. v. Kansas, 216 U.S. 1 (1910).

[32] See Southern Ry. v. Greene, 216 U.S. 400 (1910). *Southern Railway* acknowledged that the equal protection analysis follows a path similar to the earlier due process analysis. See id. at 413–18. There is good reason for the parallelism. Both the equal protection and due process clauses essentially follow the same path as the takings clause, as it applies to general taxation and regulation. In essence, it is virtually impossible to measure whether the benefits of taxation exceed the costs of the tax imposed. Hence, unequal treatment or disproportionate impact should become the proxy by which to judge whether there is an illicit transfer of wealth between groups. Cf. Armstrong v. United States, 364 U.S. 40, 49 (1960) (holding that the takings clause was intended to prevent placing a disproportionate share of burdens on a few). For an extensive discussion, see *Takings,* 195–215. The equal protection clause emphasizes equal treatment; the due process clause emphasizes the loss of property without compensation. In essence, they both look at different ends of the same set of issues.

[33] See Maurice H. Merrill, "Unconstitutional Conditions," 77 *U. Pa. L. Rev.* 879 at 879–80 (1929); S. Chesterfield Oppenheim, "Unconstitutional Conditions and State Powers," 26 *Mich. L. Rev.* 176, 176 (1927).

In *Western Union Telegraph Co. v. Kansas*,[34] for example, the Court struck down a discriminatory tax Kansas sought to impose upon Western Union, a New York corporation. The tax itself was based on the corporation's entire capital stock, not only on its local assets, and thus had a strong extra-territorial effect. Clearly, the due process clause would have struck down the tax if the firm had done no business in Kansas. The issue of unconstitutional conditions arose because the state conditioned its willingness to allow Western Union to engage in *local* commerce on its willingness to pay the discriminatory tax.[35] Without the doctrine of unconstitutional conditions, the consent of the firm would have cured the defects in extraterritorial treatment; with the doctrine in place, however, consent of the corporation did not prevent it from challenging the disputed condition.

Important consequences flow from the choice of legal regimes. The key difference between the unconstitutional conditions argument and the strong rights argument set out above goes to the set of the choices left to the state. Under the unconstitutional conditions doctrine, the state may choose either to exclude the foreign corporation altogether or to let it in on equal terms with the local corporations. By rejecting the greater/lesser analysis championed by Justice Holmes, the Court thus barred the state from allowing consenting foreign corporations to do business subject to a countless array of taxes or other burdens that did not apply to domestic corporations, but did not prevent it from exercising the "greater" power of excluding foreign corporations altogether.

How, then, will the state behave under these two alternative legal regimes? In order to answer that question, it is necessary to undertake a rough interest group analysis that takes into account three disparate sets of interests: local consumers, local businesses, and foreign corporations. When the state has complete power to admit, exclude, or admit subject to conditions, it is highly likely that the state will often choose the third path, which Kansas adopted in *Western Union*, even though it enjoyed an absolute right to exclude under *Paul*.

Start with local consumers. These individuals both gain and lose from the admission of foreign corporations subject to the discrimina-

[34] 216 U.S. 1 (1910).

[35] See id. at 4–8. The statutory decision, which subjected only purely local business revenues to the tax, probably reflected the judgment that Western Union was indispensable for the interstate business, but not for the local markets, where other firms could compete. It fits in well with a public choice model of regulation.

tory tax, when measured against the alternative of admitting them subject only to normal taxes. On the positive side of the ledger, more taxes might be collected from the out-of-state firms, thus reducing the local tax burden. (On this measure, either alternative is preferable to exclusion, which would result in no tax revenue.) On the negative side, the discriminatory tax imposes burdens on local consumers who are forced to pay higher prices for some goods and services, and to forego the benefits of other bargains that the higher tax renders uneconomical—the so-called excess burden imposed by the discriminatory tax.[36] As is usually the case with tariffs in international trade, the deadweight losses from the restriction and the political costs from setting it in place make the entire enterprise unwise from a social point of view. (Again, either alternative is preferable to exclusion, which would result in no consumers' surplus from business with foreign corporations.) For local consumers as a group, it seems plausible that these effects will tend to offset each other, although not perfectly. Local competitors for their part have far less ambivalence. They gain revenue and competitive advantages from the discriminatory tax and should support it strongly. While some might want total exclusion, the loss of both tax revenue and the opportunities to do business with foreign suppliers and customers make this an unlikely outcome. It is always possible to strike a political deal over the level of discrimination that will be embodied in the tax structure, just as it is possible to strike a deal over the level of progressivity in any broad-based income tax.

This calculus changes radically when the doctrine of unconstitutional conditions puts the state to an all-or-nothing choice. Now local consumers must be asked to support a total exclusion of out-of-state firms. Under this rule, these citizens receive no revenue offset from the foreign tax, and in addition they lose the possibility of doing business with efficient out-of-state firms who are able to overcome the tax disadvantage. Consumer losses become very large, with no obvious offsetting gains. We should thus expect that they would strongly support a repeal of the special tax when the doctrine of unconstitutional conditions puts them to the choice of nondiscriminatory entry or total exclusion of foreign firms.

[36] The term *excess burden* is applied to any tax in which the amount received from the taxing authority is less than the loss to the private parties so taxed. The deadweight loss associated with such excess burdens is analogous to that which occurs when the price set by a private monopolist exceeds the competitive price. See generally James Gwartney & Richard Stroup, *Economics: Private and Public Choice* 110–11 (4th ed. 1987).

For their part, rival sellers of goods and services may well like the total exclusion, at least for their direct rivals, but they would not desire a similar exclusion for out-of-state firms that supply inputs that these firms purchase, or for firms that purchase their products. On balance, therefore, it will be difficult to assemble a broad in-state coalition of producers who will find it in their own self-interest to keep the outsiders out permanently, or even to impose taxes so high that most of them choose to stay out. The net result would be the desired one: out-of-state firms would be allowed to compete on even terms.

Still to be considered are the interests of the out-of-state firms. In principle they would always prefer the nondiscriminatory taxes to the other two choices. But the prospect of supracompetitive profits may induce them to pay a discriminatory tax for the privilege of doing business. Thus the legal regime of *Paul,* before its demise in *United States v. South-Eastern Underwriters Association,*[37] created an extensive bargaining range between local governments and outside firms, with ample opportunities for strategic behavior on both sides. If the guess about local politics is correct, the use of unconstitutional conditions in this context would force the states to the proper social alternative—letting outsiders in on an equal basis—by precluding the use of discriminatory taxes. Under the familiar pattern, the doctrine cuts out all intermediate positions, leaving the state only the all-or-nothing alternatives of total exclusion or nondiscriminatory admission. Forced to either of the two edges of the bargaining range, the local interests are better off allowing out-of-state firms in on equal terms than excluding them entirely. The total exclusion option sanctioned by *Paul* is preserved, but as an empirical matter factional intrigue is forestalled, and the correct outcome of the ensuing political game is in most cases ensured. The subsequent histories of the decisions in *Western Union* and *Southern Railway v. Greene,* both of which struck down discriminatory taxes, bear out this hypothesis insofar as the modern versions of both statutes now

[37] 322 U.S. 533, 543–49 (1944). *South-Eastern Underwriters* held that fire insurance companies were subject to prosecution under the Sherman Act, see id. at 553–62, and explicitly rejected any argument that the business of insurance was not commerce, see id. at 539–43. Congress responded to the decision by passing the McCarran-Ferguson Act, Pub. L. No. 79–15, 59 Stat. 33 (1945) (codified as amended at 15 U.S.C. §§1011–1015 (1982 & Supp. I 1983)), which returned regulation of the insurance industry to state control. The local patterns of discrimination against foreign corporations are discussed in connection with Western & Southern Life Ins. Co. v. Board of Equalization, 451 U.S. 648 (1981). See infra chap. 9.

apply nondiscriminatory rules to foreign corporations.[38] It was simply not viable to exclude either foreign railroad or foreign telegraph companies from doing any portion of their business within any state.

This analysis applies not only to taxation of foreign corporations, but also to other kinds of regulation as well. Consider the common provisions that sought to restrict the ability of foreign corporations to avail themselves of the federal courts' diversity jurisdiction. *Terral v. Burke Construction Co.*[39] overruled several earlier cases[40] by holding that "a State may not, in imposing conditions upon the privilege of a foreign corporation's doing business in the State, exact from it a waiver of the exercise of its constitutional right to resort to the federal courts, or thereafter withdraw the privilege of doing business because of its exercise of such right, whether waived in advance or not."[41]

The justification for this result is identical to that applied in the discriminatory tax cases. Foreign corporations presumably want access to federal courts to escape the local bias of state courts. To prevent them from exercising this option is to subject them to a disguised differential tax equal to their estimated additional burdens of litigating in a hostile forum. Even so, many (but not all) foreign corporations prefer that weighted offer to total exclusion. But the resource losses still remain for two reasons: the exclusion of some foreign corporations for whom the extra burden makes the venture undesirable, and the distortion in relative prices for the firms still willing to compete. The use of the unconstitutional conditions doctrine shifts the hard choices from the foreign corporation to the state in the service of competitive equity. If forced to choose between exclusion and admission on equal terms, the states will do the latter, as happened after *Terral*,[42] which is as it should be. As with taxes, the doctrine serves in this context as an effective constraint on arbitrary

[38] In the aftermath of *Southern Railway*, Alabama law provides that foreign corporations are subject to the same "duties, restrictions, penalties, liabilities now or hereinafter imposed upon a domestic corporation of like character." Ala. Code §10-2A-227 (1987). Kansas, in the aftermath of *Western Union*, subjects domestic and foreign corporations to an identical franchise tax. See Kan. Stat. Ann. §§17-7503(c), 17-7505(c) (Supp. 1987).

[39] 257 U.S. 529 (1922).

[40] See, e.g., Security Mut. Life Ins. Co. v. Prewitt, 202 U.S. 246 (1906); Doyle v. Continental Ins. Co., 94 U.S. 535 (1876).

[41] 257 U.S. at 532.

[42] See Ark. Code Ann. §4-27-102 (1987). This statute, which corresponds to the Act of May 13, 1907, No. 313, §1, 1907 Ark. Acts 744, is identical to the 1907 Act, save for the elimination of the clause condemned in *Terral*.

power found in the absolute authority to exclude foreign corporations.[43] Again the proposition is not a necessary truth. The success of the doctrine rests solely on the (sound) empirical judgment that a state, when faced with the all-or-nothing choice, will choose to allow the outsider to compete within the state on equal terms.

### *Overriding the Nondiscrimination Rule*

Although use of the doctrine of unconstitutional conditions in state taxation cases is now well established, its success depends on the steadfastness with which it is applied. That level of resolve in turn depends upon what justifications are found appropriate to displace its underlying principle—an issue not raised in the earlier cases. In this regard, the Supreme Court's recent taxation decisions are unsatisfactory.[44] In *Western & Southern Life Insurance Co. v. Board of Equalization*,[45] California imposed an overtly discriminatory tax on some out-of-state insurance companies. The tax was not a simple discriminatory tax like the one invalidated in *Western Union*. Rather, it was styled as a "retaliatory" tax that was imposed only when the state of incorporation of the foreign company, here Ohio, charged California companies higher tax rates for doing business in Ohio than the California companies paid in California. Ohio did not impose any discriminatory tax on California life insurance companies (which it could not do under *Western Union*).[46] But Ohio did tax all insurance companies doing business in Ohio a premium tax at a higher rate (2.5 percent) than California charged for its local companies (2.35 percent). Thus, California's retaliation provision, in effect, imposed a 2.5 percent premium tax on the California revenues of

[43] The result in the case has also been supported on the ground that it protects the jurisdiction of the federal courts from state encroachment, an argument invoked, but not explored at length, in *Terral*, see 257 U.S. at 532–33, and endorsed in Merrill, supra in note 33, at 892. It was perhaps on this ground that Justice Holmes joined the decision notwithstanding his earlier dissents in *Western Union*, 216 U.S. at 52 and *Southern Railway*, 216 U.S. at 418.

[44] See, e.g., Commonwealth Edison Co. v. Montana, 453 U.S. 609 (1981) (holding a severance tax on the coal production to be nondiscriminatory even though 90 percent of the coal was shipped to out-of-state utility companies under contracts of sale shifting the tax burden to the purchaser). But see Richard A. Epstein, "Taxation, Regulation and Confiscation," 20 *Osgood Hall L.J.* 433, 445–49 (1982) (criticizing the result in *Commonwealth Edison*).

[45] 451 U.S. 648 (1981).

[46] See id. at 675 (Stevens, J., dissenting); Ohio Rev. Code Ann. §5729.03 (Anderson 1973).

Ohio corporations. The differential tax was justified as a way to pressure Ohio corporations to use their influence to lower the general premium tax in Ohio to California levels.

Despite the explicit discrimination revealed by these facts, Justice Brennan, writing for the Court, upheld the tax. He first made clear his unwillingness to reverse *Paul*'s interpretation of the term "citizen" in the privileges and immunities clause. But he did accept—heartily, though without explanation—the unconstitutional conditions gloss used to mitigate the absolutism of that decision.[47] The shift from the privileges and immunities analysis to an equal protection analysis, however, allowed Justice Brennan to place an elastic "rational basis" construction on the doctrine of unconstitutional conditions, as permissive as the rational basis review he had applied directly in equal protection cases.[48]

Applying this standard, he found that California's tax was justified as a device to induce other states to reduce the amount of taxes imposed on California businesses, and that the life insurance industry itself had supported the tax in question. In so doing, he left ajar the door to politics that had been shut more tightly by the earlier and more categorical versions of unconstitutional conditions doctrine. As Justice Stevens's dissent pointed out, the decision allows California politicians to seek influence over the general level of taxes in Ohio.[49] It is worth adding that the differential tax might be supported by insurance companies because of their determination to monopolize local markets. California's retaliatory statute is hauntingly reminiscent of New Jersey's effort to get even with New York's restrictive steamboat monopoly that was struck down in *Gibbons v. Ogden*.[50] Its motivation also seems similar to the clearly protectionist sentiment underlying the system of retaliation in the trade legislation that Congress has all too often enacted.[51] Ohio still keeps its old tax rate,[52] so that the Supreme Court's decision allows discrimination to flourish across states in a short run that lengthens as the

[47] See 451 U.S. at 656–68 (endorsing the doctrine after reviewing the long line of confused precedent in the area).

[48] See, e.g., Minnesota v. Clover Leaf Creamery Co., 449 U.S. 456 (1981) (allowing the state to ban use of plastic milk containers). I have criticized that decision strongly in *Takings*, 143–44. Justice Brennan did not originate the present judicial line of analysis, which had reached its present form in earlier decisions. See, e.g., Ferguson v. Skrupa, 372 U.S. 726 (1963); Williamson v. Lee Optical Co., 348 U.S. 483 (1955).

[49] See 451 U.S. at 677–78 n.7 (Stevens, J., dissenting).

[50] 22 U.S. (9 Wheat.) 1 (1824).

[51] See Omnibus Trade and Competitiveness Act of 1988, Pub. L. No. 100–418, 102 Stat. 1107 (1988).

[52] See Ohio Rev. Code Ann. §5725.18(B) (Anderson 1986).

shadows of the evening. As elsewhere, the rational basis test leads only to constitutional confusion and to the release of political forces far better kept in check. It is often said that the Constitution does not impose categorical restrictions upon inefficient or sneaky practices. But in hard cases, we can only make sense of the substantive provisions that it does contain in light of the social consequences generated by alternative interpretations of those provisions. We know that the creation of one national economic market, transcending state boundaries, was a major goal of the framers, and it remains a goal worthy of our support. For achieving that end, the per se rule of *Western Union* and *Southern Railway* is superior to its watered-down modern alternatives. The discrimination in tax rates against foreign corporations is a practice that should be banned. It is that result which the unconstitutional conditions doctrine achieves by moving states in the direction of a competitive equilibrium in taxation. Accordingly, discriminatory taxation forms the subject of the next chapter.

## CHAPTER 9

# Discriminatory Taxation

THE PREVIOUS CHAPTER analyzed the role of the unconstitutional conditions doctrine in connection with state regulation of foreign corporations. The major point of that analysis was that each state had a monopoly over the power to permit corporations to do business within its borders, and that this power should not be allowed to permit the state to extract economic rents from those corporations which would, if no other choice were allowed to them, be prepared to pay higher rates of taxes than local corporations in order to obtain access to local markets. By preventing each state from extracting surplus from foreign corporations, the unconstitutional conditions doctrine and the antidiscrimination rules have helped to preserve a competitive equilibrium at the corporate level and to prevent a cycle of factional intrigue within states and of retaliation across states.

A similar problem has arisen with respect to the state taxation of interstate commerce. Although the emphasis shifts from incorporation to transportation, the essential ingredients of the problem are the same as before. Each state has control over the highway system within its borders. Each trucking firm (for example) must resort to the use of the roads in many states in order to ship goods from one location to the next. With transportation as with incorporation, federalism does *not* create competition between states—competition whose effect is to reduce the risks of government power. To be sure, the basic situation is complicated because shippers have some control over the choice of routes to move goods from one destination to another. To that extent there is, at least with certain journeys, a competition between states that will serve to keep its taxation levels low regardless of the structure of state taxation of interstate commerce.

It would be a major mistake, however, to assume that these competitive elements dominate interstate transportation. Most long journeys require movement through several states, and for many trips it may not be economically feasible to avoid certain key states. In many, perhaps most, situations the cooperation of many states will be necessary to complete a single journey so that individual states, strategically located, may well enjoy a blocking position with respect to certain travel and transportation. Where the coordination of several states to facilitate interstate commerce is required, the greater the number of states, the more difficult the compliance problems. The elements are arranged in series, not in parallel. A state could impose high taxes for the use of its roads so long as the tax increase does not make some alternative route more desirable, or defeat the prospect of a trip altogether.

Given this general structure of the problem, what system of constitutional regulation should be used to constrain the power of the states to regulate, by taxation or otherwise, the use of their local highways? At one level, the unconstitutional conditions doctrine is surely implicated: while a state is under no duty to build a highway, once that highway is built, the state's (imperfect) monopoly position means that it cannot have untrammeled discretion in deciding whether foreign carriers gain access to it. (The question of domestic access is postponed to chapter 11.) Similarly, there is a hard question of whether the state, which may grant out-of-state carriers the "privilege" to use public roads, necessarily has the power to exclude them from the use of the highways altogether. That power of exclusion is not often claimed in so raw a fashion, but, if claimed and exercised, it would lead to a massive disruption of domestic transportation markets, which in turn would spur retaliatory actions by other states.[1]

The use of the term *privilege* illustrates a possible place for the unconstitutional conditions doctrine to prevent the dissipation of surplus by uncoordinated and rivalrous state action. It is commonplace for states to allow noncitizens to use their roads. Nonetheless there seems to be little explicit discussion on whether a state may formally exclude foreign carriers from using its road system. The reason is that it is not in the interest of any state to try so lonesome a policy. Excluding outsiders would only increase the costs to its own citizens in two ways. First, highway systems are expensive to maintain, and exclusion of outsiders means that local revenue sources must bear the full costs. Second, at the same time, a rule of exclusion cuts off needed goods and services that can be more cheaply supplied from out-of-state. While the language of privilege may invoke pictures of exclusion, the preferred strategy is not exclu-

[1] These instances of retaliation have occurred. See, e.g., American Trucking Ass'ns v. Scheiner, 483 U.S. 266 (1987), where Justice Stevens notes that seven states passed retaliatory taxes against Pennsylvania vehicles after it introduced marker and axle taxes that bore more heavily on out of state truckers. Id. at 285, nn.17 & 18. Stevens's opinion avoids facing the question of whether any state may totally exclude foreign transport under its claim of privilege.

sion, but discriminatory taxation of foreign carriers who use the state system. Should the state be allowed to offer a deal to foreign carriers which says "Use our roads, but pay a disproportionate share of the cost of running our system"?

To set this bargaining problem in context, suppose in the simplest possible scenario that the highway system in State A costs $1 billion per year to maintain and that this cost has to be allocated between domestic and foreign road carriers. If each group of firms is prepared to pay (say) $750 million to gain access to the system, then the state has discretion in the way in which it can allocate that joint cost. A discriminatory tax that hits foreign truckers for three times the tax on domestic truckers (a) will cover the costs of running the system; (b) will not drive those (or at least all) foreign truckers from the state; (c) will confer an enormous competitive advantage for the domestic firms that run the same routes; and (d) will result in a general reduction in local taxation for all local citizens where the foreign carrier only passes through the state without being in direct competition with local firms.

How then should that surplus be allocated? If the only issue were whether the foreign truckers were better off using the roads while subject to the taxes than they would have been without either access or tax, the answer is clearly in the affirmative. Accordingly, state "coercion" in its narrowest sense (the baseline of preexisting entitlements) cannot be found. Any form of discrimination, however explicit and overt, should be acceptable, because the exit right of foreign carriers protects them against exploitation. But if, as I have argued, the question is whether permitting discriminatory taxation creates the optimal legal regime, then there is a very different answer, as with all questions of bargaining with the state. The mere fact that discrimination in rates (unrelated to differences in cost of providing services) is possible shows that there is an exercise of state monopoly power that must be checked at a constitutional level. Out-of-state carriers must be allowed to challenge the tax, even if they are benefited by the use of the highways.

In the absence of any form of direct regulation, however, each state finds itself in a prisoner's dilemma game with all the others. Since each state occupies a holdout position, each is tempted to raise the fees on out-of-state carriers regardless of whether the other states do the same. Every state has a dominant strategy to impose discriminatory taxes on its rivals whether they retaliate or not. If the practices were to go unchecked, then it is quite conceivable that the total burden of taxation would be sufficiently great to drive out of business substantial portions of interstate transportation and trade, in contravention of the original constitutional plan that, if anything, calls for the creation of an economic common market among the states.[2] The major trick is to devise a way that allows each state, if it so chooses, to set the rate of taxes within its borders to cover the cost of running its road system, without simultaneously distorting the competitive balance among states.

The problem is one that is, in principle, susceptible to a legislative solution, but Congress has been either unable or unwilling to issue unified directives on this question—perhaps because of the great complexity of the issue and the opposition from the states. The cycle of destructive interactions could also be controlled by state action that coordinates the imposition of taxes, fees, and licenses, and this route has proved more profitable. Thus some states have entered into cooperative arrangements that subject carriers from any given state to a uniform regime of social control, and such systems have been developed to apportion registration fees across member states. But while these devices are used, they are not fully comprehensive in their scope, and they leave the field open for at least some discriminatory taxes.[3]

Owing to the imperfect legislative solutions to the coordination problem, the issue has fallen largely into the lap of the United States Supreme Court to set the ideal rules. One recurrent difficulty is whether the Court has this power, given that the commerce clause reads like an affirmative grant of power to Congress and not a restriction on the states. That point has been stressed by Justice Scalia as part of his energetic effort to cut back on the domain of the negative or dormant commerce power in the area of interstate taxation.[4] His textual argument has a good deal of force, although it has been re-

[2] "It has long been established that the Commerce Clause of its own force protects free trade among the states." Armco, Inc. v. Hardesty, 467 U.S. 638, 642 (1984). The phrase "of its own force" refers, of course, to the widely accepted proposition that the commerce clause does not operate only as a grant of power to the federal government but also, in its negative or dormant dimension, as a limitation on the power of the states.

[3] One system, the International Registration Plan, prorates the right to impose registration fees in accordance with the miles driven in each member state. The coordination plan only affects the percentage of the license fee that each state may charge, but it is understood that each state is free to set its own registration fee as high or as low as it wants. There are also reciprocal arrangements whereby State A will admit carriers who are registered in State B so long as State B will admit carriers registered in State A. These schemes are discussed in *Scheiner*, 483 U.S. at 271–73.

[4] See Tyler Pipe Indus., Inc. v. Washington Dept. of Revenue, 483 U.S. 232, 259–65 (1985) (Scalia, J. dissenting), relying on David Currie, *The Constitution in the Supreme Court: The First Hundred Years, 1789–1888* (1985).

jected by a uniform line of cases that even Justice Scalia does not wish to overturn, but only limit. But more to the point, the concerns that are expressed by the dormant commerce clause arguments go to the heart of the strengths and weaknesses of any system of federalism, and have to be addressed in more or less identical terms under either the due process clause of the Fourteenth Amendment, or more directly under the privileges and immunities clause of Article IV.[5] Indeed, if Justice Scalia is correct, then even overt and explicit discriminations against foreign corporations are not regulated by the Constitution, a result that even he would not strain to achieve. The area is one for which there is respectable authority for judicial regulation, and the critical question is how that regulation should be undertaken.

In approaching the question of discriminatory taxation generally, there are two pitfalls that the Court must avoid. First, it must make sure that its restriction on the state's power to tax does not give an unfair advantage to outsiders, relative to domestic competition. Second, it must make sure that the discretion conferred upon state governments does not allow them to impose discriminatory taxes upon outsiders. Both these substantive goals, moreover, have to be achieved in ways that do not impose impossible administrative costs on the states, that do not prevent states from satisfying their internal budget requirements, and that do not require courts to make the delicate kinds of judgments that are normally beyond the power of courts to make. The familiar prohibition against discrimination, even when applied with remorseless scrutiny, is capable of meeting the myriad constraints applicable to this area. The mere fact that some tax or burden is placed on interstate commerce is not sufficient to invalidate the state action. Only its excessive burden relative to insiders is decisive. Interstate commerce must be made to pay its way, but to assume no more than its fair share of the burden.[6] The complex case law in this area reveals both the payoffs and the risk of this form of regulation, and it is useful to summarize some of the major points of that history here.[7]

[5] "The Citizens of Each State shall be entitled to all Privileges and Immunities of Citizens in the Several States," Art. IV, §2 (discussed in chap. 8).

[6] See, e.g., Nippert v. Richmond, 327 U.S. 416, 425–26 (1946): "As has been so often stated but nevertheless seems to require constant repetition, not all burdens upon commerce, but only undue or discriminatory ones, are forbidden. For, though 'interstate commerce must pay its way,' a State consistently with the commerce clause cannot put a barrier around its borders to bar out trade from other States."

[7] On many of these issues, see Walter Hellerstein, "State Taxation of Interstate Business: Perspectives on Two Centuries of Constitutional Adjudication," 41 *Tax*

Two cases from the 1940s show the risks of imposing a regime that insulates out-of-state businesses from local taxation, giving them an unfair competitive advantage. In *Freeman v. Hewit*, Indiana sought to tax its residents and domiciliaries on "the receipt of the entire gross income."[8] The question in that case was whether the tax could be applied when an Indiana trust instructed its brokers in New York to sell shares of stock owned by the trust and remit the proceeds to Indiana. The Court, speaking through Justice Frankfurter, held that the tax, levied as it was on "the privilege of engaging in interstate commerce," could not be imposed by Indiana. *Freeman* sought to create a free-trade zone by totally immunizing interstate transactions from local taxation and was explicit in the rejection of the nondiscrimination rule as a guide for interstate taxation.[9]

*Freeman*'s critical error lay in its failure to understand that an unwarranted immunity from taxation is as much a deviation from the principles of free trade as an improper exaction of tax. The object of "tax neutrality" is to insure that there will be no shift in activities between jurisdictions as a function of the differential taxes that might be imposed. Under *Freeman*, Indiana citizens might, in a world without taxation, choose to execute their sale of shares within that state, on the ground that it is cheaper to do so. If the Indiana transaction is subject to tax while the New York transaction is not, then the relative prices of the two transactions shift, so that in some cases a more costly New York transaction is substituted for the less costly Indiana transaction. A system which allows Indiana to tax both situations avoids that distortion and prevents trade from being diverted into unwise channels. A subsidy of one transaction can

---

*Law.* 37 (1987) (generally supportive of lower levels of supervision); Daniel Shaviro, "An Economic and Political Look at Federalism in Taxation," 90 *Mich. L. Rev.* 895 (1992) (more supportive of judicial supervision over state power). See also Laurence H. Tribe, *American Constitutional Law* §§6-15 to 6-29 (1988). Some major scholarly efforts have avoided these technical waters on the ground that the cases involved defy organization and synthesis. See, e.g., Julian N. Eule, "Laying the Dormant Commerce Clause to Rest," 91 *Yale L.J.* 425 (1982).

[8] 329 U.S. 249, 250 (1946).

[9] "[T]he Commerce Clause was not merely an authorization to Congress to enact laws for the protection and encouragement among the States, but by its own force created an area of trade free from the interference by the States. . . . This limitation on State power . . . does not merely forbid a State to single out interstate commerce for hostile action. A State is also precluded from taking any action which may fairly be deemed to have the effect of impeding the free flow of trade between States. It is immaterial that local commerce is subjected to a similar encumbrance." 329 U.S. at 252. The decision was defective insofar as it precluded any taxation of foreign transactions, wholly without regard to discrimination.

distort relative prices as much as a tax on its substitutes. So long, therefore, as we live in a world in which some taxes have to be levied, an exemption of interstate commerce does not stand in the service of free trade.

Closer to the subject of interstate transportation is *Spector Motor Service, Inc. v. O'Connor*,[10] which took a similar attitude towards a Connecticut tax imposed "for the privilege of carrying on exclusively interstate transportation within the state."[11] The amount of the tax was set with reference to the carriers' use of the public highways, and it was conceded that the tax was not discriminatory and that the same amount of money could have been collected if the tax had been designated as a highway-use tax. The only objection to the tax rested upon its formal classification, not its economic effect. The problems, if any, created by *Spector* are easily cured by legislative reclassification of the relevant tax, so the decision does not amount to an important restriction on the state power to tax. In any event, the immunization of interstate commerce from the local tax did not last, for *Spector* was repudiated in *Complete Auto Transit Co. v. Brady*,[12] where the Court sustained a Mississippi tax on a trucker who removed General Motors cars from the railroads and shipped them to local dealers. All of the trucker's activities took place within the state, and it claimed immunity from taxation, not because it was hit harder than other local firms, but solely because its activities represented the last stage in an interstate transaction. In reaching its conclusion, the Court adopted the now standard four-part test which provides that the tax will be sustained "against Commerce Clause challenge when the tax is applied to an activity with a substantial nexus with the taxing State, is fairly apportioned, does not discriminate against interstate commerce, and is fairly related to the services provided by the State."[13]

The form of this fourfold test is instructive because it shows not the slightest preoccupation with a bargain theory of the sort that sustains the tax so long as the corporation taxed is left better off with the tax than it would have been without access to the state system. The status quo ante is not the baseline from which the validity of the tax is judged. Instead the four parts of this test, taken together, are designed to ensure not only that the tax in question meets the just compensation standard for any entity (domestic or foreign) subject

[10] 340 U.S. 602 (1951).
[11] Id. at 608.
[12] 430 U.S. 274 (1977).
[13] Id. at 279.

to the tax, but also that each entity so taxed is entitled to the same level of surplus from the use of the state facilities.

It is of course impossible for anyone to determine exactly what level of surplus any firm can derive from the use of public roads and highways, but the insistence that these costs be apportioned in accordance with the use of the system is a reliable proxy to ensure its maximization. The amounts of surplus per firm cannot be detected by the state, and in all likelihood are not known with precision by the private parties, so that apportionment by use is not likely to reduce or increase the level of surplus received by any group. The competitive balance between the firms is maintained, and so too the likelihood of the total size of the surplus. It may well be that the taxes imposed are too high or too low, for it is quite clear that no rule that seeks to control discrimination can by itself drive the state to adopt the optimal level of taxation with respect to its highway system.[14] But the insistence on neutrality between various users of the system at least eliminates one dangerous source of instability under federalism, and dulls the incentive for any regulated party to undertake efforts through the political process to shift some portion of its costs to its rivals.

The success of this general regime depends in large measure on the extent that its nondiscrimination test can be applied in ways that preserve the social surplus from the use of the highway. In dealing with the parallel problem of disproportionate impact under the just compensation clause, it was clear that formal inequalities in treatment are indicative of political mischief. These are the source of enormous social dislocations and are on balance easy to correct, for a court need only look at the face of the record to strike them down. Thus a tax that is twice as much per mile for the foreign carrier, or twice the cost per unit sale for a foreign seller, than it is for the local one is doomed so long as the commerce clause applies.

The more controversial question is whether the antidiscrimination principle can attack forms of discrimination that are not overt and explicit. The point is of great importance in that formal neutrality in *treatment* between different parties could well conceal vastly different effects upon the regulated parties. If states and local interest groups are bound by the general nondiscrimination principle of *Complete Auto Transit Co.*, they may nonetheless seek to subvert the ends of this rule by opting for rules that are formally neutral, but vastly disparate in their impact. Any legal approach—such as that

[14] A point stressed in Shaviro, supra note 7.

now championed by Justice Scalia[15]—that requires express or facial discrimination in order to invalidate a tax on interstate commerce will leave too much running room for state legislatures, prompted by local interest groups, to distort the relative balance between rival jurisdictions, which it is the very purpose of the constitutional restraints on state taxation to preserve.

It is clear that these initiatives have taken place and will continue to take place. One blatant illustration of the process is found in the dubious Supreme Court decision in *Commonwealth Edison Co. v. Montana*,[16] which upheld a 30 percent severance tax on Montana coal, 90 percent of which was shipped in interstate commerce under long-term contracts that shifted the incidence of the tax forward to the consumers. At the same time that the severance tax was imposed, the state repealed its state income tax—an offsetting benefit for local payers of the severance tax that was not shared by out-of-staters.

Under the *Complete Auto Transit Co.* test developed four years before, the tax should have been struck down. There is no dispute that Montana has some connection with the coal in place, so the critical question is whether the tax was fairly apportioned and fairly related to services provided by the state. One way to look at the question is to ask whether the gains that the out-of-staters received for their tax payments were proportionate to those received by the in-staters. No showing to that effect was made, or could have been made, as the in-staters received all the benefits from the tax, and the out-of-staters received none. The Supreme Court, moreover, conceded the point implicitly when it adopted a wholly discretionary standard of review on any question relating to the incidence of the tax, and refused to examine the question on its merits.[17] The most that could be said for the tax is that the out-of-staters could have avoided it by not purchasing the coal. But that argument is a mark of

[15] See his dissents in *Tyler Pipe Indus.*, 483 U.S. at 254, and *Scheiner*, 483 U.S. at 303.

[16] 453 U.S. 609 (1981). For criticism, see Tribe, §6-15, characterizing the majority opinion as a retreat from the tests announced in *Complete Auto Transit Co.*, which indeed it is.

[17] 453 U.S. at 625–26: "The relevant inquiry under the fourth prong of the *Complete Auto Transit* test is not, as appellants suggest, the *amount* of the tax or the *value* of the benefits alleged bestowed, as measured by the costs the State incurs on account of the taxpayer's activities. Rather, the test is closely connected to the first prong of the *Complete Auto Transit* test." The remark essentially obliterates the fourth prong of the test, which is directed to the preservation of the pre-tax division of surplus.

desperation. The task here is to develop an optimal set of taxation rules, and not to show how individual parties can mitigate their losses under the inferior taxation rules that are in place.

The mischief that is worked by *Commonwealth Edison* suggests the importance of finding tests to control against these forms of local abuse. The question, therefore, is whether it is possible to develop some additional guidelines that allow for the implementation of the nondiscrimination norm at an acceptable administrative cost. It is possible here to suggest two such approaches, each of which helps to achieve the correct result, both of which have analogues in the just compensation law under the takings clause. The first of these approaches is substantive, and is organized around two doctrinal points: disparate impact and the so-called "internal consistency" test, both of which reach the same result by slightly different but complementary routes. The second concerns the question of whether the discrimination found in one test may be offset by another.

## DISPARATE IMPACT AND INTERNAL CONSISTENCY

The application of these two tests is well illustrated by *American Trucking Ass'ns v. Scheiner*.[18] In *Scheiner* the state system of taxation involved a charge of $36 per axle for all vehicles that used Pennsylvania roads, regardless of the distances that they travelled.[19] As a formal matter, there was no discrimination in the axle tax, for domestic and foreign truckers were not called upon to pay different sums of money per axle. Accordingly it follows that Justice Scalia, who was concerned only with formal equality and judicial ease of administration, dissented and voted to sustain the tax. Looking more closely at the tax, however, a bare majority of the Court struck it down as unconstitutional.

The first point to note about the tax is that it differs in its consequences from another facially nondiscriminatory tax, namely one that charges so much per mile travelled within the state. The difference between the so-called flat tax (one fee for unlimited use) and the mileage tax (so much per mile) is that the former is a very poor proxy

[18] 483 U.S. 266 (1987).

[19] There are further complications ignored in the text because the overall registration fee for Pennsylvania trucks was lowered when the axle tax was introduced. See id. at 280. A second portion of the case involved the integration between the registration fee and the so-called marker charge. Apart from some complex factual questions, it raised the same flat tax issues (albeit in less- clear form) as the axle charge discussed in the case.

for either the total damage that the truck inflicts upon the road system (that is, the cost side of the equation), or the total gain that the truck derives from the use of the system (the benefit side of the equation). The mileage tax is clearly a better proxy for either side. Indeed, in the case at hand, the differential intensity of use was such that out-of-state truckers, who used the system in about the same amount as in-state drivers, were called upon to pay in excess of five-sixths of the total tax.[20] The purported justification for that result was that foreign carriers were "free to use the Commonwealth's highways as often and for whatever distances they wish," and therefore could not complain because they refused to avail themselves of Pennsylvania's generous offer.[21] But even if the marginal price for any additional use of the road system is zero, that further use will often not be forthcoming for, as the state well knows, the private costs to an out-of-state carrier (including high tolls) to use its roads may be so high as to render their use uneconomical. The offer is made on the confident ground that it will be refused by the parties to whom it is directed.

The choice of tax structures therefore has heavy influence on the distribution of the total costs of financing the system, and doubtless on the patterns of use of both local and foreign carriers. There is no question that if any explicit difference in tax had been incorporated into a use tax, it would have been struck down under the commerce clause. The question is why the tax chosen by Pennsylvania should pass muster given that it was structured to generate this same sort of rate differential. So long as it is possible to find easy measures of the disparate impact of the neutral tax, what is the objection to striking it down? The dangers the tax poses to the system of national trade are large, for we should expect this tax to foster both market and political distortions since the explicit forms of discrimination have both those effects. On the other side of the coin, the costs of controlling this particular abuse are low. Even the armchair empiricist can obtain the aggregate data that shows the massive imbalance induced by the tax. Nor does judicial invalidation pose any threat to the revenue position of the state, for at the very least, within the structure of a general-use tax it can choose whatever rates it wants, sufficient to cover the costs of running its system, wholly without regard to the rates that any other state (similarly bound by the same formula) chooses for its roads. If the sole goal of the legal system were to make

[20] Id. at 276.

[21] See id. at 279, rejecting the argument advanced by the Pennsylvania Supreme Court.

life simple for the judges, then courts should adopt the ostrich-like position of Justice Scalia and ignore the manifest improprieties that can be worked in the name of formal neutrality.

The same result can be reached by the internal consistency test that Justice Stevens invoked for the Court's five-vote majority. That test, reminiscent of the categorical norms of Immanuel Kant, provides that to pass constitutional muster "the tax must be such that, if applied in every jurisdiction, there would be no impermissible interference with free trade."[22] The word "impermissible" dulls the edge of the formulation, but should not be allowed to conceal its essential economic logic. At bottom what the test asks is this: assume that one state takes steps to maximize its revenues by a form of taxation. What would happen if all other states were to adopt the same strategy? In essence, therefore, we are asked to think in a game-theoretical way, and to ask what would happen if each state adopted the same strategy as the state whose tax is under examination. If the equilibrium that emerges is one that is consistent with the efficient operation of a competitive system across state lines, then it can resist a commerce clause challenge. If it is not, then the tax must fall. In essence the test asks the Court to determine the social desirability of an outcome in a noncooperative game.

Applying this test does not necessarily invalidate all taxes. As Justice Stevens perceptively notes in *Scheiner*, the internal consistency test allows each state to charge whatever fee it chooses for vehicles that it registers. Even if other states followed suit, there could be no differential impact because each vehicle would be subject to the tax only of a single state, and could (within limits) shop for that state which gave it the best deal. There is no degenerative equilibrium that allows the state to set the taxes as high or low as it wants. In contrast, the flat rate tax adopted by Pennsylvania flunks the internal consistency test. The test creates major distortions within the state of Pennsylvania, and these are *not* cancelled out if parallel distortions are introduced by other states that follow similar strategies. A trip from New York to California that goes through Pennsylvania and Ohio would be subject to two obstacles instead of one. Imitation of the Pennsylvania statute creates more holdouts along commercial paths and would drive us still further from the competitive equilibrium.

In essence, therefore, the internal consistency test leads to invalidation of the same tests that are struck down by viewing discrimina-

[22] Armco, Inc. v. Hardesty, 467 U.S. 638, 644 (1984), relying on Container Corp. of America v. Franchise Tax Board, 463 U.S. 159, 169 (1983).

tory taxes by their known and intended effects. The only difference is that the internal consistency approach takes an overview of the entire system while the disparate impact test looks at the impact of the rule on a single state in isolation. But the congruence between the tests seems complete. If the application of a test within a single state is the result of a negative-sum outcome, then its repetition will only increase the size of that negative. What the internal consistency test does, therefore, is to require that cumulative negative outcome be demonstrated anew in each case while the disparate impact test posits that the baleful effects of a single unsound practice will inevitably replicate themselves if undertaken on a nationwide scale.

The risks associated with state misbehavior under neutral taxes have not been uniformly perceived by the Court. Indeed Justice Stevens in his earlier decision in *Moorman Manufacturing Co. v. Bair*,[23] sustained a single-factored Iowa sales tax that appears to flunk not only the disproportionate impact test, but also the internal consistency tax that he subsequently championed in *Scheiner.* If a corporation operated within a single state, then all of its income could be taxed by that state, at whatever rates the state thought appropriate. But most corporations engage in transactions in many states, so the issue arises as to what system of apportionment should be used to allocate that income to the various states. In principle the ideal system of apportionment is one that assigns to each state some fraction of the profits corresponding to its economic activity, such that exactly 100 percent of the profits, no more and no less, are subject to state taxation. Once the apportionment has been neatly done, then each state can apply its own rate to that fraction of income that is fairly assigned to it.

When *Moorman* was decided, forty-six states (including the District of Columbia) imposed taxes on corporate income. Forty-four of those apportioned that income on a formula that took into account three elements: property of the corporation located within the state; payroll within the state; and sales within the state. Taken together these are a rough measure of the amount of economic activity concentrated in the state. Iowa for its part adopted only a single-factor test, namely sales within the state. An Illinois corporation challenged this single-factored test as unconstitutional under both the commerce and due process clauses. Justice Stevens upheld the tax by resort to two arguments. First, the tax on its face was neutral in that it did not subject the sales of foreign corporations to taxes higher

[23] 437 U.S. 267 (1978).

than those of local corporations. Second, for all one could say, any individual corporation might well have fared worse in Iowa under the three-part test than it did under the one-part test. Thus if manufacture in Illinois was extensive while sales in Iowa were small, then the Iowa rule would undertax this corporation relative to the standard three-part test.[24] So long as Iowa allows administrative deviations from its rule in the event of evident injustice, not shown here, the Supreme Court ought to stay its hand because there is not "clear and cogent evidence" of abuse.[25]

The case is one, however, in which the four dissenters, led by Justice Powell, had much the stronger arguments. There are three great advantages to the three-part test which were ignored by the Court. First, by taking into account multiple factors, it is more difficult for any state to choose that neutral form of tax that results in a disproportionate burden being placed on any outsider. Second, the use of this formula by virtually all states eliminates the prospect of inconsistent determinations of the appropriate level of taxes, and thus insures that each firm is taxed on no more, and no less, than 100 percent of its net profit position. Third, the uniform formula does not impose any constraint on the total level of revenues that a state can raise, since states retain complete freedom to raise or lower the rates on net profits for local and foreign corporations alike.

Sustaining the tax, for its part, runs afoul of both the disparate impact and the internal consistency tests. With regard to the first, it seems clear that any state will choose to deviate from the collective norm only if it believes that it can externalize some fraction of its cost. There is no reason to assume that the choice of formula is unrelated to its aggregate consequences, and Justice Stevens, by dwelling on the confused particulars of any individual case, necessarily slights the built-in bias of the general rule. Here that bias is pronounced, for as Justice Powell points out in his dissent, the use of a sales-only tax base "though facially neutral—operates as a tariff on goods manufactured in other States and as a subsidy to Iowa manufacturers selling their goods outside of Iowa."[26] Constitutional invalidation prevents these machinations from taking place without a case-by-case demonstration of the effects that local protectionism has on local policy. And the judicial intervention itself is unlikely to be the source of any new mischief, for the "safe harbor" created by the standard three-part test allows Iowa to reach whatever revenue target it chooses by changing the applicable taxing rate.

[24] See id. at 276.
[25] Id. at 274.
[26] 437 U.S. at 283.

In addition, the outcome in *Moorman* runs afoul of the internal consistency test used to good effect in *Scheiner*. Suppose that all states decided to follow the lead of Iowa and turn to the single-part test. The tariff barriers that are put in place by Iowa will not thereby be eliminated or neutralized. Other states may be encouraged to follow Iowa's lead, compounding the original allocative errors. It may well be quite impossible for any court to decree that a three-part test for allocating income across states should be applied when no states have adopted that test. But when some well-functioning system of taxation is already in place, then the Supreme Court should take steps, even constitutional steps, to insure that the favorable equilibrium obtained, whether by constitutional design or by good fortune, is not threatened or destroyed by the unilateral action of a single state. The logic of *Scheiner* extends beyond cases concerned with interstate taxation to any question of coordination between independent states within a federal system.

## COMPENSATING TAXES

There is a second state strategy for implementing a program of discriminatory taxation that should also be countered by constitutional rule. Sometimes a state will impose many separate types of taxes that, by design, do not mesh perfectly with each other. In deciding whether a particular tax imposes a discriminatory burden, the question arises whether its impermissible consequences should be offset or cancelled by those of some other tax whose effective discrimination runs in the opposite direction. Thus if Tax A discriminates against foreign business, should that tax be allowed because Tax B discriminates in its favor?

The question here is one that has antecedents elsewhere in the law. In chapter 8, I argued that it was a mistake to allow states to offer clever justifications for the imposition of taxes that were overtly discriminatory. In *Takings*, I argued that suspect social programs should not be saved by taking a "step transaction" view of the situation, that is, one which refused to look at each program in isolation, but was prepared to treat the gains associated with one legislative program as an offset for those imposed by a second independent one. The upshot would be that both the programs together could pass muster, even when either of them standing alone would fail under a disproportionate impact test.[27] The argument is the same as that developed here. Each of the programs in isolation creates a nega-

[27] See *Takings*, 209–10.

tive-sum game. It is impossible for courts to decide the size of the gains and losses generated by each program in isolation, even though its discriminatory impact is well-nigh conclusive evidence of some legislative miscarriage leading to an overall resource imperfection. Courts, in other words, have knowledge which allows them to determine whether legislation in isolation has a *positive* or *negative* effect but, given the limitations of their role, they have insufficient knowledge to determine the magnitude of these effects. Any rule that allows the state to link one program with another increases the likelihood of some overall abuse.

The potential abuses from linking distinct programs arises as much with the preservation of social surplus as it does with the basic just-compensation requirement. Fortunately, some judicial decisions are alert to the implicit perils of the set-off argument. In *Armco, Inc. v. Hardesty,*[28] West Virginia imposed a gross receipts tax of 0.27 percent on products manufactured outside the state and sold within it, but not on those which were both produced and sold within the state. The gross receipts tax on its face was discriminatory, because it applied only to out-of-state goods, but West Virginia sought to justify it by claiming that it imposed a "compensatory tax" of 0.88 percent on products manufactured and sold within the state. The Supreme Court refused to accept this justification: "Manufacturing frequently entails selling in the State, but we cannot say which portion of the manufacturing tax is attributable to manufacturing, and which portion to sales."[29] There is little burden and much abuse by having imperfect parallels between two taxes on the same activity. There is little difficulty in having West Virginia organize its affairs to provide that one tax applies to manufacture and another to sales, so that a court can then be sure that no discrimination between local and foreign producers has occurred. The task of overseeing taxes can be severely eased by forcing states to develop and justify their accounts separately, and it can be done at no revenue cost to the state, which is left free to determine the taxes as it sees fit. The refusal to allow the offsets therefore places needed teeth in the antidiscrimination principle, without imposing undue burdens on the state.

The dangers of state abuse, however, call for a very different attitude when the step transaction argument is used to *attack* legislation that has been enacted by the state. Here the adjustments in one tax by the state may often furnish strong evidence of a system-

[28] 467 U.S. 638 (1984).
[29] Id. at 643.

atic effort to force foreign persons to bear a disproportionate fraction of local expenses. The asymmetry of approach is necessary to counter the first-mover advantage that the state has in passing local taxation laws. In this regard the position is no different from that applicable in ordinary tax matters where the Internal Revenue Service is given the opportunity to recharacterize transactions to prevent tax abuse, even though the taxpayer must normally live or die with the transaction as it was originally structured. The power of evasion and abuse lies with those who structure local taxes or private business deals, and recharacterization evidence may help identify the abuse.

The pattern, moreover, is present in many of the interstate taxes that are raised before the courts. One aspect of *Scheiner* not previously discussed involved the reduction in state registration fees, usually applicable to local vehicles, at the same time that Pennsylvania imposed its axle taxes.[30] The reduction in registration fees, which inured only to local truckers, was a strong sign that the overall package of fees and taxes was skewed against outside interests, and that evidence only strengthened an already sufficient case against the tax. Similarly, in *Commonwealth Edison* it was noteworthy that Montana repealed its state income tax at the same time that it increased its severance tax. The combination of the two shows the sustained effort to shift the costs of local governance to outsiders and likewise strengthens an already sufficient case against the tax.

There are, in short, good and powerful reasons why discriminatory taxes against outsiders should be routinely struck down by the Court. The case is especially strong in the context of federalism, for there is no nagging question of income and wealth distribution that is said to justify, for example, progressive taxation within the state. Likewise, there is little reason to believe that out-of-state interests will have sufficient political clout to prevent local protectionism from running rampant within individual states. So long as each state has some monopoly power over firms that must do business in many states to survive, it is not a sufficient answer to say that those firms who do not like the tax need simply pull up stakes and move elsewhere. The exit option, however valuable, is not a sufficient defense against the misallocations that self-interested states can pursue in a regime devoid of constitutional constraints.

[30] *Scheiner*, 483 U.S. at 271: "In 1982, the registration fees for vehicles weighing more than 26,000 pounds (classes 9–25) were reduced by multiples of $36 ranging up to a $180 reduction; thereafter the maximum fee was $945."

There is today, unfortunately, some question whether the level of scrutiny of state taxation which is found in *Scheiner* and *Armco* represents the current attitude of the Supreme Court or whether it will survive the change in the composition of the Court. There are enormous crosscurrents so long as *Commonwealth Edison* and *Moorman* stand testament to how the state may be beguiled by facial neutrality; and the Court's 1991 decision in *Ford Motor Credit Co. v. Florida Department of Revenue*[31] hints that the internal consistency test may yet be on the way out as well.

Before the Court jettisons one of the few bodies of judge-made law that has worked well, it should bear these points in mind. The antidiscrimination norm is directed against a set of evils that it is worthwhile to prevent, even if certain clever stratagems are likely to escape its reach. The repeated use of that doctrine is also certain to create glitches and anomalies in its application that are hard to defend or explain[32]—accretions that are part and parcel of every set of principles that are tested in the crucible of litigation. But these criticisms have to be kept in perspective. The overall social evaluation should not concentrate on judicial foibles, much less on those that are capable of correction. It should be based upon the major evils that the test has prevented. The antidiscrimination test should not be disparaged for its imperfections. It should be preserved for the good it has done, and can continue to do.

[31] 111 S. Ct. 2049 (1991).

[32] See, e.g., the impressive list in Shaviro, supra note 7. These include inconsistent standards of judicial review; inconsistent accounts of facial neutrality; different assumptions of judicial competence to render decisions; and different allocations of burdens of proof.

CHAPTER 10

# The United States v. the States

THE MATERIAL covered in chapters 8 and 9 examined the bargaining problems between states and the individuals or corporations that wish to gain access to their markets. In this chapter I extend that analysis to deal with the separate side of federalism, the relationship between the United States and the individual states. This issue was of far greater moment before the constitutional transformation of 1937, for the then-continued validity of the enumerated powers doctrine placed effective limits on the power of the central government to regulate the affairs left within the control of the several states. The political pressures that once led Congress to seek direct regulation of local state affairs did not disappear after these efforts were struck down as falling outside the scope of the commerce clause. Other strategies to achieve the same ends were still available. Could Congress by a combination of taxation and contract achieve what it could not do by direct legislation? This entire question required courts to scrutinize the use of federal taxes to insure that their imposition did not disturb the constitutional balance of power between central government and that of the states. In this area the unconstitutional conditions doctrine has had an important role to play.

That taxation and coercion should go hand in hand is of course a point of no surprise. As is well known, taxation serves two functions. In cases of market failure, it can raise the revenues necessary to purchase public goods, such as national defense, which if supplied to one person privately must be supplied to all who benefit from it. Taxation is necessary for the service to be provided at all, and political opposition is the greatest degree of freedom that can be accorded to those who oppose either the purpose of the expenditure (e.g., pacifists) or its magnitude. More ominously, however, taxation is an effective way for governments to secure implicit transfers of both wealth and power between interest groups. These transfers can be implemented by imposing higher rates on some persons, granting exemptions to others, or by imposing conditions on the collection of taxes or on the grants of exemptions. The potential abuses in the taxing power are well captured by Chief Justice Marshall's famous dictum that the "power to tax involves the power to destroy."[1] If this tendency had been countered by a broad reading of the takings clause, then all selective taxes, exemptions, preferences, and conditions would be struck down as impermissible redistributions unless supported by a narrow police power justification.[2] But even before the 1937 constitutional watershed, the Court had taken a far more relaxed view of matters of selective taxation than Chief Justice Marshall's dictum might suggest is appropriate.[3] Only when taxation has been tied, not to individual rights, but to the distribution of power within the federal system has this pattern of judicial deference been broken. I shall address the use of the unconstitutional conditions doctrine to limit Congress's power to regulate the states under the taxing and spending powers, both as they existed before 1937 and, in far less important form, today.[4] I shall postpone a discussion of unconstitutional conditions and tax policy in the areas of individual liberties until Part Four.

## PRE-1937 CASES

In the *Child Labor Tax Case*,[5] Congress imposed a tax equal to 10 percent of the profits of any firm that employed child labor in certain specified businesses.[6] The tax imposed in this case raises the paradox of unconstitutional conditions in the following fashion: Congress

[1] McCulloch v. Maryland, 17 U.S. (4 Wheat) 316, 431 (1819).

[2] See generally *Takings*, 283–305 (applying takings analysis to taxation).

[3] See, e.g., McCray v. United States, 195 U.S. 27 (1904) (upholding a tax that discriminated against yellow margarine in favor of white margarine); Alaska Fish Salting & By-Products Co. v. Smith, 255 U.S. 44 (1921) (upholding a tax on fish produce that discriminated against the use of herrings); A. Magnano Co. v. Hamilton, 292 U.S. 40 (1934) (upholding a tax on butter substitutes alleged to discriminate against the oleo industry). The tendency continues apace today. See United States v. Ptasynski, 462 U.S. 74 (1983) (sustaining a windfall-profit tax on crude oil that contained a geographically defined exemption for certain Alaskan producers).

[4] For the most recent comprehensive account of the doctrine, see Albert J. Rosenthal, "Conditional Federal Spending and the Constitution," 39 *Stan. L. Rev.* 1103 (1987).

[5] 259 U.S. 20 (1922).

[6] Persons under the age of 16 were not to be employed in mines and quarries. Persons under 14 were not to be employed in mills, canneries, workshops, factories, or manufacturing establishments. Persons between 14 and 16 could be employed in such outfits only if they worked fewer than a prescribed number of hours. The statute also provided protections to employers who hired underage workers in good faith. See Title XII, Revenue Act of 1918, ch. 18, Pub. L. No. 65-254, 40 Stat. 1138, 1138–39 (1919).

has the power to impose a general income tax equal to 10 percent of the profits of any business; why, then, does this greater power not entail the lesser power to forgive selectively that tax payment to anyone who chooses not to employ certain forms of child labor?

The answer lies in the persistent concern over the distribution of power between the state and federal governments, and not in any concern with the desirability of child labor laws in themselves. The question of whether child labor statutes are justified depends in part on whether parents are faithful agents of their children, which in some instances they are not. But by the same token, the state may not be a perfect agent of children either, and the restrictions on child labor could well have passed with anticompetitive motivations in mind. As a matter of first principle, one might want a federal statute in this area if it were thought that parents were dubious guardians of their children, state governments inadequate substitutes, and federal regulators both better informed and motivated. But before 1937 that option was foreclosed, since the commerce clause was universally understood to confer upon Congress no power to regulate the "internal affairs" of the states. *Hammer v. Dagenhart*[7] had struck down a federal statute that forbade the shipment of goods in interstate commerce from any plant that had used prohibited forms of child labor, whether or not that labor was used on the goods shipped. *Hammer* treated the regulation as invading the reserved powers of the states as delineated under the Tenth Amendment to the Constitution:[8] "The powers not delegated to the United States by the Constitution, nor prohibited by it to the States, are reserved to the States respectively, or to the people."[9]

Although it was explicitly overruled in *United States v. Darby*,[10] I believe that *Hammer* was correctly decided,[11] for reasons that rest on the doctrine of unconstitutional conditions.[12] The ability to regulate the shipment of goods in interstate commerce is tantamount to holding vast monopoly power over all the means of transportation—highways, rails, sea, and, today, air. In essence the federal government in *Hammer* tried to use its monopoly power to extract concessions from private firms to conduct their manufacturing and mining operations in accordance with standards set by Congress at a time

[7] 247 U.S. 251 (1918).

[8] See id. at 274–76.

[9] U.S. Const. amend. X.

[10] 312 U.S. 100, 116–17 (1941).

[11] See generally Richard A. Epstein, "The Proper Scope of the Commerce Clause," 73 *Va. L. Rev.* 1387, 1427–32 (1987).

[12] See id. at 1423–24 & 1429 n.109.

when it was conceded that Congress could not set standards for local employment by direct regulation.[13] The ability to close down all modes of interstate transportation threatened to work an enormous redistribution of wealth from firms that were unwilling to comply with the restrictions to firms that were not. The statute in *Hammer* certainly had nothing to do with covering the costs of operating the interstate transportation system. If a robust form of either the takings or public trust doctrine had been applied to highways, this restriction itself would have been found invalid, wholly without regard to the commerce clause, because of its disparate impact on the rights of individual citizens: some would have gained enormously from the use of public roads, while others would have had huge portions of their gains stripped from them. But these individual rights arguments would have failed even in 1918, because the prevailing account of the police power gave broad latitude to the states to impose child labor laws.[14]

Nonetheless, because concerns of federalism were very much alive at the time of *Hammer*, a transfer of power from the state to the federal government was subject to far greater scrutiny. The effect of the child labor restriction on the interstate shipment of goods, a subject admittedly within the scope of the federal commerce power, was to induce all private firms to abide by the federal regulation. The gains that any firm achieved from the interstate sale of its goods were far greater than the gains it could hope to achieve by hiring child labor in violation of the federal statute, especially in light of the applicable state restrictions. To enforce the statute, then, was necessarily to bring about a "voluntary" acceptance of federal power. The doctrine of unconstitutional conditions is the necessary counterweight to the federal government's exercise of its monopoly power. Congress has the greater power to regulate interstate commerce and indeed to prohibit certain items from passing in interstate commerce at all.[15] But in this instance, the greater power should not

[13] For another case concerned with the balance of state and federal power, see United States v. E. C. Knight Co., 156 U.S. 1 (1895). I have defended that decision in Epstein, supra note 11, at 1432–35.

[14] Cf. New York Cent. R.R. v. White, 243 U.S. 188, 207 (1917) (recognizing state authority under the police power to enact workmen's compensation laws). All states did have child labor laws in 1917, so that the issue in *Hammer* was whether the more stringent federal standard was preferable to the lower state standard applicable in North Carolina. See Epstein, supra note 11, at 1430–33.

[15] See, e.g., Champion v. Ames, 188 U.S. 321 (1903) (lottery tickets); Hipolite Egg Co. v. United States, 220 U.S. 45 (1911) (adulterated foods). It seems clear that the power to regulate under the commerce clause allows Congress to prohibit the transfer of certain goods in interstate commerce, such as infected foods that threaten inter-

include the power to admit goods into interstate commerce subject to conditions that drastically shift the distribution of power within the federal system. *Hammer* reached the right result in striking down this statute while leaving the federal government the power to regulate the instrumentalities of interstate commerce with regard to matters pertaining directly to their use: the weight of certain shipments and the like, which are designed to prevent abuse of common assets by private users.[16]

The *Child Labor Tax Case*[17] raises the identical federalism issue as did *Hammer*, as Chief Justice Taft well understood. The only difference is that in the *Child Labor Tax Case* the federal government sought to condition its coercive powers to tax instead of its coercive power to regulate interstate commerce. The offer made was one that no firm could refuse, given that the marginal gains from using child labor in violation of the federal norm were no doubt far smaller than the 10 percent tax on profits imposed by the statute. If this tax could have been applied, then similar taxes, with higher rates if necessary, could have been used repeatedly, thus obliterating any limitation on federal power. Chief Justice Taft tried to capture these concerns in the proposition that the federal government had the power to impose "taxes" but not "penalties" upon activities within the states.[18]

The language of penalty is troublesome, however, because taxes are as coercive as penalties, given that both are backed by the use of force. The effort to distinguish between them is designed to cast the case back into the familiar libertarian mode in which only force and fraud can set aside bargains, a model that is inadequate because it does not take into account all of the risks associated with government discretion. An account of the line between penalties and taxes might delve into matters of motive—was the exaction designed to raise revenue, or to discourage primary activity, or to do both? Generally, one may conclude that a tax has some ulterior motive if its expected revenues are zero, as was the case with the child labor tax. But whether we call this exaction a tax or a penalty is quite beside

---

state commerce itself. But it is far more doubtful, even in these cases, that Congress can either regulate or prohibit the shipment of goods in interstate commerce in an indirect effort to seize the police power that each state exercises within its own territory. See Epstein, supra note 11, at 1422–25.

[16] See infra chap. 11, describing conditions intended to minimize abuse of public highways.

[17] 259 U.S. 20 (1922).

[18] See id. at 38–39.

the point. The federal power to tax can be used to the same end as its monopoly position over the public highways: to frame offers that extract a disproportionate share of the gain from some firms engaged in interstate commerce. Because this was the case with the child labor tax, it should have been struck down, even if someone could have argued that the penalty characterization was somehow mistaken.[19] The greater power to impose a 10 percent tax on all profits does not threaten the system of enumerated powers the way the "lesser" power to tax selectively does.

## POST-1937 CASES

Today, with the passing of *Hammer*, the issue in both child labor cases is moot. Since 1937, Congress has been acknowledged to have plenary powers of regulation over all aspects of the economy. Thus, what Congress was barred from achieving by indirection in *Hammer* and the *Child Labor Tax Case*, it can now achieve through direct regulation without constitutional impediment. Likewise under the Sixteenth Amendment, virtually all constitutional impediments to the federal taxing power have vanished as well.

One exception to Congress's plenary economic regulatory power, however, concerns the powers given to the states under the Twenty-first Amendment, which provides: "The transportation or importation into any State, Territory, or possession of the United States for delivery or use therein of intoxicating liquors, in violation of the laws thereof, is hereby prohibited."[20] On the plausible assumption that this amendment reserves to the states the exclusive power over

[19] The decision to strike down this tax lends support to Madison's construction of the "spending power," which authorizes Congress "to pay the Debts and provide for the common Defence and general Welfare of the United States." U.S. Const. art. I, §8, cl. 1. Madison read the clause to authorize Congress to spend only for those purposes that fell within the other enumerated powers of Article I, section 8. See United States v. Butler, 297 U.S. 1, 65 (1936). *Butler*, however, rejected the Madisonian view in favor of Hamilton's and Story's construction, which allowed any expenditure that advanced the general welfare of the United States, without regard to whether it fell into the enumerated powers.

In the *Child Labor Tax Case* the government could have argued that the power to tax for the "general welfare of the United States" covered more territory than the commerce clause and could certainly include the protection of young workers across the United States. The failure of this argument makes sense only if the general welfare is limited to the other enumerated powers, which must have been Chief Justice Taft's assumption when he linked this case so closely with *Hammer*.

[20] U.S. Const. amend. XXI, §2.

the transportation and shipment of intoxicating liquors within their borders, there would remain, even after the revolution of 1937, an area of commerce within the exclusive power of the states.

Nonetheless, in *South Dakota v. Dole*,[21] the Court held by a 7 to 2 vote that Congress could work a statutory end run around the Twenty-first Amendment. At issue in the case was title 23, section 158 of the United States Code, which allowed the Secretary of Transportation to withhold up to 5 percent of the otherwise allocable federal funds for highway construction from states "in which the purchase or public possession . . . of any alcoholic beverage by a person who is less than twenty-one years of age is lawful."[22] South Dakota's law allowed 19-year-olds to purchase 3.2 percent beer. Chief Justice Rehnquist sustained the statutory scheme. In his view, even if the Twenty-first Amendment prohibited Congress from directly regulating the age of beer drinking, Congress could do so indirectly through the use of its spending power.

Chief Justice Rehnquist's opinion is unsatisfying. The Court noted the many occasions on which Congress had been able to attach conditions to the receipt of federal funds.[23] Where such conditions do not involve any efforts by Congress to expand its effective power, however, these provisions are easily distinguishable.[24] Where the conditions involve powers reserved to the states under the Tenth Amendment, the Court has traditionally required that the federal government show a sufficiently compelling interest to override the state interest.[25] The danger that Congress will leverage its broad

[21] 483 U.S. 203 (1987).

[22] 23 U.S.C. §158(a)(1) (Supp. III 1985). The 5 percent restriction was for fiscal year 1986; for succeeding years the figure was 10 percent. See id. §158(a)(2).

[23] See 483 U.S. at 206–7

[24] See, e.g., Fullilove v. Klutznick, 448 U.S. 448 (1980) (upholding against an equal protection challenge a requirement that recipients of federal contracting grants set aside a certain portion of those grants for minority-owned subcontracting companies); Lau v. Nichols, 414 U.S. 563 (1974) (holding that a school system is required under the 1964 Civil Rights Act to offer remedial help to Chinese students who do not speak English as a condition of receipt of federal assistance).

[25] See, e.g., Oklahoma v. Civil Serv. Comm'n, 330 U.S. 127, 143 (1947). The applicable statute there provided that: "[N]o officer or employee of any State or local agency whose principal employment is in connection with any activity which is financed in whole or in part by loans or grants made by the United States or by any Federal agency shall . . . take any active part in political management or in political campaigns." Hatch Act, ch. 410, 53 Stat. 1147 (1939), amended by Act of July 19, 1940, 54 Stat. 767 (1940). The Supreme Court, relying on the broad reading given the commerce power in United States v. Darby, 312 U.S. 100, 124 (1941), sustained the statute on the ground that the Tenth Amendment is a truism. See 330 U.S. at 143. The case is far harder if the Tenth Amendment is construed as an effective limitation on federal

spending powers to subvert the Twenty-first Amendment is as great as the danger that it will leverage its power to subvert the Tenth Amendment, and should be met with the same judicial response. The state, in its effort to decide whether or not to accept the condition, has to decide whether it values the loss in federal revenues more than it values its own independence in setting the minimum age for liquor consumption. In principle, if Congress has the power to reduce highway revenues to the states by 5 or 10 percent, there is no reason why it could not exclude any state from participation in the program by cutting off its revenues entirely.[26] South Dakota must continue to pay the same level of taxes, even though the money it contributes is diverted to other states. The offer of assistance is not an isolated transaction, but must (as with the thief who will resell stolen goods to its true owner) be nested in its larger coercive context. The situation in *Dole* is scarcely distinguishable from one in which Congress says that it will impose a tax of *x* percent on a state that does not comply with its alcohol regulations—a rule that is wholly inconsistent with the preservation of any independent domain of state power. The grant of discretion, therefore, allows the federal government to redistribute revenues, raised by taxes across the nation, from those states that wish to assert their independence under the Twenty-first Amendment, to those states that do not.

Chief Justice Rehnquist conceded in effect that the doctrine of unconstitutional conditions had to apply to the spending power when he noted that

> [A] grant of federal funds conditioned on invidiously discriminatory state action or the infliction of cruel and unusual punishment would be an illegitimate exercise of the Congress' broad spending power. But no

---

power. This particular statute should be sustained against the challenge of unconstitutional conditions because it is designed to protect the United States against abuses by recipients of federal moneys. It is therefore parallel to a rule preventing private parties from obstructing public highways. The case would be quite different, however, if the statute provided that all state officials had to abide by this restriction if any state program received federal moneys. Then the overreaching by the federal government would become the greater abuse. This "relatedness" requirement as a limitation on the scope of conditions that the federal government may impose also crops up in the police power cases, see infra chaps. 11–13, and the employment cases, see infra chap. 16

26 See, e.g., State of Nevada v. Skinner, 884 F.2d 445 (9th Cir. 1989), upholding those provisions of the Highway Act which allowed the cut-off of 95 percent of federal funds to state highway systems that did not post a maximum speed limit of 55 miles per hour.

> such claim can be or is made here. Were South Dakota to succumb to the blandishments offered by Congress and raise its drinking age to 21, the State's action in so doing would not violate the constitutional rights of anyone.[27]

His defense, however, misses the essential point because the doctrine of unconstitutional conditions is not limited to the protection of individual rights against encroachment by government power. So long as the Twenty-first Amendment imposes structural limitations upon federal power, the doctrine of unconstitutional conditions should ensure that these limitations as well are not overridden by the vast discretionary power of the federal government over the distribution of its general revenues. The need to control federal power is not limited to cases of common law coercion, given the risks of strategic behavior so evident in *Dole*. As with the *Child Labor Tax Case*, the relevant question is not the desirability of the regulations the federal government seeks indirectly to impose. It is rather the proper demarcation of the division of powers between separate sovereigns.

The matter here can be usefully contrasted with that applicable to the taxation and regulation by one state, of businesses and activities in another. Each state had some monopoly power with respect to the other states, and it was the use of that power that called forth the application of the judicial limitations on state power. In this context, however, no state has a blocking power with respect to either the federal government or indeed any other state. In this context, therefore, the independence of the states does promote the competition between governments that is the cardinal virtue of a federal system of government. The imposition of the blanket federal power uses the combination of taxing and spending power to subvert that goal. As the source of the peril of monopoly power shifts, so too should the nature of the applicable doctrines.

The point is, moreover, of special importance in connection with the general regulation of state governments. With the inexorable expansion of the federal commerce power, there is little question that virtually any form of individual activity can be subject to federal regulation. The residual legal battles are only over the question of whether the federal government may control the internal operation of state governments. On this issue there are three possible positions. The first is that state sovereigns, as coequals in the constitutional order, are entitled to be free of direct regulation of their inter-

[27] 483 U.S. 210–11.

nal affairs by the federal government. The imposition, therefore, of a minimum wage law, for example, to state employees should not be within the power of the United States. The second position is that these federal regulations may be imposed on the state, so long as parallel restrictions are imposed on private parties analogously situated.[28] Under this view, the United States may extend the minimum wage to state employees so long as the same law is applied to private employees. There is no absolute state immunity from federal regulation; only the benefit of a nondiscrimination clause. A third possible position is that the federal government may select state governments out for special regulations not imposed on private parties.

In practice the third of these alternatives has not received much scrutiny, and the battle has always been between the first two, on which there has been much well-known equivocation. The Supreme Court first crafted for state governments a limited immunity from federal regulation in *National League of Cities v. Usery*,[29] for those functions that were said to be "essential to [their] separate and independent existence,"[30] such as choosing a capital city. The Court then applied this principle to invalidate the extension on the minimum wage law to state and government workers. During the next nine years, the Supreme Court never applied *National League of Cities*, and, after its rocky career, the case was in the end overruled in *Garcia v. San Antonio Metropolitan Transit Authority*,[31] which held that the federal government could extend the protection of the Age Discrimination in Employment Act to employees of state governments. No longer is the Supreme Court prepared to identify some functions essential for the preservation of the independence of the states. The matter has by degrees become a political one: states are able to maintain their structural independence only where they can exert political influence to persuade Congress to stay its regulatory hand.[32]

[28] See, e.g., New York v. United States, 326 U.S. 572 (1946), holding that a tax that applied only to the states was impermissible, but upholding a nondiscriminatory tax on bottled mineral waters that applied to states and private parties alike.

[29] 426 U.S. 833 (1976).

[30] Id. at 845.

[31] 469 U.S. 528 (1985). The decline of *National League of Cities* is traced in Tribe, *American Constitutional Law*, §5-22 (2d ed. 1987).

[32] As urged by Justice Blackmun, 469 U.S. at 546. That position has been taken up in Martha A. Field, "*Garcia v. San Antonio Metropolitan Transit Authority*: The Demise of a Misguided Doctrine," 99 *Harv. L. Rev.* 84 (1985). See, for earlier expressions of the same view, Jesse H. Choper, *Judicial Review and the National Political Process* (1980); Herbert Wechsler, "The Political Safeguards of Federalism: The Role of the States in the Composition and Selection of the National Government," 54 *Colum. L. Rev.* 543 (1954).

With the decline of *National League of Cities*, there appears to be no room left for the application of the unconstitutional conditions doctrine. Where the federal government may compel the state by direct regulation, then it should have the like power to do so by grant and by bargain as well. Thus if the federal government can order states to implement extensive programs with respect to their employees or the environment, then it should have comparable power to offer to pay the states some portion of the cost of defraying these programs as well. Any uneasiness about using conditional grants does not rest on the unconstitutional conditions doctrine, but on the prior decision to confer on the federal government the untrammeled power to regulate the business of states as states. So once these have been quieted, the doctrine looks moribund in the modern context.

The case law subsequent to *Dole* has borne out this result. Various challenges to the federal government's power to use conditional spending to regulate highway use have been sternly rebuffed. The ostensible coercion theory has been explicitly rejected, first, on the ground that there is no clear theory that explains why a 5 percent cutoff is not coercive but a 95 percent cutoff is,[33] and second, on the ground that the difficult issue in *Dole* does not arise when the federal government has unexceptionable power under the commerce clause to impose the 55-mile-per-hour speed limit on all highways including those that are not part of the interstate highway system as such.[34]

The only case in which the coercion arguments appear to have prevailed is *Clarke v. United States*,[35] where the question before the court concerned the constitutionality of the so-called Armstrong Amendment, passed as part of the 1989 District of Columbia Appropriations Act.[36] That amendment was addressed to the City Council of the District of Columbia, a legislative body that had been created by Congress for the governance of the District. The amendment did not simply override the District's statute that prohibited discrimination against gays and lesbians, as Congress was entitled to do. Rather it took the ostensibly lesser step of requiring a cutoff of all funds appropriated to the District of Columbia if its legislative body, the City Council of the District of Columbia, did not pass corrective legislation that allowed religious institutions to not recognize or

[33] See State of Nevada v. Skinner, 884 F.2d 445, 458 (9th Cir. 1989).

[34] Id. at 450.

[35] 886 F.2d 404 (D.C. Cir. 1989), mooted in 915 F.2d 699 (D.C. Cir. 1990), with the expiration of the last extension of the Appropriations Act.

[36] Pub. L. No. 100-462, 102 Stat. 2269 (1988).

support any organization "promoting, encouraging, or condoning any homosexual act, lifestyle or orientation, or belief."[37]

Judge Edwards struck down that action on the ground that "[u]nless and until Congress restructures District government to divest the Council of its legislative functions, it must respect the broad First Amendment rights" of Council members, in this instance the right to vote in accordance with their conscience and belief.[38] His decision was made easier because the government did not argue that the refusal to fund was not coercive, even though there is no duty on Congress to make any appropriation to the District at all. Instead, with the fact of coercion conceded, Judge Edwards held that the level of coercion imposed upon the members of the Council was so great that this part of the Appropriations Act had to be invalidated under First Amendment principles.

Judge Edwards's reasoning thus returns the question of degree to center stage and ignores the powers that Congress can exercise over the District. The issue of monopoly power cannot be critical to the outcome of this case, because that power is conceded to the Congress, which was under no obligation to create any institutions of self-governance within the District. If anything, the Council's ability to stand up to the Congress should be smaller than that of the states, for the states do have independent status under the Constitution even though the District does not. *Clarke* therefore should be regarded as something of a sport, and not as the sign of any judicial retreat from the dominance of Congress over the states. The broad reach of the commerce power allows Congress a royal road to condition its expenditures as it sees fit.

Although the basic pattern of the cases is both clear and inexorable, it has been accepted with discomfort even by academics who are sympathetic to the rise of federal power. Writing shortly after *National League of Cities* became law, Professor Lewis Kaden[39] expressed his uneasiness about the range of federal programs to which conditions were attached and the nature of the conditions so attached. He specifically identified the Urban Mass Transporta-

[37] The D.C. Human Rights Act, enacted by the Council, made it illegal for religious institutions to discriminate against gays and lesbians. The Act had been the subject of litigation in Gay Rights Coalition v. Georgetown University 536 A.2d 1 (D.C. 1987). That case upheld the right of the university under the free exercise clause not to "recognize" gay organizations, but upheld the Act insofar as it required Georgetown to provide gay students equal access to university's and facilities.

[38] *Clarke*, 886 F.2d at 410.

[39] "Politics, Money, and State Sovereignty: The Judicial Role," 79 *Colum. L. Rev.* 847, 871–83 (1979).

tion Act,[40] which allows states to participate in mass transit programs only if they adopt rules to ensure that "fair and equitable arrangements" are made to protect the interests of employees. These rules and regulations have been interpreted to require, for example, that states accord workers covered by these programs rights to bargain collectively even if these workers are otherwise denied these rights under local law.[41] Kaden then offered other examples of grant programs, ranging from highway beautification, to handicap assistance, to Medicaid grants and health planning, in which conditions were imposed on the internal structures of state governments that received the grants in question. All these challenges were unavailing for one reason or another—with a trend too clear to be mistakable. Kaden's uneasiness had become a lament by 1987 when Professor Rosenthal returned to the same issue after the demise of *National League of Cities*, but he too was frustrated by a similar inability to articulate workable principles for restraining federal power.[42] But whatever his sentiments, it is clear that with *Dole*, decided after he wrote, any constitutional challenges to the conditions attached to federal grants are hopeless under the current law.

But it is a pity nonetheless. Where the federal government uses tax revenues to control the power of the states, it substitutes its monopoly power for the very diverse responses of the states to common problems. The argument for diversification seems strong here because the independent course followed by individual states does not seem to create local monopolies which wise federal regulation might prevent. (Ironically the issues on which local monopolies are a real concern, such as land use planning, are cases where federal conditions do not touch state power.) But once the fatal leap was made with the expansion of the commerce clause in 1937, the continuing decline in state autonomy became but a footnote to history. The question of implied state immunity from federal regulation could not have arisen under the original view of the commerce clause that limited the reach of the clause to trade between the states. State governments do not run trading companies. But once all productive activities became swallowed under the clause, the states could not create a clear, implied immunity which allowed them to escape direct regulation and control. And where these are allowed as a matter of force, so too must conditional grants. If the national government can regulate the states with a free hand, then, alas, it can bargain with them with a free hand as well.

[40] 49 U.S.C. §§1601–13 (1976).
[41] See, e.g., City of Macon v. Marshall, 439 F. Supp. 1209 (M.D. Ga. 1977).
[42] Rosenthal, supra note 4, at 1133–42.

# Part Three

## ECONOMIC LIBERTIES AND PROPERTY RIGHTS

## CHAPTER 11

# Public Roads and Highways

THE PREVIOUS three chapters all addressed the problem of bargaining games generally, and unconstitutional conditions in particular, in connection with issues of federalism. Until the 1920s the operation of the unconstitutional conditions doctrine was confined to these governmental contexts. The legal doctrine escaped from those narrow confines in cases of state regulation of state and local highways, where again state governments enjoy the powerful local monopoly position that for familiar reasons calls into question not only their capacity to regulate, but also to bargain with their citizens. In this new setting the question was whether the doctrine of unconstitutional conditions applied when the state demands the release of constitutional rights as the price of access to public highways. The problem arises in two separate contexts: the first deals with issues of competition and economic liberty and the latter with First Amendment rights. The most important case on the first question is *Frost & Frost Trucking Co. v. California Railroad Commission*,[1] which shows the halting and ineffective development of the doctrine in the context of classic state economic regulation. A representative case of the more modern developments on freedom of speech is *City of Lakewood v. Plain Dealer Publishing Co.*,[2] decided over sixty years later.

The framework of analysis is identical in the two areas, even if the underlying constitutional rights differ. The first inquiry is to determine the extent of the government's monopoly power in its control of public highways. The second inquiry is to determine the extent to which the conditions imposed upon entry or use are designed to upset the competitive balance between rival users. The third inquiry, which is the flip side of the second, is to determine whether the restrictions in question are designed to control against opportunistic behavior by individual citizens in their use of the common pool asset, the public roads.

[1] 271 U.S. 583 (1926).
[2] 486 U.S. 750 (1988).

## ECONOMIC REGULATION

In 1917 the California Railroad Commission received the power to regulate the rates and charges of the common carriers who used California public highways.[3] A common carrier—one who carried the goods of all comers over public highways for a fee—could gain access to the public highways only after first obtaining a permit from the Commission certifying that its business was for the "public convenience and necessity."[4] In 1919 the Commission's statutory powers were extended to cover transportation companies that were not common carriers, so-called "contract carriers."[5] Frost Trucking, which had a private contract to transport citrus fruit for a single supplier, fell into this latter category, but it refused to apply for the required permit and was then ordered by the Commission to suspend its operations.[6] The Commission's decision was upheld by the California Supreme Court. In reversing that decision, Justice Sutherland wrote:

> That court, while saying that the state was without power, by mere legislative fiat or even by constitutional enactment, to transmute a private carrier into a public carrier, declared that the state had the power to grant or altogether withhold from its citizens the privilege of using its public highways for the purpose of transacting [private] business thereon; and that, therefore, the legislature might grant the right on such conditions as it saw fit to impose.[7]

In Justice Sutherland's words, the California court was willing to allow private carriers access to public roads only if they dedicated their property to the "quasi-public use of public transportation."[8]

The stage was set for the familiar unconstitutional condition argument. Justice Sutherland assumed arguendo that the state could admit or exclude persons at will from the use of public highways. Then, however, by analogy to the foreign corporation cases, he held "that it may not impose conditions which require the relinquishment of constitutional rights"[9]—in this instance the right of a private carrier not to be compelled first to assume common carrier

[3] See Act of May 10, 1917, §3, 1917 Cal. Stat. 331.
[4] Id. §5, 1917 Cal. Stat. 333.
[5] See Act of May 13, 1919, §2, 1919 Cal. Stat. 458.
[6] See 271 U.S. at 590.
[7] Id. at 591.
[8] Id.
[9] Id. at 594.

status, and then to be regulated as such against its will.[10] So stated, the argument proceeds at a very high level of abstraction and is subject to the standard objections based upon the "greater and lesser power" theory that lay at the root of Justice Holmes's general opposition to the doctrine,[11] and his dissenting opinion in *Frost*.[12] If an individual values his constitutional rights less than he does the privilege that the state is offering, why not allow the bargain to go forward? Persons have a constitutional right to keep property, yet they surrender it all the time in order to obtain other goods that they value more highly. Why not here?

The complete analysis of the case begins with its historical context. The initial problem is the now familiar one of the adequacy of a "second-best" response to government discretion. The doctrine of unconstitutional conditions arose here only after it was settled that a state has the absolute right to exclude private firms from using its highway system. That conclusion was dictated by *Buck v. Kuykendall*,[13] a precedent decided one year before *Frost* was decided. *Buck* had invalidated, under a dormant commerce clause analysis, regulatory restrictions upon interstate service between Seattle and Portland.[14] Nonetheless, this part of *Buck* did not apply to *Frost*, which concerned purely intrastate movement (as the words were understood before 1937) on state highways and was therefore beyond the scope of the federal commerce power. Without the lever of interstate commerce, *Buck* gave the states unfettered discretion to deny common carriers access to the highways:

> The right to travel interstate by auto vehicle upon the public highways may be a privilege or immunity of citizens of the United States. A citizen may have, under the Fourteenth Amendment, the right to travel and transport his property upon them by auto vehicle. But he has no

[10] See id. at 593.

[11] See supra chap. 1.

[12] See 271 U.S. at 602 (Holmes, J., dissenting).

[13] 267 U.S. 307 (1925).

[14] Justice Brandeis's reasoning in *Buck* was cryptic. See id. at 324: "The federal-aid legislation is of significance not because of the aid given by the United States for the construction of particular highways, but because those acts make clear the purpose of Congress that the state shall be open to interstate commerce." Nonetheless, the result was correct, for the alternative opens up enormous potential for strategic behavior by the states, which would be able to prevent all out-of-state common carriers from using any in-state road built without federal support. Had *Buck* gone the other way, then, short of congressional intervention, interstate business would be subject to all the intrigue and retaliation that surrounded the legislation at issue in Gibbons v. Ogden, 22 U.S. (9 Wheat.) 1, 4–5 (1824), and that finds expression today in the politics of landing rights in international aviation, and interstate taxation, see supra chap. 9.

> right to make the highways his place of business by using them as a common carrier for hire. Such use is a privilege which may be granted or withheld by the State in its discretion, without violating either the due process clause or the equal protection clause. The highways belong to the State. It may make provision appropriate for securing the safety and convenience of the public in the use of them.[15]

The phrase "a privilege which may be granted or withheld by the State in its discretion" echoes the assertion of state power over foreign corporations claimed by the Court in *Paul v. Virginia*.[16] So too does the short shrift given to the privileges and immunities clause, which nowhere is limited to personal as opposed to business activities. *Buck's* bald conclusion that "the highways belong to the State" does not begin to address the question of how their use should be allocated among the various members of the public. Instead *Buck* erroneously proceeds as though a state is in all respects a private owner devoid of monopoly power. Yet it is just that question that the doctrine of unconstitutional conditions must address. To allow the state the power to exclude or admit at will from public highways raises the problems of externalities and strategic bargaining with which the doctrine is concerned, especially in the area of commerce and trade where the state's discretion is held to be the greatest. Those firms whose entry is subject to selective conditions are at a competitive disadvantage relative to their rivals, while the bargaining range for use of the roads between the state and any individual citizen is very broad. Political discretion over licenses can only encourage the dissipation of valuable resources to achieve partisan advantage. The same numerical illustrations presented in discussing the foreign corporation cases apply without change in this context.[17]

The object of a sound highway system is to maximize the gains that are attainable from use of the public roads. That goal is attainable only if the selective power of admission to the roads is curtailed—an equal protection concern—and if the state revenues from the highways are limited to its costs of running the system—a takings or due process objective. What should be flatly prohibited is the covert redistribution of wealth between private parties in the funding and utilization of public roads by imposing unequal exactions for equal benefits. These rules are hardly novel, even at the constitutional level, for they found expression in the special assessment

[15] 267 U.S. at 314 (citations omitted).

[16] 75 U.S. (8 Wall.) 168 (1869); see supra chap. 8.

[17] See supra chap. 8.

cases for funding local improvements, including roads and sewers, that routinely came before the Supreme Court under the due process clause between the end of the Civil War and the beginning of World War I, where fair apportionment of the costs of a local improvement was the major objective of the constitutional scheme.[18]

Although in this context the proper doctrinal rules would deny the state the absolute power to admit traffic to, or exclude it from, the public road, Justice Brandeis's dictum in *Buck* set the stage for Justice Sutherland in *Frost* to use the doctrine of unconstitutional conditions as the next-best alternative. To his great credit on that occasion, Justice Sutherland recognized the importance of market structure and accepted the dominance of the competitive equilibrium as a constitutional principle, despite the state's monopolistic control over the roads: "It is very clear that the act, as thus applied, is in no real sense a regulation of the use of the public highways. It is a regulation of the business of those who are engaged in using them. Its primary purpose evidently is to protect the business of those who are common carriers in fact by controlling competitive conditions. Protection or conservation of the highways is not involved."[19]

Justice Sutherland therefore struck down the condition that the state tried to attach to the use of the roads. California could exclude Frost Trucking from the use of the highways altogether, but it could not condition its entry upon the company's willingness to assume the burdens of a common carrier. Here the Court held that the right in question was found in the due process clause of the Fourteenth Amendment, which provides that "a private carrier cannot be converted against his will into a common carrier by mere legislative

[18] See Stephen Diamond, "The Death and Transfiguration of Benefit Taxation: Special Assessments in Nineteenth-Century America," 12 *J. Legal Stud.* 201 (1983). I address this subject, within the generalized eminent domain framework utilized here, in *Takings*, 286–89.

These cases held that the due process clause imposed some limitations on the funding devices that the state could use to finance local improvements, including local roads. In each case the total sum to be raised by taxes was limited to the cost of building the road in question: excess moneys could not be siphoned off into general revenues. The difficult question was finding the right formula to match costs with benefits once redistribution was in principle ruled out-of-bounds. Individualized (plot-by-plot) assessments of benefits were costly to make, and unreliable as well. Yet automatic rules—such as assessment by front footage—could be also unreliable because they missed large pockets of subjective gain in individual cases. In large measure this choice between rival benefit rules asks which set of errors is more debilitating, so that the state has some discretion in the choice of benefit formula as long as it uses a consistent formula throughout.

[19] 271 U.S. 583, 591 (1926).

command."[20] Alternatively, the right protected could have been regarded as falling within the Fourteenth Amendment right to engage "in the common occupations of the community."[21] The doctrine is of broader scope in its first formulation than it is in the second, but both apply to the instant case. The effort to condition entry to the highways on the sacrifice of the right to remain a private carrier imposed a disproportionate burden on Frost Trucking, and would have worked an implicit transfer to the common carriers with which it competed.

The decision in *Frost* gives some indication of the type of conditions the state should be able legitimately to impose upon highway use. The clue comes from Justice Sutherland's reference to the "protection and conservation of the highways," and builds upon concerns about externalities and strategic behavior. Thus, the state can impose taxes and rules that are designed to promote the smooth flow of traffic, to prevent accidents, to resolve tort actions, and to ensure that individuals have to answer for their wrongs. These rules are necessary to prevent the exploitation of a common-pool resource by its users. Similarly, the state should be able to impose a system of weight restrictions (to control wear and tear), or tolls (to alleviate congestion). Likewise, it is appropriate to require that users of the highway take out insurance to be sure that they can meet any tort obligations they might incur.[22] In some cases courts have sustained these valid conditions by a resort to the familiar greater/lesser arguments, but these general testaments to arbitrary state power are followed in the next breath by an assertion of the reasonableness of the condition imposed, as with security provided to others in the event of accident.[23]

Owing to the monopoly position, consent in and of itself does not justify state action, so the reasonableness of the condition determines the proper scope of state action. In the cases just discussed the

[20] Id. at 592.

[21] See, e.g., Truax v. Raich, 239 U.S. 33, 41 (1915): "It requires no argument to show that the right to work for a living in the common occupations of the community is of the very essence of the personal freedom and opportunity that it was the purpose of the [Fourteenth] Amendment to secure."

[22] See Opinion of the Justices, 251 Mass. 569, 147 N.E. 681 (1925).

[23] "The power to regulate, even to the extent of prohibition of motor vehicles from public ways, includes the lesser power to grant the right to use public ways only upon the observance of prescribed conditions precedents. The requirement that every owner before being allowed to register his motor vehicle shall provide security for the discharge of his liability for personal injuries or death resulting from the presence of such motor vehicle on the public ways cannot be pronounced unreasonable." 251 Mass. at 596, 147 N.E. at 693.

consent of the user is obtained for conditions that are *justified* by the need to curtail opportunistic behavior by all road users.[24] These are the kinds of conditions that would be imposed by the private owner of a road for his own benefit and for that of his customers. The duties that they impose are reciprocal in form, and without the disparate impact that might otherwise render them suspect. To ensure that parties answer financially for their wrongs is one of the few useful heads of government regulation; if it can be imposed on firms by direct regulation, then it can be imposed under a standing offer, available on equal terms to all customers, that conditions access to public highways on compliance with the rule. From the ex ante perspective this legislation looks as though it improves the position of all parties to the road by taking advantage of an opportunity, not available in other contexts, to ensure that persons who use dangerous instrumentalities stand ready to answer for the harm that they cause. Unlike the regulations in *Frost*, they do nothing to upset competitive balance, and much to protect against the externalization of harm.

Yet how effective is the all-or-nothing approach in *Frost* in limiting abuses of governmental discretion? In the foreign corporation cases, there were good reasons to believe that if forced to an all-or-nothing choice, states would allow foreign corporations in on nondiscriminatory terms. But the same conclusion need not hold in highway cases where local political considerations are such that total exclusion of many potential commercial users of the highway will often prevail. We need think only of the airport transportation monopolies that are jealously protected by state regulations, or of private bus lines and jitneys that have routinely been kept off city streets.[25] The power of state selection within classes of carriers and between classes of carriers was hardly curtailed at all by *Frost*. The right, and unavoidable, expression of the unconstitutional conditions doctrine would be far more restrictive. The state is under no duty to build public highways, just as it is under no duty to charter corporations. If it does build public highways, however, then *all* persons, regardless of commercial status, should have equal access to them, and the state powers of regulation and taxation should be directed to the *sole* end of preventing particular users from externaliz-

[24] Cf. Hess v. Powloski, 274 U.S. 352 (1927). The statute at issue in *Hess* allowed out-of-state individuals to be sued for accidents that they caused within the state.

[25] See Ross D. Eckert and George W. Hilton, "The Jitneys," 15 *J.L. & Econ.* 293 (1972); B. Peter Pashigan, "Consequences and Causes of Public Ownership of Urban Transit Facilities," 84 *J. Pol. Econ.* 1239 (1976).

ing the costs of their own operations upon the other users of the system. *Frost* provided a weak imitation of the desired rule, because it did not attack head-on, under either a takings or public trust rationale, the state's claim of absolute ownership of the highway.

At one level *Frost* contains the seeds of this expansive approach, for it suggests the ability of the courts to develop a normative theory to distinguish between those conditions that enhance or impair competitive activity. Consistently with that view, Justice Sutherland regarded *Frost* as a kind of takings case (for a quasi-public use), because private carriers were subject to the regulation thought appropriate to common carriers.[26] But even as he applied the doctrine in the one sentence, he gutted its power in the next. In words that came back to haunt, Justice Sutherland allowed the possibility that private carriers should themselves be "subject to regulations appropriate to that kind of carrier,"[27] without indicating what they might be or what ends they might serve.

That sentence served as the opening wedge to the quick destruction of *Frost* in *Stephenson v. Binford*,[28] decided only five years later. Texas had passed a state statute for the regulation of contract carriers, similar to that in *Frost*, which required these carriers to obtain a permit before they could use the public highways. Under that statute, the state highway and the state *railway* commission were charged with setting the minimum rates that contract carriers could charge to their clients.[29] The statute then provided that the railway commission would set the levels charged on the highways, and that these should not be less than those charged by any common carriers for performing the same level of services.[30]

The functional explanation for the statutory scheme seems too obvious to require extended comment. The Texas Railroad Commission administered a cartel that covered transportation by both railway and highway. In response to political pressures, the Commission decided to drive the private contract carriers out of business, because they had underbid the common carriers. To be sure, there could be no quarrel with conditions that provide for reasonable inspection of vehicles, or require private carriers to to be insured. Yet

[26] See 271 U.S. at 591.

[27] Id. at 592.

[28] 287 U.S. 251 (1932).

[29] Tex. Rev. Civ. Stat. Ann. art. 911(b) (West 1964). Summaries of the statutory provisions may be found in *Stephenson*, 287 U.S. at 259–61, and in the decision below, Stephenson v. Binford, 53 F.2d 509 (S.D. Tex. 1931), which had sustained the statute against attack by a 2 to 1 vote.

[30] 287 U.S. at 259–62.

setting minimum rates that private contract carriers could charge their customers is a different proposition entirely. Here the Commission uses its monopoly power over transportation to suppress competition, and its minimum rate schedules should be struck down as an impermissible interference with contractual freedom between the private contract carriers and their customers.

Justice Sutherland's analysis of *Stephenson* misses the essentials of the economic situation. He rests on the usual paean of judicial deference to legislative behavior, citing with approval his own unfortunate opinion in *Euclid v. Ambler Realty Co.*[31]—the decision that has done so much mischief in the area of land use.[32] He then quotes with approval statements from the trial record to the effect that the rapid expansion in the number of contract carriers has led to a "continual decrease" in the number of common carriers, and that it is in the interest of the state to regulate the practices of contract carriers for the common good.[33] Accordingly, he credits the state's own assertion of the importance of rate regulation to the preservation of the highway system.[34] He never once explains why the shift to cheaper and more reliable means of transportation should be regarded as a public peril; nor does he consider the many ways in which the state can finance the cost of intensive road use (e.g., gasoline taxes or tolls) that do not require it to cartelize the entire market or to drive low-cost producers out of the market.

The change in perception has profound consequences for constitutional theory. No longer is the constitutional system designed to preserve competition. It is now designed to preserve state domination. *Frost*, which clearly showed sympathy for the opposite proposition, was dismissed on little more than a terminological whim.[35] The evil in *Frost* was that California sought to convert contract carriers into common carriers. In *Stephenson*, Texas only sought to subject contract carriers to their own independent system of regulation, even though "the regulations imposed upon the two classes are in some instances similar if not identical."[36] A system of regulation with two parts thus escapes the judicial invalidation of a single comprehensive scheme even though the two systems have an identical impact on the regulated parties. The structural limitations that *Frost* appeared to impose on state legislation disappeared. In their place

[31] 272 U.S. 365 (1926), cited in *Stephenson*, 287 U.S. at 272

[32] For criticism, see *Takings*, 131–34.

[33] *Stephenson*, 287 U.S. at 269–71.

[34] Id. at 272–73.

[35] Id. at 267–68.

[36] Id. at 266.

was a simple injunction: impose what regulations you will on contract carriers, so long as you do not call them common carriers.

The issues that are raised both in *Frost* and *Stephenson* relate to the efficiency of alternative market structures. In essence the state must use its monopoly over the roads just as if it were a common carrier. So long as competition among users is possible, it cannot use its power to condition entry to impose a monopolistic structure. This point was lost sight of, not only by Justice Sutherland, but also by the academic commentators on the case. Professor Robert Hale, for example, suggested that *Stephenson* could be distinguished from *Frost* on the ground that it was concerned with preservation of the highways and not the suppression of competition. More abstractly, he claimed that the outcome in *Stephenson* is justified because it is "reasonably germane to the interest in highway conditions."[37] But his naive analysis does not account for the active role of the Texas Railroad Commission in setting rates, or the means/end connection between the rate restrictions so imposed. Both cartelization and preservation of competition are germane to the operation of the public highways, and these two ends are indistinguishable on any test that seeks to validate a condition by the closeness of its nexus to its subject matter.[38] Those conditions that are most closely associated with the use of the highways may turn out to be the most mischievous. Highway preservation and rate regulation should receive different treatment because the latter works against the public welfare while the former advances it. Again, there is no shortcut to understanding unconstitutional conditions cases. The precise operation of the state-imposed condition and its effect on the marketplace must be analyzed. The damage, however, has been done. The unthinking pattern of judicial deference that was ratified in *Stephenson* sets the norm for the modern cartelization of highway use.[39]

[37] See Robert L. Hale, "Unconstitutional Conditions and Constitutional Rights," 35 *Colum. L. Rev.* 321, 350 (1935); his conclusion appears to be echoed in Kathleen M. Sullivan, "Unconstitutional Conditions," 102 *Harv. L. Rev.* 1413, 1460–61(1989).

[38] Professor Sullivan appears to approve of the outcome in *Stephenson*, see 102 Harv. L. Rev. at 1461, but she provides no analysis of the case to show that the statutory provisions there were related to conservation of the highways.

[39] See, e.g., Cal. Pub. Util. Code §§3501–3800 (West 1975 & Supp. 1992), which subjects contract carriers to maximum and minimum rate regulations, and to strict licensing requirements, see, e.g., id. §3571, under a program administered by the Public Utility Commission. The regulation has been sustained by decisions that show the same expansive respect for state regulation evidenced in *Stephenson*. One California court, for example, declared: "It is obvious that the interests of the general public, as well as those of the trucking industry, are promoted by the establishment of fair and uniform rates which tend to give stability to the industry, and to protect operators

## PROTECTION OF NONECONOMIC CONSTITUTIONAL LIBERTIES

It seems clear today that *Frost* has turned out to be a dead letter in economic regulation, the area of its birth. Nonetheless, Justice Sutherland did leave a valuable legacy in the second class of cases, which involves the kinds of suspect classifications and fundamental rights that are now closely scrutinized under the footnote-four rule of *Carolene Products v. United States*.[40] In principle the state could bargain for any number of ends wholly unrelated to the operation of the highway itself. Justice Sutherland recognized that each person acting by himself would have a strong incentive to sacrifice other protected rights in order to get the greater short-term benefit of being able to use the roads. He thus invoked in *Frost* earlier language from *Western Union Telegraph Co. v. Foster*,[41] to the effect that a state could not use its control over public streets to regulate the messages that telegraph companies wished to send.[42] He also worried about the parade of horribles that might arise if the state could use its power to "impose conditions which require the relinquishment of constitutional rights. If the state may compel the surrender of one constitutional right as a condition of its favor, it may, in like manner, compel a surrender of all. It is inconceivable that guaranties embedded in the Constitution of the United States may thus be manipulated out of existence."[43]

Justice Sutherland's concern is well founded, even though his use of the term "compel" obscures the difference between the state's bargaining strategies and the state's outright use of force, and thus mirrors the incautious use of coercion encountered in philosophical debates.[44] The question is what alternative mode of analysis might

---

against unfair and destructive competition." Orlinoff v. Campbell, 91 Cal. App. 2d 382, 387, 205 P.2d 67, 70 (1949). The case then quoted from the California decision in *Frost*, without referring to the Supreme Court case that reversed it. *Frost* is dead today on issues of economic liberties.

[40] 304 U.S. 144 (1938). See generally Bruce A. Ackerman, "Beyond *Carolene Products*," 98 *Harv. L. Rev.* 713 (1985) (dissecting the interest-group politics behind footnote four); Geoffrey P. Miller, "The True Story of *Carolene Products*," 1987 Sup. Ct. Rev. 397 (giving the unhappy special-interest history of the actual restrictions on filled milk upheld by the Court).

[41] 247 U.S. 105 (1918).

[42] See id. at 114.

[43] 271 U.S. at 594.

[44] See supra chap. 4.

be adopted. The desired results in this case are conveniently achieved by noting that the conditions that address fundamental rights are not germane to any legitimate state concern in operating the public highways. That test works as a useful proxy to the crux of the matter because those conditions that are extrinsic to the operation of the highway can hardly be said to advance their competitive utilization. But it is a mistake to rest the analysis on the germaneness test in the cases where it provides the correct outcome, given its insufficiency in distinguishing between germane conditions that are beneficial and those that are pernicious. Some alternative approach to both coercion and germaneness is needed.

The real danger in this case lies not with coercion as the use of force, but in coercion as a collective-action problem, a point hinted at by Sutherland's use of the word *manipulated*. Voting rights, for example, may be of little value to any given individual, who would surrender them gladly for a right to do business on public highways. If many individuals did so, the combined effect would be to ensure a structural tyranny and the loss of many other liberties. State officials who push this deal are not selling things that they own. They are selling "things"—for example, access to roads—that belong to the public at large. Their success may be aided by the classical prisoner's dilemma in which many unorganized users of the public highways find themselves. If all users could contract with each other in advance, none would release his right to vote. The imposition of a rule that prevents the state from making certain bargains limits the power of the dominant coalition or faction within the state to engage in strategic threats to capture the private surplus from the use of the public highways. Although public officials may still act in breach of trust, they cannot obtain as much for their pains, because they possess fewer credible threats against citizens. Once the state cannot impose restrictions on fundamental rights upon those who want to gain access to the highways, then, in this context at least, it cannot impose them at all, for any such restrictions imposed directly would fall before particular constitutional commands. It makes no difference whether we talk about the state's threats to remove access to the roads ("coercion") or its promises to grant access to them ("benefit"). Whatever the nominal baseline, the strategic games are always destructive of the social fabric. The potentially catastrophic holdout problems of treating the state as the absolute owner of the public highways are dramatically moderated even by a restricted doctrine of unconstitutional conditions.

The more difficult cases of unconstitutional conditions in the modern era do not arise in the fanciful situations that Justice Sutherland presupposes, but in those cases that are closely tied to the use and the operation of the highway. With the passing of the economic liberty questions, the public highway cases were thus transformed into the "public forum" cases,[45] and the renewed level of higher scrutiny once again proceeded from a presumption of distrust of legislative and executive behavior. Before this new orientation was adopted, there was some judicial support, again voiced by Justice Holmes, for the categorical position that the state owns the highway or park and therefore can exclude speakers at will.[46] But this absolutist position quickly fell when it was decided that state title to the public highways did not allow it to bar the distribution of literature, or to subject it to any special prior restrictions, license tax, or permits.[47] The end run tolerated in the context of economic regulation was not allowed here.

This welcome retreat from the principle of absolute public ownership limits the need for the doctrine of unconstitutional conditions, but does not render it entirely unnecessary. There is often a capacity limitation—if not for lonely leafleteers on public roads and streets, then surely on public fairgrounds—that becomes critical as the demands on public space rise.[48] Someone has to decide who will gain access and who will not. Given the level of scrutiny applied to such decisions, the issue of unconstitutional conditions should have been expected to reappear in the modern context of the public forum, and it has. One instructive illustration is *City of Lakewood v. Plain Dealer Publishing Co.*[49]

Lakewood's ordinance gave the city mayor the discretion to decide which newspaper companies would receive annual, nonassign-

[45] See generally Harry Kalven, Jr. "The Concept of the Public Forum: *Cox v. Louisiana*," 1965 Sup. Ct. Rev. 1; Geoffrey R. Stone, "Fora Americana: Speech in Public Places," 1974 Sup. Ct. Rev. 233.

[46] While still on the Massachusetts Supreme Judicial Court, Justice Holmes wrote: "For the legislature absolutely or conditionally to forbid public speaking in a highway or public park is no more an infringement of the rights of a member of the public than for the owner of a private house to forbid it in his house. When no proprietary right interferes, the Legislature may end the right of the public to enter upon the public place by putting an end to the dedication to public uses. So it may take the lesser step of limiting the public use to certain purposes." Commonwealth v. Davis, 162 Mass. 510, 511, 39 N.E. 113, 113 (1895), aff'd, 167 U.S. 43 (1897).

[47] See Lovell v. Griffin, 303 U.S. 444 (1938). Marsh v. Alabama, 326 U.S. 501 (1946), took the far more controversial step of applying a similar analysis to privately owned company towns.

[48] See, e.g., Heffron v. International Soc'y for Krishna Consciousness, Inc., 452 U.S. 640 (1981) (allowing the state to impose on Krishna groups the same time, place, and manner restrictions applicable to all others at a state fair).

[49] 486 U.S. 750 (1988).

able permits to place their newsracks on public property. The decision was to be made after considering a range of factors, including the approval of the racks' design by the Architectural Board of Review, the willingness of the permittee to obtain insurance that would hold the city harmless for all liability arising from the use of the newsracks, and "such other terms and conditions deemed necessary and desirable by the Mayor."[50] The issue of unconstitutional conditions arose when it was urged that the city was under no obligation to allow any newsracks at all on public streets, and could therefore make the right to place racks on public roads subject to whatever conditions the city wished to impose.

*Lakewood* differs from *Frost* in two ways. First, in this context city ownership of the public streets gives government far less monopoly power than was involved in *Frost*. While the public roads are the only available means of transportation, newspapers can be sold by subscription or in stores. The government power therefore is somewhat attenuated. Yet by the same token, it is by no means trivial, especially because some papers (such as those distributed without charge) rely heavily upon newsrack distributions. The scope of government power, although not absolute, is still large enough to give it substantial monopoly power. There is reason therefore to invoke the doctrine of unconstitutional conditions. Second, unlike the statute in *Frost*, Lakewood's ordinance contained no explicit requirement that the newspaper waive any constitutional right. It was not asked to agree to mayoral censorship as a condition for placing its racks on the public streets. Nonetheless, the wide level of discretion conferred upon the mayor raised the possibility that he would seek, even informally, to impose a condition that would require the waiver of First Amendment rights, such as softening opposition to one of the mayor's pet projects. The possibility that some papers might consent to this sub rosa condition could induce others to follow suit. The power to select who shall stay and who shall go made it possible for the mayor to prefer newspapers that supported his policies and to deny permits to those that opposed them, and the prospect of such mischievous behavior was far more troubling than a simple rule totally banning newsracks from the public street.[51]

[50] Lakewood, Oh., Codified Ordinances §901.181 (1984) (cited and quoted in *Lakewood*, 486 U.S. 750 n.2) (1988).

[51] Cf. Police Dep't v. Mosley, 408 U.S. 92 (1972) (invalidating a city's ban on all forms of picketing except those regarding a labor dispute). The case did not explicitly rest on the doctrine of unconstitutional conditions, and indeed the Court attached little weight to the fact that Mosley's picketing took place on the public highways. Instead the Court undertook a combined First Amendment and equal protection anal-

The sound First Amendment limitations on discretion do not, however, answer all the questions of what newsracks, if any, must be placed upon public property. Surely the First Amendment does not require that any newspaper company be allowed to place its racks on public property at will, without paying any fee at all. Public streets and roads are still a form of commons, and one risk associated with the maintenance of any commons is its overexploitation by private users who do not fully take into account the costs that their own behavior imposes upon other members of the public. Strategic behavior by the mayor is only one form of abuse; excessive use by the newspaper companies must be reckoned with as well, which is why decisions preventing excessive noise and other similar nuisances have survived to the present day under the rule that allows for appropriate "time, place, and manner" restrictions.[52]

Because of this dual hazard, there is surely some reason to allow the city to restrict the number of newsracks on public property, and perhaps even to confine them to certain locations within the town. *Lakewood* did not decide, for example, whether a total ban on newsracks in residential areas would be constitutional. There is, of course, the risk that restrictions on the locations and number of newsracks could also be more severe than appropriate. Such a restriction might be attacked in extreme cases—for example, if the ordinance banned all newsracks in order to punish one particular newspaper. Yet a facial attack on such a statute is surely out of place; some concrete evidence of official misconduct should be required. More generally, there comes a point at which the capacity to control government abuse diminishes, while the gains from controlling that abuse are small. Then it is time to quit, under the First Amendment just like anywhere else. The simple rule that the city can determine the number and location of newsracks, but must allocate them by some nondiscretionary means goes a very long way toward controlling the most obvious forms of abuse.

It is instructive to note that the First Amendment principles applicable in this case are drawn from those developed in connection with the economic liberties cases. The concern with conditional admission to the roads that animated *Frost* had to do with implicit redistribution of wealth among separate common carriers and across

---

ysis which attacked the ordinance because it distinguished among different types of speech by subject matter. See id. at 95–96. The subject-matter distinctions gave the state officials more discretion than the simple all-or-nothing ban on picketing, but far less than that contemplated by Lakewood's statutory scheme.

[52] See, e.g., Kovacs v. Cooper, 336 U.S. 77 (1949) (plurality opinion).

different sectors of the trucking business. The restrictions against excessive weight and the like were routinely allowed in order to control against the exploitation of a common resource by a single user. If that economic model had applied, *Lakewood* would have come out the same way even without resort to First Amendment principles. Indeed under the economic liberties framework, it would not be enough to guard against the possibility of favoritism to firms within the class of newspapers. It would also be necessary to worry about a reciprocal risk: whether newspapers as a class received a subsidy from the rest of the public at large in the form of below-market rents of public space. That additional constraint would be very hard to administer because there is no strong economic theory that determines the optimal number of newsracks to be allowed on public property.

The theory would, however, suggest that once the number of spaces was determined by political means, their allocation to individual newspaper companies would have to take place by bid, or perhaps by lottery. The lottery may not guarantee the most efficient use of public space, nor raise revenues for the state, but it does eliminate (ex ante) redistribution among newspapers. A system that takes the total number of spaces and divides it by the number of applicants does the same thing, but may give a boost to papers with smaller circulations that a bidding system would not. The critical point is that the First Amendment analysis of highway use generally, and the unconstitutional conditions analysis more concretely, proceed on identical terms as the previous analysis of *Frost*. The demise of economic liberties means in essence that we have to worry about only one form of error, the imposition of undue restrictions, but can ignore implicit subsidies to the newspaper companies. Whatever the Court's shortcomings in its protection for economic liberties, *Lakewood* itself is a welcome and correctly decided case in the First Amendment area.

## CHAPTER 12

# Land Use Restrictions and the Police Power

THE HIGHWAY CASES mark an area in which the government assertion of absolute ownership rights was properly countered by the doctrine of unconstitutional conditions. In this chapter, I extend my discussion of the limitations on the state's power to bargain to a second context, one in which the state has no obvious ownership rights but acts as a regulator pursuant to its prerogatives under the "police power" which in the customary formulation pertains to the health, safety, morals, and general welfare of the population at large.

Within constitutional law generally, the police power addresses the set of justifications that the state must put forward in order to override any of the substantive protections of liberty and property found in various clauses of the Constitution. Some police power justification seems to be necessary in the structure of legal rights if we are to make any sense of the Constitution at all.[1] It is difficult to conceive of a defense of private property so absolute that ownership of a handgun allows its owner to kill or maim at will, or a defense of freedom of speech so pure as to countenance securities fraud, perjury, or defamation. One possible account of the police power is overtly libertarian in its orientation and allows the state to override explicit constitutional guarantees, whether of liberty or property, when necessary to protect other persons from the threat or use of force or fraud: the power to regulate begins where the individual's liberty of action ends. The relevant restrictions are often prospective in application, like a ban on the sale of firearms or the ban on printing false prospectuses.

The police power should not in principle be construed as an unlimited charter for state action. Typically, the states and their subdivisions have a monopoly over the use of the police power, creating a risk that exercise of this power will go beyond its stated purpose. One persistent fear is that the regulation under the police power will

[1] For a longer discussion, see *Takings*, 107–45. The earlier classics on the police power include Christopher Tiedeman, *A Treatise on the Limitations of the Police Power in the United States* (1886); Ernst Freund, *The Police Power, Public Policy, and Constitutional Rights* (1904).

be used to cloak protectionist efforts to raise the cost of entry of firms and individuals into what would otherwise be competitive markets. In the pre-1937 years, the unwillingness to tolerate "labor" regulation, as distinct from health regulation, was one imperfect attempt to prevent both the federal government and the states from enacting anticompetitive laws.[2] The effort to sort out appropriate police power measures from inappropriate ones necessarily requires not only a statement of the proper ends to be served, but also an analysis of the "fit" between the ends to be served and the means to be used. The effective scope of the state power depends heavily, therefore, on the applicable level of scrutiny. So long as the perils of both overregulation and underregulation are about the same level of magnitude, some "intermediate" level of scrutiny must be adopted to determine the goodness of fit between any legitimate legislative end and the means chosen to satisfy it.[3] This analysis is perfectly general and explains why, in practice, limitations on the police power must arise from the property, speech, contract, religion, due process, and equal protection guarantees of the Constitution.

Under current doctrine, the police power is typically afforded a broad construction that covers far more than the suppression of force and fraud. In essence, the state is allowed to regulate in ways that are thought generally to advance the public good, and a very low level of scrutiny is applied both to the ends sought and to the connection between means and ends. In land use cases, the police power was extended far beyond the nuisance control rationale as early as *Euclid v. Ambler Realty Co.*,[4] during the so-called *Lochner* era, in light of the Court's acceptance of thinly disguised anticompetitive measures. Today, the police power has been broadened still further to allow states to regulate levels of population growth, to force towns to provide some minimum percentage of low-income housing, to set rents, or to pursue aesthetic ends.[5]

[2] See, e.g., Lochner v. New York, 198 U.S. 45 (1905) (invalidating a ten-hour per day statute for certain classes of bakers); Adair v. United States, 208 U.S. 161 (1908) (invalidating collective bargaining statute on railroads). For a discussion of some of the confusions in the police power jurisprudence prior to 1937, see Richard A. Epstein, "The Mistakes of 1937," 11 *George Mason L. Rev.* 5 (1988).

[3] See *Takings*, 128–29. A need to take a closer look at the police power arises whenever there is any fear of factional abuse. See generally Cass R. Sunstein, "Naked Preferences and the Constitution," 84 *Colum. L. Rev.* 1689, 1723–27 (1984).

[4] 272 U.S. 365 (1926).

[5] See, e.g., Agins v. City of Tiburon, 447 U.S. 255 (1980) (holding that a zoning ordinance restricting development of land to open space or low-density residential use is a valid exercise of police power).

Even this broad construction of the police power, however, does not give the state ordinary ownership rights over the property that it may restrict or regulate. Thus today, the state could not engage in a two-stage process whereby it first condemns all development rights in land and then turns around and sells them to new owners for cash. But even subject to this important caveat, the use of the relaxed, rational basis standard of review necessarily increases the scope of government discretion, thus opening the door to the perils associated with the improper exercise of government monopoly power. The state's ability to issue permits and licenses covers a wide range of affairs. As the scope of regulation under the police power has expanded, it has raised in its wake questions over the extent to which the state may bargain with individual citizens and corporations in virtue of these powers. As before, the central inquiry is whether the doctrine of unconstitutional conditions can control the attendant risks.

In this chapter, I examine the police power in the context of land use regulation. Although the subject is a vast one, the focus here will be on one particular issue: the extent to which the present broad accounts of the police power lead to bargaining difficulties with the state that should be subject to constitutional conditions. The first section looks at the unconstitutional conditions problem as it applies to eminent domain regulation. The second section examines the reasons why the existence of an exit right for developers is insufficient to prevent abuses under regulation. The third section illustrates the special problems of coercion that arise in connection with regulatory and temporary takings.

## TAKINGS

*Nollan v. California Coastal Commission*[6] illustrates how the generous contours of the police power in the land-use context create intensive bargaining difficulties that implicate the doctrine of unconstitutional conditions. The Nollans owned a small, dilapidated beach house that they wished to tear down and replace with a larger home. Under the prevailing construction of the police power, the Court assumed, the state could have prevented the construction of the new house absolutely, in order to preserve the public's viewing access over the Nollans' land from the public highways to the water-

[6] 483 U.S. 825 (1987). *Nollan* has generated an enormous amount of controversy. See Symposium, "The Jurisprudence of Takings," 88 *Colum. L. Rev.* 1581 (1988).

front.[7] The Commission announced that it was prepared to grant the Nollans the right to build on their land, and consequently the right to obstruct that view, if the Nollans would surrender a lateral, beachfront easement over their land for the benefit of the public at large. If the Nollans had accepted the deal, then the state would have gotten the easement without having to buy it for cash. However, it was also settled that this easement would have had to be paid for if taken by the government in a separate transaction.[8] Similarly, it seems clear that the Coastal Commission, having only the limited powers derived from the state, could not have simply declared itself the owner of the development rights over the Nollans' land solely to sell it back to them for cash.

Within these contours, the question raised in *Nollan* was whether the state could force the Nollans to choose between their construction permit and their lateral easement. Under existing California law, the exaction in question had been upheld even though there was at best an "indirect relationship" between the new construction and any local need for access.[9] Justice Brennan supported that outcome in his dissent in *Nollan*, resting his case on the model of the mutually advantageous private bargain, with its implicit rejection of the unconstitutional conditions doctrine.[10] If the state could ban construction of the new house entirely, then it could grant permission to construct on the condition that the lateral easement be deeded over to the state. Justice Scalia, writing for the majority, invoked (in all but name) the doctrine of unconstitutional conditions to hold that this particular bargain between the state and two of its citizens was impermissible because the condition imposed—surrender of the easement—lacked a "nexus" with, or was "unrelated" to the legitimate interest used by the state to justify its actions—preserving the

[7] 483 U.S. at 835–36.

[8] Id. at 834.

[9] See Grupe v. California Coastal Comm'n, 166 Cal. App. 3d 148, 212 Cal. Rptr. 578 (1985).

[10] Justice Brennan argued that: "[t]he Coastal Commission, if it had so chosen, could have denied the Nollans' request for a development permit, since the property would have remained economically viable without the requested new development. Instead, the State sought to accommodate the Nollans' desire for new development, on the condition that the development not diminish the overall amount of public access to the coastline." *Nollan* at 844–45. The clear implication is that the greater power of preventing development altogether includes the lesser power of allowing development subject to surrender of the demanded easement. Note, however, that Justice Brennan accepts the unconstitutional conditions doctrine in the speech and religion contexts. See infra chap. 15 (discussing Speiser v. Randall, 357 U.S. 513 (1958)); chap. 16 (discussing Sherbert v. Verner, 374 U.S. 398 (1963)).

view.[11] The absence of the nexus was in his view fatal to the case: "[U]nless the permit condition serves the same governmental interest as the development ban, the building restriction is not a valid regulation of land use but 'an out-and-out plan of extortion.'"[12] Who is right, and why?

A plausible first instinct is to avoid the problem by arguing that the scope of the police power gives the state far too much discretion even when it does not wish to bargain with citizens. Restrictions on height and bulk are unrelated to the prevention of any ordinary, common law nuisance, and can be obtained by neighbors (many of whom have built for themselves the very type of structures that they are trying to prevent others from building) only if they are able to purchase a restrictive covenant that limits the owner's right to build. There seems no reason why the state should be able to take without compensation for the public at large the same type of property interest that neighbors must buy. If so, then *Nollan* must be decided for the landowner without reaching the unconstitutional conditions question. The state cannot force a citizen who owns two plots of land to choose which one to keep and which to surrender to the state, because imposing such a choice amounts to taking property without just compensation. The issue is no different when the landowner must choose between encumbering his land with a restrictive covenant or a lateral easement. The choice the state puts to the citizen is no better than one which an uncommonly fastidious gunman puts by allowing his victim the choice between her watch and her wallet. The case thus falls into the familiar pattern of coercion found in the duress of goods cases.[13] Any sound delineation of property rights thus would vindicate the Nollans even before reaching the unconstitutional conditions question.

Now that this first line of defense has been overrun, why the doctrine of unconstitutional conditions? There are two possible explanations. The first returns to the question of the fair distribution of the surplus from government action. To make the case concrete, assume that there are ten landowners, each of whom loses $100 if the lateral easement is obtained by the state. Where just compensation is paid to each in cash, then each gains (or loses) the same amount from collective action as all the others. Yet now suppose that half the landowners have completed the improvements on their plots, while others have not. The *Nollan* strategy allows the state to ac-

[11] 483 U.S. at 841.
[12] Id. at 837.
[13] See supra chap. 4.

quire five lateral easements for nothing at all, while paying $100 to the others. Here there is a skewing of the surplus among the targets of government action, a telltale sign of social unfairness.

It is, moreover, possible to demonstrate how this governmental strategy can lead systematically to social losses. The situation is best explained by reverting to the basic social purpose behind the takings clause: to ensure that an interest in private property will pass into government hands only if it is worth more to the government, as the representative of the public, than its market value in private hands.[14] If the state has to purchase the lateral easement, this purpose is satisfied, because public officials have to raise the money to make the purchase. The protection so afforded is imperfect, however, because there is always the risk that one group (beach users) will be able to purchase the easement with money raised by taxes imposed upon the public generally. While the takings prohibition (unless extended to taxation) does not stop this particular form of political externality, it does at least ensure that a separate constraint against resource misallocation is observed. Making the payment requires an imperfect set of political institutions to take into account the very large losses that the single owner will suffer, losses that can be downplayed or ignored when that payment is not required.

These institutional constraints against misbehavior tend, however, to break down if the state can link the fate of the lateral easement to the issue of visual access, as the Coastal Commission tried to do. The threat to impose development restrictions on the landowner does not require any budget appropriation by either California or the local municipality. If the losses that a state regulation could inflict upon the owner are (as seems probable) far greater to the owner than the loss of a lateral easement, then there seems little prospect that the state's offer will be declined. Landowners will sacrifice an interest worth $1,000 in order to preserve development rights that are worth a hundred times as much.[15] Once this sequence runs its course, therefore, all we know are the relative values that the landowner attaches to his two separate interests—development

[14] Ideally, the state should be required to pay not the market value, but the subjective value that the individual attaches to the property. Because the latter is difficult to determine, courts have moved to the market value standard. See, e.g., United States v. 546.54 Acres of Land, 441 U.S. 506, 511 (1979). The argument in the text, however, does not depend on which standard of valuation is used.

[15] The point is not one of idle speculation, for the Nollans were the only party to fight the Commission, while forty-three other landowners had capitulated. See 483 U.S. at 856 n.9 (Brennan, J. dissenting). The number would have been forty-four if this constitutional challenge had not appeared viable.

rights and lateral easement. We do not know whether the value of the lateral easement to the state is greater than its value to the owner, because no accountable political actor has been forced to make that explicit judgment. Therefore there is the positive chance of an allocative loss if the deal goes through when the value of the easement to the state is less than its value to the landowner, which is in turn less than the value of the development rights to the landowner. The correct social choice is made by comparing the value of the easement to the two claimants. Under the Coastal Commission's strategy, however, that choice is never made. Hence the central allocative function of the eminent domain clause is effectively bypassed by allowing the state to couple the lateral easement with the construction permit.

In this context, the doctrine of unconstitutional conditions limits the abuse of government discretion by severing the denial of the construction permit from the taking of the lateral easement. This course of action is not without its dangers. It is quite possible that the easement will be purchased for cash (which is appropriate if the compensation levels are rightly set, although often they are set too low when severance damages are involved).[16] It is also possible, if the state were forced to purchase the easement, that it would deny the permit outright, so that people like the Nollans would be left worse off than they were when they could bargain away their rights. But in this case the empirical guess is that the government, as in the foreign incorporation cases, will choose not to exercise its greater power. Imposing the building restrictions necessarily deprives the community of the increased taxes generated by a new residence which probably will not increase the demands on public facilities by the same amount. The groups who are interested in lateral access (the neighbors or the public at large) may be far less interested in visual access, so that the coalition pressuring for visual access will disintegrate when the two issues are separated. Chances seem good that the "public" at large, divided among itself, would not want this permit restriction solely for its own sake. The severance, therefore, calls the bluff of the Coastal Commission by preventing it from parlaying a threat of something that interest groups do not want into the acquisition of something they do want—for free. Applied to this institutional setting, the "relatedness" or "nexus" requirement imposed by Justice Scalia has powerful, if hidden, functional roots, for it narrows the size of the bargaining range and hence reduces the state's ability to

[16] Severance damages are those damages which result to the retained interest in land when some portion of the whole has been taken for public use.

extract concessions from individual owners by coordinating separate types of government initiatives. Some "related" conditions may be improper, but the nexus requirement weeds out many "unrelated" conditions that are manifestly improper.

The necessary prerequisite for undertaking this inquiry into the subject matter of the conditions is that the takings clause limits the permissible level of redistribution between the public at large and landowners. Under the traditional rational basis test, that concern is so weak that state power (including the power to bargain) would remain unbridled. It is therefore no accident that Justice Scalia's implicit invocation of the doctrine followed a more general assertion that the deferential rational basis review does not carry over from equal protection to takings cases.[17] Even within Justice Scalia's formulation of the problem, the government's broad discretion over the nature, and type, of height, square footage, and exterior design regulations introduces various opportunities for abuse that a more rigorous account of the police power would preclude. But within very rough limits, this invocation of unconstitutional conditions does appear to place useful constraints on government power. With *Nollan* in place, the state cannot insist that the landowners deed over an easement in order to get an electrical hook-up for their house or demand that they cede land to widen a public road in order to allow their property to be zoned for commercial use. In a cautious second-best sense, *Nollan* is a fit case for using the doctrine. But it is a far cry from the best solution, which would be the return of the police power to its traditional confines.

## EXIT RIGHTS IN LAND USE CASES

Notwithstanding the functional justification just offered for it, *Nollan* has received a rocky reception in both the academic literature and the decided cases. Thus Professor Vicki Been has written at length against the outcome in *Nollan* on the ground that the "exit" rights available to real estate developers protect developers without complicating the law of zoning. Her position is directed both toward the regulatory use of the police power and the bargaining strategies of the Coastal Commission, including the exactions demanded in *Nollan*.[18] Her analysis fails here for reasons similar to

[17] See Id. at 848 n.3 (contesting Justice Brennan's advocacy of a rational basis test).

[18] Vicki Been, " 'Exit' " as a Constraint on Land Use Exactions: Rethinking the Unconstitutional Conditions Doctrine," 91 *Colum. L. Rev.* 473, 506–33 (1991). For additional criticism, see Stewart E. Sterk, "Competition Among Municipalities as a Constraint on Land Use Exactions," 45 *Vand. L. Rev.* 831 (1992). Sterk stresses that exit rights offer little protection against anti-growth ordinances, id. at 839–41, and that

those which explain its inadequacy in connection with the exit rights of corporations.[19]

First, real estate developers are not the only persons who are at risk from improper uses of the zoning power by local authorities. *Nollan* itself is a case in point. The Coastal Commission demanded its exactions from a sitting tenant who had no credible threat of exit. If the Coastal Commission had prevailed, the Nollans could not have picked up their stakes and moved their house to another locale. The imposition of zoning restrictions therefore imposes capital losses on the value of land for its *present owner*, losses that are not taken into account if only developers' interests are counted.

Second, the exit right is of little value where the restrictions on land use are imposed after annexation of unincorporated land by a nearby township. In these situations, it is not uncommon for a developer to have already received a favorable zoning determination from one set of authorities only to have to do battle against a more restrictive set of conditions after annexation takes place. The right of exit is in effect undone by the power of hot pursuit.

Third, the exit right will also fail where the developer has made investments of capital specific to a particular locale. Where that is done, the developer now assumes the position of the landowner whose exit threat is effectively gone. Yet regulation can be imposed after extensive planning has been made in reliance on the previous state of affairs.[20] The reliance could arise even before the developer sinks a single stake in the ground. Feasibility studies, architectural plans, soil tests, environmental impact studies, marketing programs, are all intensely site specific, and zoning restrictions that are imposed after these expenses are incurred cannot be met with a credible exit threat. Similarly, the exit right is not credible where a developer has completed one phase of a project and now wishes to embark on a second that is integrated with the first.[21] More generally, sunk costs cannot be recovered by the exercise of an exit option.

---

their effects are weakened as nearby locales become more imperfect substitutes for each other. Id. at 863–65.

[19] See supra chap. 8.

[20] Haas v. City and County of San Francisco, 605 F.2d 1117 (9th Cir. 1979). The California statute at issue in *Haas* provided for only limited grandfathering in projects where "substantial construction has been performed and substantial liabilities for construction and necessary materials have been incurred." Cal. Pub. Res. Code §21170(a) (West 1977).

[21] See, e.g., Avco Community Developers, Inc. v. South Coast Regional Comm'n, 17 Cal.3d 785, 553 P.2d 546, 132 Cal. Rptr. 386 (1976) (subdivision developed in stages); Lakeview Dev. Corp. v. City of South Lake Tahoe, 915 F.2d 1290 (9th Cir. 1990) (same).

Fourth, there are many forms of regulation in which the exit right is not credible, even for a developer who has not made site-specific investments. Again *Nollan* affords the textbook example. The restrictions in this case were imposed not by a single local community from which a developer could flee in accordance with the Tiebout model of competition between local governments.[22] They were imposed by a state agency whose jurisdiction extends the entire length of the state's coastline.[23] There is in constitutional law no apparent distinction between the use of the police power by states and localities, even though the exit rights are more potent in the second case than the first. If a uniform doctrine must be imposed in both cases, then the choice seems easy. A broad standard of deference causes enormous difficulties where the state exercises a uniform power by an administrative board.

Fifth, even in those cases where there are local governments in competition with each other for future business of developers, the exit option should not be regarded as a suitable, let alone perfect, substitute for constitutional limitations on the zoning power. In order for a developer to exercise an exit threat, he must be prepared to move to some alternative location. In general that location will be inferior to the first location, for otherwise the developer would have gone there first. To exercise a credible threat, therefore, means that the developer must show that the losses from shifting locales are smaller than those sustained by developing in the locale subject to the conditions set out in the plan approved. If, therefore, there is any positive probability of bargaining breakdown, the untrammeled right of local governments to bargain will produce a net social loss, whose minimum value is the difference between the best and second-best locales. The total level of developer, landowner, and consumer surplus is higher with restraints on local governments than without it. If Been's assumption that exit rights effectively constrain local government were correct, then the vast amount of litigation, which has continued unabated and without fundamental change since *Nollan* was decided,[24] would be wholly inexplicable. In a world

22 See Charles M. Tiebout, "A Theory of Local Expenditures," 64 *J. Pol. Econ.* 416 (1956).

23 Similar restrictions are still under litigation in Lucas v. South Carolina, 304 S.C. 376, 404 S.E.2d 895 (1991), reversed and remanded by the Supreme Court, 112 S. Ct. 2886 (1992).

24 "But it is apparent that *Nollan* did not revolutionize takings law." Adolph v. Federal Emergency Management Agency, 854 F.2d 732, 737 (5th Cir. 1988) (denying relief against building ordinance justified as a flood control measure); Gilbert v. City of Cambridge, 932 F.2d 51 (lst Cir. 1991) (sustaining the restrictions on apartment

of effective competition, everyone takes at the market price. There is no accounting for the mass of litigation brought against local government if the exit right eliminates the need for any direct judicial review of local government actions.

## TEMPORARY TAKINGS AND BARGAINING DIFFICULTIES

The weaknesses of the present property rights regime—a state of affairs not radically changed by *Nollan*—are shown by the bargaining behavior that can result between local governments and landowners in two related contexts. The first concerns the familiar problem of exaction ordinances, and the second involves the bargaining difficulties that arise in connection with compensation for interim takings under the Supreme Court's decision in *First English Evangelical Lutheran Church v. County of Los Angeles*,[25] decided a few months before *Nollan*. I shall examine these two problems in order.

### *Exaction Ordinances*

The recurring problem of exaction ordinances is simple enough to state. A developer proposes a project for a given locale, and the city or other local authority conditions the approval on the developer's compliance with certain onerous covenants: roads must be built, land must be donated for schools or perhaps day-care centers, or fees must be paid into the general public treasury.[26] The question in all these cases is whether the exactions represent a proper or illicit use of government power. The unconstitutional conditions doctrine is squarely raised because, in principle, a developer is entitled to attack the exaction even if he is better off with the permission and

---

owners that want to remove their units from the rent-controlled market); Naegele Outdoor Advertising, Inc. v. City of Durham, 844 F.2d 172 (4th Cir. 1988) (sustaining billboard limitations); St. Bartholomew's Church v. City of New York, 914 F.2d 348 (2d Cir. 1990) (sustaining landmark designation of church).

[25] 482 U.S. 304 (1987).

[26] For general treatments of exactions, see Symposium, "Exactions: A Controversial New Source for Municipal Funds," 50 *Law & Contemp. Prob.* 1 (Winter 1987); Robert C. Ellickson & A. Dan Tarlock, *Land Use Controls: Cases and Materials*, 737–60 (1981). In an important sense the modern exaction problem is a rerun of the nineteenth-century question of the constitutionality of special assessments, on which see Stephen Diamond, "The Death and Transfiguration of Benefit Taxation: Special Assessments in Nineteenth-Century America," 12 *J. Legal Stud.* 201 (1983).

the exaction than he is without either. The entire area arises precisely because the exit remedy is not regarded as sufficient. The question of principle is what legal scrutiny should be given to these exactions.

Initially, the question here is one that, no matter what the doctrinal approach, will raise serious problems of application and measurement. The root of the problem is that the risk of exploitation is alive and well in both directions. A developer might propose a project that will entail enormous costs on the rest of the community. The traffic densities off-site will be sharply increased, and the new demands for such standard community services as water and sewers will exceed the existing capacity. The exactions can therefore in some cases be rightly understood as a favorable local response to the developer. On this view the exaction should be understood as a waiver of the ban in exchange for the payment of fees that make both developer and community better off.

Yet there is no automatic gyroscope that says that local officials will levy exactions solely to counter developer excesses. In principle, if a project is exceedingly profitable for a developer, than the exaction might be unrelated to the additional costs imposed and serve solely to extract some of the developer's anticipated profits. The money raised could then be used to defray costs that the community must already bear even if the proposed development never were to take place at all. It is possible, for example, to tax an industrial development in order to fund the entire operation of an existing school system or water distribution system. There are of course effective limits as to how much of an exaction the municipality might impose: the exit right places some upper limit on the level of exaction, and the municipal government may be eager to attract new development to expand its tax base or increase the level of local economic activity.

When the dust settles, however, a substantial bargaining range exists between the maximum amount that the developer would pay and the minimum amount that the local government unit would accept. The insistent question is whether there is any appropriate way for courts to control the distribution of the surplus. A rule that allows all exactions as a matter of course promotes massive local abuse and destructive bargaining games, just as a rule that prohibits any special exactions may open the way to developer exploitation. The task is to identify a legal rule that reduces the resource losses from destructive bargaining games.

What attitude, then, should the courts take toward these exactions given the equal and opposite possibilities of abuse? In general, the first test that should be imposed is one of consistency. If all previous local development was allowed without special exactions of any sort, then heavy scrutiny should be given to any effort to change the rules of the game with respect to subsequent development in the community. The risk is that the existing businesses and residences will receive a disproportionate fraction of the gain from the combined endeavor, as some courts have rightly recognized.[27] In order to counter this risk, the courts should, therefore, require a clear demonstration of the additional costs that the development imposes and why the exaction, whether in cash or kind, is necessary to limit it. The dedication requirement should be limited to those expenses "uniquely attributable" to the proposed development.[28] The local government should be required to identify the additional costs that present citizens and businesses have to bear. The judicial task is to prevent implicit subsidization of the local government by the new entrant.

In principle, the same problem arises even in those cases where consistent methods of financing are adopted and special exactions are imposed on both early and late arrivals in the community. Nonetheless, the possibilities of abuse seem smaller, so that the same inquiry should take place, but without the heavy burden of justification on the municipality. In both cases, however, the ultimate end of the inquiry is to identify the additional costs imposed upon the locality by the new development and to limit the special exactions to these costs and these costs only. The inquiry is not dissimilar to one that takes place in any rate of return hearing for a regulated industry. In all cases, the charges of the local government, like the charges of

[27] See, e.g., West Park Ave., Inc. v. Township of Ocean, 48 N.J. 122, 224 A.2d 1 (1966): "But as to services which traditionally have been supported by general taxation, other considerations are evident. The dollar burden would likely be unequal if new homes were subject to a charge in addition to the general tax rate. As to education, for example, the vacant land has contributed for years to the cost of existing educational facilities, and that land and the dwellings to be erected will continue to contribute with all other real property to the repayment of bonds issued for the existing facilities and to the cost of renovating or replacing those facilities. Hence there would be an imbalance if the new construction alone were to bear the capital cost of new schools while being also charged with the capital costs of schools serving other portions of the school district." Id. at 126, 224 A.2d at 3. See also Collis v. City of Bloomington, 310 Minn. 5, 246 N.W.2d 19 (1976).

[28] Board of Educ. of School Dis. No. 68 v. Surety Developers, Inc., 63 Ill. 2d 193, 347 N.E.2d 149 (1975) (invalidating special charge for school expansion where test not met). The Illinois test is more restrictive than that adopted in virtually all other states before *Nollan.* See R. Marlin Smith, "From Subdivision Improvement to Community Benefit Assessments and Linkage Payments: A Brief History of Land Development Exactions," 50 *Law & Contemp. Probs.* 5, 13 (1987).

the local utility, should be calibrated to the cost of providing services, and all revenue streams (including ordinary real estate taxes to be collected in the future) should be taken into account.

At one time, many courts were more sensitive to the risks of exactions,[29] but notwithstanding *Nollan*, the more recent trend has been to give local governments powerful authority over the exaction question. In *Commercial Builders of Northern California v. City of Sacramento*,[30] the question was whether a "fee exaction" for all new commercial construction in Sacramento should be upheld on the ground that it was necessary to provide expanded low-income housing inside the city. The court of appeals upheld the ordinance by a 2 to 1 vote, deferring to studies that the city had commissioned which noted that some increased demand for that housing might follow in the wake of the expanded commercial development. There was no showing of any specific connection between a particular project and the changes in housing demand. The court recognized that *Nollan* imposed a nexus requirement on the subdivision exaction, but held, in line with earlier cases, that the level of scrutiny applied to these fee exactions remained unchanged by the decision. It then applied, if anything, a *lower* standard than was previously applicable in exaction cases by announcing that it was a mistake to require "too close a nexus between the regulation and the interest at stake."[31] The court also held that Sacramento had carried whatever burdens were imposed on it by hiring a consulting firm to conduct a study which indicated that some influx of low-income individuals might be expected as a consequence of the commercial development. Sacramento planned to raise about $3,600,000, or 9 percent of its anticipated budget, by fee exactions from local commercial developers.

The city's levy fails under the traditional standards applied to school and sewer exactions, for there is no showing that any of these expenditures, which are discretionary with the city in any event, are uniquely attributable to the commercial development that is taxed for their support. In addition, the consultants' study was flawed in its design because it focused only on a single consequence that might flow from the new development. But it seems clear that virtually every aspect of local life will be influenced in some degree by the

[29] See West Park Ave., 48 N.J. 122, 224 A.2d 1 (1966); City of Dunedin v. Contractors and Builders Ass'n of Pinellas County, 312 So. 2d 763 (Fla. App. 1975) (upholding hook-up charges for water and sewer where fees were proportionate to costs of future improvements and earmarked in special sinking funds).

[30] 941 F.2d 872 (9th Cir. 1991).

[31] Id. at 874.

new developments. These projects could, for example, improve the level of amenities available to others within the city, thereby increasing the value of the overall tax base. Likewise, the projects could also attract new middle-class residents to the city. Yet for all it appears, the study did not take these gains into account in assessing the overall impact of commercial development; nor did it indicate whether any portion of these ostensible costs were offset by the general real estate taxes that could be collected from the commercial property once developed.[32] Once the overall situation is taken into account, Sacramento's exaction fees look like yet another illustration of levying special assessments to provide general benefits that the community wants very much, so long as it can deflect their costs. *Nollan* itself had placed a limit on the practices of Coastal Commission, which had been previously sustained by the California courts. In the short term, the decision in *Nollan* appears to have reined in some excesses of local government. Unfortunately, *Commercial Builders* honors *Nollan* more in the breach than in the observance by returning to the status quo ante and ushering in a new age in which the connection between the exaction imposed and the benefit provided is tenuous at best.[33]

### *Waiver of Interim Damages*

The *Nollan* decision has also had an important role to play in the subsequent response to a second of the key Supreme Court decisions during the 1987 term: *First English Evangelical Lutheran Church v. County of Los Angeles*.[34] *First English* held that a landowner was entitled to compensation for a temporary regulatory taking just as if the state had taken possession of the property for a limited but indefinite period of time. Prior to the decision, California law held that whenever the state imposed restrictions on land use that were determined to amount to a regulatory taking, the sole remedy of the land-

[32] Note that one reason why local governments have moved to special assessments is that they afford a partial escape from the general limitations on real estate taxes that are found in many states, including Proposition 13 (the Jarvis-Gann amendment) in California. Cal. Const. art XIIIA (1978). See Gus Bauman & William H. Ethier, "Development Exactions and Impact Fees: A Survey of American Practices," 50 *Law & Contemp. Probs.* 51, 52 (1987).

[33] See, e.g., Sigfredo A. Cabrera, "Taxman, Spare That Golf Course," *Wall St. J.*, July 11, 1991, at A10, noting that Honolulu was considering an ordinance that would impose a tax on the Japanese developers of a golf course in order to fund low-income housing.

[34] 482 U.S. 304 (1987).

owner was an injunction to lift the ban.[35] *First English* overturned that rule on grounds that are, I believe, unassailable.[36]

One critical question left open in *First English* was how and when the landowner asserted the right to compensation for interim takings. Even before *First English*, the Supreme Court had held that a takings claim "is not ripe until the government entity charged with implementing the regulations has reached a final decision regarding the application of the regulations to the property at issue."[37] The Supreme Court has held that there cannot be any action against the state for a taking of property "until just compensation has been denied,"[38] and that time is very late in the process, for individual landowners can be required to exhaust all administrative procedures, including a request for a variance, before bringing a damage claim under the just compensation clause. For example, the mere fact that a permit is required never furnishes the occasion for suit, because the permit could always be granted, so that the landowner could use the land as desired.[39] This body of law has been carried over in toto to the claims for interim damages, so after *First English*, all administrative remedies need to be exhausted before judicial relief may be sought under the just compensation clause.

This set of rules sets the stage for a bargaining problem similar to that in *Nollan.* Can a landowner be required to waive his claim for interim damages in order to obtain the appropriate permits? That waiver was upheld, for example, in *Rossco Holdings, Inc. v. California Coastal Commission*,[40] a case which arose out of a dispute over whether the Coastal Commission could impose certain restrictions, relating to density and the need to purchase transferable development rights, on the developer. As part of an omnibus settlement, the Coastal Commission demanded and received a *waiver* from the developer of all claims for interim damages under the *First English* rule. The California court held that the waiver was binding.

In order to see why the question is important and the outcome in *Rossco* incorrect, consider the following view of the situation, which does not postpone the right to claim compensation. On this view, what is done is done. Once it is established that the temporary

[35] Agins v. City of Tiburon, 24 Cal. 3d 266, 598 P.2d 25, 157 Cal. Rptr. 372 (1979).

[36] For my views of the case before the subsequent developments, see Richard A. Epstein, "Takings: Descent and Resurrection," 1987 *Sup. Ct. Rev.* 1.

[37] Williamson County Regional Planning Comm'n v. Hamilton Bank, 473 U.S. 172, 186 (1985).

[38] Id. at 194, n. 13.

[39] United States v. Riverside Bayview Homes, Inc., 474 U.S. 121, 126–27 (1985).

[40] 212 Cal. App. 3d 642, 260 Cal. Rptr. 736 (1989).

restrictions amount to a taking, the meter starts to run on the just compensation award. The total bill is the present value of the losses that the landowner suffers during the period in which the restrictions are in place. The only settlement between the landowner and the state is over the dollar value of the relevant calculations. Negotiations over future use are conducted separately as a matter of course. The landowner can collect the money owed under *First English* at any time, whether or not the ongoing dispute over future use has been resolved. Under this regime, there is nothing that the state can do in future planning decisions that can undercut the claim for interim damages. Instead, by virtue of the fact that it acts under the police power, the state remains under a fiduciary duty to pass on the developer's plan under applicable constitutional standards. Since there is no linkage between the two halves of the case, the state (whether through a municipality or coastal commission) has a powerful incentive to pass, quickly and correctly, on any application in order to avoid the damage payments. By keeping the two matters—past compensation and future use—in hermetically sealed compartments, the state is foreclosed from adopting a variation on the strategy that it used in *Nollan*, namely, to insist that the *First English* claim be waived in order for the land use decision to be made.

The alternative approach adopted in *Rossco* leads to radically different outcomes in the bargaining game. There the state is allowed to condition its approval of future development on a waiver of past rights because there is no right to assert a claim for damages until the full case has run its course. Here we should expect in each and every case that the state will insist upon that waiver, just as was done in *Rossco.* Can the landowners afford to refuse? The answer is, most likely no, even if the interim regulation was an undisputed taking. The local authority tells the landowner that unless it waives all claim to interim damages, then it will not be able to obtain final approval for the project. By a classic Catch-22, it can then remind the landowner that the takings damage claim cannot be brought until the entire matter has been resolved. Therefore, since the local authority can drag out the internal review procedures indefinitely, the project remains on hold, which may be just what the dominant political faction wants.

This pattern of negotiation represents a classic illustration, not of the refined bargaining problems in *Nollan*, but of the standard common law model of duress of goods.[41] Stated in its simplest terms, the landowner is given the choice between the right to press the past

[41] See supra chap. 4.

claim and the right to pursue a development project, when in principle he should be able to press both. The case is therefore no different from the situation where the gunman puts the victim to the choice between her money or her life, or the cleaner gives his customer the choice between the recovery of his garment at a higher price and a lawsuit to secure its recovery at the contract price.

The temptation to yield to the threat is as great as it is in private commercial contexts. The exit right is of course useless in this context, for the object of the local government may be to have the project disappear, and the breaking off of negotiations results in the loss of both the project value and the claim for interim damages. The legal remedy is always insecure as a matter of principle, given the amorphous standards of takings law, and it is always possible that some elements of damages (the depreciation in the value of marketing or soil studies) will be sufficiently difficult to prove that they will turn out to be noncompensable. There seems to be no risk of exploitation if the rules are fixed in the opposite direction. The correct solution thus requires that the state must pay for what it has taken on an accrual basis, while the landowner can pursue the interim damage claim. This last option, limited to accrued losses, prevents him from exerting any holdout power over the state. In essence the procedural preconditions to the claim for interim damage allow the state to adopt a linkage strategy that will result in few *admitted* temporary takings receiving just compensation. The legal rules should be restructured to eliminate the possibility of strategic bargaining that the state now possesses.

But it might be asked, why all this concern with property rights and the plight of the developer? The answer comes from asking this question: who is represented by markets and who is represented by the political process? The answer to the question is that the political process is responsive to local interests, that is, to those who vote because of their residence in the community. If one person owns land worth $1 million and the remaining 100 people in a region own property worth a tenth that in value, the will of the 100 shall prevail over that of the one unless that owner can find a way to obtain the permission to develop land by buying off the local government, that is, by yielding to conditions and exactions in the regulatory process. Indeed, the patterns can be both more complex and more insidious. Thus a local government may make a deal with one developer that allows that developer to pursue its project on the understanding that development of other parcels will be delayed so as to preserve its price structure.

The market system, freed of permits and exactions, works in quite the opposite way. It will register the preferences of those persons who do not live inside the community and who cannot vote in local elections. The market process therefore allows, via a credible system of virtual representation, a greater level of participation in the land development than the regulatory process, which systematically attaches no weight to the interests and desires of persons who are affected by the developments within the jurisdiction but who have no territorial nexus to it: under current legal rules those who purchase from a developer have no standing to protest restrictions on development. The absent and the silent have their own self-appointed champion, and a far broader class of preferences can be taken into account. So long as the police power is preserved within its proper boundaries, the risk of exploitation running in the opposite direction can be effectively thwarted. Not only will local governments be able to prevent garden-variety nuisances, but they will be able to demand that developers compensate them for the additional costs that their development will cause to the community in the form of sewer hookups and other special services that will not be compensated by the ordinary real estate and other taxes that are currently imposed. But the bargaining range over these factors is far smaller than that which is currently allowed under the police power. *Nollan* and *First English,* read broadly, promised some level of supervision over regulation and bargaining by local governments that should be welcome from a social perspective. It seems a shame that the opportunity offered by these cases has been frittered away.

CHAPTER 13

# Licenses and Permits

LAND USE regulation is only one area where the state holds a monopoly position by virtue of its ability to act under its police power. The state's power to license various kinds of business activities creates another domain of monopoly power of great importance and equally subject to abuse. In this chapter, I examine three separate contexts in which the state's exercise of its licensing power has been challenged, usually under the doctrine of unconstitutional conditions. The first section addresses the licensing of medical and legal professions. The second section deals with the licensing of insurance firms. Finally the third section examines the use of police power regulations over gambling.

## PROFESSIONAL LICENSING OF PHYSICIANS AND LAWYERS

The traditional justification for licensing learned professionals, such as lawyers and physicians, has a familiar ring: the assurance through government action of a minimum level of competence for persons who are engaged in activities that call for a high level of training and sophistication. In a world without licensing, or so the argument goes, individual practitioners of the various professions might deceive those whom they serve by providing them with inferior or dangerous services. As information is costly for private persons to collect and assemble, the state takes over that function for them by providing a centralized system of control that bars entrance to a profession for those individuals thought unfit to ply it. The strong critique of the licensing system, with which I largely agree, is that consumers can make the necessary judgments about professional services, or can hire other persons to help them with their choices. On this view licensing is but a transparent effort by professionals to cartelize their own trades by excluding their rivals.[1] Simple certifica-

[1] See, e.g., Keith B. Leffler, "Physician Licensure: Competition and Monopoly in American Medicine," 21 *J. Law & Econ.* 165 (1978); Lawrence Shepard, "Licensing Restrictions and the Cost of Dental Care," 21 *J. Law & Econ.* 187 (1978); Note, "On Letting the Laity Litigate: The Petition Clause and Unauthorized Practice Rules," 132 *U. Pa. L. Rev.* 1515 (1984).

tion that persons have passed certain tests, or have met the membership requirements of certain societies, is all that is necessary to control information, and consumers should be allowed to purchase lower quality goods at lower prices, when they so choose.

One feature common to both sides of this debate, however, is that the legitimate functions of licensing are limited to the protection against fraud and misconduct by incompetent practitioners. The critical question for constitutional law is whether the standard justifications for licensing practices limit the reasons that the state may invoke to refuse to grant licenses, or to grant them on condition. This framework can be accepted in constitutional terms even by persons who think that restraint of trade provides a more persuasive, self-interested account of the way the system operates. The key question therefore is whether it is unconstitutional to withhold the license for conditions that are unrelated to the competence of any individual to practice the chosen profession. Within this framework of analysis, the constitutional right protected is (or at least was)[2] the right to engage in a trade or profession as one sees fit, just as it was in the highway cases, and the unconstitutional condition is that imposed by the licensing requirement, which limits that degree of professional autonomy.

In the earlier cases, there was clearly some strong tendency to take this point of view both at common law and under the Constitution. In *Hurley v. Eddingfield*[3], the plaintiff claimed that the defendant, in virtue of the license to practice that he received from the state, was under a legal duty to tender services to a patient in need who was willing and able to pay his customary fee. The cause of action was rejected emphatically: "The [licensing] act is a preventive, not a compulsive, measure. In obtaining the State's license (permission) to practice medicine, the State does not require, and the licensee does not engage, that he will practice at all or on other terms than he may choose to act."[4] The case reflects the traditional understanding about licensing, but it is not decisive on the constitutional question: what would happen if the state did impose conditions of service on those who sought to obtain or retain licenses within the state?

The same basic attitude has been revealed in a constitutional setting in connection with licenses to practice law. In *Schware v. Board of Bar Examiners of New Mexico*,[5] the Court held that, under the due process clause, the state improperly denied the plaintiff admis-

[2] Truax v. Raich, 239 U.S. 33 (1915).
[3] 156 Ind. 416, 59 N.E. 1058 (1901).
[4] 156 Ind. at 417, 59 N.E. at 1058.
[5] 353 U.S. 232 (1957).

sion to the practice of law on the ground of his past arrests (without convictions), use of aliases (to escape anti-Semitism in the 1930s), and affiliations with the Communist Party, when other evidence spoke to his exemplary character. In reaching this decision Justice Black, speaking for a unanimous Court, held, consistent with the unconstitutional conditions doctrine, that it did not matter whether a license to practice law was a "right" or a "privilege."[6] He then reverted to the familiar nexus requirement: "A state can require high standards of qualification, such as good moral character or proficiency in its law, before it admits an applicant to the bar, but any qualification must have a rational connection with the applicant's fitness or capacity to practice law. Obviously an applicant could not be excluded merely because he was a Republican or a Negro or a member of a particular church."[7]

Neither of these cases is dispositive on the next, and relevant, round of constitutional litigation, which concerned the attachment of very different kinds of conditions to licenses: the requirement that lawyers be prepared to do pro bono work as a condition to obtain licenses, upheld in *United States v. Dillon*,[8] or the requirement that physicians not charge patients on Medicare sums in excess of those for which reimbursement is obtained from the federal government, upheld in *Massachusetts Medical Society v. Dukakis*.[9] *Hurley* is not decisive, because it deals only with the conventional, and common law, understanding that licensees practice in open markets. It did not say what, if anything, should happen if the state legislated a change of its licensing practices. For its part, *Schware*, while a constitutional decision, was concerned with reasons for denying licenses that were tied to First Amendment concerns of freedom of speech and association. Justice Black's illustration of political and religious affiliations and race are far removed from the strictly economic issues raised in *Dillon*.

[6] Id. at 239, n.5.

[7] Id. at 239 (citations omitted).

[8] 346 F.2d 633 (9th Cir. 1965); see also Williamson v. Vardeman, 674 F.2d 1211, 1215 (8th Cir. 1982) (citing cases).

[9] 637 F. Supp. 684 (D. Mass. 1986). The statute provided: "The [Board of Registration in Medicine] shall require as a condition of granting or renewing a physician's certificate of registration, that the physician, who if he agrees to treat a beneficiary of health insurance under Title XVIII of the Social Security Act [Medicare], shall also agree not to charge or collect from such beneficiary any amount in excess of the reasonable charge for that service as determined by the United States Secretary of Health and Human Services." Ann. Laws Mass. C. 112, §2, Chapter 475, Massachusetts Acts of 1985. The statute banned the so-called practice of "balance billing" whereby recipients under Medicare could pay additional fees to physicians from either their own pockets or from medical insurance.

How then ought these issues to be resolved? Within the current system, which affords only weak protection for economic liberties, the results are foregone. Just as comprehensive price fixing and similar regulations may be imposed, so too economic conditions may be attached to the licenses.[10] In some cases this result is said to depend on the evident fact that lawyers (or doctors) are "aware of the traditions of the profession" and therefore are bound by them when they become members of the bar (or medical community).[11] Yet a closer analysis indicates that this use of state monopoly power has the same mischievous consequences as in other settings and should be struck down for the same reason: that there should be more powerful protection of economic liberties generally.

The general argument in favor of regulation, here as elsewhere, places far too much weight on the idea of *notice* as a justification for regulatory action under the licensing power.[12] Notice in the law is a mixed blessing. In those cases where parties receive notice of the legal rights of other individuals, they can conduct their affairs in a way that allows them to avoid serious disputes over the ownership of various assets. The entire system for the recordation of title to land is rightly justified as a means to insure that potential purchasers of real estate understand who has what interest in property, so that they will deal only with those persons who have valid ownership claims. It strengthens the system of property rights by preventing fraud and double-dealing. But notice takes on a more dangerous complexion when tactically invoked by persons who wish to claim what they do not own. The standard tort hypothetical is the landowner who gives notice that he will not be responsible for accidents caused by animals or pollution on his land, so that others should take care to mitigate their losses.[13] Here the strategy of the landowner is not to facilitate a system of voluntary exchange but to allow strategic threats to extort precautions from others without paying for them, and the proper legal response is to insist (a) for the state, that the party that gives notice pay for the precautions that he recommends, or (b) for everyone else, that the notice be disregarded by others whose entitlements are threatened.[14]

Licensing functions in an impermissible context when it is conditioned upon the willingness of attorneys to provide pro bono services

[10] Thus the predictable reliance on Nebbia v. New York, 291 U.S. 502 (1934) (upholding minimum price regulations on dairy products).

[11] See, e.g., *Dillon*, 346 F.2d at 635.

[12] See *Takings*, 151–58, for criticisms of these arguments.

[13] See, e.g., Susan Rose-Ackerman, "Dikes, Dams, and Vicious Hogs: Entitlement and Efficiency in Tort Law," 18 *J. Legal Stud.* 25 (1989).

[14] See *Takings*, 151–58.

to individual clients on court order. Under the traditional regime of licensing, the accumulated human capital associated with running a profession is allocated uniquely to the professional who holds it, subject only to those costs necessary to pass the bar. But once services of any sort can be extracted at below-market value from that professional, then this accumulated capital is subject to dissipation, by the struggle over its division between the state (or those to whom it furnishes services) and the holder of that human capital. More and more services can be demanded of lawyers. These conditions will of course be accepted in most cases because the opportunity to earn income with the license is greater than the opportunities to earn income in some alternative employment for which this license is not required. The conditions will bite especially heavily on persons already at the bar, but even if their effect is purely prospective (as for college seniors), the imposition of the condition will have unfortunate allocative effects as well: some persons will decide not to enter the profession, given the implicit tax (here in the form of forced labor) that the state imposes.

In principle, the threat to exercise the exit right will be available in all cases. Nonetheless, as with the land use case, that threat is not credible for most lawyers who will consent to the condition in question in order to preserve some of their professional surplus. But the allocative effects are demonstrably inferior to those which are achieved under the (more) open market when licenses are limited to matters of professional competence. With the condition attached, there will be partial foreclosure of marginal entrants into the business; and there will now be the ceaseless machinations by individual lawyers to avoid service for which adequate compensation is not tendered by the state. Nor is the insistence that requiring pro bono work is unconstitutional under a takings or due process analysis (or for that matter as a form of involuntary servitude) inconsistent with the view that the state should supply legal services for those who need it. What the rule does insist on is that this social obligation should fall on the public at large and not on some segment which is said to be uniquely situated to provide it. The state can impose general taxes to collect the revenues it needs, which can then be used to hire lawyers at market wages. It does not have to conscript lawyers whose knowledge of criminal procedure is nonexistent, and whose other clients are forced to scramble to find other representation at great cost to themselves and the efficiency of the system. The unconstitutional conditions doctrine, with its focus on preserving the cooperative surplus achieved in open markets, thus requires the invalidation of a condition that has been uniformly sustained by the courts.

A similar analysis applies to the Massachusetts Medicare statute. The maximum fee condition is wholly unrelated to any question of competence to perform services and is no more legitimate if imposed as a condition for licensing than if imposed by direct regulation on all physicians. As a matter of first principle, it does not matter whether the condition is imposed on new physicians entering the market or on those who seek a renewal of license—the statute carefully covers both cases, for the argument against the condition is not merely that retroactive conditions are unfair because there was no notice that they were imposed, but also that *prospective* conditions are inappropriate because of the way in which they disrupt the market. Judge Keeton, in sustaining the statute, did so in large part because he thought that the laws of supply and demand were of no descriptive relevance to the supply of medical services. He relied on the "common sense expectation that physicians faced with a limit on fees will have an incentive to increase the volume of services provided in order to maintain their income level."[15] He further asserted that, in addition to income incentives, physicians were influenced by "a physician's pride in his or her work, commitment to the ethic of care of the profession, personal concern for his or her patients, and intellectual curiosity in the best and newest forms of treatment."[16]

His decision represents all too well the muddled economic thinking that leads to misguided constitutional results. The effects of a limitation on the fees that can be charged patients will induce physicians to take steps that will maximize their income, given their options, subject to the new constraints. Keeton's reference to the ostensible efforts of physicians to maintain income levels by increasing the level of services is an inadvertent effort to invent an economic rationale for the statute, albeit a wrong one. A more complete explanation would stress that the definition of an office visit or procedure will shrink in order to increase the number of billing occasions. It would also stress that if, notwithstanding these evasions, regulated prices are set below cost (as will be the case for some physicians), then no increase in volume will permit the maximization of profits. Finally, that explanation would note that the nonpecuniary elements of providing medical services should be taken into account under any complete economic analysis of the situation, when they receive the opposite effect that Judge Keeton attributes to them. First, these noneconomic benefits are reduced by state orders that remove a level of physician self-control and with it a level of physi-

[15] *Massachusetts Medical Soc'y*, 637 F. Supp. at 697.
[16] Id. at 698.

cian self-respect. Second, even if these benefits remain constant, so long as the pecuniary elements of compensation are reduced, the total compensation package is necessarily reduced as well, and with it the supply of services rendered in the regulated sector.[17]

The law of supply—that increased prices bring forth increased quantities—may have been repealed in the federal District Court of Massachusetts, but it should be respected everywhere else. The constant effort to tinker and control health care in Massachusetts and elsewhere works no better when it is tied to a licensing scheme than when it is run through direct regulation. Striking down this condition on licensing does not necessarily end a system of redistribution for the provision of medical care; it only requires that the state or the federal government pay out of general revenues for the services they provide the poor. As with the pro bono requirements, individual physicians with large investments of specific capital will find it impossible to exit the market and hence will consent to the condition. But so long as a doctrine of unconstitutional conditions is available, this option should be systematically denied to the state. The goal of constitutional law should be to maximize overall surplus by the maintenance of competitive markets. The proper antidote to the monopoly elements that remain under a system of licensing is to allow greater ease of entry (as by admitting, as a matter of course, to the practice of law or medicine those persons who have practiced in another jurisdiction). The evils of a licensing system are not offset by using it to achieve redistributive ends better achieved by other means.

## EXIT RESTRICTIONS AND INSURANCE REGULATIONS

The use of the licensing power has, as of late, also proved extremely important in the area of insurance rate regulation. Rate regulation in the insurance industry has always been problematic as a matter of principle. Rate regulation may well be appropriate for public utilities, for if left unregulated these entities could wield substantial amounts of monopoly power. The system of regulation imposes heavy administrative costs and, if unchecked by a fair return requirement, could allow the state to expropriate the invested capital of the utility under the guise of rate regulation. The due process and just

[17] Note that exit here could take the form of abandoning the Medicare market but remaining in practice, which would reduce the costs of medical care in other sectors at the expense of a general misallocation of resources.

compensation clauses have been brought to bear in this area to forestall such a possibility, and the vast bulk of the debate and litigation has been on the proper form of the constitutional constraints on rate regulation.[18] In large measure the function of this regulation has been to make, to the extent that legal rules can devise, the utilities price their services as if they were in a competitive industry.

The carryover of this system of public regulation to the insurance industry is problematic to say the least. To be sure, there is a case for some regulation of the industry if only to prevent firms from becoming insolvent before they can satisfy their claims. But today regulation often goes beyond these solvency requirements and seeks to duplicate the rate of return regulation applied to public utilities. There is no justification for this system given that the market is in the competitive state that regulation normally seeks to achieve. Therefore, it is quite impossible as a matter of principle to see how firms in a competitive industry can be asked to increase their costs and lower their rates, while still earning the same profit. If revenues are down and costs are up, then profits must be reduced below levels needed to maintain a constitutionally required rate of return. In my view there is never any need to engage in any complex inquiry before striking down all rate of return regulation for competitive industries on constitutional grounds. The formal case against the system of regulation is that decisive.

As one might expect, the modern law takes a more relaxed view of the subject and allows rate of return regulation in principle so long as the reasonable rate of return is required in fact.[19] The matter obtains overtones of an unconstitutional conditions case when the state, in addition to imposing rate regulation and rollbacks on the industry, seeks to control the right of exit as well. Thus, in New

[18] For the most recent Supreme Court foray into the area, see Duquesne Light Co. v. Barasch, 488 U.S. 299 (1989). The two dominant standards have been the "bottom-line" standard of Federal Power Comm'n v. Hope Natural Gas, 320 U.S. 591 (1944), and the "used and usable" standard of Smyth v. Ames, 169 U.S. 466 (1898). By the former, the state is allowed to proceed as it will so long as at the end of the day the utility investors have a just return on their invested capital. By the latter, only that capital which is actively used in the business is entitled to a return, but at a higher level to compensate the investors for risk. The bottom-line standard does not give the utility appropriate incentives to maximize return on investment, but the used and usable standard creates major difficulties of valuation. The judicial response is to allow the state to take its pick between the two, with the bottom-line standard of *Hope* being by far the more common choice.

[19] See, e.g., Calfarm Ins. Co. v. Deukmejian, 48 Cal. 3d 805, 771 P.2d 1247, 258 Cal. Rptr. 161 (1989) (striking down an automatic 20 percent rollback for the next year, but subjecting all insurance regulation to rate of return requirements).

Jersey, FAIRA (The Fair Automobile Insurance Reform Act of 1990),[20] in addition to its onerous rate of return regulation,[21] contains a critical provision that destroys the viability of the exit right. The statute provides that "any insurance company of another state or foreign country" that wishes to exit must make "a submission of a plan which provides for an orderly withdrawal from the market and a minimization of the impact of the surrender or discontinuance on the public generally and on the company's policyholders in particular," and further, that the commissioner "as a condition of approval" of such plan require the company to surrender its other licenses to do business within the state.[22] It is consistent with the general statutory scheme that another of the conditions on withdrawal is payment of exit taxes and fees.[23]

One line of attack against this statute is to argue that it switches the rules in the middle of the game, without providing those firms that previously entered the insurance industry in the state adequate notice of the conditions for doing business within the state. While general solvency legislation is surely subject to change, and rate of return regulation might be regarded as foreseeable if undesirable, the exit restrictions and the license removals are outside the normal scheme of legislation. I have a certain sympathy for these procedural and administrative type of objections, but, even when given their due, they do not go to the heart of the matter. The more urgent question of principle goes to the power of the state to announce clearly and unambiguously these conditions to any new firm that seeks to enter its local markets. In essence the question is whether it may condition entry into local markets, be it for corporations or anyone else, on the willingness to abide by future regulations of the sort involved here.

As with the cases of medical and legal regulation just considered, only the negative answer is appropriate. The question in these cases is not whether the firm can protect itself by deciding not to do busi-

[20] N.J. Stat. Ann. c. 17:33B, 1990 N.J. Sess. Law Serv. 8 (West), sustained against a facial constitutional challenge in State Farm Ins. Co. v. New Jersey, 124 N.J. 32, 590 A.2d 191 (1991).

[21] For my general criticisms of this statute, see Richard A. Epstein, "A Clash of Two Cultures: Will Tort Law Survive Automobile Insurance Reform?" 21 Val. U.L. Rev. 173 (1991).

[22] N.J. Stat. Ann. §17:33B-30 (West 1990) (New Jersey Fair Automobile Insurance Reform Act of 1990 (N.J. FAIRA)).

[23] See Massachusetts General Laws, ch. 175, §22H. Under the statute, any insurer that wishes to abandon its license to sell automobile insurance and retain its other state licenses must make payments into the assigned risk pool for an eight-year period after it withdraws from that market.

ness at all, so that it can be said to assume the risk of any exaction that the state chooses to impose. The question instead is whether the conditions that the state seeks to attach to doing business within its borders are ones that advance or retard the operation of a competitive market. Here the major social loss will be that new firms will *not* enter the market in the first place, which might throw a protective mantle over the firms already there. In principle any firm that enters the state should be allowed to attack the conditions and proceed to do business as if they did not exist. Likewise firms that are within the state should be able to leave unilaterally and resist any tax or license removal when doing so. When the conditions are imposed while the firm is doing business, they should be subject to immediate facial invalidation, whether the firm chooses to leave or stay.

The explanation for this configuration of restrictions is not difficult to find. The exit right is one that will restrain the power of the state to confiscate wealth from private parties even where the system of rate of return regulation provides (as is typically the case) insufficient protection against the regulated firm.[24] To be sure, all firms will have some sunk costs, and will therefore be reluctant to leave if the level of future confiscation is below the capital losses that will be sustained from discontinuing business within the state. The state has some running room even if there are no legal restraints on exit. But these restraints are limited, for the firm can make a credible threat to leave if the level of confiscation exceeds that limit, and by so doing adds an additional constraint against the abuses inherent in rate regulation.

By imposing the tax, the state increases its opportunities for exploitation. Similarly, the ability to lift other licenses places firms that are losing money on one line of insurance (e.g., homeowner's or automobile) in the position of having to sacrifice the profits on other lines in order to make their escape. For those firms that have only a single line, this threat may be of little consequence, but for major firms that have multiple lines of business the threat is devastating,

[24] One possible strategy is to exclude recoverable items from the rate base. Another is to give low valuations of the various items, especially intangibles, that are properly included in the base. A third strategy is to delay the implementation of rate increases with procedural requests. A fourth is to argue that current losses can be made up with future rate increases, which, while authorized, cannot be captured in the marketplace. All of these have been adopted with marked success in the rate regulation imbroglios in both California and New Jersey. See Benjamin Zychar, "Automobile Insurance Regulation, Direct Democracy, and the Interests of Consumers," *Regulation*, Summer 1990, at 67.

especially if profits in other lines are large relative to the level of losses in the single regulated line.[25]

The free exit right should be constitutionally guaranteed even where the market is unregulated. A fortiori, it should be applied where rate of return regulation of a competitive industry is constitutionally permissible. If it requires calling a condition coercive in order to invalidate it, so be it. The important point is that the state should not be allowed to adopt any scheme of regulation that pulls an industry away from its competitive form. A firm could well accept the regulation in the hopes that it will still be able to garner profits with the sword of Damocles hanging over its head—perhaps because the refusal of other firms to enter has given it a short-term opportunity to extract monopoly rents. But the doctrine of unconstitutional conditions is intimately concerned with market structure. The theoretical reasons why a firm should not be bound by its own consent in the face of state monopoly power apply with especial force when the state licenses firms to do business within its jurisdiction.

## COMMERCIAL SPEECH AND PUBLIC MORALS

A similar police power problem can arise in the First Amendment context. There too the freedom of speech conferred by the Amendment is nowhere regarded as absolute. Instead the key question is what forms of speech may be restrained under the police power. While the scope of this power is far more narrowly construed than it is with property,[26] it is clear that the police power is at least implicated, however cautiously, in cases that involve the threat or use of force, such as "fighting words," and likewise of fraud.[27] With speech, as with other forms of human activity, the most difficult branch of the police power is its so-called morals branch.

It was just that branch that was called into question in *Posadas de Puerto Rico Associates v. Tourism Co.*[28] There, Puerto Rico wished to encourage tourists to come to Puerto Rico to gamble. It did not

[25] In New Jersey, the Hartford Insurance Company abandoned plans to take a small subsidiary out of the auto business for fear that its licenses for its lucrative health insurance business would be lifted.

[26] See, for an extensive comparison, Richard A. Epstein, "Property, Speech, and the Politics of Distrust," 59 *U. Chi. L. Rev.* 41 (1992).

[27] See, e.g., Brandenburg v. Ohio, 395 U.S. 444 (1970) (subversive advocacy); New York Times Co. v. Sullivan, 376 U.S. 254 (1964) (defamation).

[28] 478 U.S. 328 (1986).

make gambling illegal for local citizens, but it did prevent any local advertisement of gambling on the island proper, leaving Posadas, a Holiday Inn franchisee, free to advertise its gambling facilities on the mainland. It was conceded that the control of gambling fell within the traditional "morals" head of the police power of the state, so that the state could have made gambling illegal across-the-board. In upholding this statute, Justice Rehnquist implicitly rejected the doctrine of unconstitutional conditions when he argued that Puerto Rico's plenary power to ban gambling itself gave it the lesser power to license gambling, subject to the condition that the licensee accept a ban on local advertisement[29]—itself a limitation on a First Amendment right. Do First Amendment principles require that such advertisements be tolerated, given the decision to allow the gambling itself? Where the advertising was neither misleading nor fraudulent, the canonical version of the constitutional inquiry is that "the speech may be restricted only if the government's interest in doing so is substantial, the restrictions directly advance the government's asserted interest, and the restrictions are no more extensive than necessary to serve that interest."[30] Justice Rehnquist's deferential exploration of these issues upheld the restrictions, which Justice Brennan, who championed the greater/lesser logic in his *Nollan* dissent, would have struck down.[31]

For our purposes, the central question is whether the doctrine of unconstitutional conditions, as applied in this context, effectively checks government misbehavior. The picture is decidedly murky, but in one sense it does. The Puerto Rican policy is cynical: gambling has terrible consequences for the social fabric, so Puerto Rico attempted to externalize its costs by taking the money of tourists, who will take their social and psychological problems home with their other belongings. The possible interests of other states, which cannot prevent their citizens from gambling outside their borders, are not registered in the local political calculus, and in all likelihood are of faint importance in the congressional politics over Puerto Rico's status and preferences. On the domestic front, the ban on casino

[29] See id. at 346.

[30] Id. at 340 (citing Central Hudson Gas & Elec. Corp. v. Public Serv. Comm'n, 447 U.S. 557, 566 (1980)).

[31] See 478 U.S. at 350 (Brennan, J., dissenting). Although he employed a high level of scrutiny, Justice Brennan claimed that he would have struck down the law even under the Court's more permissive standard. See id. at 350–51. For a spirited denunciation of Justice Rehnquist's opinion for its application of low-level scrutiny, see Philip B. Kurland, "*Posadas de Puerto Rico v. Tourism Company*: ''Twas Strange, 'Twas Passing Strange; 'Twas Pitiful, 'Twas Wondrous Pitiful,'" 1986 *Sup. Ct. Rev.* 1.

gambling does not extend to such noble pastimes as horse racing, cockfights, and the Puerto Rican lottery.[32] In essence this exercise of the police power has a clearly anticompetitive component, for as Justice Brennan, writing in the spirit of a public-choice economist, suggested "it is surely not far-fetched to suppose that the legislature chose to restrict casino advertising not because of the 'evils' of casino gambling, but because it preferred that Puerto Ricans spend their gambling dollars on the Puerto Rico lottery"[33]—which, it might be added, tourists are not very likely to play.

*Posadas* is extremely difficult to make sense of because the statute, as applied to both Puerto Ricans and to visitors, can plausibly be characterized either as a traditional exercise of the police power or as an attempt by Puerto Rico to exploit those within its borders. The unconstitutional conditions inquiry in *Posadas* is in a sense the opposite of the one in *Nollan*: should the Court require the bundling of the two issues—casino gambling and casino advertising—in order to forestall the political abuse that threatens commercial speech?

Perhaps it should. One advantage of the bundling is that the advertising ban, permissible only if gambling itself is banned, is of no consequence: who would advertise what he could not sell? This means that governments and citizens would not become comfortable with large bureaucracies whose sole function is to suppress or regulate speech. Yet in another sense this linkage is very hard to sustain. One reason to legalize gambling is simply damage-control: it is better that people not gamble, not only for their own personal character, but also for the corrosive effect gambling has on family and business obligations. Nonetheless, it is just too costly to try to control gambling by criminal sanctions. Better therefore to legalize the "disfavored" activity, which can then be taxed to keep participation within reason. Disfavored activities, moreover, need not be treated like all other business activities. Advertising stimulates business, so it might be proper for a state to decide that, while it should not ban gambling, it should nonetheless moderate its growth by banning advertising. Surely if the issue were the legalization of marijuana and other drugs, a respectable argument could be made to allow their sale, subject to a general tax and to prohibitions or restrictions on advertising which, because of advertising's public visibility, should be reasonably easy to enforce. In effect we have adopted such a strategy with respect to cigarettes, which are sold, heavily taxed, and subject to advertisement restrictions, at least on television and radio.

[32] See 478 U.S. at 342.

[33] Id. at 353–54 (Brennan, J., dissenting).

Given the absence of any coherent social attitude toward gambling (or toward drugs, alcohol, tobacco, or prostitution), courts should exercise some deference to state restrictions on such activities under the traditional "morals" head of the police power as it relates to *both* property and speech.

Nonetheless there are reasons to doubt that the regulation at issue in *Posadas* meets that test. The social disruptions of gambling, if real, should be manifest in all its forms. When the state seeks to divide markets—with local customers directed toward the state's own lottery and well-heeled, out-of-state customers toward its posh casinos—it looks as if the anticompetitive motives dominate the protective motives. Forcing an all-or-nothing choice between banning all advertisement or banning none allows the state to pursue its legitimate police power objectives without running the risk of rigging local markets. If total bans are thought to be too damaging to the pocketbook, then it is still possible to have a rule that allows all forms of gambling to use print but not broadcast advertising, or perhaps the reverse. Perhaps the state should be able to disengage the decision to allow gambling from its decision to ban its advertisement, but some very powerful justification must be offered to show why different forms of gambling should operate under different regulatory regimes. Here, as in other First Amendment contexts, the *selective* nature of the ban calls for an extra measure of scrutiny. Justice Rehnquist might have been correct in insisting that the doctrine of unconstitutional conditions is inapplicable to the connection between gambling and advertising. But the explicit discrimination between government-run and privately-run gambling raises the prospect of abuse that calls for a stronger use of the doctrine of unconstitutional conditions in its equal protection guise.

There is a second strand to *Posadas* that is still more disturbing. Present law freely allows general economic regulation of all sorts and descriptions.[34] Under Justice Rehnquist's logic, the power to ban an activity implies the power to ban its advertisement. It follows, therefore, that First Amendment protections afforded commercial speech can be no greater than the meager protections given to economic liberties. In order to provide adequate protection for speech, then, it becomes necessary to build a Maginot Line between the relaxed attitude toward economic liberties and the stricter scrutiny on matters of speech. The doctrine of unconstitutional conditions again

[34] See, e.g., City of New Orleans v. Dukes, 427 U.S. 297 (1976); Ferguson v. Skrupa, 372 U.S. 726 (1963); Williamson v. Lee Optical Co., 348 U.S. 483 (1955); Kurland, supra note 31, at 13.

serves as a second-best tool to limit the ominous implications of the modern economic liberties cases. But this larger problem, and the horribles it suggests, would disappear if we returned to the older cases on occupational freedom requiring the state to show a strong justification before banning any ordinary commercial activity.[35]

Even if we do not take that hard line, it is still possible to limit *Posadas*, which should be understood not as an ordinary commercial speech case, but as a police power morals case. Constitutionally, it may be a close question whether gambling may be banned, and hence a close case whether advertising of gambling can be banned even if the gambling is allowed. The difficulty of these questions thus weakens the constitutional protection for gambling and its advertising alike. But these substantive doubts do not eliminate the equal protection dimension of the case. It is still imperative that the state treat all forms of any suspect activity such as gambling under the same standard unless some powerful justification for differential treatment can be demonstrated. By this logic, *Posadas* should stand only for the proposition that constitutional protection of speech is at its lowest ebb in the morals cases. It need not overrun the constitutional protection of commercial speech generally.

[35] See, e.g., Truax v. Raich, 239 U.S. 33, 41 (1915).

## CHAPTER 14

# Labor and Employment Contracts

THE SCOPE of the state's power to bargain is not confined to its exercise of the police power. Bargaining with the state also can give rise to difficulties in the broad range of labor and employment contracts. The state, of course, can only discharge its public functions through agents, and these agents must be hired by contract, either with individual workers or through independent contractors. These contracts are governed by the ordinary principles applicable to private parties on such matters as offer and acceptance, contract interpretation, and defenses of fraud, incompetence, and duress. But there are also distinctive contracting problems, similar to those encountered in other contexts, stemming from the state's bargaining role. The first of these is the takings risk: the government acquires its property through taxation, so that its revenues are impressed with a trust which dictates that these moneys be spent in ways that benefit the public, that is, the same people from whom they were exacted. The risk is that state officials will become faithless agents and enter into sweetheart transactions in which public funds are given away to private parties—either themselves or their friends. The second risk is the familiar one of unconstitutional conditions. The state will use its monopoly power to extract the waiver of some constitutional right, which will lead to an elimination of a competitive equilibrium or a distortion of the political process, or both. In this chapter, I shall examine these two risks in tandem, for in practice the division between them is far from watertight.

In the previous contexts, e.g., highways and licensing, the bargaining risk loomed larger than the takings risk, given the state's extensive monopoly power. With labor contracts, the weights of the relevant concerns shift, for now the risk of diversion of public assets for private gain is substantial. On the other hand, labor markets are by and large competitive, at least in the sense that there are many interested parties on both sides of the market, so the monopoly power that undergirds the unconstitutional conditions issue is usually not present. To see why this is so, suppose the state announces that it will offer jobs only to persons who agree to forgo any claims for compensation should the government condemn their property at some future time. The condition itself is not germane to the employment relationship, in the sense it does not enable the government to better perform the mission for which the individual worker has been hired. Courts, with their suspicions raised, might be tempted to strike down this condition on that ground alone. But that judicial determination is likely to be an unnecessary act, for cases of this sort are not likely to arise even if the government had the power to impose this demand on its employees.

Assume that the government is paying the worker a competitive wage, and then tries to impose this condition. If the worker has any property of value, or contemplates its future acquisition, then the effective wage for the job will be reduced by the anticipated losses should this confiscation right be exercised. That de facto diminution in wages would be large enough to induce most employees to shift into their next-best line of employment unless the government is prepared to pay them, up-front and in cash, some premium that is sufficient to offset the loss attendant to the possible condemnation. But it is difficult to find what dollar figure will satisfy the worker's competitive-wage constraint while preserving the profit for the government. Whether that confiscation takes place is wholly within the control of the government. So too is its extent. If the government compensates at a level below the value of the property owned (or to be acquired) by the employee, then it will make a losing bargain from its side unless it exercises its confiscation power. But if the government can profit only by exercising that power, then the worker's signing bonus must equal the value of the property that will be condemned. It will hardly be worthwhile for the government to pay that hefty sum, and take the risk of overpayment. An alternative strategy dominates: the government can sever employment from condemnation and choose the proper objects for condemnation in a separate proceeding initiated at some later time.

The tie-in between employment and confiscation, then, makes no sense as a business matter for either side. The government and the worker are both better off if the understandings governing employment relations are kept wholly distinct from those governing condemnation. Indeed, even if the government had some substantial element of monopoly power in the employment setting, demanding this waiver of a constitutional right would be a foolish way to exercise it: insisting on wage levels below those applicable in a competitive market offers a better way for the state to exploit its monopoly position. The unrelated condition, then, will not be imposed for business reasons alone, even if no doctrine of unconstitutional conditions were on the books. The legal concerns will gravitate to those conditions that are in some sense "germane" to the work, to conditions that satisfy Justice Scalia's "relatedness" requirement in *Nollan*.

The relevant class of cases, therefore, will be those in which the condition imposed will be related to the task or job in question, for here the ratio of gains and losses is such that it will be in the interest of government to impose the condition and in the interest of a private party to accept it, if the only available alternative is to do without the deal altogether. Deciding which conditions are acceptable and which are not is, moreover, likely to be difficult because the problem of bilateral opportunism, which played a secondary role in most of the previous discussion, comes to the fore in this setting. Employees have substantial obligations to their employers, and whenever work can be done, it can be done badly. Contractual restraints against employee misconduct should be expected as a matter of course. Within this class of cases, therefore, it is important to ask in each individual case whether the state's restriction represents a strategic gambit or whether it is designed to counter a similar gambit by the individual worker.

How then should a court decide which form of opportunism is dominant? In principle, one ready test is at hand: a court can ask whether the kinds of restrictions that the government seeks to impose on its own employees are similar to those that private firms in competitive labor markets impose on their employees. This test is not perfect because firms that adopt sound and novel practices should be able to reap great rewards. A test that matches government practices with those of private firms will look with suspicion on desirable government innovations. It is also the case that different firms in the private sector will have good reasons to adopt contracting practices tailored to the particulars of their work force. A firm with experienced workers earning high salaries may impose fewer conditions on its workers than a firm that hired relatively new workers at lower salaries. The increased reliability in the work force offsets the need for certain forms of supervision. The vitality of the private market, therefore, may (but need not) preclude uniformity in the terms of employment contracts. The best test that can be hoped for is this: does the condition imposed by the government match those which are adopted by some significant fraction of the market? If it does, then there is a strong presumption for its validity. If not, then the presumption should be set the other way.

The formula, even as modified, may not work in all cases, for some government jobs may be so unique as to defy any private analogue. But even in governmental settings, the large number of separate government employers at all levels may help to create a competitive labor market, even with services uniquely provided for by the state.[1] For the broad range of office workers, executives, policymakers, and bureaucrats, the connections are very close indeed. It is very hard to create monopolies in labor markets without explicit government intervention to block free entry.

It follows, therefore, that the law should find fewer occasions to invoke the unconstitutional conditions doctrine in the context of government employment than in other contexts. In many cases there is a commendable reluctance to invoke the doctrine of unconstitutional conditions. But in other cases the opposite trend is observed. The law puts both sides to an all-or-nothing choice even when there is no risk of monopoly excess. In these cases, modern conceptions of inequality of bargaining power or contracts of adhesion are used in this context with the same disruptive influence that they have in other contexts. In the materials that follow it is possible to trace the influence of both conceptions of the doctrine.

## THE CASES

### *Competition and Economic Liberties*

The first of the unconstitutional conditions cases in employment arose shortly before *Lochner v. New York*[2] invalidated the ten-hour per day maximum hour provisions for certain bakers. In *Atkin v. Kansas*,[3] a Kansas statute required all municipal corporations to employ day laborers in highway construction for a maximum of eight hours per day. Kansas instituted criminal prosecution against Atkin, a local contractor, who had knowingly hired and paid a day laborer for a ten-hour day in violation of the Kansas statute. It was stipulated that the work in question was not dangerous or injurious to health, and it was regarded as an open question as to whether the state could impose this condition by regulation upon private employers and employees with whom it had no state regulation, given the general constitutional protections for liberty of contract.[4] Nonetheless, Justice

[1] This theme is developed in Stephen F. Williams, "Liberty and Property: The Problem of Government Benefits," 12 *J. Legal Stud.* 3, 27–31 (1983).

[2] 198 U.S. 45 (1905).

[3] 191 U.S. 207 (1903).

[4] Id. at 219. Harlan himself was not insensitive to those concerns. He subsequently dissented in *Lochner*, but only because he was persuaded that the New York statute was justified as a means to protect the health of bakers. But where health issues were not involved, he struck down a statute requiring mandatory collective bargaining on the railroads as interference with freedom of contract. See Adair v. United States, 208 U.S. 161 (1908).

Harlan, speaking for a six-member majority, held that the state in virtue of its position as a market actor could impose this (or indeed any) condition on contractors with whom it did business. After noting that municipal corporations for these purposes are the creatures of the state and are to be treated as such,[5] he concluded:

> [W]e can imagine no possible ground to dispute the power of the State to declare that no one undertaking work *for it or for one of its municipal agencies*, should permit or require an employee on such work to labor in excess of eight hours each day, and to inflict punishment upon those who are embraced by such regulations and yet disregard them. It cannot be deemed a part of the liberty of any contractor that *he* be allowed to do public work in any mode he may choose to adopt, without regard to the wishes of the State. On the contrary, it belongs to the State, as the guardian and trustee for its people, and having control of its affairs, to prescribe the conditions upon which it will permit public work to be done on its behalf, or on behalf of its municipalities. No court has authority to review its action in that respect. Regulations on this subject suggest only considerations of public policy. And with such considerations the courts have no concern.[6]

This passage has proved of enormous influence in a wide range of areas[7] because it signals the adoption of a view that the government, which may be heavily constrained as a regulator, may nonetheless be accorded great freedom as a market actor. *Atkin*, and the broad-scale deference that it adopts, misconceives the nature of the problem. In the course of his opinion, Harlan addresses only one of the two risks associated with the government contract, namely, the unconstitutional conditions doctrine. In dealing with that question he rightly does not consider the matter after the statute has been violated, because the employer had knowledge of the limitation before hiring took place and could have conducted himself accordingly. Indeed from the perspective of the present dispute, the evident gamesmanship is that of Atkin, not of the state. He knew the terms of the deal when he accepted the initial contract and was able to extract a higher price as an offset to the condition imposed: he then turned around and acted as though he were free of the contractual constraint.

Harlan's argument turns on the common-sense distinction between the government as contracting party, regulating its own af-

[5] 191 U.S. at 220–21.

[6] Id. at 222–23.

[7] See, e.g., Reeves, Inc. v. Stake, 447 U.S. 429, 438 (1980) (upholding, against a commerce clause challenge, South Dakota administrative order not to sell state cement to out-of-state customers).

fairs, and the government as regulator, regulating the affairs of two private parties. There is no question that the government will be somewhat more hesitant to impose conditions on bidders to its contract when it will have to bear some of the increased costs attached to the condition. So viewed, there is no individual "liberty" interest that has been jeopardized by the statute, even if Atkin is left worse off by doing business under the restrictions required by the state. The unconstitutional conditions doctrine does not apply, for the state has no monopoly power in the construction market. (Indeed, if it did, requiring or forbidding special labor terms would hardly limit the use of that power.)

There is a second side to the problem, however, which is ignored in the quoted passage: the position of the citizens and taxpayers in the state. Harlan takes the view that the state is the trustee for its people: so far so good. But the hard question is: what method can be used to insure that the trust has been faithfully discharged in passing the statute? For Harlan, there is no constitutional mechanism or theory for maintaining the challenges. Taxpayers' suits to object to unconstitutional legislation were unheard-of in his time[8] and are maintainable only under limited circumstances at the present time.[9] The net effect is that there is no one who is in a position to ask whether the state has acted in response to interest-group politics when it imposes that condition in the first place. The higher costs of procuring the labor needed to construct public improvements will lead either to a reduction in the number or quality of these improvements, or to an increase in taxes in order to cover the bill. If there is no strong government interest that justifies the increase in cost, then presumably *someone* should have standing to challenge the statutory framework, say, on the ground that it represents an illicit interest-group transfer to protect some workers from competition by others. In the world as Harlan has devised it, the legislature has acted in violation of its public trust but is wholly insulated from any remedy.

So viewed, the question is whether the absence of taxpayer suits

[8] For the first unsuccessful attempt, see Frothingham v. Mellon, 262 U.S. 447 (1923) (prohibiting taxpayer suit to challenge the federal Maternity Act of 1921, which called for federal grants to states to prevent infant mortality).

[9] See, e.g., Flast v. Cohen, 392 U.S. 83 (1968) (allowing taxpayer challenges because of the special status of the establishment clause), distinguished in Valley Forge Christian College v. Americans United for Separation of Church and State, Inc., 454 U.S. 464 (1982) (refusing to allow standing to challenge disposition of excess lands to church). See also Schlesinger v. Reservists Committee to Stop the War, 418 U.S. 208 (1974) (disallowing citizen challenge under incompatibility clause governing dual status in both Congress and the military).

can be offset by allowing the prospective recipients of these programs to challenge them on their own behalf. Initially, it is not clear that this device will often prove to be effective, because the amounts at stake for potential contract recipients may be too small to warrant the protracted legal fight that is sure to ensue. It is likely to be only in the context of criminal prosecutions, such as in *Atkin*, or for major government grant programs where compliance is at issue, that these challenges are likely to be forthcoming. But the difficulty of mounting this challenge is surely not a reason for banning the only means to attack illegal government practices. No one should be required to risk criminal prosecution in order to challenge a set of illegal constitutional practices. At the bidding stage, therefore, Atkin should be allowed to challenge that condition unless some alternative device for taxpayer suits is created by statute, which at the federal level at least, Congress, ever anxious to preserve its own prerogatives, has not chosen to do.[10] Indeed if the constitutional rules are sufficiently clear, then the challenges will be routine and all parties will bid on the (correct) assumption that the bid restriction is void and of no effect.

Assuming, therefore, that the standing obstacles can be surmounted, the substantive issues must still be resolved. In this context, the government officials should have the same fiduciary obligations as ordinary private trustees, which in turn means that they must obtain the most favorable terms for their beneficiaries that are available within the market. The government cannot give away public property, either outright or through a disguised or bargain sale.[11] The first question is: what justification can the state offer for the restrictions that it seeks to impose in apparent violation of its trust? One easy avenue of justification is this: the state has imposed by contract only those same restrictions that it has imposed by way of general regulation on private contracting parties. Today that test yields an "anything goes" result. But in the pre-1937 environment, the inquiry led back to the question that Harlan sought to evade in *Atkin*: could the state impose this restriction on private parties? Stated otherwise, is this restriction justified on the score of health, or is it a simple "labor" statute that interfered with the competitive balance of the market? Within its own time, the Kansas statute, if

[10] There is, for example, no general authorization of taxpayer suits under the major administrative law statute, the Administrative Procedure Act, ch. 324, 60 Stat. 237 (1946) (codified at 5 U.S.C. §§551 et seq., 701 et seq., 3105, 3344 (1988)).

[11] For elaboration, see Richard A. Epstein, "The Public Trust Doctrine," 7 *Cato J.* 411 (1987).

applied to private parties, would have been struck down under *Lochner* because of its weak relationship with health. So why not here? Just as the unconstitutional conditions doctrine is designed to prevent government distortion of the competitive process, so too the public trust doctrine, designed to deal with the risk of improper diversion of public assets, should be construed with the same end in view. The state may participate in a private market only for the benefit of its taxpayers, not for some select group thereof. Here it is difficult to see any benefit that the state receives, qua state, from restrictions that it imposes on the way in which a contractor hires or manages its laborers.

If the competitive solutions are in general more efficient, then taxpayers are protected, and public welfare is advanced *only* if the government acts just like another market participant when it participates in the market. It should not matter whether the exceptional condition is imposed as part of a special-interest arrangement, or out of a sense of misguided public benevolence. In either case, the increased burdens are greater than the increased benefit, judged by the usual standards of voluntary exchanges. The concerns of limited government are of equal force no matter which role government takes, for its participation as a market actor is heavily dependent on its antecedent coercive power to tax. The split standards for regulation and contract introduced by Harlan, therefore, fail because they follow the flawed analogy between private and government actors. The principles of sound government impose strong limitations on the principal of freedom of contract for state officials.

Within the modern context, the consequences of this error are small, given the plenary power that the state today may exert over the employment relationship. But the dislocations that can be caused in this context are broad indeed given the systematic disregard of one of the major risks of government contracting. Within the employment area, the Davis-Bacon Act,[12] which requires bidders on construction projects for the United States to pay the "prevailing"

[12] Chap. 411, 46 Stat. 1494, March 3, 1931 (codified as amended, at 40 U.S.C. §§276a et seq. (1988)). David Bernstein, "The Supreme Court and 'Civil Rights,' 1886–1908," 100 *Yale L.J.* 725, 742 (1990). It should also be of some interest that the original impulse behind the statute was to protect northern white construction workers from competition by itinerant black construction workers from the South, as is evident from the congressional debates on the subject. "Reference has been made to a contractor from Alabama who went to New York with bootleg labor. That is a fact. That contractor has cheap colored labor that he transports, and he puts them in cabins, and it is labor of that sort that is in competition with white labor throughout the country. This bill has merit, and with the extensive building program now being entered into,

local (read: *union*) wage on government projects, could not withstand the slightest scrutiny if government bargains were subject to the same standards that should be applicable to government regulation of private firms. The statute represents a large wealth transfer from the public at large to protected unions, by shielding them from competition by nonunion firms. Under the standard view of monopoly, the gains to the union members are smaller than the losses imposed upon the government at large. Yet there is no procedural means nor substantive doctrine which allows the invalidation of the statute.

The force of the prohibition sweeps further. Federal and state law frequently authorizes collective bargaining for government employees at the state or federal level. But these rules (whether implemented by statute or executive order) are unconstitutional on their face, given the position taken here, and given the implicit diversion of public assets when the state creates a monopoly bargaining position for those that sit on the other side of the table. Similarly, today's various affirmative action programs all began by executive orders imposing heavy affirmative action obligations on government contractors, which also added substantially to the cost of public programs, while providing interest-group transfers.[13] Outside the employment area, state governments have been allowed to restrict the sale of their products to in-state customers, even though the loss in revenue to the public at large is smaller than any gains to the private customers who benefit from the rule.[14]

In short the great vice of the current legal regime stems from its assumption that the Constitution is, and ought to be, indifferent to the shape of the market, notwithstanding the allocative inefficiencies that result when the legislature is free to impose monopolistic practices by contract or by regulation. The proper view of the subject, I believe, is that the state is no more free to create inefficient structures by bargaining with public funds than it is through direct

---

it is very important that we enact this measure." 74 *Cong. Rec.* part 7, 6513 (1931) (statement of Rep. Allgood). Similar references to "cheap" or "imported" labor dot the debate. See, e.g., id. at 6516. (statement of Rep. McCormick).

[13] I develop the case against their constitutionality at greater length in Richard A. Epstein, *Forbidden Grounds: The Case Against Employment Discrimination Laws* 421–37 (1992).

[14] See Reeves, Inc. v. Stake, 447 U.S. 429 (1980). Here the challenge was mounted under the commerce clause, given the overt discrimination against out-of-state consumers. It failed because these purchasers did not have any contractual claim. The losses borne by local taxpayers deprived of the increased revenue flow were left out of the calculus, as irrelevant to the commerce clause challenge.

regulation. Putting the proposition in this fashion should make it easy to distinguish between the improper conditions at issue in *Atkin* and similar cases, and the conditions relating to price, time of performance, payment schedules and the like which should be part and parcel of all contractual arrangements. The limitation on state power to bargain in employment contexts and elsewhere does not strip the state of its power to protect its citizens by searching for the lowest price and the best quality goods and services. It is only designed to ensure that it does not stray from the proper path.

## *Modern Applications*

The judicial refusal to afford any constitutional protection for economic liberties has not led to the end of litigation over the kinds of contracts that the government may make with its citizens. It has only shifted the focus of the inquiry as the new challenges have asked whether particular contracts run afoul of other substantive provisions, most notably those contained the First Amendment. In these cases too, the concerns have been directed to both of the risks endemic to state contracts: the diversion of public assets and the unconstitutional conditions doctrine. It is useful to analyze some of the most important developments here in light of the general approach to the problem taken above.

### PATRONAGE HIRING

The task of controlling does not end with the demise of constitutional protection of economic liberties. If anything, the reverse relationship is true, for the expansion in the size and power of government only opens new opportunities for misconduct, both public and private. Political patronage, whereby employment with the state is conditioned on membership in, or contributions to, the dominant political party, is a textbook illustration of the danger. Systems of patronage have long been part of the American scene, and the judicial attack on them has taken place, not under the public trust doctrines that might seem ideal for the purpose, but under the First Amendment, on the ground that the condition attached to the contract requires an impermissible waiver of constitutional rights to one's own political belief and speech.

The decisive case is *Elrod v. Burns*,[15] which upheld a challenge to the patronage system in Cook County brought by various persons in

[15] 427 U.S. 347 (1976). The decision was extended to assistant public defenders in Branti v. Finkel, 445 U.S. 507 (1980).

the sheriff's department, none of whom filled high policymaking positions. That decision is clearly correct as a matter of principle, but as with other forms of employment restraints, it is often difficult to locate the proper source of concern—is it with the status of the individual claimant or with the effect of the general practice on the overall operation of the system? As regards the first, the person who finds political support uncongenial is able in a competitive market to seek roughly comparable employment, and may in any event have been the beneficiary of the patronage system operated by the party that has just been voted out of office. These individual claims, therefore, do not have any special appeal. But the systematic issues are of much greater importance. In essence, the filling of all government jobs with persons who have both official and political ties to the incumbents works a serious distortion of the political process. Money which is paid by the public at large works its way by indirection into benefit, whether in cash or in services, for the political incumbent, which in turn increases his or her probability of reelection. In effect one party is allowed to use public funds, denied to the other, in order to increase its partisan chances of success. To counter this action, allowing suits by the individual workers "coerced" (though not subject to threat of force) by the arrangement induces interested private parties to attack a set of practices that might otherwise be immune from judicial review.[16]

The principles at stake here are of broad application, but are not always followed. Thus in *Messer v. Curci*,[17] Judge Danny Boggs refused to extend *Elrod* from discharge to political refusals-to-hire, and argued that patronage does not work any dislocations in the political system because of the competitive nature of party politics at all levels of government. The advantage that is given to one party today will be enjoyed by the other party tomorrow. Competitive balance will therefore be retained, not at any given point in time, but in the long haul through the alternation of the parties in power. In essence two forms of parity are possible: the system in which both parties may resort to patronage, and the system in which both sides are restrained from so doing.

The resort to a principle of parity rules out the obvious cases of selective protection: Democrats get to use patronage, but Republicans do not. But Boggs's argument does not explain which type of parity should be preferred, any more than it explains why a universal prohibition against the use of force and fraud is preferable to a universal free-for-all. The relevant question is not whether competition

[16] See the discussion of coercion in chap. 4, supra.

[17] 881 F.2d 219 (6th Cir. 1989).

exists, but whether the rules under which that competition takes place are likely to lead to the proper social results. Here a system without patronage should fare far better. If each party is entitled to root out members from the opposition when it takes office, then a number of consequences will follow: initially, there will be a sharper competition for obtaining political power because of the greater private benefits that can be dispensed through the system. If and when incumbency is a strong advantage, there will be fewer turnovers and a greater risk of entrenched parties and political corruption. When turnovers do take place, there will be greater discontinuity in the conduct of public affairs, given dismissals that are wholly unrelated to the work product of the employees who are dismissed. No matter who is in power, the day-to-day administration of justice is apt to be compromised if the political loyalties of private individuals become a litmus test for the sort of public protection and service that they receive from public employees who are all drawn from one party. A system of alternating patronage allows each side to commit abuses, which cumulate, and do not cancel out. What is required is a constant limitation on public power. One approach is to hew to the course taken in *Elrod,* while a second, which veers in the opposite direction, is to refuse to allow *any* participation of public employees in political debates. That last course of action has rightly been sustained against a First Amendment challenge.[18] Prohibiting all political speech by government officials avoids the distortion that the patronage system creates: the political control of government that lurches between rival parties.

The general condemnation of the patronage system has far-reaching consequences. Although *Elrod* was concerned with the discharge of employees from their present positions, the prohibition should extend to all other variations of the basic employment arrangement. The issue here is the prevention of political abuse, so it matters not one whit whether the dismissed worker had a long-term contract, was not rehired at the end of a contract for a term, or was not hired in the first place.[19] The danger of political abuse cuts across all stages in the life of contract. By the same token, it seems clear that the prohibition against patronage hiring should not require that all positions be filled on a merit basis. Within a democratic system, a

[18] United Public Workers of America (C.I.O.) v. Mitchell, 330 U.S. 75 (1947) (sustaining the Hatch Act for federal employees); Oklahoma v. United States Civil Serv. Comm'n, 330 U.S. 127 (1947) (sustaining same, as applied to state programs receiving federal aid).

[19] For the contrary result by a sharply divided court, see Messer v. Curci, 881 F.2d 219 (6th Cir. 1989), discussed supra.

change at the top carries with it some mandate to institute the policies on which the public official was elected to public office. Policy-making officials, and those who work in confidence with the elected officials, should rotate in and out of office with changes at the top. The decisions of the Supreme Court make it clear that the prohibition against patronage employment practices does not extend to these key positions.[20]

Even so limited, it should not be supposed that the judicial supervision of hiring practices comes without cost. The contract at-will (on which patronage depends) is far cheaper to administer than any system of for-cause hiring and firing that is necessarily introduced when the patronage system is limited. To be sure, most of the appellate decisions (including the three considered here) have been well-cultivated test cases in which the *sole* motive for discharge or nonhiring has been political. But once the crack is open in the door, the mixed-motive cases (was it incompetence on the job, was it political loyalty?) will arise, just as they necessarily arise under any other for-cause type regime, whether concerned with the antidiscrimination laws, with collective bargaining agreements, ordinary wrongful dismissal cases, or retaliatory dismissals against whistleblowers.

The key question is whether there is any social payoff that justifies the burden of running the system. That inquiry in turn cannot be answered in the abstract, but depends upon the reasons for scrutinizing motives in the first place. With the antidiscrimination and the labor laws, I believe that the case is very weak, because both systems are meant to displace competitive markets, which dominate their regulatory substitutes on both counts: ease of administration and creation of desirable incentives.[21] With whistleblowing, the balance probably shifts in the opposite direction, at least for certain legal infractions. With patronage hiring, the case for the limitation is very strong indeed, while the costs of running the system are relatively low. So long as the basic principle of *Elrod* prevents the sweeps and purges that used to be attendant to the transfer of political power, the occasional litigated case does little to compromise, and something to advance, the integrity of the political system. The patronage cases, then, offer in a modern setting a textbook illustration of when judicial intervention can improve the overall operation of the political system.

[20] See *Elrod*, 427 U.S. at 375 (opinion of Stewart, J., limiting case to "nonpolicymaking, nonconfidential government" employees).

[21] See Epstein, *Forbidden Grounds*, supra note 13, chaps. 3, 8.

PROCEDURAL RIGHTS

The case for invoking the doctrine of unconstitutional conditions becomes far weaker when the political overtones are removed from the case. Now it is no longer possible to view the claim of the aggrieved employee as a convenient way to get at political imperfections within the system. Instead it becomes a pure claim for just treatment, to which the freedom of contract arguments generally provide a sufficient answer. The nature of the difference is made evident by looking at the role of the doctrine of unconstitutional conditions in ordinary employment situations. Suppose that the government has offered an individual an at-will employment contract which by design provides the employee with no procedural protections against government dismissal. The case presents no colorable First Amendment claim based upon government interference with political beliefs. Indeed, even though the protection of the classical forms of private property have been dismantled, under current law the decisive question is whether this contractual provision infringes the constitutional guarantee that no person shall be deprived of property without due process of law.

In an early foray into the issue, Justice Rehnquist, in *Arnett v. Kennedy*,[22] adopted a view containing strong freedom-of-contract strains: "where the grant of a substantive right is inextricably intertwined with the limitations of the procedures which are to be employed in determining that right, a litigant in the position of appellee must take the bitter with the sweet."[23] In one sense his statement is surely too broad, for the government is surely not in the position of an employer under a contract at-will given the prohibition on patronage hiring. And Justice Rehnquist is far too eager to embrace the freedom-of-contract language even in other circumstances where the doctrine of unconstitutional conditions should apply.[24] Nonetheless, despite the many sustained attacks on his position in this context,[25] Justice Rehnquist's contractual logic is far stronger once cases involving forbidden motives are put aside. *Arnett* itself in-

[22] 416 U.S. 134 (1974) (plurality opinion).

[23] Id. at 153–54. *Arnett* is one of many cases that raise this issue. See, e.g., Bishop v. Wood, 426 U.S. 341 (1976); Board of Regents v. Roth, 408 U.S. 564 (1972).

[24] See supra chap. 8, for a discussion of his views on corporations.

[25] See, e.g., Frank I. Michelman, "Formal and Associational Aims in Procedural Due Process," in *Due Process*, Nomos 18, at 126 (J. Pennock & J. Chapman eds., 1977); William W. Van Alstyne, "Cracks in 'The New Property': Adjudicative Due Process in the Administrative State," 62 *Cornell L. Rev.* 445, 462–66 (1977). But see Williams, supra note 1, at 27.

volved the most attractive facts for the dismissed employee, insofar as he was fired for allegedly defaming the very government official who was supposed to render an initial judgment on his case.[26]

Whatever the right result in cases of this sort, the basic logic of *Arnett* seems unassailable. The government here hires workers in an intensely competitive environment, which is why its own rules and procedures do in fact contain fairly extensive procedural protections for them, including the possibility of back-pay awards after an evidentiary trial-type hearing on appeal.[27] Given the wide range of possible employment opportunities outside the government, there is little danger of state monopoly power in this context. However, there is considerable concern with substandard government service by lax, incompetent, or dishonest employees. The decision to steer clear of constitutional entanglements in the employment area removes a host of thorny issues from the judicial agenda, freeing the Court from having to determine what kind of hearing is required and when it should be offered. There are quite enough political pressures to turn government employment into a civil service sinecure without the Court placing its own unsteady thumb on the scales.

The sound logic of *Arnett* has been decisively repudiated by the subsequent decision in *Cleveland Board of Education v. Loudermill.*[28] Loudermill, a security guard who had been dismissed from his job on charges that he had dishonestly filled out his employment application, challenged the constitutional adequacy of the city's procedures. His claim was sustained, 8 to 1, with only Justice Rehnquist dissenting.

Speaking through Justice White, the Court first noted that no one disputed that Loudermill's contract created the necessary "property right," because all state employees were allowed to retain their position "during good behavior and efficient service."[29] Justice White then concluded that the procedures necessary to protect this substantive right could not be determined solely by the Ohio statute, but had to be tested against constitutional requirements. He curtly rejected Justice Rehnquist's "bitter with the sweet" rationale:

[26] Justice Rehnquist deliberately sidestepped the thorny constitutional question of whether some independent party would be required to make the initial hearing determination. See 416 U.S. at 155 n.21.

[27] See id. at 145–47.

[28] 470 U.S. 532 (1985).

[29] Ohio Rev. Code Ann. §124.34 (Anderson 1984). The statute in fact provided for a review procedure under which grievances could be filed with the state personnel board of review. The board could appoint a trial board to hold a hearing, from which appeals could be taken to the State Court of Common Pleas. The statute did not provide for a pretermination hearing.

> The point is straightforward: the Due Process Clause provides that certain substantive rights—life, liberty and property—cannot be deprived except pursuant to constitutionally adequate procedures. The categories of substance and procedure are distinct. Were the rule otherwise the Clause would be reduced to a mere tautology. "Property" cannot be defined by the procedures provided for its deprivation any more than can life or liberty.[30]

Justice White's argument may capture the state of current doctrine,[31] but it misses the key analytical point. The reason why life and liberty are not "defined by procedures" is that they are not, in any system of limited government, acquired by grant from the state. Property, to the extent that it is acquired by first possession or private purchase, should stand in exactly the same position as life or liberty. Because none is a grant from the state, ordinary procedural guarantees must be met before any may be taken away. In this context, it is imperative that the state not be allowed to "redefine" the private interest so as to remove constitutional protections. But contracts for public employment do have their origins in transactions with government. So long as private contracts can specify both the terms of employment and the terms of dismissal, public contracts should be able to do the same, absent the threat of abuse of government monopoly power. In this context, substance is not separate from procedure. Both are part of a complex package of contractual benefits that an employee receives in exchange for services rendered.

The doctrine of unconstitutional conditions should not apply solely because the attached condition is important, nor because it is good policy for the state to keep an employee on the job until the charges against him are fully resolved,[32] nor because dismissal will impose some measure of hardship upon the worker.[33] Nor does the validity of the condition turn upon some effort to advance individual dignity.[34] The state does not need judicial oversight to make its own

[30] 470 U.S. at 541.

[31] See, e.g., Logan v. Zimmerman Brush Co., 455 U.S. 422, 430–32 (1982) (holding that state law defines "property" interests, whereas the Constitution defines applicable procedural guarantees); Vitek v. Jones, 445 U.S. 480, 488–90 (1980) (holding that due process guarantees attach to "liberty interests" created by the states).

[32] See 470 U.S. at 543. The same theme is echoed in Justice Marshall's partial concurrence. See id. at 549 (Marshall, J., concurring in part and concurring in the judgment). Justice Marshall would have required a full-dress evidentiary hearing before any stopping of an employee's wages. See id. at 548.

[33] See 470 U.S. at 544.

[34] For an attempt to develop such a dignitary theory, see Jerry L. Mashaw, "Administrative Due Process: The Quest for a Dignitary Theory," 61 *B.U. L. Rev.* 885 (1981).

prudential judgment of whether it is riskier to keep workers suspected of improper conduct on the job pending hearings, taking into account the costs of hiring substitutes or training replacements. Likewise, individual employees are capable of deciding whether procedural benefits are more important than the wage and other benefits provided by the job. Unconstitutional conditions doctrine should be invoked only when there are structural concerns relating to monopoly power, collective action problems, and externalities to suggest that individual consent will generally be an insufficient check against systematic government misbehavior. Freedom-of-contract rules should have prevailed in *Loudermill.*

## PREGNANCY BENEFITS

The problem of unconstitutional conditions also crops up with many of the substantive terms of an employment contract. One critical issue is whether a public employer is under a constitutional obligation to provide pregnancy benefits for its female employees as part of its system of mandatory disability coverage.[35] In *Geduldig v. Aiello,*[36] the Supreme Court rejected the contention that the equal protection clause required this coverage on the ground that the economic benefits at issue had to satisfy only a minimal level of judicial review. Justice Brennan in dissent argued that the higher standard of review applicable to sex discrimination should govern the case. In his view, the higher level of scrutiny invited the application of the unconstitutional conditions doctrine: the state was under no obligation to establish a system of disability benefits at all, but *if* it did so, then it had to include pregnancy on the list of benefits.

Let us assume that Justice Brennan's initial call for higher scrutiny is correct. Even so, it hardly follows that the state ought to be put to the all-or-nothing choice dictated by the unconstitutional conditions doctrine. Initially, the state does not have the monopoly power to permit it to extract surplus from any of its employees, male or female. Nor would the refusal to treat pregnancy as a disability amount to such extraction, even if the state possessed any monopoly power. Even when pregnancy is excluded, women as a group receive more from the disability pool than men. In the California plan at issue in *Geduldig,* for example, women contributed 28 percent of the dollars to the plan but received 33 percent of the benefits. Adding

[35] A more extended treatment of this issue is found in Epstein, *Forbidden Grounds,* supra note 13, at 329–58, especially 338–39.

[36] 417 U.S. 484 (1974).

in pregnancy benefits was no inconsequential detail, but boosted their payouts to 45 percent of the plan funds without increasing their contributions.[37]

Brennan's insistence on the all-or-nothing choice does nothing therefore to drive the market back to the competitive solution, but only increases the deviation from it. In any market setting, state employers who keep their disability plans will seek other means to reduce their burdens, either by hiring fewer women of child-bearing age or by paying them a lower cash salary than they would otherwise receive. In the alternative they could decide to eliminate the disability coverage altogether, or to scale down the level of benefits provided in all cases, thereby reducing the gains that both women and men receive from the plan. Demanding that pregnancy be treated as another form of illness does not have merely distributional consequences. It decreases the net gain from employment for men and women alike. To put numbers to ideas, the likely pattern of outcomes is as follows: if pregnancy is not covered, then the combined surplus is 8; if all health coverage is excluded, then the gain is 0; if pregnancy is covered, then the total gain is –5. It is not possible to hazard a guess as to separation of gains and losses by sex, for some women lose as much by the mandated coverage of pregnancy as do men. The unconstitutional conditions doctrine therefore has no role to play in this situation, for the all-or-nothing choices posed will reduce and not advance social welfare. Ordinary employment markets will outperform the intervention of either courts or legislatures.

Unfortunately, the basic point has been totally obscured. After *General Electric Co. v. Gilbert*[38] held that the refusal to cover pregnancy under a standard medical plan was not a form of sex discrimination under Title VII of the Civil Rights Act, an outraged Congress promptly reversed that determination with the Pregnancy Discrimination Act of 1978. Today the unconstitutional conditions choice is imposed on all employers, public or private: if they wish to provide medical coverage of any sort, then they must include pregnancy in the plan. The allocative inefficiencies of this interference with ordinary contracts are as great in the public as in the private sphere. The nondiscrimination principle in this context scarcely operates as a check against monopoly power. Instead it operates as a crude lever to mandate an ill-disguised subsidy from male and nonpregnant female

[37] George Rutherglen, "Sexual Equality in Fringe Benefit Plans," 65 *Va. L. Rev.* 199, 220 n. 98 (1979).

[38] 429 U.S. 125 (1976).

workers to pregnant female workers, where the net gains to recipients are, as always, smaller than the net costs required to generate them. A doctrine designed to maximize the cooperative surplus from social arrangements is now used to destroy that surplus.

## TESTING FOR DRUGS AND HIV

The doctrine of unconstitutional conditions has also been critically important in dealing with the conflict between employee claims to privacy and the government's claim, as employer, to control and monitor misconduct. Perhaps the most controversial area involves various sorts of testing to determine whether an employee is HIV-positive (as a precursor to AIDS), is on drugs, has taken alcohol, and so on, down the line. In a line of recent cases the government has prevailed in its effort to require testing of various sorts on workers who are engaged in safety-sensitive jobs.[39] The bottom line in all these cases is that the minimal restrictions on privacy are justified by the strong public interest in safety, and that random tests impose sufficient limitations on government discretion to allow their use.

In most testing situations, the federal tests are imposed on employees of private firms, so that the government acts solely in its regulatory capacity. But when the government regulates its own employees, as with customs inspectors or air controllers, the question could be asked whether the government can require persons to waive their Fourth Amendment rights against unreasonable searches and seizures as a condition of employment. Most contemporary approaches to the problem[40] do not distinguish between re-

[39] See, e.g., Bolden v. Southeastern Pa. Transportation Auth., 953 F.2d 807 (3d Cir. 1991) (union contracts allowing randomized drug testing binding on all employees); National Treasury Employees Union v. Von Raab, 489 U.S. 656 (1989) (upholding random drug testing of federal custom employees); Skinner v. Railway Labor Executives Ass'n, 489 U.S. 602 (1989) (upholding testing of employees of private railways). These decisions have been followed in the Courts of Appeal. See Bluestein v. Skinner, 908 F.2d 451 (9th Cir. 1990) (upholding random drug testing of airline pilots); International Bhd. of Teamsters, Chauffeurs v. Department of Transp., 932 F.2d 1292 (9th Cir. 1991) (upholding random drug testing for commercial drivers). In all these cases the holdings can be summarized in a single proposition: the safety justification advanced by the government justifies the minimum infringement of the privacy interest.

[40] See, e.g., *National Treasury Employees Union*, where there was, at most, an oblique reference to the unconstitutional conditions doctrine, 489 U.S. at 671. See also Institute of Bill of Rights Law, *Proposal: Drug Testing in the Workplace* 7 (1991): "The Task Force members believe that this is a propitious time for balanced, uniform legislation on drug-testing." No distinction is made between public and private employers, and a "national approach" is urged to combat a "national problem."

strictions imposed by public and private employers, but instead seek to develop an elaborate set of "for-cause" rules which indicate the persons, substances, occasions, and procedures under which testing should be allowed. The implicit assumption behind these programs is that any determination on testing should be made by collective decision that rests on constitutional standards of reasonableness, equally applicable to the public and the private sector. The object of this collective enterprise is to balance two powerful and competing interests, one in individual privacy and the other in maintaining a drug-free environment within the workplace, or an HIV-free medical staff, and so on.

The major error in these proposals lies not in their assumption that some balance of interests is necessary, but in the further assumption that this balance is attainable only by collective means. This approach thus overlooks the decisive advantage a market solution has over a legislative one in dealing with government employees. The legislative solution must postulate that there is a uniform intensity of preferences, both in the workers' demand for privacy and (across broad occupational categories) the employers' demand for testing. But in so doing, it ignores the inevitable variation in the intensity of preferences, both across employers and individual workers. An unregulated solution will permit voluntary sorting by the intensity of preference: those individuals who are relatively indifferent to being tested will be able to pair themselves with employers that have a strong demand for testing. Those persons who have strong hostility to testing will in turn pair themselves with firms that require little or no testing as a condition of employment. The matches should minimize the frictions associated with the testing problem in all its manifestations far more than any legislative dictation of a single standard for all workers and all firms. The vice of the legislation is that it neutralizes in advance any desirable selection pressures that would otherwise emerge. Both the firm and the worker have strong incentives to make honest estimation of their own preferences. They should be allowed to do so.

The above arguments have their greatest power for prospective relationships, where there are no specific ties between employer and employee. But the matter becomes more complex when the question of testing applies to ongoing employment relationships in which both sides have invested substantial specific capital. In practice, the contract (or the employer's handbook, or company practice) may cover this contingency, and if so, then those guidelines should be respected in the courts. Unfortunately, there are doubtless many cases in which the drug testing requires both employers and employees to venture into untested waters, where the readjustments are likely to be painful. But even in this more difficult context, there is little that regulation can do to ease the pain—the firm that insists upon testing may suffer from employee turnover and a loss of goodwill. Firms are likely to be sensitive to these issues, and to take care to limit the scope of any testing program, to explain their purposes in company meetings and brochures, to allow persons to transfer within the firm, and perhaps to offer some increase in severance pay for those who decide to leave. And when all is said and done, there will still be unhappy employees for whom any combination of these measures are likely to prove inadequate. But transitions are never clean. There are countless other settings in which revised demands on the employment relation come into tension with established practices within the firm. The sorting mechanism will continue to work, although less well than in the prospective situation; however unpretty the results are, there is little that any system of across-the-board regulation can do to solve the problem.

This analysis of the private market response provides a convenient benchmark from which to evaluate the argument that any government imposition of testing should fall under the unconstitutional conditions doctrine. Government has no monopoly in the relevant employment markets, and private firms that have to operate within competitive labor markets often impose similar conditions on their employees. These conditions do not seek to constrain private practices and relations of employees that are unrelated to their employment—even though *any* drug use might be regarded as job-related. Those workers who are opposed to the testing are free to go elsewhere or to voice their protests, individually or collectively, in order to influence government rules. There is no necessity that uniform standards be imposed across all job categories. Any insistence on testing is, in any event, far superior to the use of criminal sanctions to pursue individuals who seek to avoid government conduct. It is far cheaper and more effective to control drug abuse by allowing market mechanisms to help check its spread. Similarly, within the context of individual employment contracts, there appears to be little risk of a prisoner's dilemma game that, under the guise of multiple, separate, private contracts, could work a fundamental change in overall government structure by a system of sham cash payments. That outcome is of course possible if the private use of the public highways is conditioned upon the waiver of all protection against search and seizure, for the government possesses an element of monopoly power not available in the employment context.[41]

A parallel risk could arise by an improper use of the taxing power. Thus the government could give $100 to each person to waive his Fourth Amendment rights, only to raise the necessary sums by taxing each person in an equal amount. Thus, the money that any person receives directly is exactly offset by his forced contribution to the public fisc. Once the cross-payments are netted out, the compensation that is received is strictly in-kind, subject to the usual bureaucratic charges. In exchange for the release of my Fourth Amendment rights, you hereby agree to release your Fourth Amendment rights. It is not clear that one person should regard the release of Fourth Amendment rights by others as a benefit to him, given its tendency to increase government powers. Rather it is a situation in which every private citizen loses. Yet again the employment context is quite different because there is no single person who can bargain with all persons to waive their constitutional rights. The close connection between employment and testing seems to preclude any system-wide loss that calls for using the unconstitutional conditions doctrine.

The second risk of government bargaining likewise seems small in this context, for it is virtually impossible to identify any diversion of public assets for private gain. The costs of running these programs may be substantial, but there is a return benefit that is worth the price, and there is no set of individuals who receives gifts or bargain sales of public assets. It is of course a weighty and often acrimonious question as to whether, when, and how drug testing should be required. But it is a struggle that is best resolved through ordinary bargaining and not statutory innovation.

## NATIONAL SECURITY

The possible restrictions on government employees may also present acute conflicts among freedom of speech, national security, and employee misconduct. In *Snepp v. United States*,[42] the Supreme Court held that the United States could require Snepp, an ex-CIA agent, to adhere to the terms of an employment contract in which he agreed, first, that he would "not . . . publish . . . any information or material relating to the Agency, its activities or intelligence activi-

[41] See supra chap. 11.

[42] 444 U.S. 507 (1980). The analysis given here is similar to that provided in Frank H. Easterbrook, "Insider Trading, Secret Agents, Evidentiary Privileges, and the Production of Information," 1981 *Sup. Ct. Rev.* 309, 339–52.

ties generally, either during or after the term of [his] employment, without specific prior approval by the Agency," and second, that he would not "disclose any classified information relating to the Agency without proper authorization."[43] Snepp published his book without first obtaining the contractually required clearance, and the book may or may not have contained classified information—an issue that the CIA had a strong incentive to keep out of court. But wholly apart from the disclosures contained in the book, there was an evident breach of contract—assuming that the state could impose the contract condition consistent with the First Amendment guarantee of freedom of speech. Most directly, the case thus again raises the question of unconstitutional conditions: does the greater power not to hire at all include the lesser power to hire subject to this condition on publication?[44]

Why shouldn't it? Any breach of the system of prior clearances creates the risk of improper disclosure, which can only undermine the ability of the CIA to obtain needed information from sources that rely on the review process for their protection. Thus any relatedness requirement seems to be met. More generally, the operation of any government agency requires the sharing of restricted information which will be inhibited if personnel can obtain information for one purpose, only to turn around and use it for another. The restriction in question is no doubt similar to those that private employers impose upon employees entrusted with sensitive information, and it is difficult to see how the public is ill-served by ensuring that its intelligence agents keep confidential information secret. Should the government, through pre-publication review, seek to stifle political criticism of the agency that does not rest upon classified information, then the problem can be handled on a case-by-case basis, by in-camera hearings if necessary, without disturbing the basic structure of the statute. Here as elsewhere, one must worry about abuse not only by the government, but also by parties doing business with it. The bargain here does not seem to be a cloak for any hidden government abuse, and it thus should be sustained, as the Court held, absent some specific showing of misbehavior.[45]

It has been suggested that this defense of government power is too pat, given the enormous public interest in the details of the internal

[43] 444 U.S. at 507–8 (quoting appendix to Petition for Certiorari at 58a-59a, *Snepp* (No. 78–1871)).

[44] See generally Easterbrook, supra note 42, at 349 (arguing against the Court's use of the unconstitutional conditions doctrine in *Snepp*).

[45] See 444 U.S. at 509 n.3.

operation of the government.[46] The decision to stop publication is harmful not only to Snepp, but also to all individuals who might rely on that information in order to criticize government operations, a central First Amendment function by any standard. There is no question that the suppression of information always has external effects that are not taken into account by the parties to a voluntary agreement. But the critical question with information is the direction of the external harms so created. There is no partial release of information. The information that provides useful ammunition for government critics is the same information that might provide useful ammunition to our national enemies. It is not clear that the government should be left in the position to make an independent determination of the risk of publication when its duty and interest are in opposition. But by the same token, it is absolutely clear that Snepp should not be allowed unilaterally to make that determination when his interest necessarily conflicts with his duty. The statute in question only called for submission to the pre-publication review, and the sensible accommodation therefore is to allow judicial reexamination of any material which the CIA wishes to keep from publication. Intermediate solutions are therefore possible to make the appropriate accommodations. Given the risk of both government and individual misbehavior, however, no corner solution, including that urged by Snepp, should be adopted.

## THE INTERNAL OPERATION OF GOVERNMENT SERVICES

Another setting in which there is conflict between the First Amendment and the employment contract arises when individual employees criticize the government officials for whom they work. There is no question that outsiders may criticize the government service with impunity, and the question is whether some restrictions may be placed on government employees. In a sense the stakes are apt to be higher on both sides. Criticism from within carries with it greater conviction than criticism from without. Yet it also involves the possible dissemination of confidential information and the demoralization of the public service. The question is how to balance these risks.

In *Connick v. Myers*,[47] The Supreme Court enforced the limita-

[46] See Howard Abrams, "Economic Analysis and Unconstitutional Conditions: A Reply to Professor Epstein," 27 *San Diego L. Rev.* 359, 382–87 (1990). My more extensive answer to Professor Abrams is found in Richard A. Epstein, "Unconstitutional Conditions Obscured," 27 *San Diego L. Rev.* 397, 403–5 (1990).

[47] 461 U.S. 138 (1983).

tions on speech found in the plaintiff's employment contract with the federal government. There the plaintiff, an assistant district attorney in New Orleans, protested her transfer to another division and circulated questionnaires inside the office concerning office morale, the need for grievance committees, and the alleged misconduct of her supervisors. She was then dismissed for leading a "'mini-insurrection'" in the office.[48] The decision on balance is correct. The government does not have anything like a monopoly position over the district attorneys it employs, for both local governments and private firms hire criminal lawyers. The conditions imposed upon the plaintiff were similar to those private firms impose on the public protests that their employees can make. The unconstitutional conditions claim thus founders on the inability to show a government monopoly or an exceptional restriction on the plaintiff's personal activity.

Similarly, as was the case in *Snepp*, there seems little reason to allow the plaintiff to prevail on her claim in order to vindicate the diffuse interests of the public at large. There are other powerful checks against official abuse. There are the normal channels of administrative review within the office, extending up, where necessary, to elected officials. There is free rein for criticism by persons who have no contractual relationship with the office. And criminal and civil sanctions can be brought to bear against officials who have abused their public office. No one can claim that these sanctions are sufficient in all cases. But the available sanctions should work often enough that disregard of a government contract is not called for under the circumstances. On balance this First Amendment claim should fail.

## CONCLUSION

In sum, the employment cases analyzed in this chapter reveal an important tension. The modern analysis of these cases in the government arena follows a pattern of analysis that is familiar to standard-form contracts. It assumes that these are often "contracts of adhesion" and should be set aside because the sheer size of government gives it extensive bargaining power.[49] The limitations on govern-

[48] See id. at 141.

[49] The most influential piece in this tradition is still Friedrich Kessler, "Contracts of Adhesion—Some Reflections About Freedom of Contract," 43 *Colum. L. Rev.* 629 (1943). See also Morris R. Cohen, "The Basis of Contract," 46 *Harv. L. Rev.* 553 (1933).

ment contracts therefore fill out the same generous contours that they fill out in ordinary private agreements. But the position cannot explain why anyone would enter into a contract voluntarily that leaves him worse off than before. The upshot, however, is to encourage a more extensive invalidation of employment contracts, especially on matters of procedural due process and government testing, than is achieved under the view taken here: the only two special risks of bargaining with the state are monopoly power and diversion of private wealth through the power of taxation. The model of exploitation through contract is wrong at a basic descriptive level because it cannot explain why workers ever earn positive wages for their labor: why shouldn't the oppressive employer drive those wages down to zero if the worker's threat to quit is not credible? Likewise, the theory of exploitation has no descriptive power in explaining the operation of contracts made between individuals and the state. The uniform framework set out in this book applies to employment contracts every bit as much as it does to the other endeavors of the state.

# Part Four

## POSITIVE RIGHTS IN THE WELFARE STATE

## CHAPTER 15

# Tax Exemptions

THE PREVIOUS three chapters have examined the problems of bargaining with the state in connection with those types of government action routinely undertaken by the traditional minimal state. Within that framework it was both possible and necessary to ask whether the particular restrictions placed on the government's freedom of contract advanced the competitive ideal. With the rise of the welfare state, the older functions of these contractual restrictions have lost their pride of place in the constitutional hierarchy, as the New Deal has vastly expanded the catalogue of permissible government activities. In celebration of that development, Professor Charles Reich, writing in 1964, spoke of the new role that government had taken, not only in protecting traditional interests in contract and property, but also in creating various kinds of government "largess" in the form of "money, benefits, services, contracts, franchises, and licenses."[1] With these new forms of entitlement comes an increase in the scope of state power and level of government activity, bargaining and granting included. The concomitant increase in official discretion thus necessarily expands the potential number of applications of the doctrine of unconstitutional conditions. This chapter discusses the use of tax exemptions in connection with the constitutional guarantees of both speech and religion. The next two chapters consider the same problem in connection with a wide array of government benefits that are routinely a part of the expanded welfare state. Chapter 18 then completes the analysis by looking at the conditions attached to various educational programs undertaken by the federal government.

[1] Charles A. Reich, "The New Property," 73 *Yale L.J.* 733, 733 (1964): "Increasingly, Americans live on government largess—allocated by government on its own terms, and held by recipients subject to conditions which express 'the public interest.'" Reich's category of largess includes many of the traditional functions of government, such as licensing and regulation of highways, along with their modern counterparts in the welfare state. In this part, the greater emphasis is upon a subclass of the new property that is tied to the welfare state.

## TAX EXEMPTIONS AND FREEDOM OF SPEECH

In dealing with the problems of tax exemptions, it is important to recall the qualified sense in which taxation in general should be regarded as coercive. When the government says that it will tax certain activities, or the income they generate, it does not, save with the rare exception of a head tax, impose a categorical obligation on the citizen to pay a definite sum of money into the public coffers. Rather, it makes an implicit offer of the form which says, *if* you decide to undertake certain activities, *then* we shall impose upon those activities a tax calculated in a given fashion. The tax can therefore be avoided if the activity is not undertaken. The general scheme of taxation thus represents a set of implicit state offers setting the terms on which private parties are allowed to undertake their ordinary activities. The undertaking of these activities with knowledge of the tax operates as an acceptance of the offers so made. The very fact that all activity does not fall to the zero level is conclusive evidence that engaging in some activities subject to taxation is preferable to not engaging in any activities at all.

One way for the government to influence the pattern of private activities is through the imposition of selective taxes. People are less willing to engage in those activities that are taxed than in those which are not. The flip side of this power is the provision of tax exemptions, which have the opposite effect upon the ordinary pattern of people's activity. People are more likely to engage in activities that are exempt from taxes relative to those which are not. The incentive effects of tax rules are evident across the entire spectrum of economic activities, although today they normally receive almost no constitutional examination under the prevailing rational basis test. If direct regulation proceeds largely without constitutional interference, then there is no reason to subject taxation to any higher level of review. The situation is quite the opposite when speech is affected. Here taxation and exemptions have the same effects as they do in other contexts, and they are subject to the same high levels of scrutiny imposed on direct regulation generally. What is true of taxes is also true of exemptions.

Speiser v. Randall[2] is an early manifestation of the problem, and it shows how the conditions attached to a tax exemption can properly be struck down on First Amendment grounds. The California Constitution provided that World War II veterans were entitled to prop-

[2] 357 U.S. 513 (1958).

erty tax exemptions only if they signed an oath stating that they did not advocate the overthrow of the governments of the United States or California by force or violence or aid hostile foreign states in time of war.[3] The state argued that it could give its "privilege" or "bounty" to whomever it saw fit,[4] but Justice Brennan regarded the denial of the exemption as tantamount to a "fine," and struck it down accordingly for the want of the proper procedural protections.[5] The doctrine of unconstitutional conditions is implicated because the benefit conferred by the exemption is conditioned on the willingness of individual taxpayers to adhere to certain political views. The selective tax exemption, no less than a selective tax, necessarily results in a redistribution of wealth and political influence from those who are unwilling to sign the oath to those who are. It may well be that the general property tax exemption for veterans is proper. It is on that ground that the U.S. Supreme Court has upheld various government preferences that were not tied to the beliefs or political preferences of their recipients.[6] But redistribution on grounds of political belief is a very different matter. Coercive tax burdens cannot be waived selectively for those whose views conform to the dominant political position, any more than additional taxes can be imposed on those whose views do not. State gifts work as much of an illicit redistribution of wealth and power across political viewpoints as do state fines.

The California Supreme Court had recognized the point when it held that the exemption could be denied only for speech or advocacy that could be punished directly, thereby mooting the objection that the state was punishing indirectly what it could not punish directly. But once the statutory exemption received that construction, it was then fair to ask whether the statute afforded the same procedural protections as an ordinary criminal trial, which it did not. As Justice Brennan demonstrated, the statute was rendered vulnerable to attack on procedural due process grounds. *Speiser* involved excessive

[3] The full oath read: "I do not advocate the overthrow of the Government of the United States or of the State of California by force or violence or other unlawful means, nor advocate the support of a foreign government against the United States in event of hostilities." Id. at 515.

[4] See id. at 518.

[5] Id. at 518–29.

[6] Cf. Regan v. Taxation with Representation, 461 U.S. 540 (1983) (upholding against First Amendment and equal protection challenges a statute that exempted from taxation charitable contributions to support lobbying by veterans groups, but not to support lobbying by other groups); Personnel Adm'r v. Feeney, 442 U.S. 256 (1979) (holding that a statute giving preference to veterans in awarding civil service jobs does not discriminate against women in violation of the equal protection clause).

reliance upon an unexplicated idea of fines or coercion.[7] But its result is correct when tested against a theory of unconstitutional conditions designed to thwart the abuses arising from unchecked government discretion.

Since *Speiser*, the question of tax exemptions has come up in a somewhat more difficult form. In *Arkansas Writers' Project, Inc. v. Ragland*,[8] the Arkansas statute exempted from its general sales tax the "[g]ross receipts or gross proceeds derived from the sale of newspapers" and from certain types of magazines, including "religious, professional, trade and sports journals and/or publications printed and published in this State."[9] The plaintiff's general-purpose magazine fell into neither of these two categories, and hence it had to pay the tax.

*Arkansas Writers' Project* again raises the problem of unconstitutional conditions because Arkansas did not have to give any publication an exemption in the first place. Thus, the sole issue was whether the state could condition the exemption on the willingness of a magazine to publish material of a particular subject matter. The statute would have been a manifest violation of the First Amendment if it had tied the exemption to the adoption of any particular viewpoint, which it did not. Nonetheless, the statute did single out certain types of publications for benefits that other types of magazines were denied. By changing the relative costs of producing various kinds of magazines, the statute in effect brought about a mix of publications different from the one that would have arisen in a tax-free world, or indeed in any world with a uniform tax on all types of publications. As a matter of marketplace economics, these distortions deviate from the competitive ideal, and could be condemned on those grounds alone. But with the waning of economic liberties as a constitutional doctrine, this argument can be directed only to the legislature, not to the courts. Indeed, Justice Scalia would have upheld the tax because he regarded *Arkansas Writers' Project* as an economic regulation case,[10] scarcely distinguishable from other

[7] See 357 U.S. at 518: "To deny an exemption to claimants who engage in certain forms of speech is in effect to penalize them for such speech."

[8] 481 U. S. 221 (1987).

[9] Ark. Stat. Ann. 84-1904(f), (j) (1947), quoted in 481 U.S. at 223–25. This statute seems unconstitutional in its explicit discrimination against out-of-state newspapers. The issue, however, is more complicated, because it now seems that states may provide differential subsidies for local firms, but not impose differential taxes. See *New Energy Co. of Ind. v. Limbach*, 486 U.S. 269 (1988) (disallowing a discriminatory tax while appearing to tolerate discriminatory subsidies).

[10] See 481 U.S. at 235 (Scalia, J., dissenting).

cases of selective exemptions that have thus far survived constitutional attack.[11]

Nonetheless, the evident connection between the exemption and speech makes this clearly a First Amendment case. In this context, it is hard to demonstrate how any economic misallocation leads to an unwanted distortion in the marketplace of ideas, especially one that could be seized upon by political actors to advance their own interests. Still, the Court was correct to strike the statute down because there was so little to be said on its behalf. A uniform system of exemptions could end all objection to the statute without requiring a detailed analysis of its content while still allowing the state to advance newspapers and magazines as against other activities. In the unlikely event that a uniform exemption created a budget shortfall, the state could adopt a partial uniform exemption as necessary to meet its revenue requirements. Finding the condition attached to the exemption unconstitutional thus achieves the right result, even in a case that seems to present only limited opportunities for government abuse.

The same analysis yields different results in two other cases, one decided before, and the other after *Arkansas Writers' Project*. Its sequel, *Leathers v. Medlock*,[12] concerned another provision of the Arkansas Gross Receipts Act that exempted from its reach receipts obtained from the sale of newspapers by subscription or over-the-counter,[13] but which by a 1987 amendment imposed a sales tax on cable television activities.[14] The Court upheld this tax on two grounds. First, there was no viewpoint or subject matter discrimination as there was in *Arkansas Writers' Project*, and second, there was no evidence that any small group of firms was singled out for taxation. The tax imposed reached a wide range of ordinary commercial activities and applied to over 100 cable systems operating within the state. At most the tax could be said to induce a modest shift from cable to other forms of exempt communications, and that shift was not regarded as sufficient to strike down the tax.

*Leathers* represents one of those cases that poses a small danger to freedom of speech for which the state is able to offer only a weak public justification: there is no good reason for treating magazines

[11] Justice Scalia pointed out the special mail rates given to religious, educational, scientific, philanthropic, agricultural, labor, veterans', and fraternal organizations. See id. at 237–38. These classifications are broader than those involved in *Arkansas Writers' Project*, and thus they probably would, and should, survive challenge.

[12] 111 S. Ct. 1438 (1991).

[13] Ark. Code Ann. §§26-52-401(4), (14) (Supp. 1989).

[14] 1987 Ark. Gen. Acts. No. 188, §1.

and newspapers differently from cable TV. If the Court had treated this as a takings or an economic liberties case, then the result would have come out the other way, for Arkansas could have met all its revenue objectives with a uniform gross receipts tax which could have eliminated all specter of political favoritism and factional intrigue. The risks involved with this tax may be small, but I agree with Justice Marshall's dissent that, since high levels of scrutiny are applied under the First Amendment, the tax should have been struck down unless it applied to all forms of communication.[15]

*Regan v. Taxation with Representation*[16] (*TWR*), decided prior to *Arkansas Writers' Project*, raises a more troublesome question. *TWR* challenged a system of charitable exemptions on the ground that they could not be applied to moneys raised for lobbying activities. The taxpayer in *TWR* was a political organization that attacked two provisions of the Internal Revenue Code, one that failed to grant it tax-exempt status, and one that failed to grant deductions to its contributors.[17] The unconstitutional conditions challenge came in two parts. The first was that it was impermissible to attach any limitations restricting the ability of otherwise exempt organizations to participate in lobbying. The second part was that it was impermissible to permit veterans organizations to operate free of the restrictions made applicable to other political groups.

Justice Rehnquist, speaking for the majority, rejected both challenges, relying heavily upon the norm of "broad discretion" in taxing matters.[18] "This Court has never held that Congress must grant a benefit such as TWR claims here to a person who wishes to exercise a constitutional right."[19] But this account suppresses the equal protection component of the argument. The objection is not to the fail-

[15] 111 S. Ct. at 1447. Note that if this case were an economic liberties case, then the defect could not be cured simply by exempting cable from the gross receipts tax. The entire tax would have to be repealed. Arkansas would, of course, retain the object of enacting it across the board, subject only to exemptions that could withstand a very high level of scrutiny.

[16] 461 U.S. 540 (1983).

[17] The two provisions involved were §501(c)(3) and §501(c)(4) of the Internal Revenue Code. Both provide tax-exempt status for various kinds of charitable organizations. The Court specified two principal differences between organizations receiving §501(c)(3) status and those receiving §501(c)(4) status: "Taxpayers who contribute to §501(c)(3) organizations are permitted by §170(c)(2) to deduct the amount of their contributions on their federal income tax returns, while contributions to §501(c)(4) organizations are not deductible. Section 501(c)(4) organizations, but not §501(c)(3) organizations, are permitted to engage in substantial lobbying to advance their exempt purposes." 461 U.S. at 543.

[18] Id. at 547.

[19] Id. at 545.

ure to grant the subsidy as such, but to granting the subsidy to charitable organizations while denying it to lobbying organizations.

Properly formulated, the critical question is whether this broad type of condition creates any distortion in the political process. It is doubtful that it does, even when the statute is tested against the more demanding First Amendment standards of scrutiny. The religious, political, and educational activities exempted under the statute cover the full range of activities without subject-matter or viewpoint discrimination, and the ban on lobbying is imposed at the same high level of generality. The differences in tax treatment may well induce some moneys to go into, say, academic work that would otherwise have gone into direct lobbying, but it is hard to see what political groups, if any, would systematically gain from this effect. Here, unlike the tax exemption situation posed by *Arkansas Writers' Project*, there seems to be a powerful government counterweight on the other side. One great peril in political life today is that the broad discretion of federal and state government over economic affairs increases the potential gains to partisan activities, of which lobbying is only the most visible. Why that conduct must be subsidized, even if charitable organizations are subsidized, is therefore something of a mystery. The doctrine of unconstitutional conditions should be invoked precisely when the conditions attached to government action increase the risk of political polarization, the opposite of the case in which lobbying efforts proceed without tax dollars. The distinction between lobbying and charitable activities thus survives even a higher level of constitutional scrutiny.[20]

The standard of review becomes far more important on the second question: whether veterans organizations alone should receive preferred tax status for their lobbying activities. Justice Rehnquist, still employing a degree of judicial deference, simply noted that all veterans organizations qualified regardless of their views.[21] If veterans groups only had disagreements among themselves on issues of no concern to others, a tax subsidy to them might not affect the denial of a parallel subsidy to other organizations. But although these groups may differ among themselves on some issues, they must surely act in concert with respect to others, where they operate in direct competition with unsubsidized lobbying groups. In these cases the differential tax treatment does distort the outcome of the

[20] It is therefore unnecessary to adopt Justice Blackmun's position. Using a high level of scrutiny, he allowed the denial of exemptions for lobbying organizations under §501(c)(3), but only because of the ability of affiliate organizations to use tax-exempt funds to lobby under §501(c)(4). See id. at 552–53 (Blackmun, J., concurring).

[21] See 461 U.S. at 548.

political process in ways that the First Amendment and the equal protection clause should preclude. It appears, therefore, that Congress at least should be put to the all-or-nothing choice of granting exemptions to all lobbying organizations or to none.

I reach that conclusion with a fair bit of trepidation, lest Congress take the bait and extend the tax benefit to all lobbying groups, including the vast number that are totally unconcerned with veterans activities. The unconstitutional conditions doctrine again achieves only a second-best goal. The grant of universal tax exemptions to lobbying organizations subsidizes all special-interest groups at the expense of the general public, introducing yet another set of tax distortions. There is a prisoner's dilemma game here, in which all persons can be made better off if no lobbying group receives a tax subsidy. Perhaps the proper response is to treat all tax subsidies of political lobbying as beyond the power of Congress to grant. That more vigorous approach controls not only tax distortions between one lobbying group and another, but also tax distortions between lobbying and socially productive activities.[22] Lobbying may well be a protected constitutional right,[23] but it is not one that is either deserving of or entitled to a political subsidy.

## TAX EXEMPTIONS AND RELIGIOUS FREEDOM

### *Universal Exemptions*

The question of tax exemptions is also important in connection with protection of religious freedom. In principle the arguments here should be identical to those available for freedom of speech. Initially, however, the entire issue is clouded because of one threshold question: should any state decision to exempt religious organizations be treated as equivalent to an in-kind subsidy of religious organizations? In the modern context, there is a well-nigh irresistible urge to adopt that conclusion, so that the debate only goes to the justification for the subsidy so provided. But this approach takes a distinctly modern view of the entire subject. Earlier in our history, church-

[22] It would of course be irresponsible for the Court to take such an extreme step in any case where veterans organizations did not have a chance to present their side of the argument. Indeed the best justification for *Regan* is prudential: the Court did not want to resolve the various difficult issues that would have arisen if the veterans' tax exemption had been found unconstitutional.

[23] See, e.g., Eastern R.R. Presidents Conf. v. Noerr Motor Freight, Inc., 365 U.S. 127, 138 (1961): "The right of petition is one of the freedoms protected by the Bill of Rights."

state relationships assumed a form very different from what they have today. The Church asserted an independent jurisdiction that was beyond the power and authority of the King.[24] The early assize utrum asked whether certain activities fell within the domain of the Church or within the domain of the King.[25] Where these matters were church-related, then the question of tax-exemption did not arise, for the King had no power to impose the tax in the first instance. The Church was master of its own house, much the way in which a foreign government is regarded as sovereign over its own embassy in another nation.

The recognition of two separate domains was of economic significance as well. In order to find out whether there is an implicit subsidy from any scheme of taxation, it is necessary to match the costs imposed with the benefits received. In a regime of strict separation, religious organizations do not receive any services from the secular authorities. The question of subsidy cannot arise without economic interaction, when there are both zero benefits and zero costs. It is only when religious organizations become subordinate to the secular sovereign that the genuine economic complications begin. The state provides a variety of public goods which benefit religious organizations and their memberships. In a community in which all persons belong to the same church, the question of exemption from taxation carries with it few complications. The persons charged with the extra tax burden are identical to those who receive its benefits. The decision to exempt or not has no redistributive consequences across persons, even though it may increase the level of religious relative to nonreligious activities.

The situation, however, becomes vastly more complicated when many different religions coexist under the same government and when some people partake in no religious activities at all. In this setting, a decision not to tax a religion is certain to contain within it elements of subsidy whose extent will depend on the uses to which the forgone tax revenues might have been put. To take a couple of simple examples, if the money raised from the tax is used to fund

[24] See, e.g., Theodore F.T. Plucknett, *A Concise History of the Common Law* 17–18 (5th ed. 1956), with a brief account of the jurisdictional dispute between Henry II and Thomas Becket, Archbishop of Cantebury.

[25] "A fourth assize called utrum also began as a preliminary proceeding in order to ascertain whether litigious land fell under the jurisdiction of the Church or the Crown, but in course of time the decision in this preliminary question became in effect a decision upon the principal question" Id. at 360. See also id. at 17, 111, 360; F.W. Maitland, *The Forms of Action at Common Law* (A.H. Chaytor & W.J. Whittaker eds., 1968).

public education, then exemption from the tax should hardly count as a subsidy for a religious organization whose own schools may compete with public education. Yet by the same token, if the tax revenues are used to supply garbage collection and police protection to the church, then the effect of the exemption is quite different. As regards the garbage collection, there is an implicit subsidy if the state continues to supply the service free of charge. But there is none if the church arranges for garbage collection from other sources or pays the state an appropriate user fee. Police protection raises somewhat different issues because the church is likely to derive some benefit from overall police protection in its neighborhood, even if none of it is directed to the church.[26] Yet the courtesy is likely to be repaid if the separate security measures undertaken by a church also reduce the overall incidence of crime in the community at large. There are, in short, several layers of analysis that must be undertaken before the "net" subsidy conferred by an exemption can be determined.

The question then arises, where the exemption does confer some subsidy on a religious organization, should it be tolerated? In important respects the analysis here parallels that afforded to the general exemption of speech-related activities from taxation. If the Constitution continued to provide strong protection for economic liberties, then any subsidy to any sector creates distortions from the tax-free world, and should be struck down forthwith, notwithstanding the long tradition to the contrary. But once these economic redistributions fall within the scope of legislative judgment, then the narrower question under the establishment clause is whether this exemption to religion amounts to an impermissible subsidy.

In *Walz v. Tax Commission of New York*,[27] the Court sustained New York City's exemption from real estate taxation for religious organizations. At times Chief Justice Burger wrote as if the tax exemption was not a subsidy,[28] and at other places he wrote as though the long tradition of tax exemptions was decisive on the constitutional question.[29] But his more persuasive argument within the con-

[26] To be sure, there are further complications, for if police protection is provided to secular institutions only, it could induce potential criminals to prey on church members and church property.

[27] 397 U.S. 664 (1970).

[28] "The grant of a tax exemption is not sponsorship since the government does not transfer part of its revenue to churches but simply abstains from demanding that the church support the state." Id. at 675. The "simply" conceals the difficulties with the distribution of the tax revenues so raised.

[29] Id. at 676–80.

text of the religion clause is that the subsidy created is distributed to a class of institutions sufficiently broad that there is little risk of favoritism for religious institutions, relative to a wide class of charitable institutions generally. Thus it is clear, as with the speech case, that any *selective* exemption from real estate taxation instantly fails. But as the relevant statute covers a multitude of religious and nonreligious charitable and benevolent purposes, the case cannot be looked upon as one where religious organizations receive subsidies that are denied to other charitable organizations.[30] If anything, it must be viewed as one that asks whether religious organizations should be denied the benefits given to other charitable organizations. Here there is no obvious theory which determines what organizations fall into the broad basket of exempt organizations—unions and chess clubs are both excluded. But so long as that basket contains all religious (including some antireligous groups) and lots of nonreligious institutions besides, then the exemption should be sustained on the familiar nondiscrimination grounds, as held in *Walz.*

### *Selective Exemptions: The Case of Racial Discrimination*

The question of exemptions becomes far more troublesome when these are granted on a selective basis. The problem is presented in its most exquisite form where the religious organization practices some form of voluntary racial discrimination. In *Bob Jones University v. United States*,[31] the constitutional issue was whether Bob Jones University should be able to keep its charitable tax exemption, even though it had adopted, out of sincere and genuine religious beliefs, a ban against interracial dating and marriage for its students.[32] For the

[30] The Constitutional framework of New York State provides, Art. 16, §1: "Exemptions from taxation may be granted only by general laws. Exemptions may be altered or repealed except those exempting real or personal property used exclusively for religious, educational or charitable purposes as defined by law and owned by any corporation or association organized or conducted exclusively for one or more such purposes and not operating for profit." The statute implementing the constitutional provision provides "Real property owned by a corporation or association organized exclusively for the moral or mental improvement of men and women, or for religious, bible, tract, charitable, benevolent, missionary hospital, infirmary, educational, public playground, scientific, literary, bar association, medical society, library, patriotic, historical or cemetery purposes." New York Real Property Tax Law, §420, subd. 1.

[31] 461 U.S. 574 (1978).

[32] See id. at 580–81, 602–3. Also at issue in the case was whether the university's discriminatory practices disqualified it from tax-exempt status under the "public policy" doctrine, a question that the Court answered affirmatively. See id. at 592–96.

Court, the case was easy. It started with the premise that "there can no longer be any doubt that racial discrimination in education violates deeply and widely accepted views of elementary justice,"[33] and cited its decision in *Brown v. Board of Education*[34] to reaffirm its opposition to any system of state-sponsored segregation. Set against this background, the free-exercise objection to the statute under the religion clauses received short shrift, given that "the Government has a fundamental, overriding interest in eradicating racial discrimination in education."[35] The Court concluded that "[d]enial of tax benefits will inevitably have a substantial impact on the operation of private religious schools, but will not prevent those schools from observing their religious tenets."[36] The contrast with *Speiser* is manifest, for there the denial of benefits was regarded as a fine even though Speiser was perfectly able to express his political beliefs without receiving the tax benefit from the state.

Notwithstanding its sharp break with the usual judicial attitude toward selective exemptions, *Bob Jones* has generally received a warm response,[37] but once the problem of unconstitutional conditions is forthrightly considered, the decision is nonetheless clearly incorrect. The initial inquiry is whether the state could decide that its "compelling interest" in eradicating racial segregation in education is sufficiently strong to allow the state to impose a direct fine or criminal punishment on the school for imposing those conditions on its students. The answer, I take it, is no. The free exercise clause of the First Amendment does not pertain only to the liturgy but to the full range of religious activities, of which schooling is most definitely a part.[38] Indeed, if *Bob Jones* is correct, then the compelling state interest test is endowed with infinite elasticity. The government could condition its tax exemptions to religious institutions on their compliance with a prohibition against sex discrimination as practiced by Roman Catholics and Orthodox Jews in the selection of

[33] Id. at 592.

[34] See id. at 593 (citing Brown, 347 U.S. 483 (1954)).

[35] Id. at 604.

[36] Id. at 603–4.

[37] See, e.g., Joel L. Selig, "The Reagan Justice Department and Civil Rights: What Went Wrong," 1985 *U. Ill. L. Rev.* 785, 817–21; see also Meyer Freed & Daniel Polsby, "Race, Religion, and Public Policy: *Bob Jones University v. United States*," 1983 *Sup. Ct. Rev.* 1, 1–2 (noting the various editorials and columns of the *New York Times* and the *Washington Post* denouncing the University and the Reagan Administration's position).

[38] See, e.g., Wisconsin v. Yoder, 406 U.S. 205 (1972).

their religious leaders.[39] After all, they are not hurt just because their rivals are benefitted.

Even if it is assumed that the denial of a tax benefit does not operate like a "fine," there still remains the question whether the government can deliver its economic benefits in ways that favor one religious set of beliefs over another, given its obligation not to use its coercive powers to advance or retard religion.[40] It is often said that the general public should not be forced to subsidize institutions like Bob Jones University in their religious beliefs. But the argument has the subsidy claim backwards. Under *Bob Jones*, the University and its supporters are forced to bankroll in part the subsidies provided for other institutions, without receiving any parallel benefits of their own, thereby skewing the relative power of the two sets of institutions from what it would be in the tax-free world. The use of selective grants on matters of religious belief shows government power at its most dangerous. In this context it becomes idle to say that the greater power to withhold tax exemptions includes the lesser power to condition an exemption on the sacrifice of the prospective recipient's own religious convictions. As is usually the case, the setting of conditions on government grants is the result of powerful political pressures against which the Bill of Rights was designed to guard. Bob Jones University may be unfashionable and perverse in its religious beliefs and practices, but it is entitled to the same level of constitutional protection as everyone else.

[39] The tension between Title VII and the religion clauses did surface in Corporation of Presiding Bishops v. Amos, 483 U. S. 327 (1987), in which the Court held that the exemption from Title VII for religious organizations, see 42 U.S.C. §2000e-1 (1982), did not offend the establishment clause. The Court did not ask the harder question whether the exemption was required by the free exercise clause, to which I would answer in the affirmative. See generally Richard A. Epstein, "Religious Liberty In the Welfare State," 31 *Wm. & Mary L. Rev.* 375 (1990). If that conclusion is correct, then *Bob Jones* must be clearly wrong. If the state cannot coerce compliance with the antidiscrimination norm against religious organizations by the use of force, then it cannot discriminate against them in the receipt of tax benefits.

[40] For a parallel discussion of the more difficult case of Sherbert v. Verner, 374 U.S. 398 (1963), see infra chap. 16.

## CHAPTER 16

# Unemployment Benefits

THE PREVIOUS fifteen chapters of this book have demonstrated how a rigorous respect for the limits on government power is able to secure the benefits of a competitive regime even where the government's power to bargain is enhanced by its power to tax and by its monopoly position. With the advent of the welfare state, it is no longer possible to treat public support for a competitive system as the sole proper function of government. The question then arises whether the strategies that were used to constrain the power of the state within its traditional context may be fruitfully applied within the expanded frontiers of the welfare state.

It has been suggested that an "unconstitutional conditions doctrine built on pre–New Deal foundations is poorly adapted to the regulatory state."[1] But why? The major prohibitions required for the maintenance of a competitive order are two: no monopoly exactions and no forced redistribution. The rise of the New Deal state reduces the force of these limitations by allowing redistribution, but it does not eliminate them altogether. The New Property embraces many forms of government largess and government benefits,[2] but it does not mark the end of constitutional government. There may be redistribution, but there may still be some restraints on the persons from whom it is taken, the persons to whom it is given, or the purposes for which it is transferred. Indeed, Charles Reich's own account of the New Property fairly invites the use of an unconstitutional conditions doctrine: "Increasingly, Americans live on government largess—allocated by government on its own terms, and held by recipients subject to conditions which express 'the public interest.'"[3] Surely not just any conditions will do, unless we regard the New Deal as a return to a regime of unfettered legislative supremacy, which it emphatically is not. In order to make sense of the new constitutional order, and to flesh out what is meant by the *public inter-*

[1] Cass R. Sunstein, "Why the Unconstitutional Conditions Doctrine is an Anachronism (With Particular Reference to Religion, Speech, and Abortion)," 70 *B.U. L. Rev.* 593, 601 (1990).

[2] Charles A. Reich, "The New Property," 73 *Yale L.J.* 733 (1964).

[3] Id. at 733.

*est*, therefore, it is necessary to know which forms of government actions are prohibited, and to see that those ends are not achieved through improper bargaining any more than they are through direct government regulation.

Within broad areas of social life, the remaining constraints in the welfare state have genuine bite. Even if the state is not under a constitutional obligation to promote the competitive equilibrium, there may be two separate activities (e.g., religious and nonreligious schools) whose parity it must respect. Thus the state may, in a style consistent with the welfare state (as well as pre–New Deal understandings), provide extensive subsidies to education, but the distribution of that subsidy between religious and nonreligious institutions will nonetheless remain subject to serious constitutional scrutiny. Although it may no longer be possible to reach a competitive optimum that covers all activities, it is still possible to insist upon some constitutional balance between religious and nonreligious activities, as well as a balance between the educational activities of different religions.[4] That requirement of balance translates into a prohibition of differential subsidies or penalties that might distort relative preferences within the subsidized fields. Whether or not those subsidies have been created depends on the methods of analysis that have been developed throughout this book. No matter what the context, the rise of official discretion that comes with the expansion of state power can never be regarded as a matter of indifference.[5] The limitations on the power of the state to bargain are therefore as much a part of the new constitutional order as they are of the old.

Accordingly, the focus now shifts to the full range of government benefits that are provided by the welfare state. In order to organize this material I shall divide it into three separate groups of benefits. In this chapter, I shall consider the conditions that may be attached to unemployment benefits, first as they come in tension with the religion clauses of the First Amendment, the equal protection clause as it relates to sex differences, and finally in connection with purely economic issues raised by unemployment benefits to striking workers. In chapter 17, I shall examine the role of conditional grants for

[4] Michael W. McConnell & Richard A. Posner, "An Economic Approach to Issues of Religious Freedom," 56 *U. Chi. L. Rev. 1* (1989).

[5] The theme resonates with administrative lawyers as well as small-government types like myself. See, e.g., Kenneth Culp Davis, *Discretionary Justice: A Preliminary Inquiry* (1969). Indeed much of the impulse behind modern administrative law has been to constrain the levels of abuse that seem to be an inseparable part of the elaborate system of government offices and agencies.

welfare benefits, both procedural and substantive. The procedural issues are those raised by the claim for pretermination hearings in welfare cases, and the substantive issues are raised by the divisive question of whether the state may provide medical benefits for pregnant women, but refuse to subsidize abortions. Finally, in chapter 18, I shall examine the question of educational benefits, first as it applies to the funding of religious and public schooling, and second as it applies to funding for the arts.

## THE RELIGION CASES

### *The Basic Unconstitutional Conditions Dilemma*

Unemployment compensation programs typically limit their benefits to people who are unemployed through no fault of their own and remain available for work. While these complex systems raise many interpretive difficulties, the salient initial inquiry for these purposes is whether the state can deny these benefits to people who will not work because the only jobs available require them to violate their religious beliefs. Can the state refuse to provide unemployment benefits to persons unwilling to take these jobs? The current answer is no. The Supreme Court's major decision is *Sherbert v. Verner,*[6] which was followed in the 1980 Term by *Thomas v. Review Board of the Indiana Employment Security Division,*[7] and in the 1986 Term by *Hobbie v. Unemployment Appeals Commission,*[8] and ominously limited in *Employment Division, Department of Human Resources v. Smith.*[9]

*Sherbert* illustrates the basic pattern. Sherbert, a Seventh-Day Adventist, was dismissed from her job because she refused to work on Saturday, when to do so violated her religious convictions. The state system of unemployment compensation restricted payments to persons who were unable to work through no fault of their own.[10] The state employment board decided that Sherbert had quit for personal reasons, and that jobs were "available" to her within the region. Accordingly her claim for compensation was denied.[11] The Supreme Court was then forced to decide whether the refusal of the state to pay her benefits constituted a limitation on the free exercise of religion, or, alternatively, whether the decision to pay unemployment

[6] 374 U.S. 398 (1963).
[7] 450 U.S. 707 (1981).
[8] 480 U.S. 136 (1987).
[9] 494 U.S. 872 (1990).
[10] See 374 U.S. at 400–401.
[11] See id. at 401.

compensation constituted a de facto establishment of religion. The case raised an unconstitutional conditions question because two propositions have been settled under applicable law: first that a state need not have any system of unemployment compensation at all and, second, that a state may operate its system of unemployment compensation to promote the "common good."[12] Does the state unconstitutionally condition its grant of unemployment benefits on Sherbert's waiver of her First Amendment rights?

*Sherbert* brings to a head the tension between the religion clauses in the Bill of Rights on the one hand, and one common form of "New Property" on the other. In a world of limited government, each of the two religion clauses operates within a relatively self-defined sphere.[13] The free exercise clause guarantees that the government cannot interfere with the "negative liberties" of the citizen with respect to religious practices. It cannot prohibit religious worship, and it cannot fine, license, tax, or punish religious practices in any way. The obligation of the state is to leave people alone. The establishment clause governs the other side of the line, prohibiting the state from going into the business of religion. Certainly it cannot support one religion to the exclusion of the others. In the modern view, neither can it give aid to all religions equally, if nonreligious groups are excluded from the program.[14] In a world of limited state and federal power, the pressure on each of the religion clauses is tolerably small, and the possibility of their collision reduced, being limited primarily to cases in which the government is forced to recon-

[12] Carmichael v. Southern Coal & Coke Co., 301 U.S. 495 (1937). For my criticisms of that decision, see *Takings*, 309–12.

[13] As of late, the coercive power of the state has begun to chop away at the free exercise clause in alarming proportions. See Michael W. McConnell, "Academic Freedom In Religious Colleges," 53 *Law & Contemp. Probs.* 303 (1991), for a defense of the institutional academic freedom of religious institutions—a position once eloquently advanced by Justice Frankfurter, see Sweezy v. New Hampshire, 354 U.S. 243, 263 (1957). Academic freedom includes "the four essential freedoms of a university—to determine for itself on academic grounds who may teach, what may be taught, how it shall be taught, and who may be admitted to study." Note that the antidiscrimination laws are a powerful qualification to that principle, which in the end, I believe, will undermine it substantially. For an egregious illustration of government interference in religious institutions, see Babcock v. New Orleans Baptist Theological Seminary, 554 So. 2d 90 (La. Ct. App. 1989), requiring a religious institution to grant the plaintiff a master's degree in marriage and family counseling, even though he had allegedly abused his wife. The court held that the grounds for refusing the degree were irrelevant because they did not "touch upon theological or ecclesiastical matters." The narrow tests of relevance here are wholly inconsistent with the subjective determination of preferences required by any liberal theory of contract.

[14] See, e.g., Everson v. Board of Educ., 330 U.S. 1, 15–16 (1947).

cile the religious interests of its employees with the requirements of public service.[15]

The situation becomes far more difficult once the government goes beyond its role as an enforcer of private rights to create and administer a system of positive welfare rights. The greater scope of government action necessarily makes it easier for the state to offend either or both of the religion clauses. Moreover, as long as the government remains in the business of managing all phases of the economy, a simple line that requires government "nonfeasance" in certain areas or a "strict separation" between the state and religion becomes indefensible. The misfeasance/nonfeasance line works well only on a small canvas, to keep strangers apart, but it does not offer a workable litmus test in such areas as medical malpractice, for either individual responsibility or state power. The strict separation approach for its part is far too rigid because it rules out any cooperative efforts between church and state (even for the joint funding and use of public roads and sanitation facilities) that work for the advantage of both groups.

Some more sophisticated test to distinguish among government actions is needed. In 1961 Professor Philip Kurland proposed the following standard:

> [T]he thesis proposed here as the proper construction of the religion clauses of the first amendment is that the freedom and separation clauses should be read as a single precept that government cannot utilize religion as a standard for action or inaction because these clauses prohibit classification in terms of religion either to confer a benefit or to impose a burden.[16]

Reduced to a single catchword, "neutrality," is said to have become the guiding principle in religion cases. So stated, however, the principle gives rise to many serious questions when a neutral principle has disparate impact upon religious and nonreligious groups, or on individuals from different religious groups. The problem here is

[15] See, e.g., Goldman v. Weinberger, 475 U.S. 503 (1986) (upholding a military regulation barring the use of religious headgear).

[16] Philip B. Kurland, "Of Church and State and the Supreme Court," 29 *U. Chi. L. Rev.* 1, 5–6 (1961); see also Wilber Katz, "Freedom of Religion and State Neutrality," 20 *U. Chi. L. Rev.* 426, 429 (1953) (noting the tension between the two clauses "where the state takes over the ordering of the lives of groups of citizens, as in the armed forces, in prisons, and in institutions to which delinquent or dependent children are committed. Here the effect of strict separation would be seriously to limit the religious freedom of the citizens concerned."). For a more recent treatment of the same issue, see Michael W. McConnell, "Neutrality Under the Religion Clauses," 81 *Nw. U.L. Rev.* 146 (1986).

but a subset of the more general problem that exists with all takings, that is, with rules that restrict or tax the use or disposition of property more generally.[17] Explicit special classifications are *usually* strong evidence of a subsidy, but in some circumstances may be justified in order to offset special burdens that might otherwise exist. By the same token, facial neutrality is *usually* evidence that both sides benefit equally from the restrictions imposed. Yet there are exceptions to these rules in ordinary property transactions *in both directions*, and similar problems, with similar difficulties can easily arise under the religion clauses, where they receive an enigmatic response.[18]

Start with special treatment. A rule that allows members of one religion to pray on military bases to the exclusion of all others is surely bad. There is no powerful reason not to make the use of military facilities universal. But in other cases the exceptions have stronger grounding. A dispensation from the rule ordinarily prohibiting Orthodox Jewish psychiatrists from wearing religious headgear while on duty is a violation of the neutrality principle, but one that seems fully justified as an accommodation of religion. The privilege may not have to be extended to members of other religions (or even other branches of Judaism) in order for them to practice their faith in the service, and the refusal to grant the dispensation is a wholesale exclusion of certain individuals from military service, without any showing of how that practice advances some government interest—an interest that the government itself is not prepared to assert. In effect there is no neutral position: the question is whether the burdens from exclusion are greater than the burdens from accommodation, where the muted constitutional imperative is to choose that position with the smallest level of net inconvenience—a kind of Kaldor-Hicks test for religious affairs—when any form of direct cash compensation seems singularly inappropriate. On balance, a rule that allows the government to make this accommodation should not be attacked as an establishment of religion, even though there are no parallel accommodations that can be made for non-

[17] See *Takings*, chap. 14 (dealing with the relationship of disparate impact to the compensation criterion).

[18] Michael W. McConnell, "The Origins and Historical Understanding of Free Exercise of Religion," 103 *Harv. L. Rev.* 1409 (1990), concludes, after an exhaustive evaluation of the pre-1787 evidence, that "exemptions were not common enough to compel the inference that the term 'free exercise of religion' necessarily included an enforceable right to exemption," but by the same token that this evidence was "more consistent" with this view than with the alternative that demands strict facial neutrality.

religious persons, such as those who do not have any need to wear specialized religious clothing.

There is a second side to the preference question that is still more difficult. Suppose that the government refuses to make this accommodation by statute or rule. May that refusal to grant the exemption be challenged as an infringement of individual liberty under the free exercise clause, given the explicit preference built into the rule? An uneasy Supreme Court gave a negative answer to this question by a divided vote.[19] But surely the Kurland rule does not begin to capture the relevant questions because of its mistaken insistence that any rule of formal neutrality necessarily blocks both a subsidy (conferring a benefit) and a penalty (imposing a burden), when in fact that neutral rule can operate as either subsidy or penalty, depending on circumstances. As much as one dislikes balancing tests, here is one area in which the demand for accommodation fairly requires them.

Likewise a neutral rule can be attacked from the other side. Happily, in many cases, it may preserve the relative balance between two groups, so that the law will be enacted only when both sides are left better off.[20] Yet where its impact is disparate, one side may be better off and the other worse off. In the context of religion it is not possible to predict the direction of the implicit shift solely from a knowledge that disparate impact exists. Indeed its religious motivation seems strong enough to condemn the practice notwithstanding its facial neutrality, even if the Supreme Court had decided the question the other way in *Braunfield v. Brown*.[21] Kurland's joint account of the two clauses, however, misses the difficulty of these cases, because they possess both formal neutrality *and* provide an implicit subsidy for some groups at the expense of others. The neutrality test is at most an imperfect proxy for the ultimate question of penalty or subsidy, which in many cases may have no clear answer.

Given the unavoidable tensions in the religion cases, it is not surprising that none of the Justices in *Sherbert* was able to give a satisfactory account of the clash between the religion clauses and the

[19] Goldman v. Weinberger, 475 U.S. 503 (1986). The vote was 7 to 2, but the concurring opinion of Justice Stevens, joined by Justices White and Powell, recognized the force of the individual claim, and concurred only because they feared the slippery slope—a concern that hardly seems stronger here than in many other cases of unavoidable balancing.

[20] For a discussion of the political dynamics that lead to this conclusion, see *Takings*, chap. 14.

[21] 366 U.S. 599 (1961).

unemployment benefit programs. The Court, speaking through Justice Brennan, recognized that the state did not seek to impose "criminal sanctions,"[22] but held in essence that the elimination of the unemployment benefits was a form of coercion:

> Here not only is it apparent that appellant's declared ineligibility for benefits derives solely from the practice of her religion, but the pressure upon her to forego that practice is unmistakable. The ruling forces her to choose between following the precepts of her religion and forfeiting benefits, on the one hand, and abandoning one of the precepts of her religion in order to accept work, on the other hand. Governmental imposition of such a choice puts the same kind of burden upon the free exercise of religion as would a fine imposed against appellant for her Saturday worship.
>
> Nor may the South Carolina court's construction of the statute be saved from constitutional infirmity on the ground that unemployment compensation benefits are not appellant's "right" but merely a "privilege." It is too late in the day to doubt that the liberties of religion and expression may be infringed by the denial of or placing conditions upon a benefit or privilege.[23]

Thus the doctrine of unconstitutional conditions surfaced to fill the void in Sherbert's case. It is clear that the state need not provide any benefits at all. The "fine" becomes a measure of relative deprivation: if the government chooses to provide those benefits, it cannot condition them upon the willingness of people to work in ways that contravene their religious beliefs.

Justice Stewart's concurrence shows that Justice Brennan's "fine" analogy is far from dispositive. In Justice Stewart's view, any effort to apply the free exercise clause to these facts would conflict with the Court's own establishment clause jurisprudence:

> If the appellant's refusal to work on Saturdays were based on indolence, or on a compulsive desire to watch the Saturday television programs, no one would say that South Carolina could not hold that she was not "available for work" within the meaning of its statute. That being so, the Establishment Clause as construed by this Court not only permits but affirmatively requires South Carolina equally to deny the appellant's claim for unemployment compensation when her refusal to work on Saturdays is based upon her religious creed. . . . [T]he Estab-

[22] 374 U.S. at 403.
[23] Id. at 404 (footnote omitted).

lishment Clause forbids the "financial support of government" to be "placed behind a particular religious belief."[24]

In this passage, Justice Stewart treats the unemployment program as a subsidy to religion because people who do not work on Saturday for religious reasons obtain a benefit that other non-Saturday workers do not receive. Justice Brennan finds a penalty by comparing the claimant to other persons who actively seek work but cannot find it. Justice Brennan's "penalty" suggests free exercise difficulties in upholding the statute as applied, while Justice Stewart's "subsidy" suggests establishment clause difficulties in striking it down. The neutrality principle could be invoked to support both positions or neither. Clearly something has to give. What?

It is necessary again to return to fundamentals. Notwithstanding their differences, Justice Brennan and Justice Stewart share two premises. Both start from the assumption that the unemployment compensation programs are constitutionally sound, for otherwise the unconstitutional conditions issue could never arise. Both then explore the limitations that the state might place upon receipt of the benefit. While they disagree about the proper analysis in *Sherbert*, neither Justice would tolerate a program that provided public unemployment compensation programs only to those who agreed to practice Judaism or Christianity, or only to those who agreed not to observe one of those faiths. They thus agree on the vital issue. They both reject the now familiar argument that because the state need not establish an unemployment compensation program at all, it can therefore choose the objects of its affections as it pleases, for such selection confers too much power on the state. Thus the doctrine of unconstitutional conditions is not a point of contention between the two Justices. It is in fact their second common premise.

The question arises, however, as to the doctrine's scope. Here the constitutional acceptance of income redistribution through employment compensation programs is important because it marks a clear break from *Frost*,[25] whose imperfect efforts to preserve competition had an explicitly anti-redistributive bias. Once general takings and public trust arguments are no longer sufficient to forestall all forms

[24] Id. at 414–15 (Stewart, J., concurring in the result) (quoting Engel v. Vitale, 370 U.S. 421, 431 (1962)). Justice Stewart concurred in the Court's result because he thought that "the Court's mechanistic concept of the Establishment Clause is historically unsound and constitutionally wrong." Id. at 415. His concurrence reflects his view of the dominance of the free exercise clause over the establishment clause, see id. at 415–16; Braunfield v. Brown, 366 U.S. 599, 616 (1961) (Stewart, J., dissenting), a view that makes *Sherbert* a relatively easy case.

[25] See supra chap. 11.

of redistribution, whether covert or overt, between A and B, then additional pressure is placed upon the religion clauses to forbid redistribution both from or to any religious group. In this context it thus becomes clear why it is important to reformulate the idea of neutrality into its more precise economic analogue: the government cannot engage in activities that either penalize or subsidize the practice of religion.[26] Judicial scrutiny is high, for whether the government program is sustained or struck down, there is a substantial risk of constitutional error. This test is more stringent than that found in the speech area, where only restrictions that burden private speech are suspect, while those that subsidize it are not. In contrast, *every* form of error in the religious context is subject to constitutional scrutiny, for to avoid the perils of free exercise may be to land in the thicket of establishment, and vice versa. The question of subsidy or penalty, then, requires the selection of the right baseline, but that in turn is possible only after careful treatment of the insurance and funding issues in *Sherbert.*

This approach allows us to go beyond the metaphor of the "fine" that appealed to Justice Brennan. The state does not take Sherbert's money when she quits work. It refuses to pay her "its" money. Therein lies the rub. The state is not a person, but a complex network of arrangements among people, of which only some are voluntary. As with public highways and foreign taxation, the state does not spend its own money. It spends money that it raises from private individuals, including Sherbert. To make the analysis tractable, assume that all the contributions to the unemployment system are collected from a tax imposed directly or indirectly on the workers and the firm. Assume further that random redistributions of wealth between, say, plumbers and pipefitters, are permitted under ordinary unemployment compensation programs. Now divide the world into two classes of people, those who might quit jobs for religious reasons and those who would not. The question that the religion clauses ask is whether there is an implicit redistribution of wealth across those two classes—*either way.* If the redistribution runs from religious persons to nonreligious persons, then we have a free exercise clause violation. If it runs in the opposite direction, then we have an establishment clause violation. Which is it?

At first blush, the argument seems to be that there is an implicit subsidy conferred upon Sherbert, and hence an establishment clause violation. She is entitled to recover for all the normal cases of unemployment specified in the statute, plus one additional type of case:

[26] See infra chap. 17.

not working because of religious conflict. If she pays the same premium as everyone else, but receives more extensive insurance coverage in exchange, then she looks like the net recipient of a forbidden state subsidy.

This argument, however, is wrong, or at least incomplete. The proper insurance inquiry is whether Sherbert is, other things being equal, in the same risk classification as other people within the state. Thus, suppose it could be shown that people with religious beliefs have steadier work habits and therefore quit jobs far less frequently than those whose work habits are inferior in part because they are not anchored in religious beliefs. If Sherbert is denied benefits, then she is forced to subsidize nonreligious workers. Indeed, even after she is allowed to obtain coverage when she refuses to work on Saturdays, it remains unclear whether that subsidy is fully reversed. It could be that the additional coverage afforded her is quite negligible, given her other personal characteristics (of the 150 Seventh-Day Adventists in Spartanburg only two were unable to find non-Saturday employment),[27] so that on balance she contributes far more to the unemployment fund than her expected payout from it. Alternatively, it may well be that the coverage for her refusal to work on the Sabbath gives her a better-than-expected deal from the fund. If one considers the religious benefit in isolation, then it looks as though there is an establishment clause violation. If one considers that benefit in the context of the entire program, then (combining effects) the outcome is unclear. It may well be that the plan is skewed against Seventh-Day Adventists. The only way to find out for sure is to check the contributions to and payments from the fund. Justice Stewart's establishment clause view is more defensible on the view that each item of coverage should be considered in isolation. Justice Brennan's is more defensible on the aggregate view. The problem simply could not arise if all premiums paid to any state unemployment compensation system reflected the risk of each covered worker accurately, for then any elements of systematic redistribution already would have been squeezed out of the system.

What should be done when, as is now the law, one form of redistribution (between or within occupational groups) is allowed while another form of redistribution (between religious classes) is prohibited? The ostensible solution would be to create two separate risk pools at the outset.[28] But how? One possibility is to allow individuals who want to have coverage against Sabbath layoffs to pay an addi-

[27] See *Sherbert*, 374 U.S. at 399 n.2.

[28] Implicitly rejected in United States v. Lee, 455 U.S. 252 (1982), see infra chap. 18.

tional premium with respect to that risk. The insurance should be viable because these workers can still be required under the policy to conduct a search for other employment. But will they be able to escape the terrible dilemma that Justice Brennan described, of having to choose between economic welfare and their religious beliefs when responding to a distinct offer? In effect, that cost is brought forward to the time that workers first enter the market, where the extra cost borne by the religious workers properly eliminates any subsidy that they might otherwise receive for their religious beliefs. The small extra premium to cover this religious risk is borne only by those workers who think it important to get it, and the economic biases otherwise built into the system can continue apace. Still another possibility is to place all these religious workers in a separate risk pool, with their own insurance premiums. This prospect is far more radical, and it might well result in a substantial revision of premium levels for workers in both classes, given other differences in risk characteristics between workers of the two classes. There would still be some redistribution within each class of workers on nonreligious grounds, but the total level of residual redistribution would probably be far smaller than it is under the present program.

Either of these systems of separate charges costs money, if only to administer the proper "pass-throughs" to individual employees. With modern actuarial and payroll techniques the costs should be small, but the cost of setting and collecting the premium might still exceed the premium itself, if that too is small. Even private insurance markets do not have perfect calibration of risk groups, because the costs involved in separating them are too high. If that situation exists, we are forced to decide which distortion matters most: the hard choices that are stressed by Justice Brennan, or the ostensible subsidy to religious activities noted by Justice Stewart. On balance Justice Brennan's conclusion seems to be correct. The amount of redistribution from a failure to subdivide this risk pool is small, given the infrequency of unemployment payments necessitated by a recipient's religious beliefs. On the other hand, the ex post dilemma of religious people—who are forced to participate in this system against their will in the first place—seems palpable. Where some imperfection must be tolerated, better to choose the smaller, as Justice Brennan did.

Even if it were feasible to charge Sabbatarians separate premiums for religious layoffs, or even to place them in their own separate risk group, one problem would remain. Suppose a worker takes a job when she has no religious convictions; she then acquires religious convictions only to be dismissed promptly because she will not work on Saturday. Does this case differ in any degree from *Sherbert*? The Supreme Court in *Hobbie*, following its earlier decision in *Thomas*, held that this new circumstance was immaterial. Justice Brennan's opinion is perfectly conclusory: "The First Amendment protects the free exercise rights of employees who adopt religious beliefs or convert from one faith to another after they are hired. The timing of Hobbie's conversion is immaterial to our determination that her free exercise rights have been burdened."[29]

From an insurance point of view, however, the difference between the two cases is critical. In a world in which religious conversions are random, it may make more sense to allow unemployment compensation benefits to people who convert after they were hired. If, when employment was undertaken, all persons had an equal chance of converting, then there would be no redistribution ex ante. In contrast, the redistribution problem in *Sherbert* arose precisely because the risk of Sabbath employment was known before employment had begun, when the separate premium could have been collected. Still, *Hobbie* is problematic. Allowing the benefits may not work a redistribution across members of the nonreligious pool, but it will necessarily work a redistribution from nonreligious people (who pay into the system) to religious people (the only ones who collect) in a way the establishment clause prohibits. One way to solve that problem is to require an additional premium to cover this risk, for now there will be redistribution across employees (which is allowed) but not across religions (which is prohibited).

Nonetheless there are doubtless limits beyond which this analysis of subsidy and penalty cannot go. Suppose that there were a single pool of unemployment benefits, and that it were known from the outset that, while religious and nonreligious workers contribute equally to the fund, the religious workers will, over time, draw down far smaller payouts from the fund than the nonreligious workers. Does the requirement that all workers join the same formally neutral fund result in a free exercise violation because of the disparate impact in payouts that is thereby created? Traditional analysis would hold that it does not, given the other legitimate state purposes for the program, so that the redistribution, even if known, would be dismissed as "incidental." Indeed the result seems, in practical terms, to be strictly necessary because if the redistributions are not tolerated between religious and nonreligious persons, then the same objection could be made to the implicit transfers between members of different religions if the payout levels differ, as they surely must. The whole unemployment compensation system would become un-

[29] 480 U.S.136, 144 (1987) (footnote omitted).

glued. The qualified defense of *Sherbert* must therefore make a distinction between this case and the situation in *Sherbert* itself, which can only be done with reference to the inescapable dilemma to which Sherbert was subjected by the South Carolina rule.

Admittedly, this approach to interpreting the religion clauses quickly becomes very technical, and it may seem odd that resolving particular religion clause cases should turn on the fine points of insurance contracting as applied to unemployment compensation or social security benefits. But this conclusion is really inescapable. Together the religion clauses function to prohibit redistribution, in either direction, between religious and nonreligious persons. Skewed insurance contracts and massive welfare systems offer almost unlimited opportunities for implicit redistribution, which must be policed if both clauses are to be given their full effect. In the days of limited government action, the somewhat stricter separation of religious and government activities reduced the possibilities of redistribution. Now with the pooling of resources through government ventures, combating redistribution on religious lines is far more difficult, for the benefits and burdens to both groups must be both identified and measured. Even so, with the major normative premise set by the religion clauses, the rest is economic technique, for which a knowledge of insurance contracts and plans is indispensable. The simpler rhetoric of freedom, fines, and coercion must be replaced with a closer analysis of whether this state system of forced contribution and disbursement works implicit transfers along religious lines.

### *Justification*

The analysis thus far has focused on the question of whether in general the state should be allowed to put employees to the test to which South Carolina put Sherbert. There is, however, a second portion of the inquiry which asks whether some special justification exists for denying persons unemployment benefits for the practice of their religion. That issue was presented squarely in *Employment Division, Department of Human Resources v. Smith*,[30] easily the most

[30] 494 U.S. 872 (1990). For a critique, see Michael W. McConnell, "Free Exercise Revisionism and the *Smith* Decision," 57 *U. Chi. L. Rev.* 1109 (1990), critiqued in William P. Marshall, "In Defense of *Smith* and Free Exercise Revisionism," 58 *U. Chi. L. Rev.* 308 (1991). The root of the difficulty in construing the religion clauses lies in the fact that the free exercise clause provides special benefits to religions, while the establishment clause subjects them to special disabilities. It is often difficult to decide which clause should control given the wide range of government activities in the welfare state.

controversial free exercise case in many a year. Oregon passed a general criminal statute that classified peyote as an illegal substance under its drug laws. Smith, a member of the Native American Church, admitted that he used peyote as part of his religious practice.[31] Justice Scalia, writing for a divided Court, held that the criminal nature of Smith's actions gave Oregon sufficient cause to deny him unemployment benefits when Smith was dismissed from his job because of the drug use.

At one level the case is a simple rerun of *Sherbert* in that Oregon has placed Smith in the position of having to forgo one of the rituals of his faith in order to qualify for unemployment benefits that are generally available. The difference arises because of Oregon's argument that the criminal nature of Smith's conduct obviates his dilemma: if the state could prosecute Smith for his use of peyote, then surely it can forsake the prosecution and content itself with denying him employment benefits. The issue, then, is whether the criminalization of peyote use in religious services is maintainable under the First Amendment. In sustaining the state's position, Justice Scalia first argued that there were two levels of protection to free exercise: "first, and foremost, the right to believe and profess whatever religious doctrine one desires."[32] He recognized that the scope of the clause surely had to go further to protect some forms of religious conduct, but with respect to this second class of actions, he was prepared to strike down only those statutes that singled out and attacked certain religious practices because they were religious.

Under Scalia's two-tier test, it followed that the state was within its rights to apply its criminal statute to Smith provided two conditions were satisfied: first, that the statute was facially neutral and general in its application; and second that it was passed wholly without any motivation directed toward Smith and his church. Fearing a slippery slope that would allow religious attacks on a variety of commonplace institutional arrangements—"ranging from compulsory military service, to the payment of taxes, to health and safety regulation such as manslaughter and child neglect laws, compulsory vaccination laws, drug laws, and traffic laws, to social welfare legislation such as minimum wage laws, child labor laws, animal cruelty

[31] So stated in the opinion, at 494 U.S. at 874–75. A story in the *New York Times* suggests that neither Smith, nor his coworker Black, were members of the Native American Church, but participated in their rituals as drug abuse counselors for the American Indians. "Oregon Peyote Law Leaves 1983 Defendant Unvindicated," July 9, 1991, at A14 (reporting the passage of an Oregon law that legalized the use of peyote for "a good faith practice of a religious belief." Oregon Rev. Stat. 472.992 (5)(a)).

[32] 494 U.S. at 877.

laws, environmental protection laws, and laws providing for the equality of opportunity for the races" [33]— he refused to budge one step further.

Justice Scalia has offered a long and impressive list, but its mere recitation misses the major points about the debate. First, there is the question of what standard of review should be brought to bear in these cases. Justice Scalia's approach guarantees that these statutes are immune from facial attack, no matter how severe the impact on the religious practice in question, and how trivial the gain to the state interest involved. Surely, the better approach in the face of an explicit constitutional guarantee of religious freedom is to ask for some special justification for the restriction of the state criminal law in this context, wholly without regard to government intention or singling out. There is no strength to the argument that a compelling state justification is required only to limit religious beliefs and their profession, to the exclusion of the religious conduct that those religious beliefs require. The troubled line between action and expression that explains so little in ordinary First Amendment law is of still less help in this context, where the verbal distinction between speech and conduct is not available at all. By Scalia's test a general statutory prohibition on the use of alcoholic beverages could prevent their use in all religious ceremonies, unless the state chooses to create religious exemptions.

The position seems so unsatisfactory that some alternative has to be found. The scope of the criminal law cannot be taken as a given regardless of its content. Instead there must be some showing that its general rules are also consistent with the free exercise of religion as such. Some signposts mark the way. The free *exercise* of religion covers more than speech. It reaches conduct as well. Religious freedom is a subset of human freedom, so that the ordinary restrictions on force and fraud that normally apply to individual conduct are applicable to religious conduct as well. Conscripting strangers for human sacrifice or polluting public waters seem to be easy cases; and so too obedience to ordinary traffic laws. A different analysis has to apply to regulations that are inconsistent with the older principles of economic liberties. The state interest with respect to minimum wage laws and rules on health and safety seems far weaker where they involve activities within church groups, and stronger where they involve the commercial activities of the church. But whatever the hard cases, *Smith* seems easy, for Smith's use of peyote in religious observance poses no threat of harm to others. The specific drug

[33] Id. at 888–89 (citations omitted).

use itself is sharply limited by time, place, and circumstance and carries with it none of the risks normally associated with general drug use. There will no doubt be many twists and turns on the road, but the drawbacks of the simple categorical rule announced by Justice Scalia seem so substantial as to warrant the greater fuzziness that comes with a more nuanced approach. If the criminal prosecution should fail, so too should the state's effort to use conduct (now lawful, and indeed protected) to deny unemployment benefits otherwise required by state law.

### *Social Security Benefits*

The difficulties raised in connection with unemployment benefits have also surfaced in connection with social security, most notably in *United States v. Lee*,[34] where the Supreme Court's analysis was seriously defective. In *Lee*, the appellee, a member of the Old Order Amish, refused to file the appropriate social security returns or to withhold social security payments from his employees' paychecks. His argument, not contested, was that the Amish religion requires its followers to look after their own elderly and sick and considers it sinful either to pay any funds into, or to receive any benefits out of, the social security system. The statute is thus a more massive infringement on religious liberty than the unemployment statute in *Sherbert*, because the social security tax means that the Amish can hire workers, and remain in business, only if they are prepared to violate their religious beliefs.

The entire case for the statute therefore turns on the strength of the government's interest in the social security system. The traditional requirement calls for the state to demonstrate an "overriding governmental interest," but no reader of *Lee* can escape the impression that the Court at best paid lip service to its own standard. The Court was content to quote a congressional report to the effect that mandatory participation was "indispensable" and that the social security system would collapse if participation were made "voluntary." Its argument, however, is woefully weak in this context.

First, the concern with a voluntary social security system rests upon the obvious conclusion that younger workers (among others) will abandon a system in which the present value of their contributions is greater than the present value of their expected receipts. If everyone did this, the system would collapse, leaving the federal

[34] 455 U.S. 252 (1982).

government unable to pay off benefits to present and future recipients, at least without resorting to general taxation. But even if the Amish as a group could opt out of the system on religious grounds, all persons whose religious beliefs were not affronted would remain as both contributors and recipients. The massive amounts of redistribution within the social security system could continue apace, without making the Amish be part of it. Indeed it is unclear whether the system would be stronger or weaker unless some detailed accounting were made to determine whether the Amish as a group were net payors or recipients. (Because of their refusal to accept the money to which they are entitled, they are at present clearly net contributors to the system.)

To be sure, the case would be different if the Amish wanted the benefit of the social security system without having to bear any of its costs. That was, for example, the situation in *Bowen v. Roy,*[35] in which two applicants for welfare benefits claimed that their religious beliefs prevented them from having their two-year-old daughter's social security number used in processing their claims. That free exercise claim was rightly rejected because the applicants were seeking the benefits of the system without assuming its burdens, which in this instance were imposed to prevent fraud. A religious belief that it is blessed to receive but sinful to pay need not be funded by those who disagree. But in *Lee,* the Amish made no effort to capture the sweet without the bitter. To be sure, the Amish claim would be suspect if some Amish opted into the system while others did not. But there is no hint of any selective participation designed to wring dollars from the system. Indeed, all self-employed Amish are already out of the system by virtue of a specific statutory exemption from Congress.[36]

Nor is there any reason to think that exempting the Amish from social security offers a peril to the nation. The services rendered here are not the classic public goods that are provided under a regime of limited government. Quite the contrary, the benefits received under social security are all separable, and thus sharply distinguishable from the hypothetical cases put by the Court, such as defense and public order, from which the Amish benefit whether they contribute or not. Thus the Court is surely wrong when it writes as though there were a slippery slope problem: "If, for example, a religious ad-

[35] 476 U.S. 693 (1986)

[36] See 26 U.S.C. §1402(g) (1982). The Court in *Lee* refused to reach the question whether the free exercise clause compels this exemption, or whether the establishment clause forbids it. See 455 U.S. at 260 n.11.

herent believes war is a sin, and if a certain percentage of the federal budget can be identified as devoted to war-related activities, such individuals would have a similarly valid claim to be exempt from paying that percentage of the income tax."[37] With social security contributions, there is no free-rider problem at all.

In sum, the Amish's case regarding social security is compelling because as a group they are willing to disaffirm both the benefits and the burdens of the social security system. The analysis of *Sherbert* showed that the best way to fend off both establishment clause and free exercise claims is to adopt a set of rules whereby religious groups neither receive a net subsidy nor suffer a net tax from participation in collective financing plans—which is one reason why it was a major mistake for the government to have gotten involved in the business at all. In *Lee,* it was possible to guarantee that result by having a complete separation between social security and the Amish system of self-help for their own elderly. Why the Court should have found any overriding governmental interest in preventing this arrangement remains a regrettable mystery.

## UNEMPLOYMENT BENEFITS FOR STRIKING WORKERS

We come now to the last of the variations on the problem of government benefits in the employment context: may the government deny unemployment benefits to workers out on strike? The question here is devoid of the special overtones that were found in all previous cases because there is no (evident) claim of a constitutional right apart from those associated with the now-rejected doctrines of economic liberties. Religion appears nowhere in the area, and matters of equal protection, and freedom of association, while asserted, are (as we shall see) especially weak in this context.

The case that raises these issues to the fore is *Lyng v. International Union, UAW.*[38] In *Lyng,* the union mounted a two-prong attack on the legislative decision to exclude striking workers from the food stamp program when other workers who voluntarily quit their jobs are disqualified from receiving benefits only for a period of 90 days.[39] First, the union claimed that this exclusion operated as an impermissible "burden" upon their First Amendment rights of asso-

[37] See 455 U.S. at 260

[38] 485 U.S. 360 (1988).

[39] Omnibus Budget Reconciliation Act of 1981, Pub. L. No. 97-35, §109, 95 Stat. 361 (1981) (codified at 7 U.S.C. §2015(d)(1)(B)(ii), (3)) (1988).

ciation; second, it claimed that the disparate treatment between these striking workers and other workers eligible for food stamps constituted an impermissible classification that offended equal protection guarantees.[40] Stated otherwise, the union's claim is that the state uses impermissible "coercion" when it denies a benefit to striking workers that it grants to others. The rival position is that the state has chosen to "subsidize" certain kinds of workers, and is not duty-bound to extend that subsidy to workers who have chosen to strike. The case thus raises the unconstitutional conditions question of whether the greater power to eliminate the entire food stamp program entails the lesser power to exclude striking workers from the receipt of this set of government benefits.

As before, the plaintiff's claim can be evaluated only if this legislative decision is placed within its larger constitutional context. The initial point of departure involves the National Labor Relations Act (NLRA). The statute itself represents a deliberate decision to displace market mechanisms with a system of collective bargaining, under which the majority of workers within a given bargaining unit are able to require their employer to negotiate with them in good faith. The central feature of this statute is that it explicitly repudiates the competitive norm and substitutes in its place a monopolistic structure whereby the employer is required to negotiate with the workers as a group. Ironically, the major historical opposition to the NLRA was that its duty to bargain in good faith violated the employer's right to freedom of association, by denying it the right to do business with whomever it saw fit. The inevitable consequence of the present labor statutes is to block free entry and exit, and thereby to increase the role of strategic behavior, given the attendant expansion in the size of the bargaining range.[41] Hard, protracted negotiations over the division of the gains from trade become the rule, with strikes resulting from breakdowns in negotiations that both create private losses for the parties and inflict extensive social costs on third parties. In my opinion, the pre-1937 constitutional law on the subject was sound: the NLRA should have been struck down on both

[40] 485 U.S. at 363–365.

[41] See NLRB v. Mackay Radio & Tele. Co., 304 U.S. 333 (1938), which in allowing the employer to hire permanent replacements for an economic strike (as opposed to an unfair labor practices strike) effectively reduced the threat potential of the union, relative to what it might have been. The reversal of that decision is the major item on the labor agenda today. See, e.g. H.R. 5, National Labor Relations Act Amendment—Strikebreakers Replacement Bill, 102d Cong., 1st Sess., July 18, 1991, which seeks to make it illegal to promise or threaten to hire permanent replacements for union members.

commerce clause and takings grounds,[42] in which case the dilemma in *Lyng* quickly disappears. However, for present purposes, that position is quite irrelevant. The explicit rejection of a strong system of property rights made possible a level of government discretion in labor relations that had not previously existed. The question then becomes whether the doctrine of unconstitutional conditions can sensibly confine the use of that power.

Probably not, at least in this case. The doctrine of unconstitutional conditions was used in the contexts just considered to forestall redistribution of wealth along forbidden dimensions. In the foreign incorporation cases and the early highway cases, the competitive ideal forbidding economic redistribution by government still held sway. In the religion and speech cases, the marketplace of ideas is more than an idle economic image, as redistribution along political or religious lines continues to be prohibited even though unrelated economic redistributions are allowed. However, once redistribution of wealth and power is tolerated under the rational basis test in all relevant dimensions, then there is no forbidden use of government power to which the doctrine of unconstitutional conditions could attach. The search for some fundamental right or freedom falls short on both the question of economic liberties, given the NLRA, and of welfare benefits, given the food stamp program. The intersection between two programs over which Congress has an acknowledged broad discretion does not yield any principle under which the discretion over the whole is less than the discretion over the parts.

Start with the legacy of the NLRA. The chief significance of the constitutional decisions in this area has been the repudiation of the system of private property and competitive markets as the baseline against which permissible legislative enactments were measured. Without accepting that baseline, the shift from competitive markets to cartel arrangements cannot be regarded as a "penalty" or a "taking" from employers made subject to the new restrictions. By the same token, the legal structure of the original 1935 Wagner Act[43] was held constitutionally permissible, although not constitutionally required. As long as union members have no "fundamental right" to the protection of labor statutes, then the current statutory frame-

[42] On application of the commerce clause, see Richard A. Epstein, "The Proper Scope of the Commerce Clause," 73 *Va. L. Rev.* 1387 (1987). On application of the takings clause, see *Takings*, 279–82, and Richard A. Epstein, "A Common Law of Labor Relations: A Critique of the New Deal Legislation," 92 *Yale L.J.* 1357 (1983).

[43] National Labor Relations (Wagner-Connery) Act, ch. 372, 49 Stat. 449 (1935) (codified as amended at 29 U.S.C. §§151–166 (1982)).

work, however well-entrenched, does not establish any new definitive constitutional baseline against which subsequent legislative decisions must be tested. One immediate result was that the 1947 Taft-Hartley Act,[44] which created a new category of union unfair labor practices, could not be regarded as a penalty or a taking from workers that itself should be subjected to some form of heightened constitutional scrutiny. Any number of structural permutations of the employment relation have equal constitutional dignity. There is no impediment against oscillating between different economic orders, just as there is none against the repeal of Taft-Hartley in its entirety.

In response, it might be suggested that the collective interest of the workers presents a fundamental claim of associational freedom that requires continuation of the system of collective bargaining. Yet under present law it is impossible to see how that might be done without repudiating the modern understanding that the state's police power trumps all economic liberties. Unions are large and complex organizations, making it implausible to claim that their members enjoy an "intimate" right of association such as that found in marriage and perhaps certain other highly personal forms of association.[45] The function and structure of unions are driven by the same economic considerations that govern ordinary business firms. In addition, unions themselves are not organizations formed by unanimous consent, but receive under statute the extraordinary power to bind individual dissenters by their majority vote. The "freedom" of association involved here is antithetical to any traditional libertarian conceptions of freedom, as they have evolved both in connection with property and with speech. The bargaining privileges conferred by this special-interest statute do not offer a firm foundation on which to rest the unconstitutional conditions doctrine.

The new constitutional order thus comes to us bereft of the old common law baseline, and without a new baseline to replace it. Given this legal void, it is quite impossible to say that a certain reform introduces either a subsidy or a penalty that needs to be constitutionally justified. Rather, it is just a change among the class of equally permissible permutations. Once all baselines are extin-

[44] Labor-Management Relations Act of 1947, ch. 120, §8, 61 Stat. 136, 140 (codified as amended at 29 U.S.C. §158 (1982)).

[45] Cf. Roberts v. United States Jaycees, 468 U.S. 609, 620 (1984) (noting that "[a]s a general matter, only those relationships" that are "distinguished by such attributes as relative smallness, a high degree of selectivity in decisions to begin and maintain the affiliation, and seclusion from others in critical aspects of the relationship" qualify as intimate associations protected by the First Amendment).

guished, the doctrine of unconstitutional conditions has nothing on which to anchor itself, for there remains no dimension along which strategic behavior or the redistribution of wealth is forbidden. If the state can limit the power of unions under the Taft-Hartley Act, then it can also do so under the food stamp program. Neither side in *Lyng* shows mastery of the appropriate constitutional discourse. The Court should not have described the food stamp program as a "subsidy."[46] By the same token, the dissent improperly called the exclusion of striking workers from the program a "penalty."[47] In the present constitutional regime devoid of firm baselines, the 1981 food stamp legislation is neither.

The two errors are not, however, of equal magnitude. Justice White, writing for the Court, need not have shown that the provision of food stamps to striking workers is a subsidy in order to sustain the statute's constitutionality. He could have prevailed by showing that the want of any discernible baseline leaves the matter squarely in the lap of Congress. That escape-hatch was not open to Justice Marshall in dissent who *had* to show that the withholding of the food stamps is a forbidden "penalty"—that is, that it works a redistribution of income or wealth along some forbidden dimension. The obliteration of all constitutional landmarks in the labor relations area therefore does no damage to Justice White's majority position, but is fatal to Justice Marshall's dissent.

Justice Marshall tried to escape his problem by arguing that the mirage of government "neutrality" cannot possibly be used to uphold the statute.[48] After all, employers themselves receive many benefits from the welfare state that are in no way conditioned upon their behavior in labor disputes. To hit union workers with an exclusion from this program fits poorly with the maintenance of government benefits on the other side. But his claim about neutrality fares no better in this context than his claim of statutory penalty. The complete response to Justice Marshall's point is that in the present constitutional world of labor relations, Congress could exclude employers from a wide variety of economic benefits, whether or not they were enmeshed in a labor dispute, without fear of overstepping its constitutional limitations. In this case, for example, the statute places heavy pressure on employers not to lock out workers, who would then be able to receive their food stamp benefits, but surely

[46] 485 U.S. at 371: "Public policy demands an end to the food stamp subsidization of all strikes."

[47] Id. at 383.

[48] Id. at 380–83.

no one would say that this provision is unconstitutional because it "coerces" employers (who have long been forced to surrender their freedom of association) to abandon their rights not to do business with the union. The conscious, systematic elimination of all recognizable baselines makes the idea of neutrality, so powerful in a common law world as an argument against the NLRA, an empty vessel along with the claims of penalty and subsidy that are parasitic upon it. Again this absence of constitutional principle presents no obstacle to the party that wants to sustain the statute. It is fatal only to the party, be it management or labor, that wants to strike it down.

One must reach the same conclusion starting at the opposite pole with the food stamp program. Here too we have a system of in-kind benefits provided to recipients by the public at large. Yet there is a long line of Supreme Court cases holding that poverty is not a suspect classification,[49] and that the state is under no duty to redistribute wealth from rich to poor. Again there is no right to which the doctrine of unconstitutional conditions may be anchored. The decision to exclude striking workers from the program is based upon the sensible notion that the removal of payments to striking workers reduces the incidence of strikes. In turn, reducing the incidence of strikes is an end the state could pursue directly (as, for example, by repealing the collective bargaining rules), so it becomes one that the state may pursue by indirection as well. Looked at in retrospect, the exclusion of striking workers from the food stamp program may well treat persons with equal need differently, but it is hardly an instance of failing to treat "like cases alike," as Justice Marshall's dissent implicitly argues.[50] There is still the question of incentives to be considered, and here Congress has decided that it is willing to suffer some inequality after the fact in order to reduce the frequency and severity of strikes. The weak rational basis test offers no reason to control the power of such state discretion, on which the entire unconstitutional conditions doctrine rests.

The same conclusion follows when the matter is considered from the point of view of its funding. Here there is no way to match the taxes paid by striking workers with the level of food stamp benefits that they are entitled to receive. It is quite possible that, even if they cannot recover benefits while on strike, they receive a net benefit from the system, because they are still covered for the same contingencies as all other recipients. If so, then some other parties must be

[49] See, e.g., Kadrmas v. Dickinson Pub. Schools, 487 U.S. 450 (1988); Ortwein v. Schwab, 410 U.S. 656, 660 (1973).

[50] See *Lyng*, 485 U.S. at 374 (Marshall, J., dissenting).

net losers, but they are not allowed to complain either, even if they are shareholders whose tax dollars are being used to support those workers out on strike against their businesses. Who wins and loses is all quite impossible to determine anyway. There is no tracing mechanism to allow us to decide which set of benefits were funded by which person. More fundamentally, there is no normative criterion to render any forms of redistribution impermissible. Without fundamental right or suspect classification, we remain mired in a constitutional wasteland.

The depths of this difficulty are, moreover, revealed if we assume but one pertinent change to the current balance of power: the workers who go out on strike are doomed to forfeit their food stamp allotments for life, even if their eligibility is wholly unrelated to any union activities. There is little doubt that this alteration increases the cost to workers of going on strike and extends the reach of the statute to matters that are not, at least at first impression, germane to the ongoing strike. The remoteness of the claim may indeed make it impossible for employers to muster the political muscle to pass the statute in the first instance. But should such a statute pass, it should not be struck down, so long as the right to strike under collective bargaining agreements is given special protection under statute. The Congress could here bar all strikes outright as a condition for receiving the protection of the labor statutes, just as unions often enter into no-strike pledges as a condition for obtaining favorable contracts.[51] If justification is needed, it could argue that the long-term denial of food stamps is germane to the workplace after all, because it reduces the incidences of strikes in the first place. The economic burden therefore can be avoided, not by surrendering a constitutional right, but only by surrendering a desired privilege under statute. The question here would be far closer if the right to strike in a common law world were conditioned on a forfeiture of unemployment benefits, at least in a constitutional regime that afforded protection to the economic liberties of workers. (The hard issue is whether the restriction against striking is an appropriate limitation on labor monopolies.) But in a landscape barren of constitutional landmarks, there are no places of apparent safety for anyone.

Correctly understood, therefore, *Lyng* is a far cry from *Sherbert* and its progeny. Outside the context of the establishment clause,

[51] Boys Markets, Inc. v. Retail Clerks Union, Local 770, 398 U.S. 235 (1970) (enforcing a no-strike clause notwithstanding the general anti-injunction statute in labor law).

there exists no general requirement that persons not be taxed for benefits they do not receive. Nor does *Lyng* involve a state-imposed choice between the receipt of a government benefit and the waiver of constitutionally protected rights. Without the food stamp program, the workers know that they will have to fend for themselves. After the passage of the food stamp program with this exception, they still have to fend for themselves. Basically they face the same costs and benefits from striking with the statute as they did striking before the food stamp programs were first introduced. At most the statute works a change in the incentives faced by union workers who might delay striking in order to induce the employer to lock them out first (just as the employer may seek to delay the lockout in order to induce the strike). The dominant feature of this case is that the unions have lost in a struggle over political power, and the broad gulf between power and entitlement cannot be crossed when, of sheer necessity, judicial deference is the order of the day.

## CHAPTER 17

# Welfare Benefits

THE ROLE of the welfare state extends beyond the employment relationship to direct forms of public assistance given to the poor and the needy. These public grants are not simply outright grants of cash, services, or goods to persons who earn less than a certain income, but are typically coupled with conditions that determine who is eligible to receive the grant, the purposes for which it may be spent, and the conditions under which it may be terminated or forfeited. The welfare system is not an ordinary contract, in the sense that it is not a bargain: there is no consideration that moves from the individual to the state. But by offering a package of benefits subject to conditions, the state keeps an iron fist concealed within its ample velvet glove: if the conditions are not satisfactory, then the potential recipient is free to reject the grant altogether, and to remain no worse off than he would have been if the program had not been instituted in the first instance. The question is what limitations, if any, should be imposed upon this implicit pattern of bargains between the individual and the state.

As a matter of first principle, both of the generic risks associated with government bargaining are present in welfare grants. First, the money which is paid over to welfare recipients, or used to fund them with in-kind benefits, is all raised by taxation from individuals who do not receive full compensation, either in cash or in-kind, from the program in question. In a world in which the takings clause precluded all forms of redistribution, this objection might well prove fatal to the emergence of any welfare system at either the state or the federal level.[1] But for these purposes we may assume that any objection against welfare as such has been overcome. The funds in question, at least if raised from general revenue taxation, may be spent on welfare programs, notwithstanding any principled objections of the persons so taxed.

At this point, the sole question at hand involves the second of our two familiar risks: does the condition run afoul of the doctrine of

[1] For one version of this argument, see *Takings*, 314–24; see also Richard A. Epstein, "Luck," 6 *Soc. Phil. & Pol.* 17 (1988).

unconstitutional conditions? The problem at this point assumes a somewhat different cast from that where the state uses its monopoly power over interstate commerce, public highways, or limited liability corporations, for there is no effort to obtain from welfare recipients restrictions that will benefit their competitive rivals or require the parties so restricted to fund more than their proportionate share of the public costs associated with their own ventures. Therefore much of the sting normally associated with the doctrine of unconstitutional conditions is absent in this context, for the chief argument (made most powerfully in connection with the abortion funding cases)[2] concerns the differential incentives that are created for the waiver of a constitutional right.

In this chapter, I shall consider under two separate headings the unconstitutional conditions questions that do arise. The first deals with the procedural conditions that may be attached to the receipt of a welfare grant—inspections, hearings, and the like. The second concerns the most conspicuous substantive issue: whether the state that provides financial support for pregnant women who wish to carry their children to term is also obligated to fund the abortion right otherwise protected against criminal sanctions under *Roe v. Wade*.[3]

## PROCEDURAL LIMITATIONS ON THE WELFARE RIGHT

### *Site Visits and Inspections*

On first impression, the line between a bargain and a gift is sharp and clear. In the context of a bargain, the party surrenders something that it values in order to receive something of value in exchange. Within this framework, it is hard to conceive of how any bargain could work without some conditions attached to the promises so made. The party that delivers goods today does so on the strength of a promise that they will be paid for tomorrow. The party that pays money in advance does so on condition that the goods will be delivered tomorrow. The entire network of conditions is designed to expand the scope of bargains by making the order of performance immaterial: a party is more likely to perform first because it believes that thereafter it can compel the return performance on the other side.

[2] See infra chap. 18 .

[3] 410 U.S. 113 (1973).

The pure case of a gift does not involve conditions of this sort. A father can make an outright gift to his daughter, secure in the knowledge that he will be happier if she improves her own position by spending the money as she sees fit. But while this unconditional grant is common within family situations, it is far from universal. In many instances the grantor subjects gifts to conditions, about the time at which the money can be spent (to A to be held in trust until she reaches 35); or for the occasions on which it may be spent (to B in trust, but only to be spent on his college education); or the circumstances on which it may be forfeit (to C at 35, but should he resign his commission from the air force in the interim, then the gift is void). What is common about all these conditions is that the grantor retains an interest in the way in which the funds are spent even though he or she receives no consideration in return from the grantee. Notwithstanding the obvious opposition between the commercial bargain and the completed gift, the class of conditional gifts (both in and out of trusts) constitutes an important group of family and charitable transactions.

At one level, systems of public welfare look like private gifts: there are conditions for eligibility, but no return promise of goods and services to the state. But, as is the case with private benefits, the public grant of cash and in-kind benefits is rarely offered without conditions. Food stamps may provide income supplements, but they cannot be spent on alcohol, candy, or dog food. The state retains an interest in seeing that the funds are spent in ways that are associated with the purposes for which the subsidy is given, and limitations to healthy and nutritious food surely come at the top of the list. Stated more generally, one major function of conditions in the public arena is to introduce the safeguards against recipient misbehavior similar to those found in routine commercial transactions. Thus money given to a welfare recipient may be intended for the benefit of children, and the conditions could be imposed to see that it is spent for those purposes.[4]

In the context of welfare the state may adopt one of two broad strategies to counter the problem of recipient abuse. The first of these is to provide the benefits in kind and not in cash. The food stamp program, for example, is but one illustration of that strategy, for in giving stamps, not cash, to recipients, the government seeks to insure that its revenues are spent in certain ways and not in others. The use of stamps is subject to counterstrategies by welfare recipi-

[4] For the criminal complications in food stamp fraud, see Liparota v. United States, 471 U.S. 419 (1985).

ents. First, they can try to sell their stamps for cash. That bargain works to the advantage of the purchaser who would otherwise spend hard cash to get the same foodstuffs that are covered by the stamps. And it works to the advantage of the recipient who prefers a smaller sum in cash to a larger (face) value in food stamps. In order to counter that risk, the government can impose a nontransferable condition on the stamps and seek to enforce it by rules that require stamp recipients to show a picture identification to the supermarket or other retail proprietor before redeeming the stamps in question. But even that strategy may be defeated in some cases if the food stamp recipient engages in a somewhat more complex transaction of buying specified foodstuffs for his prospective purchaser and receiving cash in exchange, either before or after the delivery of those foodstuffs.

The cycle of restriction and evasion may lead to the second strategy for monitoring the behavior of welfare recipients. The state can inspect and supervise the conduct of a recipient more generally. Thus one strategy is to conduct "interviews" or "inspections" at the home of a welfare recipient, to see that he or she is in compliance with the wide range of restrictions that are part and parcel of the welfare system. The introduction of any such restriction necessarily raises the traditional problem of unconstitutional conditions, in two possible ways. First, the Supreme Court has recognized a right of privacy in family associations sufficient to defeat the usual low standards of review in zoning cases.[5] Second, the requirement of social worker interviews or inspections, however delicately expressed, appears to constitute a search under the Fourth Amendment for which no warrant has been required under statute.

The question here is whether the consent to the search excuses the need for a warrant and vitiates a charge that it is "unreasonable" under the Fourth Amendment prohibition. That issue was faced by the Court in *Wyman v. James*,[6] where the use of warrantless

[5] See Moore v. City of East Cleveland, 431 U.S. 494 (1977) (striking down ordinance that forbade a grandmother from living with her two grandchildren who were only cousins to each other.)

[6] 400 U.S. 309 (1971). For extensive commentary and cautious defense of the decision, see Lynn Baker, "The Prices of Rights: Toward A Positive Theory of Unconstitutional Conditions," 75 *Cornell L. Rev.* 1185 (1990). Baker's positive theory which holds that "[t]he Court declines to defer to the legislature only when the challenged condition requires persons unable to earn a subsistence income, and otherwise eligible for the pertinent benefit, to pay a higher price to exercise their constitutional rights than similarly situated persons earning a subsistence income." Id. at 1188. Baker claims her theory supports the result in *Wyman*, but it is unclear why. Her only explanation is that "the challenged condition did not therefore involve any constitutionally protected activity by the claimant." Id. at 1225. But her point makes it seem

searches was upheld against a Fourth Amendment challenge, with the standard lawyer's evasion: the interview was not a search,[7] and if it was, it was justified nonetheless, in this instance to see that the funds given to the mother were spent for the benefit of the child.[8] This decision has generally been greeted uneasily by commentators, who fear its ostensible "coercive" impact.[9] But the decision seems easy the other way. The concern with recipient misconduct seems very powerful, and the conditions here are surely no different from those which a private lender exacts when it demands the right to inspect the borrower's books and to audit its plant and operation, or when the government, as lender, advances money to small businesses and requires access to their premises to see that the money has been properly spent. The grantor and lender have fully performed their part of the deal with the payment of the cash or the transfer of the in-kind benefit, so that the risk of misconduct (which could reduce the funds available for other program recipients) must dominate the analysis. The political process that creates the welfare program in the first instance has strong incentives not to overstep on the privacy limitation. Indeed, it is noticeable in *Wyman* that, wholly apart from the constitutional obligations, the state had already committed itself (too generously perhaps?) to give advance written notice before conducting any interview, and not to resort to any form of snooping or forcible entry, or even examination of public records.[10] The political risks of public misbehavior seem small relative to those of private misconduct, so the condition of inspection should stand, given the enormous costs of doing any form of recipient monitoring.

### *Pretermination Hearings*

The analysis of *Wyman* is sufficient, I believe, to show the errors in the most well-known of the Supreme Court's decisions on welfare

---

as though it denies that a search has taken place. It does not address the relative prices paid by persons not on welfare to receive government grants, or even establish that there are grant situations sufficiently comparable to make her test operable.

[7] *Wyman*, 400 U.S. at 317, on the ground that the "rehabilitative" function dominated the "investigative" one, which if true seems irrelevant.

[8] Id. at 318–21.

[9] See Kathleen M. Sullivan, "Unconstitutional Conditions," 102 *Harv. L. Rev.* 1413, 1437, n. 88 (1989). Robert A. Burt, "Forcing Protection on Children and Their Parents: The Impact of *Wyman v. James*," 69 *Mich. L. Rev.* 1259 (1971).

[10] 400 U.S. at 321.

rights—*Goldberg v. Kelly*.[11] There Justice Brennan, writing for the Court, held that welfare benefits are a form of property that can be terminated only after the welfare recipient receives a hearing on the grounds for termination.[12] The decision rests upon two key assumptions. First, that welfare benefits are a form of (new) property which is protected against arbitrary state action under the due process clause; and second, that, given the fidelity to the rule of law, a pretermination hearing is necessary to reduce the risk of arbitrary misconduct.

The response to that two-pronged attack comes at both levels. The new property here is a far cry from other forms of new property instanced by Reich and others: licenses, patents, copyrights, corporate shares, broadcast frequencies, and the like. In each of these cases, the state seeks to imitate the ordinary rules for property applicable to land in order to increase the overall efficiency in the operation of the economic system.[13] There is no redistributive element involved at all. In this context, the benefits in question are made subject to conditions, and if the conditions are valid, then the recipient should take, as has often been said, the "bitter with the sweet."

But is the condition itself one that should fail under the unconstitutional conditions doctrine? At root the question raises the same issue as *Wyman*: is there any evidence of state misconduct that requires the condition be set aside? The answer to that question appears to be no. In order to see why, assume first that the state has a fixed budget, determined through the political process, which it is prepared to spend on welfare recipients. Its task is to find a way that maximizes the net value of the public assistance that it hands out. One possible extreme is to use all the money to provide assistance to eligible recipients, and none to monitor their behavior. Here the risk of abuse is so great, that some conditions (such as the inspections

[11] 397 U.S. 254 (1970). I have analyzed the unconstitutional conditions and other aspects of *Goldberg* in Richard A. Epstein, "No New Property," 56 *Brook. L. Rev.* 747 (1990). Many of the ideas from this section are drawn from that article. The article was part of a symposium which contained several strong defenses of *Goldberg*. See, e.g., Owen M. Fiss, "Reason in All its Splendor," 56 *Brook. L. Rev.* 789 (1990); Sylvia Law, "Some Reflections on *Goldberg v. Kelly* After Twenty Years," 56 *Brook. L. Rev.* 805 (1990); Charles Reich, "Beyond the New Property: An Ecological View of Due Process," 56 *Brook. L. Rev.* 731 (1990); William Simon, "The Rule of Law and the Two Realms of Welfare Administration." 56 *Brook. L. Rev.* 777 (1990).

[12] For Justice Brennan's extra-judicial defense of the case, see William J. Brennan, Jr., "Reason, Passion, and the 'The Progress of the Law,' The Forty-Second Annual Benjamin N. Cardozo Lecture," 42 *The Record of the Association of the Bar of the City of New York* 948 (1987).

[13] For further discussion, see Epstein, supra note 11, at 754–60.

upheld in *Wyman*) should be used to constrain that risk. Termination for improper use of public funds seems to be one proper ground of forfeiture, as is the receipt of income from other sources, which removes the recipient from the class of eligible persons. The state might clearly choose to spend some of its money to monitor recipients, although it would be obviously unwise for it to spend its entire budget on that task.

The question then arises, does the political process create any built-in incentive to set the wrong set of conditions? That would surely be the case, to use the stock examples, if benefits were denied to persons who voted against the incumbent political party, or who participated in political activity, or who wished to practice their religion, or even to have an abortion paid for by charitable sources. But the denial of a pretermination hearing does not fall remotely into any of those categories. To be sure, there would be grave risks to the soundness of the system if benefits could be terminated on a whim, but the political process (here, as in *Wyman*) has developed extensive rules governing the withdrawal of benefits. Written statements of reasons have to be provided seven days before termination, and these have to be reviewed by a superior inside the welfare system, after being provided to the recipient.[14] It is far from clear that this approach is inferior to that adjudged a constitutional imperative under Justice Brennan's decision. While the rule may result in some persons being discharged without proper hearing, it also makes it easier to add new persons to the welfare rolls, persons whose plights may be far greater than those of present welfare recipients.[15] It also reduces the need for caseworkers to enter into adversarial relationships with their clients, and to redirect the internal audits of welfare departments to cut out excessive payments instead of seeking to remedy cases of underpayments that crop up within the system.[16]

Nor, ironically, is there any reason to suppose that the political process will continue to allow terminations without prior hearings if the demands for it increase. If popular and professional sentiment shift, the rules could be reversed. Indeed, *Goldberg* may have institutionalized a set of reforms that the political process would have adopted on its own within a few years. But the method of introduc-

[14] *Goldberg*, 397 U.S. at 257–660.

[15] As noted by Justice Black in his dissent, 397 U.S. at 278. See also Paul R. Verkuil, "Revisiting the New Property After Twenty-Five Years," 31 *Wm. & Mary L. Rev.* 365, 369 (1990).

[16] See, for discussion, Jerry L. Mashaw, *Due Process in the Administrative State* 34–35 (1985).

tion is as important as choosing what is introduced. Keeping the hearing question outside of the constitutional order allows the political process to inch toward some workable solution, without having to face under the due process clause the questions of what sort of hearings should be required, who should give them, when they should be conducted, and the like. To resolve this issue by constitutional litigation entrusts these decisions to judges who are largely without administrative knowledge or experience. And it does so in the absence of any evidence of a miscarriage in the political process that might call for such intervention.

In the end, therefore, *Goldberg* seems to founder on its fundamental misapprehension of the relationship between means and end. No one could dispute Justice Brennan's judgment that if a welfare system is established, it should be operated in a just, humane, and efficient matter. But the means to reach that end are as treacherous here as they are everywhere else. The constraints of scarcity do not disappear because welfare is provided; and the risk of recipient misconduct is no less for welfare recipients than for anyone else who receives government largess. The indirect effects of constitutionalizing one portion of the welfare system are greater than Justice Brennan supposed. This situation is not one where the government seeks to use its monopoly power (if such it has) to reshape the conduct of its recipients; to shift the behavior patterns that they would have adopted in a world without welfare benefits; or to extract some special monopoly rent for the benefit of competitors. The fundamental concerns of the unconstitutional conditions doctrine are absent from this case, and their absence suggests that *Goldberg* shows how it is possible for good intentions to lead to mistakes of constitutional proportions.

## MEDICAID BENEFITS AND ABORTIONS

The bargaining difficulties that surround the government programs of welfare benefits are not confined to procedural issues, but extend to substantive questions as well. Of these the most controversial is whether the state can refuse to provide funding for abortions when it pays for its alternative, the prenatal care of pregnant women. The Medicaid program established by the Social Security Act in 1965 is generally designed to provide medical benefits for needy persons.[17]

[17] Social Security Act, Pub. L. No. 89-97, tit. I, §121(a), 79 Stat. 343, 343 (1965) (codified as amended at 42 U.S.C. §1396 (1982 & Supp. IV 1986)).

Since 1976, the Hyde Amendment to the statute has provided, subject to narrow exceptions, that Medicaid benefits could not be used to reimburse otherwise-eligible women for the costs of obtaining abortions,[18] which had become constitutionally protected by the Court's 1973 decision in *Roe v. Wade*.[19] The Hyde Amendment was spurred on by the widespread opposition to *Roe* and represented an undisguised legislative effort to limit *Roe's* impact by changing the rules for funding medical care. *Roe* manifestly prohibits any explicit fines or penalties to be placed upon a woman's right to have an abortion. The Hyde Amendment sidesteps the obvious by offering the indigent woman a clear financial inducement to carry the fetus to term.

The constitutional challenge to the Hyde Amendment, rejected in *Harris v. McRae*,[20] presents the issue of unconstitutional conditions in yet another guise. Before 1965 there was no Medicaid program at all. If Congress had passed a Medicaid program which excluded all care for pregnant women, then it could have excluded without difficulty funding for abortions as well. Abortion is generally regarded as the alternative to live births. So long as the government does not provide funding for live births, then it has not upset the relative balance of the two alternatives to Medicaid recipients. But Medicaid does fund care for pregnant women. The problem of unconstitutional conditions arises as follows: if the state does not have to fund care any care for pregnant women, does it then have the lesser power to withhold funding for abortions while providing funding for live births?[21] The greater power is that the state can decide not to fund

[18] The amendment provides that "[N]one of the funds provided by this joint resolution shall be used to perform abortions except where the life of the mother would be endangered if the fetus were carried to term; or except for such medical procedures necessary for the victims of rape or incest when such rape or incest has been reported promptly to a law enforcement agency or public health service." Joint Resolution of Nov. 20, 1979, Pub. L. No. 96-123, §109, 93 Stat. 923, 926 (1979); see also Joint Resolution of Dec. 21, 1982, Pub. L. No. 97-377, §204, 96 Stat. 1830, 1894 (1982) (providing that appropriated funds can be spent on abortions only when the mother's life is endangered).

[19] 410 U.S. 113 (1973). For the record I should note that I view *Roe* as incorrect largely for the reasons that I set out in 1973. See Epstein, "Substantive Due Process by Any Other Name: The Abortion Cases," 1973 *Sup. Ct. Rev.* 159. The literature on *Roe* of course continues to be produced at a fever pitch, but I do not wish to reargue *Roe* on its merits here. Instead the material that follows assumes that *Roe* is rightly decided and only asks about its implications for the abortion funding cases insofar as they depend upon the doctrine of unconstitutional conditions.

[20] 448 U.S. 297 (1980).

[21] For an exhaustive account of the problem, in comparison with funding for religious education, see Michael W. McConnell, "The Selective Funding Problem: Abortions and Religious Schools," 104 *Harv. L. Rev.* 989, 1000–1006 (1991).

the care of pregnant women. The lesser power is that the state can exclude certain procedures—abortions—from coverage under the program.

If one treats the state, as the Court did, like a private person, then the case becomes easy—too easy: there is no "coercion" in the form of either force or fraud. Those women who want to get an abortion can still do so, even if they do not receive the "subsidy" from the state. Those who now think that the provision of external benefits makes bearing a child worthwhile have their opportunities expanded, not contracted. While their choices may be shifted, as a group they are better off because they have received options that previously they had been denied; so too are the fetuses that survive. The fact that the public at large has to bear the costs of running a Medicaid system remains beyond constitutional scrutiny, given the explicit constitutional approval of redistributing income and wealth to improve the health of the public at large.

The hurdle faced by the dissenters is to show that the special powers of the state present prospects of illicit behavior sufficient to displace this simple model of the socially useful bargain. In his dissent Justice Brennan relied upon two familiar strands of the unconstitutional conditions doctrine: *Frost* (for highways)[22] and *Sherbert* (for unemployment benefits).[23] *Harris* is critically different from both cases, however.

In *Frost*, the unique power of the state lay in its ability to exclude everyone from the public highways, instrumentalities of commerce for which there are no clear substitutes—arguably no substitutes at all. The unconstitutional conditions doctrine was used, albeit ineffectively, to constrain that substantial monopoly power. But there is no monopoly in the abortion market, for *Roe* in effect established a rule of free entry that ensures that indigent women, like all others, can receive abortions at a competitive price. The only pull the Hyde Amendment gives the state over the Medicaid recipient is its ability to withhold funds for an otherwise readily available abortion. To be sure, there are many costs of an abortion that are high—the emotional aftermath, the physical operation, the potential stigma from the process—and should never be overlooked in any discussion of the issue. But these costs have to be borne whether or not the state funds the abortion through Medicaid, so that the Medicaid makes a difference only on the cost of the abortion itself, which while far

[22] See 448 U.S. at 336–37 (Brennan, J., dissenting). I do not discuss the dissents of Justices Marshall, Blackmun, and Stevens because they do not expressly address the unconstitutional conditions aspect of the case.

[23] See id. at 334–36.

from trivial is relatively low, at least in comparison with aggressive neonatal care. Nor is there anything to prevent other private individuals or charitable organizations from making up the shortfall, and doing so in today's world with an implicit tax subsidy. We are far removed from a world in which private charity would have to construct an entire rival highway system in order to escape the clutches of the state monopoly.[24]

*Sherbert* poses the much closer challenge, for it too involved the provision of state financial benefits without the powerful monopolistic structure of the state. Read in one sense, *Sherbert* treats the differential benefits between what one gets if willing to work on the Sabbath and what one gets if not, as though it were a "fine." Analogously in *Harris*, the failure to provide medical payments for abortions also could be regarded as a "fine," bringing the case within the general prohibition of *Roe*, insofar as the state will pay in full for the alternative medical procedures.

Yet the differences are also critical. *Sherbert* was decided within an extraordinarily strict constitutional framework, where the free exercise and the establishment clauses worked as powerful pincers to constrain government action. The full analysis of *Sherbert*, given earlier, shows the weakness of the "fine" metaphor and requires that one take into account both the incentive effects and the insurance consequences of the unemployment compensation system. That same analysis should be brought to bear here, where it points, cautiously, in support of sustaining the Hyde Amendment.

Start with the problem of differential incentives. The winning argument in *Sherbert* was that the promise of unemployment benefits induced the applicant to behave in a manner that necessarily vio-

[24] Kathleen Sullivan has criticized this argument in the text as "overstated" on the following grounds: "As with public education, government's entry into the business of providing subsistence to the needy and insuring against loss of livelihood from unemployment has altered cultural expectations and substantially displaced private alternatives. In the modern welfare state, "[c]ertain key social goods have been taken out of private control . . . and are now provided by law." Walzer, "Socializing the Welfare State," in *Democracy and the Welfare State* 13 (A. Gutman ed. 1988). As the state has absorbed welfare functions, private voluntary substitutes such as charitable organizations and self-help societies have tended to dry up. See id. at 19–20." Sullivan, supra note 9, at 1453, n. 161. Her arguments are better directed as an attack on the welfare system than upon the point made in the text. First, Walzer is incorrect to state that welfare has been "taken out" of private control, for there is no ban against the private funding of this sort. Second, his argument leads to the conclusion opposite to that Sullivan argues for. Once it is clear that the state cannot fund abortion, then private funding for that purpose (relative to funding for live-birth care) should increase.

lated her religious convictions. The right to an abortion may be subject to constitutional protection, but having an abortion is not a religious or moral obligation. The state may have given the woman a financial inducement to do what she would otherwise not choose to do. But it has not forced her to sacrifice religious scruples in order to retain financial benefits, as in *Sherbert*. Can the two choices be regarded as the same?

The answer must come, if at all, from what we think of as the constitutional status of the woman's choice of the abortion. It is here that the counterargument gains strength. Justice Brennan correctly insisted that *Roe* does more than just decriminalize abortion. Rather, *Roe* works a double transformation at a single leap: abortions move from the status of criminal acts into "fundamental rights," which are as strongly protected as religious beliefs. As Brennan writes, "[i]t would belabor the obvious to expound at any great length on the illegitimacy of a state policy that interferes with the exercise of fundamental rights through the selective bestowal of governmental favors."[25]

This elevation of the abortion right must go down very hard with foes of abortion who believe both that the Constitution does not prevent abortions from being criminalized and that those who perform abortions should be punished criminally. These beliefs are critical to the funding side of the analysis, which was ignored by Justice Brennan, who silently assumed that government money is like manna from heaven: it is not traceable to the individuals from whom it was collected.[26] But once we pierce the government veil, it becomes necessary to examine what correlative duties this expanded fundamental right of abortion may properly impose upon the opponents of *Roe*.

On this side of the issue, we must confront the claims of the free exercise of religion. Suppose that a special tax to fund Medicaid abortions were placed upon only those individuals who opposed abortions for religious reasons. The question thus arises whether those persons who have to pay this tax may maintain a colorable free exer-

[25] 448 U.S. at 334. The point is taken up in Michael Perry, "Why the Supreme Court Was Plainly Wrong in the Hyde Amendment Case: A Brief Comment on *Harris v. McRae*," 32 *Stan. L. Rev.* 1113 (1980); Sullivan, supra note 9, at 1476 n. 280 (1989). Again the "interference" does not involve the use of force, but the failure to fund.

[26] See also Laurence H. Tribe, "The Abortion Funding Conundrum: Inalienable Rights, Affirmative Duties and the Dilemma of Dependence," 99 *Harv. L. Rev.* 330, 339 (1985). But Tribe would be quick to trace funds from dissenting individuals paid to establish an official church out of general revenues when the context changes. See McConnell, supra note 21, at 1009, n. 63.

cise claim against it. The takings risk is thus set in opposition to the bargaining risk. In principle, these people should be entitled to object to the tax on much the same ground that union members can object to dues payments that are used to support political programs and candidates to whom they are personally opposed.[27] The free exercise of religion, like the free exercise of speech,[28] can be limited as much by direct taxation as it can by prohibitions. The point may not be decisive, but by the same token it cannot simply be ignored. The right to escape this form of state coercion seems as "fundamental" as the woman's right to have the abortion in the first place: to put the claim in the baldest way possible, who wants to be coerced into paying for what they view as the murder of unborn children?

Thus the flip side of the "fundamental right" claim of the Medicaid recipient is far more powerful in *Harris* than the parallel establishment clause argument in *Sherbert*, for no one thinks that the modest subsidy, if any, to individuals like Sherbert affronts the core religious beliefs of the persons who are made to pay it. Pushed to the limit, this free exercise argument would make it unconstitutional for the government to use public funds to fund abortions. Thus the unconstitutional conditions argument suggests that the Hyde Amendment is unconstitutional, given *Roe*, while the free exercise argument suggests that the amendment is constitutionally mandated. Both risks in bargaining with the state are present: the danger of state distortion of private choices *and* the danger of impermissible state exactions through its taxing power. Neither argument allows a middle ground, and both together account for the genuine difficulty presented by the case.

The matter is still more complex because there are also establishment clause arguments that can be brought to bear against the Hyde Amendment. In this context, that argument turns largely on motive, a factor that looms large in these cases.[29] Many of those who oppose the funding of abortions do so on religious grounds. When they turn

[27] See Lehnert v. Ferris Faculty Ass'n, 111 S. Ct. 1950 (1991); Communications Workers of Am. v. Beck, 487 U.S. 735 (1988); Abood v. Detroit Bd. of Educ., 431 U.S. 209 (1977).

[28] For examples of taxes found to violate the free speech clause, see Minneapolis Star & Tribune Co. v. Minnesota Comm'r of Revenue, 460 U.S. 575 (1983), and Grosjean v. American Press Co., 297 U.S. 233 (1936).

[29] See, e.g., Wallace v. Jaffree, 472 U.S. 38, 55–56 (1985) (discussing the permissible degree to which a statute can be motivated by a religious purpose). Note too that even after *Smith*, 494 U.S. 872 (1990), discussed supra at chap. 16, motivation can bring down a facially neutral statute under the free exercise clause, and also under the establishment clause.

their preferences into law, they have established, at least in part, their religious beliefs under the Medicaid statutes. This argument, however, seems more strained in this context than does its free exercise alternative. If the foes of abortion were able to exclude both abortion funding *and* all pregnancy and neonatal care from Medicaid solely for religious reasons, would their motives void this neutral exclusion once the issue of differential incentives is removed from the case? It seems highly doubtful that any court would reinstitute all these programs, including public funding for abortion.

The funding issue thus reveals a house divided. A substantial fraction of taxpayers objects to abortions on religious grounds. Other taxpayers strongly support abortion funding for indigent women, and counter any free exercise claim with an establishment claim of their own. The obvious lesson is that it is troublesome to use extensive government power to force collective decisions in the teeth of these wide and wholly irreconcilable divergences of opinions: any such decision leaves a minority, or perhaps a majority, deeply disaffected with the collective outcome. The deep moral and political divisions over abortion cannot be papered over simply by writing, as Justice Brennan did, solely about the differential incentives the Hyde Amendment places on Medicaid recipients.

One problematic line of escape, analogizing to the proper treatment of unemployment benefits in *Sherbert*,[30] would segregate contributions to the Medicaid program. The state could determine in advance its budget requirements for Medicaid abortions and then allow individual taxpayers to decide whether or not they wished their moneys spent on abortions. It could further insist that only those opposed to abortions on religious grounds may refuse to contribute to the fund. If the budget target were met without the contributions of those opposed to abortions, then the program could go forward. If not, then the program would have to cease, or operate on a reduced basis.

The suggestion in turn presents some serious internal difficulties of its own. It would be difficult to determine who refused to contribute out of sincere religious conviction and who simply wanted others to bear that portion of the social burden. Free-riding could thus distort collective choice. On the other side, if the abortions were so funded, then something would have to be done with the tax revenues from those people opposed to the program on religious grounds. If these moneys were simply put into general revenues, then nothing would really have changed at all. If any substantial fraction of the

[30] See supra chap. 14, at note 6.

population supported abortions, then all federal programs, whether for abortions or anything else, would be funded exactly as if no one were opposed to abortions for religious reasons. Perhaps money is too fungible for such a separation to work. Even if these financing difficulties could be addressed, one problem would remain: what is to be said to people who are opposed to their government paying for something that they find morally reprehensible?

The problems raised in the abortion funding cases, moreover, do not disappear even if we reevaluate the theory of *Roe*, most notably by converting it, as seems fashionable today, from a privacy/liberty case to a sex discrimination/equal protection case.[31] The motivation for the switch seems clear enough. Privacy speaks of autonomy and is a cousin to traditional forms of property rights. Sex discrimination allows matters of "constitutional caste"[32] by which some persons stand higher in the class hierarchy than others, and the subordination of women, understood either in historical or contemporary terms, to be factored into the debate. Yet this switch in emphasis does nothing to advance the debate on either criminality or funding.

On the first question, the sex discrimination charge is problematic in at least three ways: generalization, necessity, and justification. As regards the first, there is no critic of *Roe* who would shrink from the prospect of an anti-abortion statute that is perfectly general in form. "No person shall have, perform, procure, or assist in the abortion of any person" is a statute that could, and would, apply to men as well as women. Men could be freely prosecuted for performing, procuring, and assisting in an abortion. And they too would be prosecuted if they became pregnant and had abortions. At the facial level, then, there is no discrimination.

The charge of illicit discrimination then shifts to the disparate impact of the statute on women, for only they are subject to the direct prohibition against having an abortion, while the other lesser offenses are all directed against that particular goal. But here necessity of the disparate impact must influence the overall evaluation. In most cases of sex discrimination—pregnancy is an exception—a statute is attacked when it applies to only men or women when it is capable of being applied to both. A minimum-wage law for

[31] See Cass R. Sunstein, "Why the Unconstitutional Conditions Doctrine is an Anachronism," 70 B.U. L. Rev. 593, 617 n.76 (1990). Among those who have adopted the equal protection rationale are Catharine MacKinnon, Sylvia Law, Fred Schauer, David Strauss, and Laurence Tribe. The ACLU, which has fought many of these cases, remains committed to the traditional privacy line.

[32] See Sullivan, supra note 9, at 1497.

women, but not for men is one illustration of the problem,[33] as is a draft registration statute applicable to men but not to women.[34] With abortion, however, the limitation to one sex is not a legislative determination but a biological imperative, at least until men are able to become pregnant. There is discrimination to be sure, but the necessity of discrimination removes much, if not all, of the associated taint. The legislature could not have made the statute broader even if it had tried.

Finally, there is the third question of justification, which at this juncture follows exactly the same course as it does on the usual liberty and privacy justifications for abortion. If the fetus is a person, then the liberty of the women ends because of the injunction against killing another person. So too, if the fetus is a person, then the justification for criminalization is just as powerful where the initial claim rests on equal protection grounds. To show that there is a prima facie case, without meeting the justification for criminalization, is to evade the central problem with abortion. To be sure, even if the fetus is a person, there may yet be further justifications for vindicating the woman's right to abort, but at this point they do not turn in the slightest on the sex discrimination issue, but depend upon the idea that women who have been subject to involuntary pregnancy, as with rape or incest, or more generally, should not be pressed into unwilling servitude for the benefit of their unborn children. The strength or weakness of these arguments is a matter of extensive debate, but it is a debate that takes exactly the same form that it did under the privacy model of the abortion right. At the first level, then, the soundness of *Roe* is not strengthened by the move from privacy to discrimination, from due process to equal protection.

Suppose, however, that the sex discrimination approach swept the boards, and the privacy approach was dismissed as bankrupt. The shift in constitutional fortunes of rival theories makes no difference at all for the funding issue in *Harris*. That debate started with the assumption that *Roe* was unassailable on its own terms, and then asked whether there was a syllogism that said "whenever conduct cannot be made criminal, it cannot be subject to a selective exclusion from funding." The shift from liberty to equal protection is relevant only to the first stage of the analysis—is *Roe* right? As that point was assumed ab initio, it matters not that further reflection proves beyond a shadow of a doubt what had previously only been

[33] See, e.g., West Coast Hotel Co. v. Parrish, 300 U.S. 379 (1937).

[34] Rostker v. Goldberg, 453 U.S. 57 (1981).

assumed. The question in *Harris* was not whether *Roe* was correct, but whether it should be extended.

In the end, therefore, no revitalized defense of *Roe* can avoid the central dilemma raised in *Harris*. It is not possible to protect the free exercise rights of opponents of abortion under a system that involves any affirmative government support of abortions. The problem here is in a sense the obverse of that with unemployment benefits to striking workers. There the difficulty with the unconstitutional conditions argument was that there were no constitutional benchmarks at all. In this case the difficulty is that there are too many constraints, given two powerful but inconsistent constitutional claims. The analysis at this juncture has to leave the land of constitutional absolutes and turn to the muddy waters of balancing and accommodation.

In this context, I can offer only one compromise position that has the virtue of being satisfactory to neither side. The funding of abortions solely through tax-deductible charitable contributions has at least the modest advantage of keeping the government from the middle of the abortion battle. Yet charitable deductions still, in effect, make religious people bear part of the costs of the subsidized abortions, to which it can be said in reply only that the current tax system uses charitable deductions that allow religious people to fund their institutions and practices at the expense of nonreligious ones. The only way to avoid these problems is to get the government totally out of both medicine and religion, which, although the only principled answer, is unlikely to be done in the near future. Until that day, however, the unconstitutional conditions question in *Harris* is far closer than the one in *Sherbert*, and far more divisive. The claim of indigent women to be free of direct financial incentives not to abort cannot be ignored. But it is not as important as a state policy offering a woman a financial inducement to have an abortion inconsistent with her religious beliefs—which would be the precise *Sherbert* analogue. On the other side, the use of public moneys to support abortions taxes, and therefore coerces, other individuals to support practices that are against their religious convictions. As with *Sherbert*, none of these problems could arise in a constitutional order that imposed restrictions upon redistribution through taxation and state welfare benefits. Once that redistribution becomes part and parcel of the system as we know it, the proper strategy should be to choose the lesser of two evils, a very hard call here. On that uneasy note, the unconstitutional conditions challenge to the Hyde Amendment should fail—but perhaps only by a bare 5 to 4 vote.

## CHAPTER 18

# Educational Benefits

### A THIRD POSITION?

The ever-expanding role of government in modern life has brought forth public funding of educational, as well as welfare, programs. What kinds of conditions may the government attach to its grants for educational purposes? At one level it seems clear that government may impose some subject-matter restrictions, given the inevitable economic constraint of scarcity. If the government decides to fund programs designed to deal with adolescent education, it is not thereby bound to fund programs to teach physical education to the elderly. No matter how great the level of national prosperity, limited public funds necessitate hard choices about which parties will receive what funds, and for what purposes. But the omnipresence of scarcity does not eliminate the persistent concern stemming from extensive state activities. Rather, scarcity only sets the stage for yet another round of difficulties and conflict in which both the bargaining risk and the takings risk must be confronted.

Of the many educational programs that the government runs, I shall content myself to address three here, two of which have been the subject of critical Supreme Court opinions, and one of which has been the subject of an extensive and ongoing congressional, popular, and academic debate. The first of the issues is a direct sequel to *Harris v. McCrae.*[1] The Supreme Court in *Rust v. Sullivan*[2] upheld regulations under Title X of the Public Health Service Act prohibiting the use of federal funds "in programs where abortion is a method of family planning"[3] against challenges raised both on First Amendment and fundamental rights, or due process, grounds. The second issue was squarely raised in *Bowen v. Kendrick,*[4] which upheld those provisions of the Adolescent Family Life Act[5] that allowed religious

[1] 448 U.S. 297 (1980).

[2] 111 S. Ct. 1759 (1991).

[3] Pub. L. No. 91–572, §6(c), 84 Stat. 1508 (1970) (codified as amended at 42 U.S.C. §300a-6 (1988)).

[4] 487 U.S. 589 (1988).

[5] Pub. L. No. 97–35, 95 Stat. 578 (1981) (codified as amended at 42 U.S.C. §§300z, et seq. (1988).

programs to participate in providing "educational services relating to family life and problems associated with adolescent premarital sexual relations,"[6] against an establishment clause challenge. Finally, the 1989 Helms Amendment stipulates that grants made under the National Endowment for the Arts could not be used "to promote, disseminate, or produce materials" that the NEA could consider "obscene."[7]

The issues raised by these three separate educational and funding programs contain their fair share of irony, chiefly because there is a protracted and uneasy tension between political orientation and constitutional commitment. It is difficult to identify anyone who uniformly defends or uniformly opposes the various conditions associated with these three separate programs. Instead the political fault lines are drawn so that those in favor of striking down the conditions on the abortion counseling and NEA funding generally support conditions that exclude all religious organizations from participation in the Adolescent Family Life Act.[8] Similarly, I suspect that those who are in favor of allowing religious organizations to participate in the Adolescent Family Life Act programs are also likely to support the conditions that the federal government seeks to attach in the abortion and NEA speech and funding disputes.[9]

I wish to stake out a third position here that calls for the wholesale cessation of government activities in these controversial areas. Even if all barriers against extensive government involvement are lifted in economic matters, they should remain in place on matters of abortion, sex education and art. The tensions between the bargaining risks and the takings risk so evident in *Harris* do not disappear in these educational contexts. The only way in which the struggle between the two warring sides can be mitigated is to get the government out of the funding business altogether, easily done with adolescent counseling and artistic support, but accomplished only with great difficulty on the matter of abortion counseling, given the extensive and apparently unshakable federal commitment to providing and funding medical services. To the extent that these activities are suitable for state subsidy, a far less divisive system lies at our disposal: the government can grant charitable deductions to all persons who wish to involve themselves in these activities. The change in

[6] 42 U.S.C. §300z-1(a)(4) (1988).

[7] Act of Oct. 23, 1989, Pub. L. No. 101–121, tit. III, 103 Stat. 741 (to be codified at 20 U.S.C. §954).

[8] See, e.g., Kathleen M. Sullivan, "Religion and Liberal Democracy," 59 *U. Chi. L. Rev.* 195, 209–14 (1992), supportive of *Rust* and critical of *Kendrick*.

[9] I have been not able to locate written material that draws the comparison, but from workshops and conversations, the point seems tolerably clear.

funding method should help diffuse much of the acrimonious public debate by removing the burden of making choices from the collective arena. Increased debate and communication has in this area, as in so many others, only led to more fractious public discourse, which is best attacked by restricting the scope of the public effort, not by reshaping its contours.

## ABORTION COUNSELING

*Rust v. Sullivan* is a complex piece of litigation that involved questions of both administrative discretion and constitutional law. These restrictions have been lifted by the Clinton Administration, but the issues that they present remain important as a matter of principle even though the controversy has for the moment abated. The initial condition set out in Title X of the Public Health Act, that federal funds not "be used in programs where abortion is a method of family planning," clearly prohibits the use of federal moneys for the funding of abortions themselves. The statute, however, does not simply say that federal money is "not to be used to fund abortions." Instead it has a somewhat wider reach, covering programs in which abortion is a method of family planning, even if no abortions are performed. The burning question is how much further this language goes. Pursuant to administrative regulation in 1988, it was held that recipients under a "Title X project may not provide counseling concerning the use of abortion as a method of family planning or provide referral for abortion as a method of family planning."[10]

The threshold question in *Rust* was whether this regulation fell within the scope of the statute, which Chief Justice Rehnquist resolved by an unfortunate two-step analysis: first he noted that the statute was ambiguous, and then he deferred to the decision of the administrative agency as to its proper scope and content.[11] The decision is unfortunate because it transfers the locus of decision-making power from the Congress to an administrative agency which, especially in an age of divided government, may have a vastly different political agenda from the Congress that had enacted the relevant statutory scheme years before. It was therefore urged, both by Justice O'Connor in her dissent[12] and by others as well,[13] that the regulation

[10] 42 C.F.R §59.8(a)(1) (1991).

[11] *Rust*, 111 S. Ct. at 1767–71. In so doing, he relied on Chevron U.S.A., Inc. v. National Resources Defense Council, Inc., 467 U.S. 837 (1984).

[12] *Rust*, 111 S. Ct. at 1788–89.

[13] See Guido Calabresi, "Antidiscrimination and Constitutional Accountability (What the Bork-Brennan Debate Ignores)," 105 *Harv. L. Rev.* 80, 140–42 (1991).

should be struck down, and that constitutional adjudication should have been avoided, by throwing the entire matter back into the hands of Congress, which (for the record) rejected the administrator's gloss of the Public Health Act by a clear majority (but not one that was veto-proof).[14]

There is surely much to be said for avoiding constitutional disputes when they need not be resolved, but it is not clear that *Rust* allows that easy escape from matters of first principle. To be sure, nothing is more dangerous than entrusting administrators to make decisions on the scope of their own powers, for whatever expertise they have on this issue—and it is surely minor—is more than dwarfed by their inherent bureaucratic bias to expand the scope of their own jurisdiction and to stamp their own policy agendas on their statutory mandates. But the appropriate remedy in this context is *not* to throw up the collective judicial hands at the first sign of textual difficulty; it is to read the administrative regulation and the statute without any presumption one way or the other, and to decide a difficult question of construction as best one can. The choice cannot be avoided by any "remand" to Congress. That remand does not ask the Congress to clarify its initial act. Rather, it gives a different Congress the advantage of starting from a blank slate when its own sensibilities are vastly different from the Congress that enacted the disputed statutory provision.

The problem raised in *Rust* therefore concerns the best way to resolve the ambiguity, given that (whether or not the regulation is upheld) Congress can enter the fray yet a second time. Here, on balance, the standard rules of construction are sufficient to support the administrative gloss wholly without Chief Justice Rehnquist's illegitimate interpretive ploy. "Programs where abortion is a method of family planning" covers more than giving abortions. If it does not cover the incidental counseling and referral activities, then what activities, beyond abortions themselves, does the prohibition reach? I am hard-pressed to think of *anything* that could fall into this intermediate category without covering counseling and referral itself. Certainly, it would be incongruous to allow literature to be distributed under a Title X project while prohibiting the performance of the very act that the literature promotes as a legitimate social alternative.

[14] The vote to override George Bush's veto failed to obtain the necessary two-thirds majority by twelve votes in the House, 276 to 156, with three abstentions. For an account, see Tanya Melich, "Will the Democrats Stand Up for Choice? *N.Y. Times*, July 30, 1992, at A13.

The administrative regulation seems, then, to be consistent with the scope of the statute, so that the constitutional questions are themselves unavoidable, both with regard to the ability of Title X grantees and their employees to say their piece on abortions, and to the women who enroll in the program to exercise their fundamental right to abortion, as conceived in *Roe v. Wade*.[15] With both these questions, the battleground is similar to that which was fought in *Harris* itself. The sharp divide over the desirability of the funding of abortion carries over to the question of abortion referral and counseling, and the new First Amendment complication does nothing to ease the pain of the analysis. On the one hand, program participants who want to speak out on this alternative now find themselves muffled by an abhorrent administrative ukase. On the other hand, some portion of the public finds it utterly inappropriate that its tax dollars should be used to urge the commission of acts of homicide. Both groups raise insistent First Amendment claims, the former because their speech is restricted, and the latter because they are asked to fund speech with which they disagree on matters in which they have strong moral or religious preferences.[16] The same tension extends to any proposal that *requires* Title X employees to give abortion referral or advice when they are personally opposed to the practice. If the current ban on advice is upheld, then so too should the requirement that such advice be routinely given.

The key question is whether there is any reason to be concerned with a uniform state position on the subject, either way. The answer

[15] 410 U.S. 113 (1973).

[16] See Abood v. Detroit Bd. of Educ., 431 U.S. 209 (1977). The scope of the doctrine is now the subject of major uncertainty, see Lehnert v. Ferris Faculty Ass'n, 111 S. Ct. 1950 (1991), where the Court was hopelessly divided over the question of for what purposes union funds could be spent over the objection of dissident members. A majority of the Court allowed union funds to be spent on "non-political" information services on teaching, job placement, and professional development, but it was unwilling to allow the expenditure of union funds for lobbying or electoral activities, or for securing additional state funds for education, or for improving the public reputation of the teaching profession. In my view, the overtly political activities (lobbying and state expenditures) are more objectionable than moneys spent on image development. The whole problem could be obviated by purely voluntary unions which, for their members at least, could settle the permissible forms of expenditures by contract. It is the coercive structure of the National Labor Relations Act that requires some limitations on union expenditures, just as it requires limitations on collective bargaining and secondary boycotts. Note that any system of labor negotiations creates a risk that nonunion members will free ride on union agreements with the employer, although in this case the expenditures that the union seeks to make to advance its own position will probably be opposed by nonunion members, thereby negating the free-rider issue in this context.

to that inquiry again depends on the relative strength of the bargaining and takings risks. On the first question, does the state wield monopoly power in this area—in which case *both* uniform rules, you can't speak or you must speak, should be struck down? Alternatively, is the availability of private counseling and referral services sufficiently great, and the possibility of entry sufficiently free, that the government should be allowed to impose either condition? On this point, the bargaining risk is decisive, because there are no obvious barriers to entry that impede setting up rival programs to pick up the slack or to counteract the impression of the desirable options that government creates. But even here there is reason to be cautious. Market power is defined relative to a geographical market, and the menu of alternatives to government programs may be far greater in New York or San Francisco than it is in Amarillo or Fargo. Similarly, the takings risk here is aggravated if the state takes either extreme position because some citizens will necessarily be forced to fund programs with which they are in strong philosophical or intellectual disagreement. The irreducible tension of *Harris* thus carries over to this case, which points to striking down either a prohibition or a requirement on counseling.

In light of the evident difficulties, one possible solution is to insist that there be *no* collective government position on the abortion referral or counseling business. In a first variation, each participating employee could make up his or her mind, so that the advice varies with the person who happens to give it. At one level this solution seems to invite a form of administrative chaos, for why should the luck of the draw determine what advice a pregnant woman receives by enrolling in a Title X project? The inconsistency and confusion in programming when individual physicians make their choices based on personal conscience alone is something that government should be able to avoid, with abortion referral and counseling, as with everything else. Nonetheless, this objection does not carry over with comparable force if the individual *projects* funded under Title X are allowed to make, at the project level, their separate collective choices as to whether they will refer or counsel on the question of abortion. Each separate project can organize its internal affairs as it sees fit, so that the government in effect can expand the realm of choice (as it does with the voucher system) by funding competitive institutions that take different views on the fundamental problem. Under this view, the bargaining risk is obviated, because grantee institutions can adopt a pro-choice or a pro-life stance, or any position and nuance in between. Similarly, the takings risk is reduced because all citizens know that some fraction of tax revenues goes to the organizations whose views match their own. Or if they think that their money is used to fund ideas of which they do not approve, then they can take secret satisfaction in the knowledge that people whose views are opposed to their own have been forced (if only to make the accounts balance) to fund views that they find totally unacceptable as well. The key point is that competition in programs avoids the all-or-nothing outcomes normally generated by the political process.

This freedom-of-choice plan among project grantees therefore escapes many of the objections that are raised to any all-or-nothing approach (and the outcome in *Rust* will haunt pro-life supporters now that the Presidency has fallen into Democratic hands), but it is still subject to strong objections on its own. Who chooses which projects participate? No automatic criterion makes federal grants. Instead, Title X provides for the Secretary of Health and Human Services to "make grants to and enter into contracts with public or non-profit private entities to assist in the establishment and operation of voluntary family planning projects which shall offer a broad range of acceptable and effective family planning methods and services."[17] At the very least, there must be some assurance that the grantees have staff and plant and program before they receive their federal funds. The discretion afforded in making grants could skew the balance of sentiment within the class of successful grant applications. The abortion question is so charged that it can easily become the tail that can, and would, wag the dog. If the Secretary could not impose any conditions on the advice given to program participants, then he would be unwilling (save under heavy legal and political duress) to accept as project participants those groups whose agenda differed from his own. A pro-life Secretary could bar the pro-choice groups, and vice versa. The skewing effects in the selection process could undo the safeguards that decentralized markets normally provide.

I do not believe that any set of administrative remedies could control the bias in either direction, and thus think the combined bargaining and takings risks doom *any* program that seeks to provide counseling and referral, at least so long as *Roe* is on the books. If the counseling and referral program is separable from the rest of the Medicaid package (which appears to be the case),[18] then the only course of action consistent with the full range of constitutional im-

[17] 42 U.S.C. §300(a) (1988).

[18] "Most clients of Title X-sponsored clinics are not pregnant and generally receive only physical examinations, education on contraceptive methods, and services related to birth control." General Accounting Office Report, App. at 95, quoted in *Rust*, 111 S. Ct. at 1765, n. 2.

peratives in this area is to close up shop altogether. If there is perceived to be some important social reason to subsidize family planning (say, to reduce the human and financial costs of illegitimate children), then that subsidy can be provided through charitable deductions, which do a better job in negating the relevant risks. Any group, regardless of its position on abortion, can raise funds for the program, so the bargaining risk is controlled. Similarly, the takings risk is moderated because each group receives a matching federal grant only to the extent that it can obtain citizen contributions for its positions.

Most importantly, perhaps, *no* government official decides who receives the money and who does not, thereby negating the risk that only preferred applicants will receive grant support at any given time. Far from having a radical redirection of grant efforts that depend on the vagaries of politics, the level of support that each group can muster will rise and fall incrementally in proportion to its privately secured contributions, and be immune from the shifts in political power that are often triggered by small changes in the overall political sentiment of the nation at large. If it be said that the charitable subsidy is too small (perhaps because the marginal tax rates are too low), then the short answer is that one can increase the deductions (say, to 200 percent of that normally allowable) in order to counteract a problem of great importance *without* running the political risks that are exemplified in *Rust*. It seems therefore a pity that the wooden decision of the Supreme Court should rule the day; and equally a pity that the strident criticisms of that decision[19] should be regarded as the only viable alternative to that position. Getting out of the counseling and referral business, save by charitable deduction, is preferable, both on prudential *and* constitutional grounds.

## ADOLESCENT FAMILY PLANNING

The Adolescent Family Life Act (AFLA), which was sustained against facial constitutional attack in *Bowen v. Kendrick*,[20] raises many of the same issues as *Rust*. The key purpose of the AFLA was to provide federal moneys to private agencies to help stem what Congress perceived to be the epidemic of pregnancies among unwed teenage mothers in the United States. As part of the public/private partnership, the money provided under the grants went to organiza-

[19] See, e.g., Walter Dellinger, "Gag Me With a Rule: Bush and Abortion Counseling," *New Republic*, Jan. 6, 1992, at 14.

[20] 487 U.S. 589 (1988).

tions that were designed to help adolescents to "promote self discipline and other prudent approaches" to teenage pregnancy, "within the context of the family."[21]

In *Kendrick*, the Court addressed the question whether the establishment clause of the First Amendment prohibited religious organizations from participating in the AFLA program on even terms with nonreligious organizations. In sustaining the statute against facial attack, the Supreme Court analyzed the program in terms of its traditional, but by no means unproblematic, three-part test developed in *Lemon v. Kurtzman*.[22] *Lemon* asks whether the challenged program is motivated by an impermissible religious purpose, whether its primary effect is to advance or retard religion, and whether it results in an excessive level of entanglement between secular and religious agencies. The Court (but only with two concurrences and with three dissents) concluded that the stated purpose was secular, and that its primary effect was care and advice on pregnancy. Most controversially perhaps, the Court also ruled that there was no evidence of excessive entanglement, even though religious organizations had to promise, and the government had to monitor, the program requirement of keeping religious overtones from creeping into a secular program. Because the program was neutral with respect to religion on its face, and because the grantee organizations were a diverse lot, the risks involved were thought insufficient to warrant a per se ban against the participation of religious organizations in the program. But the Court left open the possibility that the conduct of any religious organization might warrant, on a case by case basis, its exclusion from the program.

The Supreme Court's conclusion in *Kendrick* is perhaps weakly defensible, but its argumentation is not persuasive. As with so many of the Court's recent religion decisions, the statute was sustained in deference to the stated congressional judgment that religious organizations possessed the skills needed to communicate with adolescents, and could do so without imparting religious messages to their youthful charges. But the concerns with the program run much deeper. The key question under both the free exercise and the establishment clauses is whether there is an implicit transfer through regulation from religious to nonreligious persons, or vice versa: redistribution along religious or sectarian lines is the major danger addressed by both the free exercise and the establishment clause. Here the AFLA was funded through general revenues, raised from the reli-

[21] 42 U.S.C. §300z (b)(1) (1988).

[22] 403 U.S. 602 (1971). For a recent critique of these factors, see Michael W. McConnell, "Religious Freedom at a Crossroads," 59 *U. Chi. L. Rev.* 115, 127–34 (1992).

gious and nonreligious alike. If the AFLA had been sustained, and religious organizations had been excluded from participation, then its net effect would have been to work a redistribution of resources from religious to secular activities.[23] There would have been a tax on religious organizations with no offsetting advantages, and perhaps the uneasy sensation that the moneys spent by secular organizations might well undermine the values that these religious organizations, or at least some of them, uphold.

The point here can be taken one step further. As drafted, the AFLA imposed sharp conditions on the participation of religious organizations by requiring them to suppress their religious orientation when using these public funds. Clearly the organizations are better off participating in the program subject to that condition than they are from being totally excluded. But why the condition at all? In a world in which family planning programs are conducted without government support, religious organizations are entitled to tie their views on family planning to their religious beliefs. The same linkage seems appropriate even where religious organizations are funded in part by charitable contributions, for it would be a mistake to have selective charitable funding distort the balance between religious and nonreligious organizations that would otherwise exist in a tax-free world.[24] Why then should the balance shift when the Congress makes the shift from tax exemptions to direct grants? The conditions here amount to a partial exclusion of religious organizations from public funds that are raised in part from their own supporters. The level of subsidy for the secular from the religious is somewhat smaller than it would be from the total exclusion, but the subsidy is there nonetheless.

It might be said in response that any inclusion of religious organizations on the public payroll violates the time-honored principle of separation of church and state. But it is that principle which stands in need of reexamination in an age of extensive government activities.[25] Thus, so long as the minimal nightwatchman state characterizes our constitutional order, it appears relatively easy to insist upon the separation. There are few gains that might be obtained from the cooperative activities between church and state, and much abuse

[23] It is just this position that leads me to reject the position taken in Sullivan, supra note 8, which, while announcing a strong defense of religious autonomy, argues for the exclusion of religious participation in public-funding programs, on the ground that their interests should yield to a "secular public moral order." 59 *U. Chi. L. Rev.* at 198.

[24] See supra chap. 15.

[25] For discussion, see Richard A. Epstein, "Religious Liberty in the Welfare State," 31 *Wm. & Mary L. Rev.* 375, 386–99 (1990).

that can take place if church is subsidized by state, or state is subsidized by church. The categorical principle of separation therefore represents a studied judgment to give up on the gains from coordinated activities in order to avoid the far greater risks of abuse.

Yet even here the principle is in some measure illusory. The minimal state may engage in few government activities, but it does not engage in none at all. The principle of separation of church and state could run so far as to provide that ordinary police protection does not extend to religious organizations who would (if the argument were carried to its extreme) be allowed to maintain police forces of their own. Yet that system could quickly be the source of massive embarrassment, given the jurisdictional disputes that could arise between various organizations: if a member of one religion vandalizes property owned by a member of another religion, which organization should hear the case? There is ample precedent for these jurisdictional tussles in the history of English law.[26] A single police force, funded out of general revenues, should provide protection for all persons. The only difficult question, already canvassed, is whether religious organizations should be entitled to an exemption from the tax, which they now receive along with many other charitable organizations.[27] And similar arguments could be raised about the provision of other public services: religious organizations should be allowed to use the highways on even terms with others; they should have access to the judicial system on equal terms, and so on.

These counterexamples should raise genuine concern even among the supporters of rigid separation between church and state. So long as the state, however small, maintains its monopoly on the provision of any public service, then the appropriate response is not one of sharp separation, but of nondiscrimination between the two groups. To insist on sharp separation is always to require a subsidy of nonreligious individuals and groups by religious ones, and it is that implicit transfer that the nondiscrimination principle, of such great importance elsewhere, attacks. As the state expands to cover ever more activities, the dangers of the strict separation principle become still greater, and it is just that frame of mind that makes the qualified defense of the AFLA in *Kendrick* so unsatisfactory.

There is, however, no reason for optimism. The nondiscrimination principle may not suffice either, for it faces the same difficulties

[26] The medieval law included the writ of assize utrum, where the question had to be decided whether certain matters belonged to the jurisdiction of the church or the state. It was a sign of secular supremacy that the decision over jurisdiction quickly became lodged on the civil side. For a brief account, see Theodore F.T. Plucknett, *A Concise History of the Common Law* 111, 360 (5th ed. 1956).

[27] See, e.g., Walz v. Tax Comm'r of New York, 397 U.S. 664 (1970).

that render any federal funding that touches on the abortion issue so problematic. There is, quite simply, no way to insure that the participation of various organizations in the funding under the AFLA will proportionately reflect the general sentiment of the population on this issue. Many nonreligious persons are violently opposed to religious organizations receiving federal funding; there are other nonreligious persons who might want religious groups to participate in federal programs; there are some religious organizations that might refuse to apply for the funding; and others that are all too eager to have it. The government grantors could have a strong bias for inclusion or exclusion based on their general political orientation, so that there is little reason to expect that universal participation in AFLA grants will eliminate the subsidies in question. It is far more likely to create a new set of subsidies that will be difficult to track down because they are so embedded within the system, and thus likely to shift with political fads and fortunes. As before, therefore, the radical proposal becomes still more appealing relative to available alternatives. Keep the government out of this business altogether. Any federal subsidy is better provided, and more fairly distributed, by a system of charitable deductions for money spent on these programs—no strings attached.[28] It is just too dangerous to have the government be the teacher of individual virtue in a society in which there is no agreement as to how that message should be conveyed. The preferred remedy is to strike down the AFLA. Broad-scale inclusion of religious organizations, subject to conditions that limit their religious input, is an inferior second-best alternative.

## PUBLIC FUNDING OF THE ARTS

The risks of extensive government funding of educational matters have also come home to roost in the ongoing saga of public funding for the arts through the National Endowment of the Arts. The history of this episode has been so often discussed and recounted,

[28] In other contexts, other forms of government support might be appropriate. See Witters v. Washington Dep't of Servs. for the Blind, 474 U.S. 481 (1986), which allowed a blind person who received funds for vocational rehabilitation to use his grant to train for the ministry at a religious institution. The key feature of the rehabilitation program is that government funds are available for use anywhere, and only the recipient makes the decision as to how they are spent. The system shortcuts government discretion in exactly the same fashion as the charitable exemption. The exclusion of religious organizations thus creates a subsidy for nonreligious organizations, and in my view runs into serious constitutional difficulties of its own.

that it is hardly necessary to dwell on its particulars here. The simmering controversy reached its peak over the NEA funding of a 1989 retrospective exhibition of the photographic works of Robert Mapplethorpe, a gay photographer who died of AIDS at age 42. His collection included explicit photographs of gay men photographed in homoerotic poses or engaged in homosexual activities, and other photographs which could be regarded by some as sadomasochistic, including one of a man urinating into the mouth of another.[29] One question about these photographs is whether they could be regarded as obscene and thus subject to prosecution under the criminal statutes.

Under the current law, obscenity is determined under a three-part test of suitable vagueness and limited utility. The standard thus asks (a) whether "the average person, applying contemporary community standards" would find that the work, taken as a whole, appeals to the prurient interest; (b) whether the work depicts or describes, in a patently offensive way, sexual conduct specifically defined by the applicable state law; and (c) whether the work, taken as a whole, lacks "serious literary, artistic, political, or scientific value."[30] As applied to the Mapplethorpe case, it is highly doubtful that his work could be found obscene given the enormous critical praise that has been heaped upon it by his peers within the field.[31] And the criminal prosecution for obscenity brought in Cincinnati against the museum and director who exhibited the show resulted in an acquittal, after the prosecutor presented a case that contained no expert testimony by any serious art critic who was prepared to brand the exhibit, or any part of it, as obscene.

If the Mapplethorpe exhibit, and others like it, could have been found obscene, then the question of unconstitutional conditions simply disappears from view. There is no government obligation to fund work that is subject to criminal prosecution, because its obscene content takes it outside the ambit of First Amendment protection. But once the opposite conclusion is reached, then the familiar dilemma is upon us: may the government withhold funding from certain works of art which are not obscene? At one level the answer is again trivial: the scarcity constraint precludes unlimited funding. But the inquiry here is far more pressing because the exclusions from funding are explicitly based on the viewpoint and general orienta-

[29] A very careful description of the photographs is found in Owen M. Fiss, "State Activism and State Censorship," 100 *Yale L.J.* 2087 (1991).

[30] Miller v. California, 413 U.S. 15, 24 (1973) (citation omitted).

[31] See Ingrid Sischy, "White and Black," *New Yorker*, Nov. 13, 1989, at 124.

tion involved. Thus in the aftermath of the Mapplethorpe affair, the Congress passed the Helms Amendment which provided that:

> None of the funds authorized to be appropriated for the National Endowment for the Arts or the National Endowment for the Humanities may be used to promote, disseminate, or produce materials which in the judgment of the National Endowment for the Arts or the National Endowment for the Humanities may be considered obscene, including but not limited to, depictions of sadomasochism, homoeroticism, the sexual exploitation of children, or individuals engaged in sex acts and which, when taken as a whole, do not have serious literary, artistic, political, or scientific value.[32]

As drafted, the statute could be read innocuously, as simply making the current legal standards part of the grant proposals. But in fact the scope of the prohibition looks to be broader, both because of the use of the enigmatic "may be" instead of the more restrictive "are," and because the list of obscene materials looks as though it were drawn up by a reviewer critical of the Mapplethorpe exhibit. Once the broader reach is made we are driven back to the familiar tension between takings and bargaining risks from which there is no easy escape. Those who oppose any restrictions beyond those allowable under the criminal law will shout, as they have shouted, that government censorship is utterly inconsistent with the command of the First Amendment. Yet those who are in favor of the restrictions will deeply resent the use of public money—of their money—to fund the kind of artwork to which they take deep offense. As before neither risk disappears simply because the other one is present. Indeed, both risks are compounded, and the effort of government officials to split the difference in passing on grant applications is likely to add further layers of political confrontation, as each side will be all too eager to place the most ominous interpretation on the actions of its rivals. Even after the change of guard at the NEA, there have been continuous battles in the grant-making process. Individual panels have recommended the approval of grant proposals that have been rejected by the program director. And all the while funds are moved from national to state and local programs, as part of another set of intrigues to bypass the panel system entirely.[33]

[32] Act of October 23, 1989, see note 7, supra.

[33] See William H. Honan, "Arts Agency to Bypass Defiant Panel," *New York Times*, August 1, 1992 at 13. The story details how the NEA, and its new acting Chairwoman Anne-Imelda Radice blocked funds for two highly controversial sculpture projects, and then shifted the money for that program to regional councils, whose activities are concerned less with creative arts and more with public service functions, the

We are thus left with the following unhappy choices. One is to yield to the demands of artistic supporters that any and all conditions be removed from the NEA grants, so that the NEA and its panels are allowed to continue to make funding decisions just as they did before the controversy over Mapplethorpe. A second is to make some form of retreat, one that makes it possible to refuse a few very controversial grants in order to keep afloat the entire program of government funding for the arts. A third is to close down the NEA on the ground that divisions of opinion are so strong that it is best to use the route of charitable deductions for the reasons that were stated before. Instead events have played out in exactly the opposite fashion. Compromise legislation has been passed which has weakened the control that individual panels have had in the selection of grants by including more lay people on the individual panels, and a greater portion of the total funding now goes through state affiliates in support of local artists. The attacks on John E. Frohnmayer by Patrick Buchanan and others have borne fruit and have resulted in President Bush asking for, and receiving, his early resignation.

The entire episode shows the fragile nature of successful government enterprises. So long as there is a broad and powerful social consensus in support of the actions of a government agency, its funding will be secure even when its internal operations are left within the control of professionals within the field. But once that consensus breaks down, then any defense by experts within the field will be viewed as apologetics by persons outside of it, and only give additional reason to rein-in an operation sponsored by "the" taxpayer but wholly beyond his control. The opposition to the NEA funding programs should not be based on their performance in funding particular exhibitions, or particular artists (such as Karen Finley, whose application was granted only after being placed on hold), but on the long-term structural risk that public funding places on the safety of the arts in a political society. The greater the levels of funding, the higher the levels of political dependence, and hence the greater the dislocations within the political and artistic realm when the conflicts over value become too great to cover up. It is better to avoid the dangerous decline in popular rhetoric, and the dangerous risk of populist and intolerant rhetoric, by keeping the government out of these activities *before* the issue of conflict arises.

Are these general observations relevant only to the wisdom of the NEA or do they provide the foundation for constitutional analysis?

---

preparation of catalogues and the like. The decision was preceded by bitter internal wrangling.

That some connection may be forged between politics and constitutional analysis is a common-enough insight. Indeed, in some cases the connections are thought to run in the opposite direction: that the importance of art for the well-being of the nation is so great that there is a constitutional duty to fund the NEA without strings attached.[34] But the attendant difficulties are too great to convert an amendment designed to limit the scope of government into a provision that calls for its perpetual involvement in the funding, and hence the evaluation of art. If the First Amendment mandates federal support, does its incorporation through the Fourteenth Amendment impose similar duties upon the states? And what are the levels of funding that have to be provided by each branch of government, and the procedures to make individual determinations?

But is the opposite position, calling for a separation of state from direct subsidy, so untenable? There is a long line of cases which indicate that First Amendment concerns are raised whenever taxation is used to force unwilling persons to engage in political or religious speech. These concerns are surely very great in this area, and raise at least a presumptive difficulty with any funding program. In view of the total breakdown on the question of *which* grant proposals are to be funded at *what* levels, by *which* persons, the necessary injection of politics into art and art into politics calls for some modest degree of separation between art and state, and state and art. There is a vast difference between the matching grants provided by charitable contributions and the hands-on activities of a divided government. The dilemma between coerced expenditures and improper conditions can only be resolved by getting the government out of the business altogether.

The one question that remains is how far does this prohibition run. The government is engaged in the support of many other enterprises of a research and academic nature. In addition to the NEA, it sponsors the National Endowment for the Humanities, and the National Science Foundation, the National Institutes of Health and the Institute of Medicine, to fund a myriad of scientific projects across-the-board. In each of these cases there is the possibility of abuse, and in each case the charitable deduction can be, and indeed is, used to support the desired activities. It is a fair question, for which there is no easy answer, as to whether any First Amendment attack on the idea of the NEA carries over to other academic endeavors funded by government, and if it did, whether this would be a good idea.

The inquiry, however, is so vast that it is almost impossible to

[34] See Robert Brustein, "Disaster at the NEA," *New Republic*, Dec. 11, 1989, at 28.

know how to answer it responsibly. If there were no strong division of opinion on who should receive grants and why, then public funding would be a sensible alternative: there are public benefits from the creation of good ideas in any discipline that are not captured by the market prices for which art (or history, or science) product can be sold, even in a world that grants extensive copyright protection.[35] The public funding thus makes up for the inability to privatize all the information generated by grant recipients. But the risks of capture remain, and leave me, at least, profoundly disturbed by concentrating so much power in the hands of government-sponsored organizations whose prestige is so great and whose word is all too often taken without critical restraint. If the question had to be resolved on a blank slate, we surely would have been better never to have created the National Endowment for the Humanities, which may well be caught in the undertow brought about by the attacks on the NEA.

Scientific research (at least until the advent of AIDS) has proceeded by means that were largely independent of politics, but which have become far less so over time. There is now, for example, a constant effort to condition the grants awarded to researchers in ways that are said to be designed to ferret out the risks of academic fraud and scientific misconduct. While these ends of government are surely legitimate, the means of control in many cases are not, for with government money comes the assertion of government power, and with it the demand to centralize investigations of scientific misconduct in Washington, where the political situation—think only of the enormous battles of David Baltimore and Robert Gallo—makes it likely that inept and politically charged investigations will only undermine the morale of the system as a whole.[36]

Nonetheless, the gainful activities from scientific research, and the cost and scale of its activities are such that the same concerns that should lead to closing down the NEA and even the NEH do not apply here. The subject matter is just far enough removed from politics most of the time that the bargaining and takings risks do not together call for an invalidation of the total enterprises, even though they call for considerable care as to how it is undertaken.[37] The most that can be said is that in these cases it seems likely that the attacks on government power will depend only partially on constitutional

[35] William M. Landes & Richard A. Posner, "An Economic Analysis of Copyright Law," 18 *J. Legal Stud.* 325 (1989).

[36] See, e.g., "Profile: AIDS Dispute; Robert Gallo Toughs Out Controversy," *Scientific American* Jan. 1991, at 36.

[37] Abbs v. Sullivan, 963 F.2d 918 (7th Cir. 1992) (Posner, J.).

doctrines that seek to limit the power of government to do good deeds, and bad, by bargaining with its individual citizens. The enormity of the task of fettering the leviathan we have created may well fail, because of the enormity of the establishment that is now in place.

Whatever the future course of events, however, it should not blind us to the central thesis of this book. The power to contract and to grant, when lodged in the hands of government, may well prove to be as dangerous as the power to take and to regulate. The effort to create an unfettered source of government power at root rests on an apparent position that private parties are entitled to contract for good reason, bad reason, or no reason at all. It then exaggerates the scope of freedom of contract in private transactions, and imputes the same level of freedom to a government whose power must always be questioned for the two reasons identified at the outset of a book: the takings risk that results from its power of taxation and the bargaining risk that results from its monopoly position in all areas of life. A government that can tax, and hence take, at will should never be totally free in choosing the parties with whom it contracts and to whom it makes grants. And a government that has any level of monopoly power cannot be trusted to impose whatever conditions it wants on these same parties. The conventional wisdom has it that government is subject to extensive limitation when it regulates and none when it contracts. But the conventional wisdom contains only a tiny portion of the truth, for it ignores the need to limit government in all its activities. Government and statecraft are always a high-risk enterprise, and bargaining by the state has to be watched as closely, and with the same level of concern and suspicion, as taking, regulation, and taxation—the traditional forms of government power.

# *Table of Cases*

# Author Index

## Subject Index